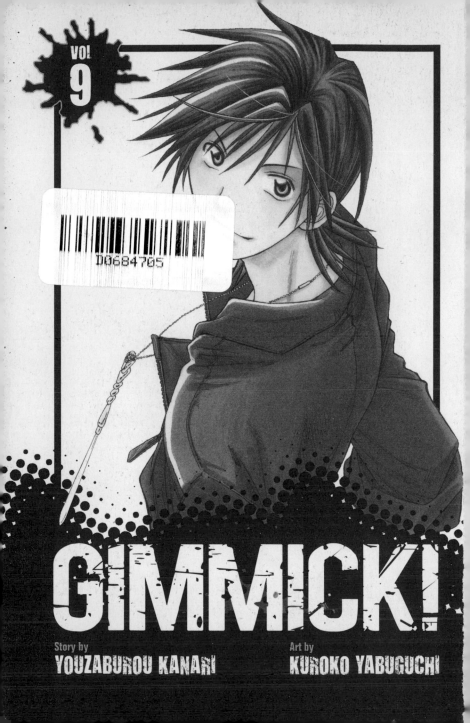

VOL 9

D0684705

GIMMICK!

Story by
YOUZABUROU KANARI

Art by
KUROKO YABUGUCHI

GIMMICK!

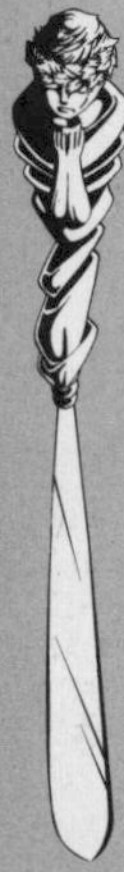

CONTENTS

VOL 9

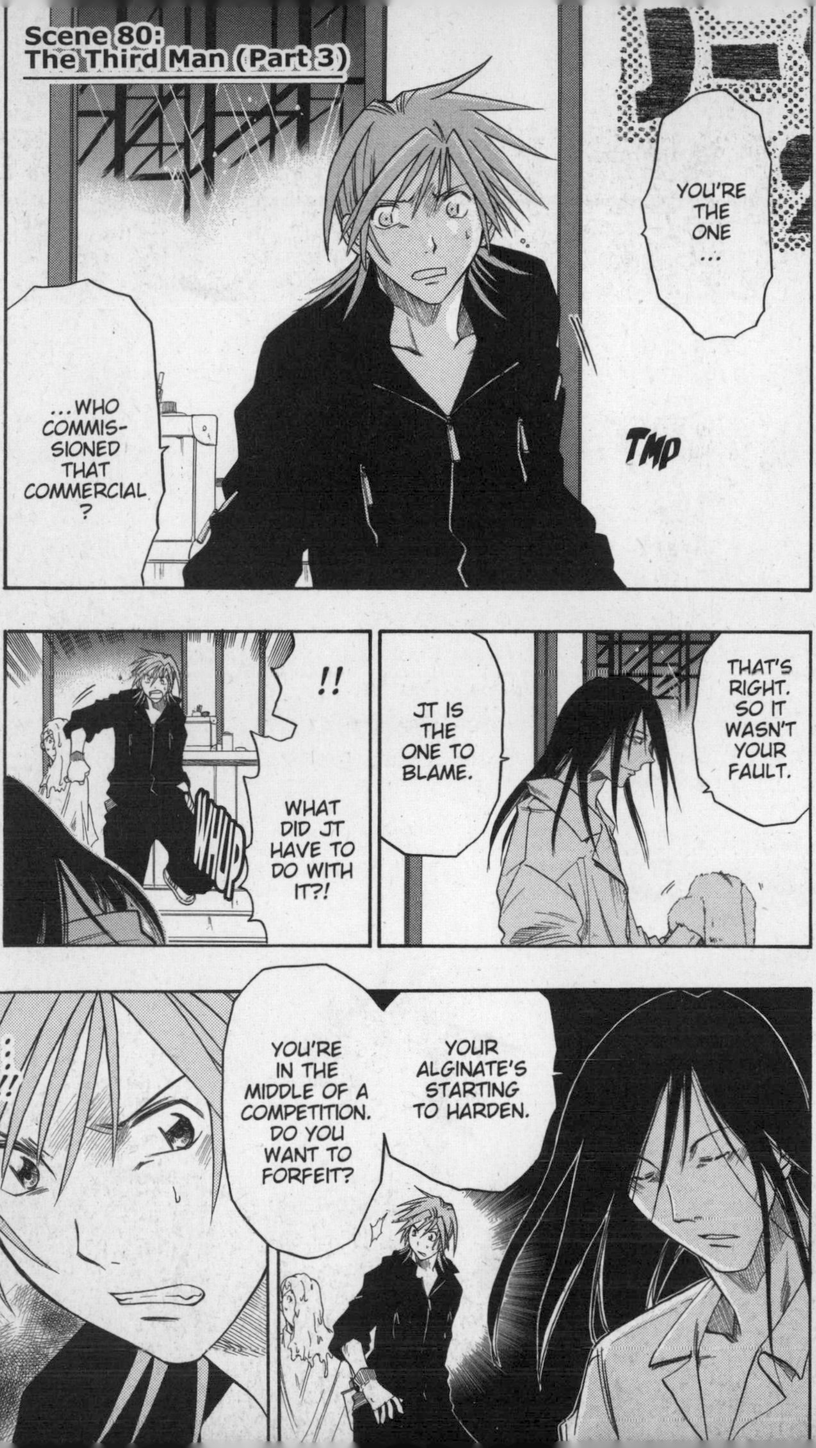
Scene 80: The Third Man (Part 3)
YOU'RE THE ONE ...
...WHO COMMISSIONED THAT COMMERCIAL?
TMP
THAT'S RIGHT. SO IT WASN'T YOUR FAULT.
JT IS THE ONE TO BLAME.
!!
WHAT DID JT HAVE TO DO WITH IT?!
WHUP
YOUR ALGINATE'S STARTING TO HARDEN.
YOU'RE IN THE MIDDLE OF A COMPETITION. DO YOU WANT TO FORFEIT?
...!!

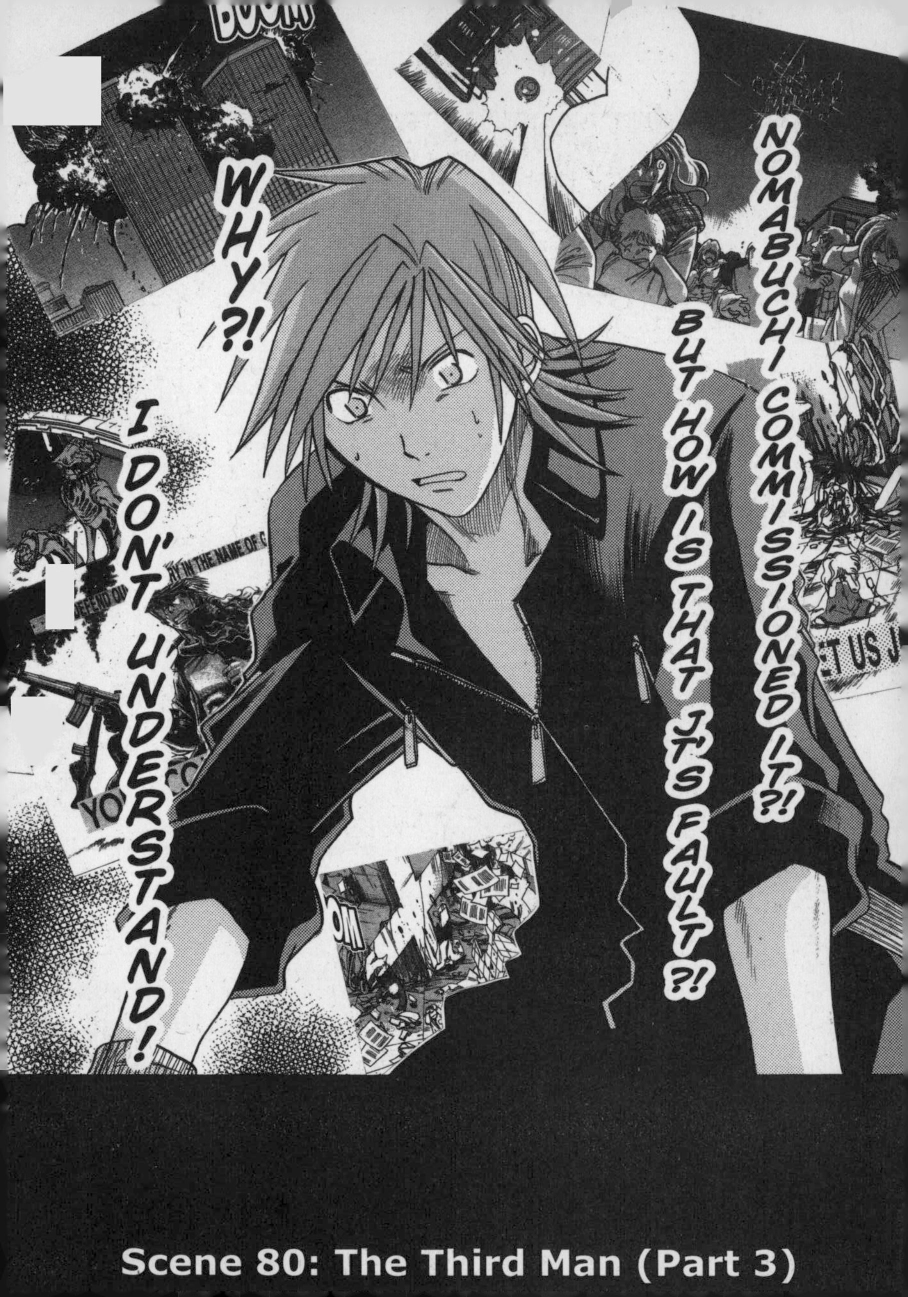
NOMABUCHI COMMISSIONED IT?!
BUT HOW IS THAT JT'S FAULT?!
WHY?!
I DON'T UNDERSTAND!
BOOM

Scene 80: The Third Man (Part 3)

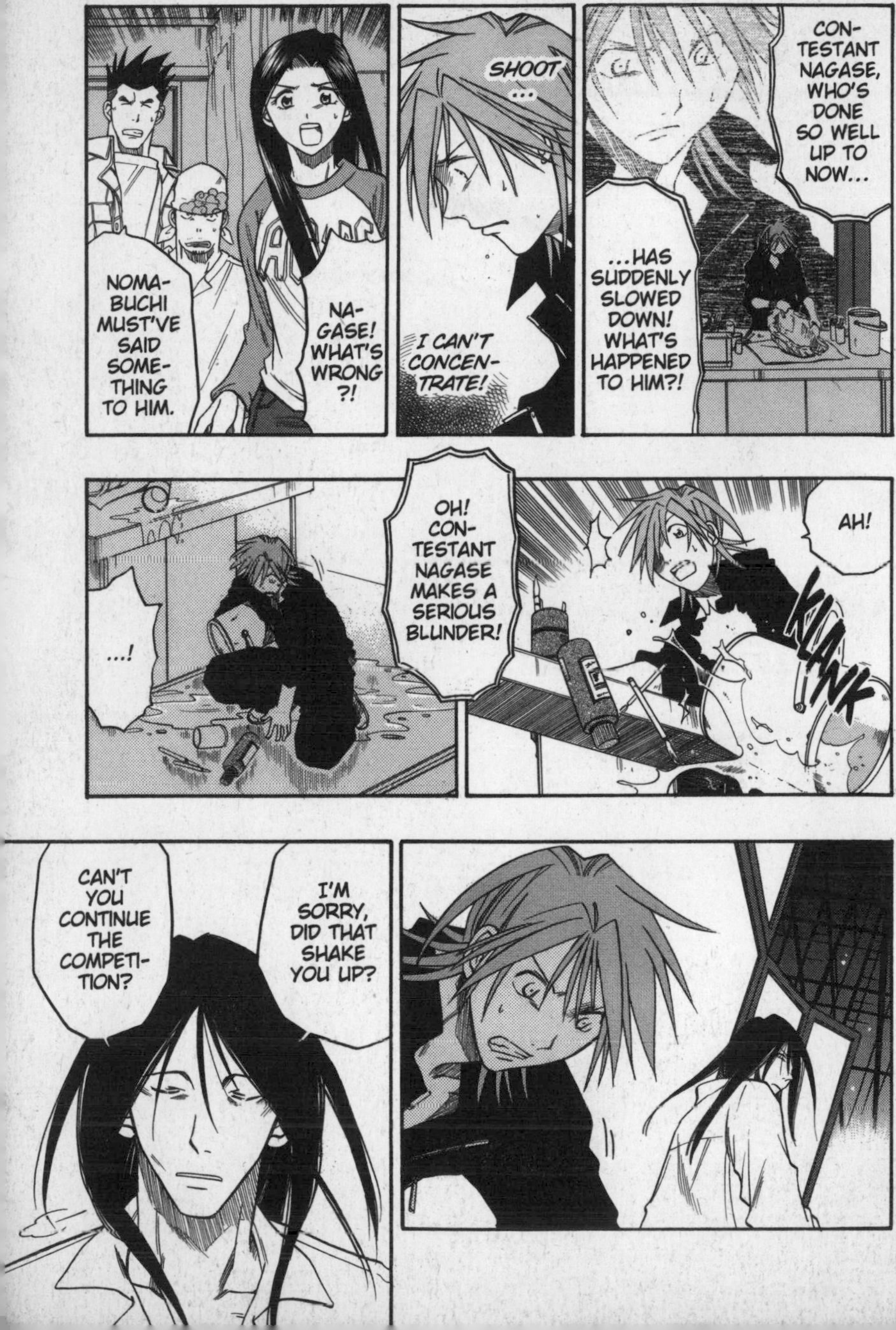
CON-TESTANT NAGASE, WHO'S DONE SO WELL UP TO NOW...
...HAS SUDDENLY SLOWED DOWN! WHAT'S HAPPENED TO HIM?!
SHOOT...
I CAN'T CONCENTRATE!
NA-GASE! WHAT'S WRONG?!
NOMA-BUCHI MUST'VE SAID SOME-THING TO HIM.
AH!
KLANK
OH! CON-TESTANT NAGASE MAKES A SERIOUS BLUNDER!
...!
I'M SORRY, DID THAT SHAKE YOU UP?
CAN'T YOU CONTINUE THE COMPETI-TION?

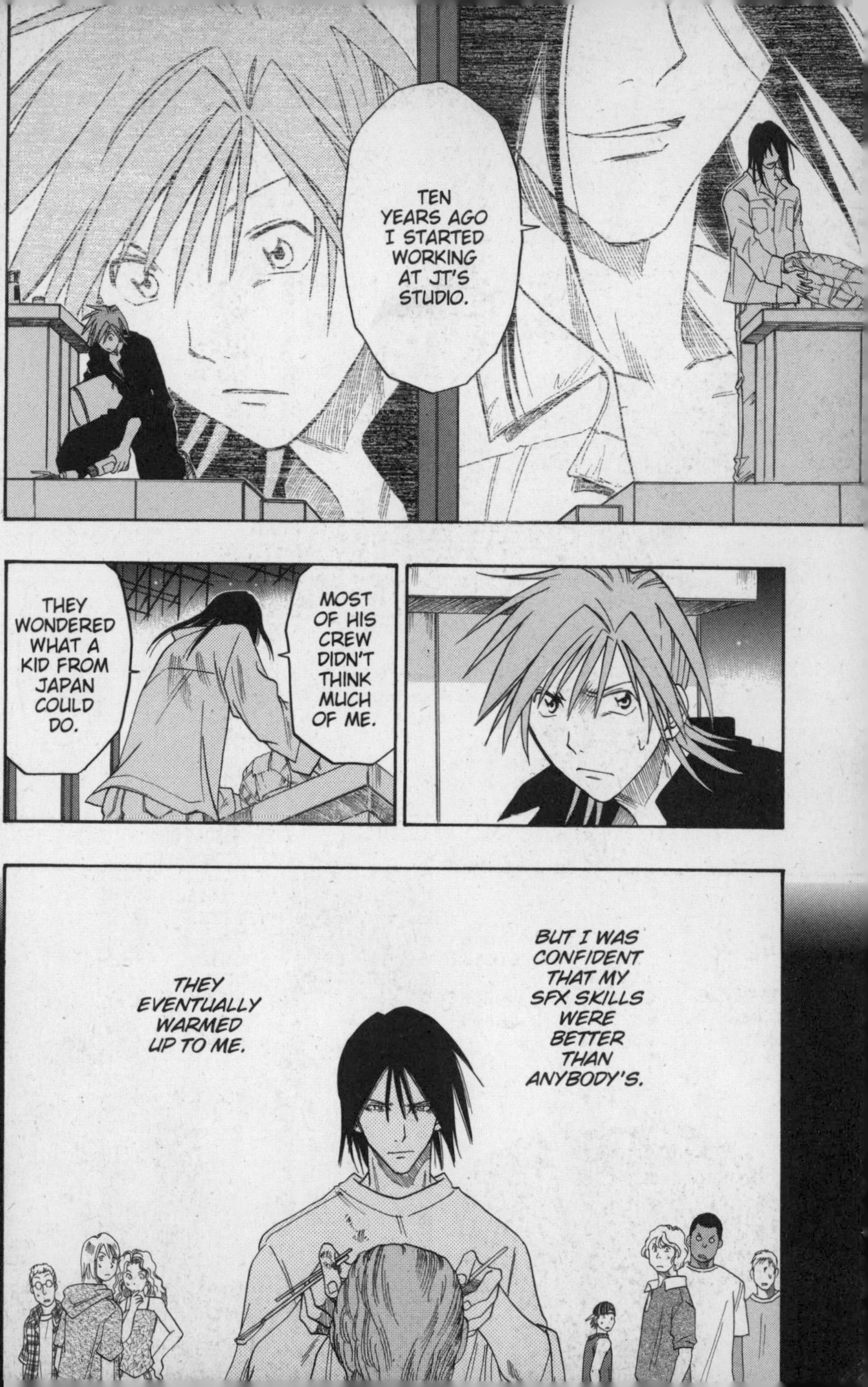
TEN YEARS AGO I STARTED WORKING AT JT'S STUDIO.
MOST OF HIS CREW DIDN'T THINK MUCH OF ME.
THEY WONDERED WHAT A KID FROM JAPAN COULD DO.
BUT I WAS CONFIDENT THAT MY SFX SKILLS WERE BETTER THAN ANYBODY'S.
THEY EVENTUALLY WARMED UP TO ME.

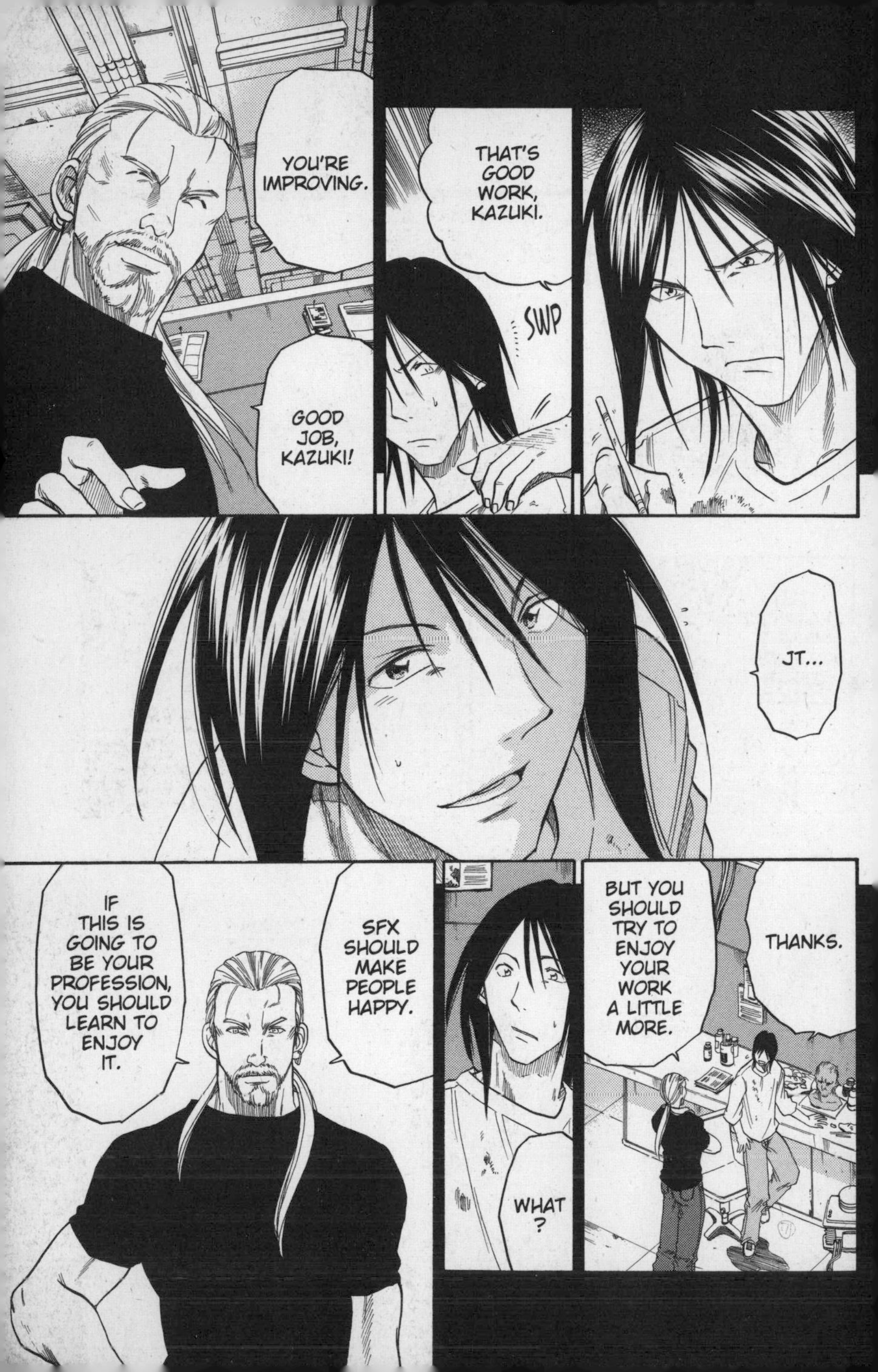
THAT'S GOOD WORK, KAZUKI.
SWP
YOU'RE IMPROVING.
GOOD JOB, KAZUKI!
JT...
THANKS.
BUT YOU SHOULD TRY TO ENJOY YOUR WORK A LITTLE MORE.
WHAT?
SFX SHOULD MAKE PEOPLE HAPPY.
IF THIS IS GOING TO BE YOUR PROFESSION, YOU SHOULD LEARN TO ENJOY IT.

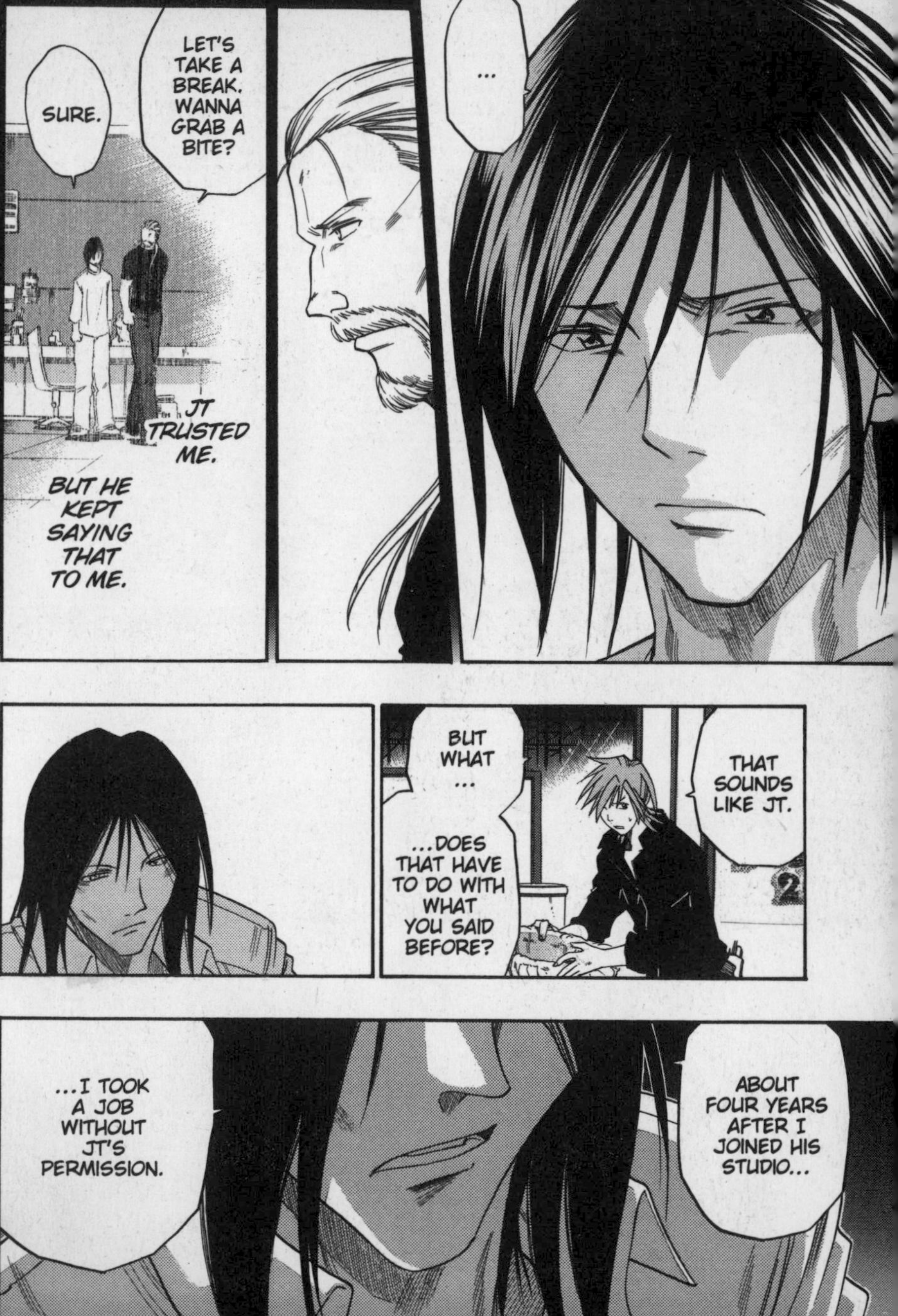
...
LET'S TAKE A BREAK. WANNA GRAB A BITE?
SURE.
JT TRUSTED ME.
BUT HE KEPT SAYING THAT TO ME.
THAT SOUNDS LIKE JT.
BUT WHAT ...
...DOES THAT HAVE TO DO WITH WHAT YOU SAID BEFORE?
ABOUT FOUR YEARS AFTER I JOINED HIS STUDIO...
...I TOOK A JOB WITHOUT JT'S PERMISSION.

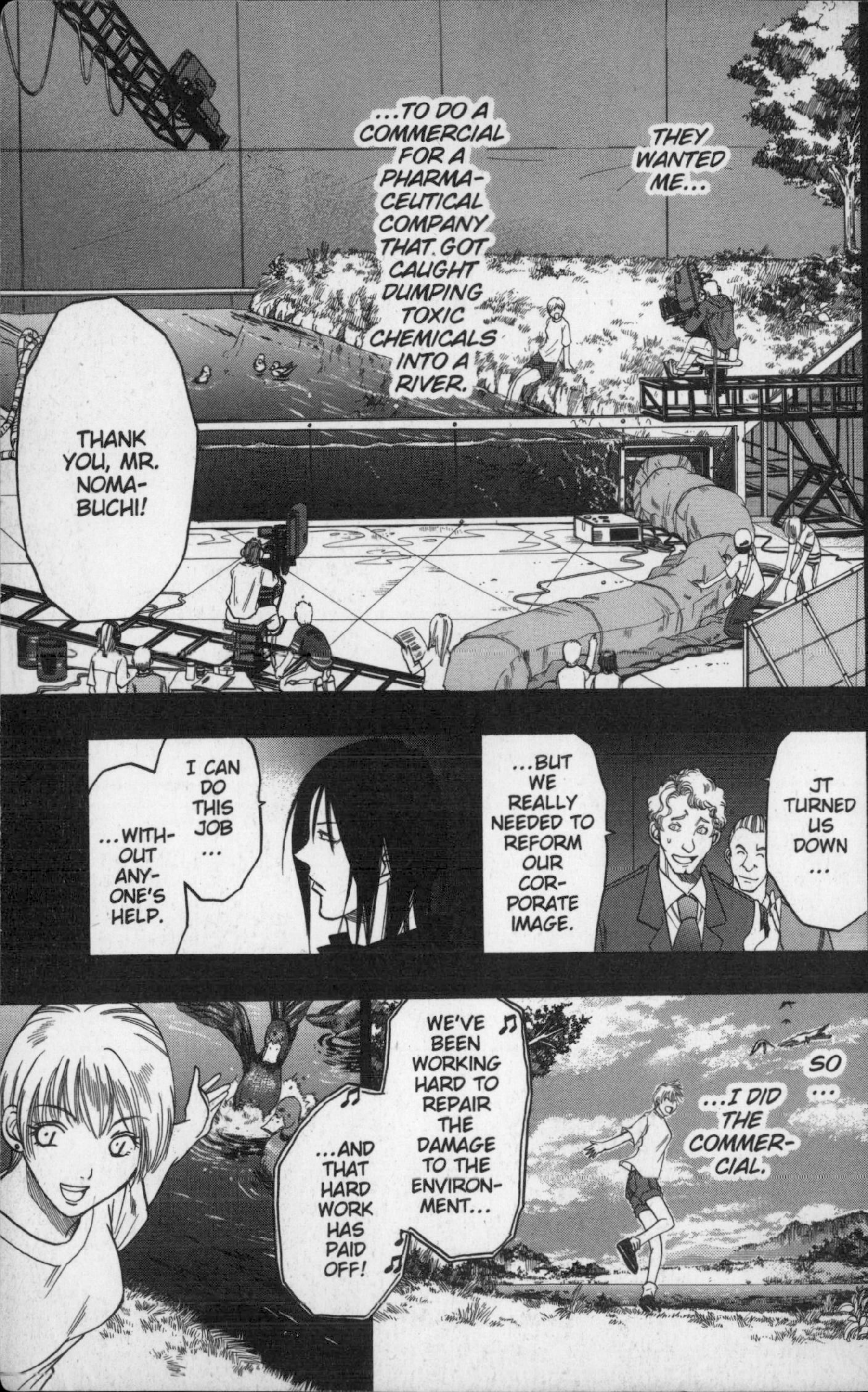
THEY WANTED ME...
...TO DO A COMMERCIAL FOR A PHARMACEUTICAL COMPANY THAT GOT CAUGHT DUMPING TOXIC CHEMICALS INTO A RIVER.
THANK YOU, MR. NOMABUCHI!
JT TURNED US DOWN...
...BUT WE REALLY NEEDED TO REFORM OUR CORPORATE IMAGE.
I CAN DO THIS JOB...
...WITHOUT ANYONE'S HELP.
SO...
...I DID THE COMMERCIAL.
WE'VE BEEN WORKING HARD TO REPAIR THE DAMAGE TO THE ENVIRONMENT...
...AND THAT HARD WORK HAS PAID OFF!

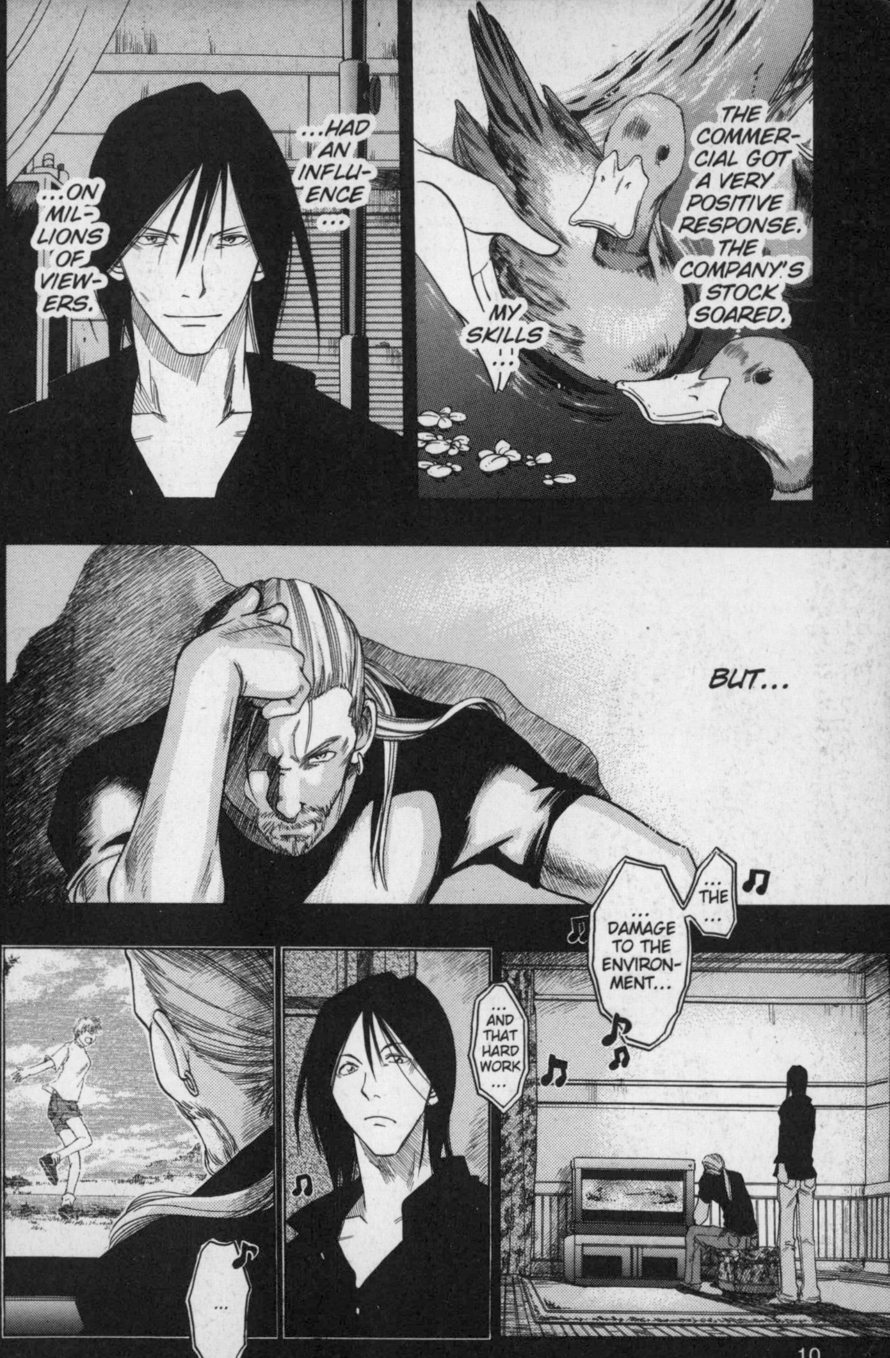
THE COMMERCIAL GOT A VERY POSITIVE RESPONSE. THE COMPANY'S STOCK SOARED.
MY SKILLS...
...HAD AN INFLUENCE...
...ON MILLIONS OF VIEWERS.
BUT...
...THE...
...DAMAGE TO THE ENVIRONMENT...
...AND THAT HARD WORK...
...

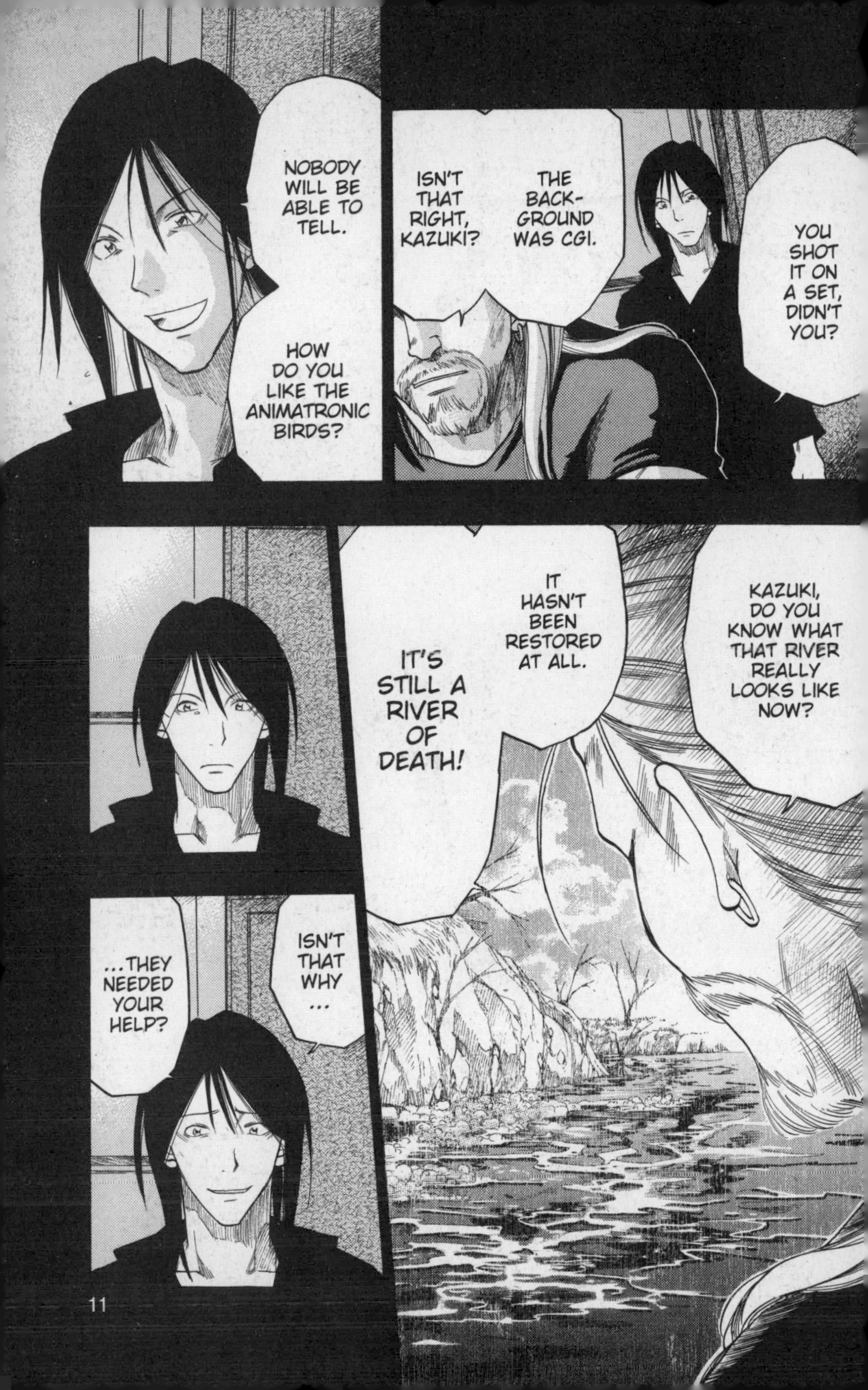
YOU SHOT IT ON A SET, DIDN'T YOU?
THE BACK-GROUND WAS CGI.
ISN'T THAT RIGHT, KAZUKI?
NOBODY WILL BE ABLE TO TELL.
HOW DO YOU LIKE THE ANIMATRONIC BIRDS?
KAZUKI, DO YOU KNOW WHAT THAT RIVER REALLY LOOKS LIKE NOW?
IT HASN'T BEEN RESTORED AT ALL.
IT'S STILL A RIVER OF DEATH!
ISN'T THAT WHY...
...THEY NEEDED YOUR HELP?

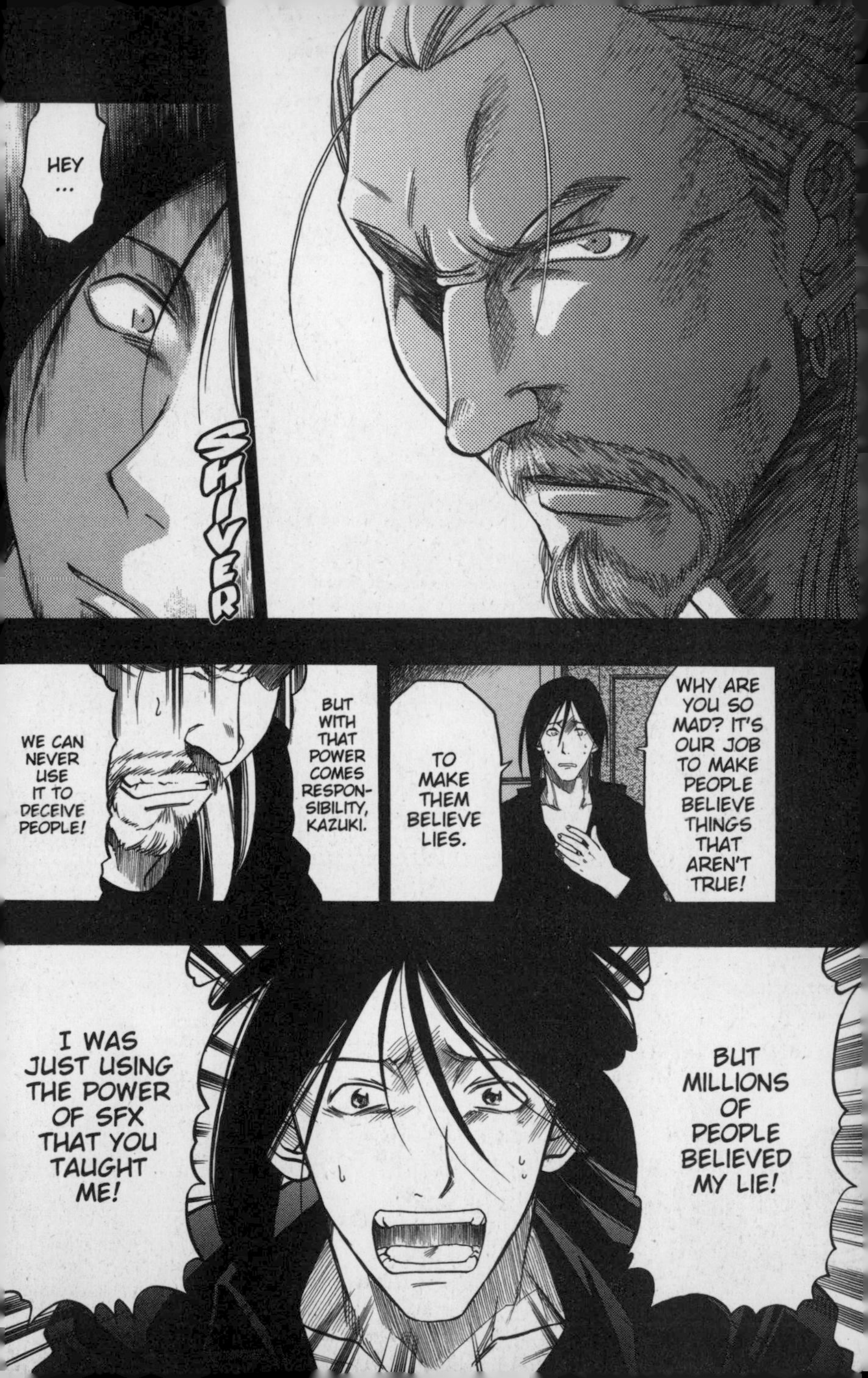
HEY ...
SHIVER
WHY ARE YOU SO MAD? IT'S OUR JOB TO MAKE PEOPLE BELIEVE THINGS THAT AREN'T TRUE!
TO MAKE THEM BELIEVE LIES.
BUT WITH THAT POWER COMES RESPON-SIBILITY, KAZUKI.
WE CAN NEVER USE IT TO DECEIVE PEOPLE!
BUT MILLIONS OF PEOPLE BELIEVED MY LIE!
I WAS JUST USING THE POWER OF SFX THAT YOU TAUGHT ME!

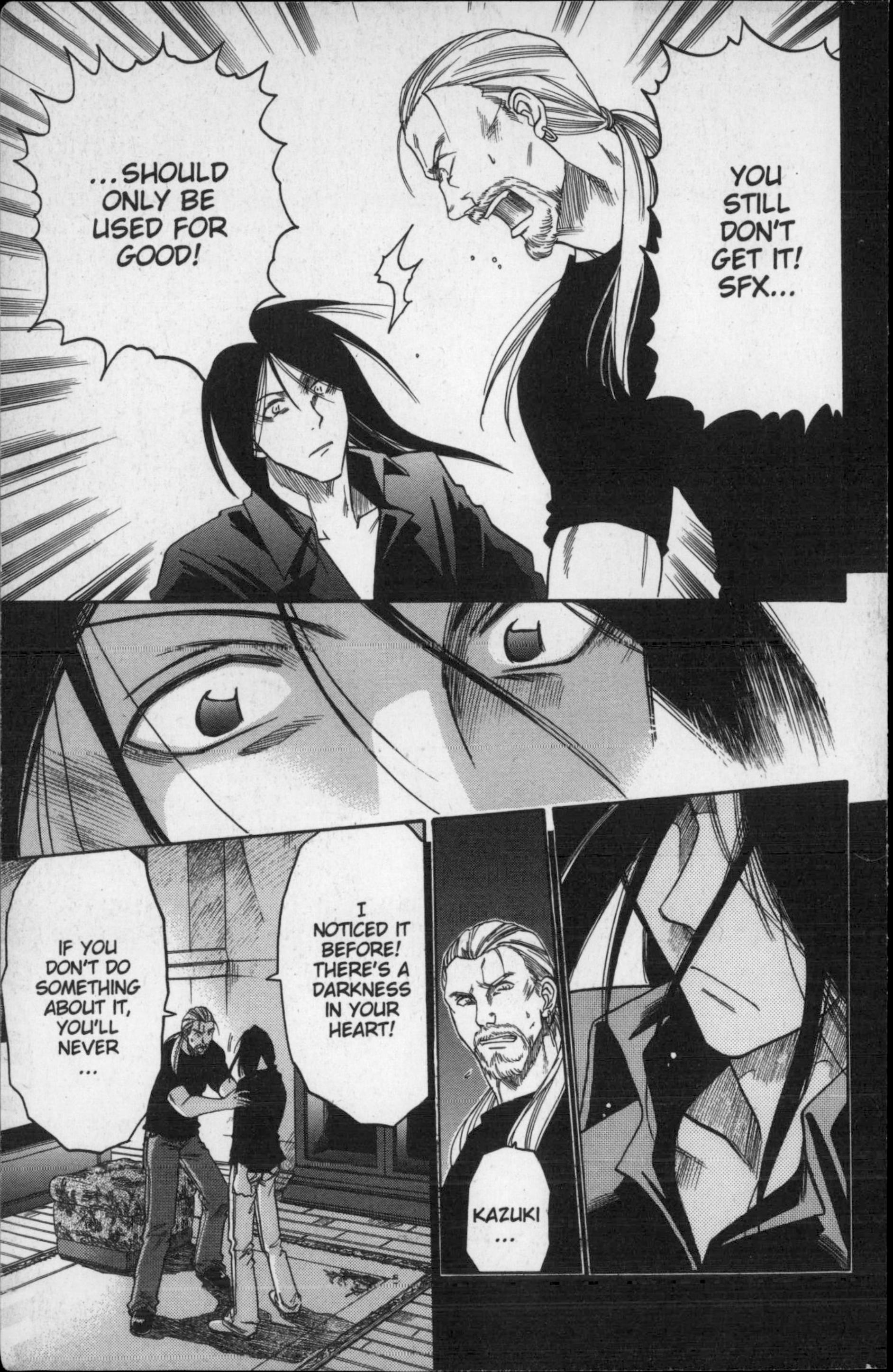
YOU STILL DON'T GET IT! SFX...
...SHOULD ONLY BE USED FOR GOOD!
KAZUKI ...
I NOTICED IT BEFORE! THERE'S A DARKNESS IN YOUR HEART!
IF YOU DON'T DO SOMETHING ABOUT IT, YOU'LL NEVER ...

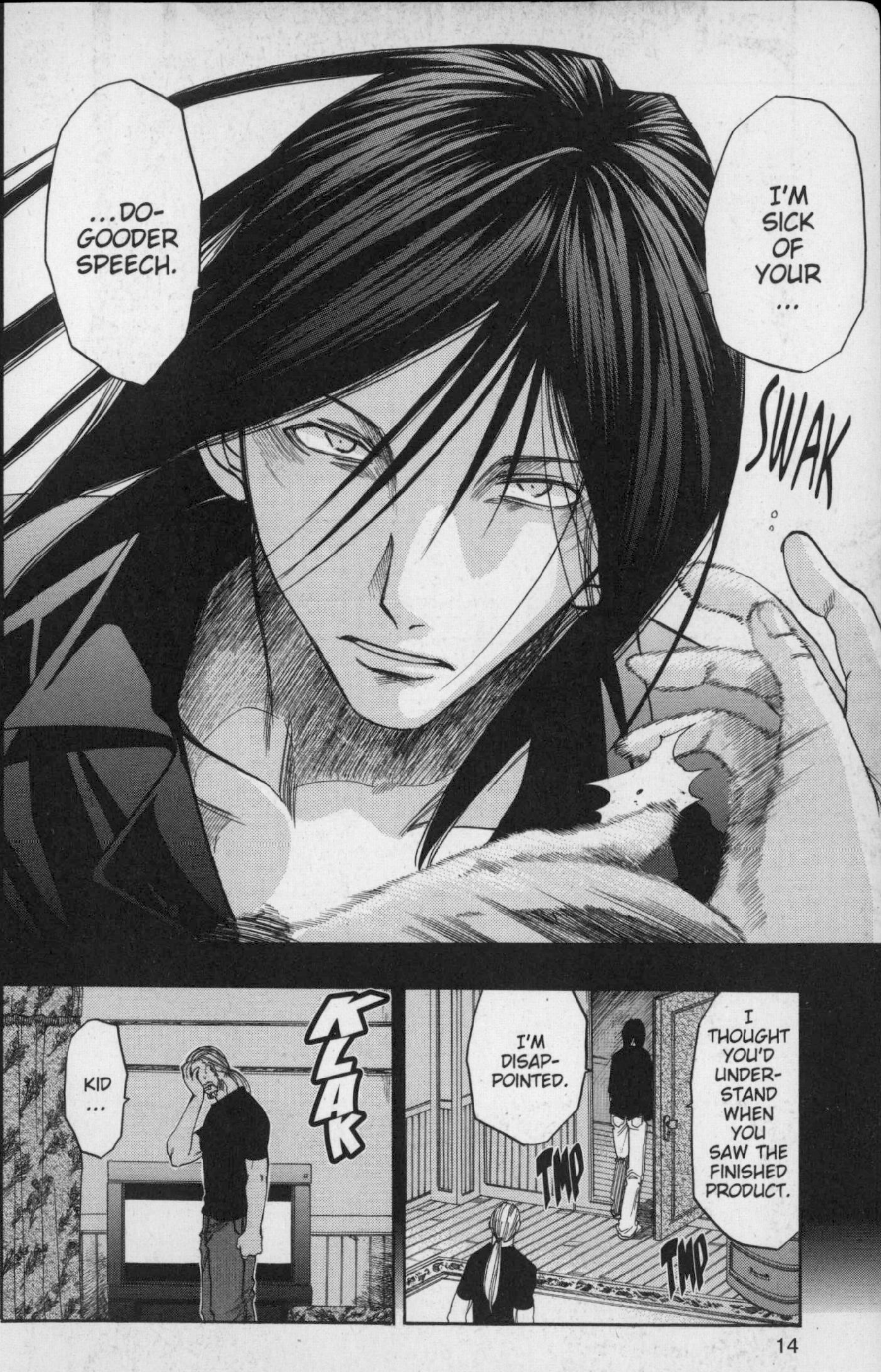
I'M SICK OF YOUR ...
SWAK
...DO-GOODER SPEECH.
I THOUGHT YOU'D UNDERSTAND WHEN YOU SAW THE FINISHED PRODUCT.
I'M DISAPPOINTED.
TMP
TMP
KLAK
KID ...

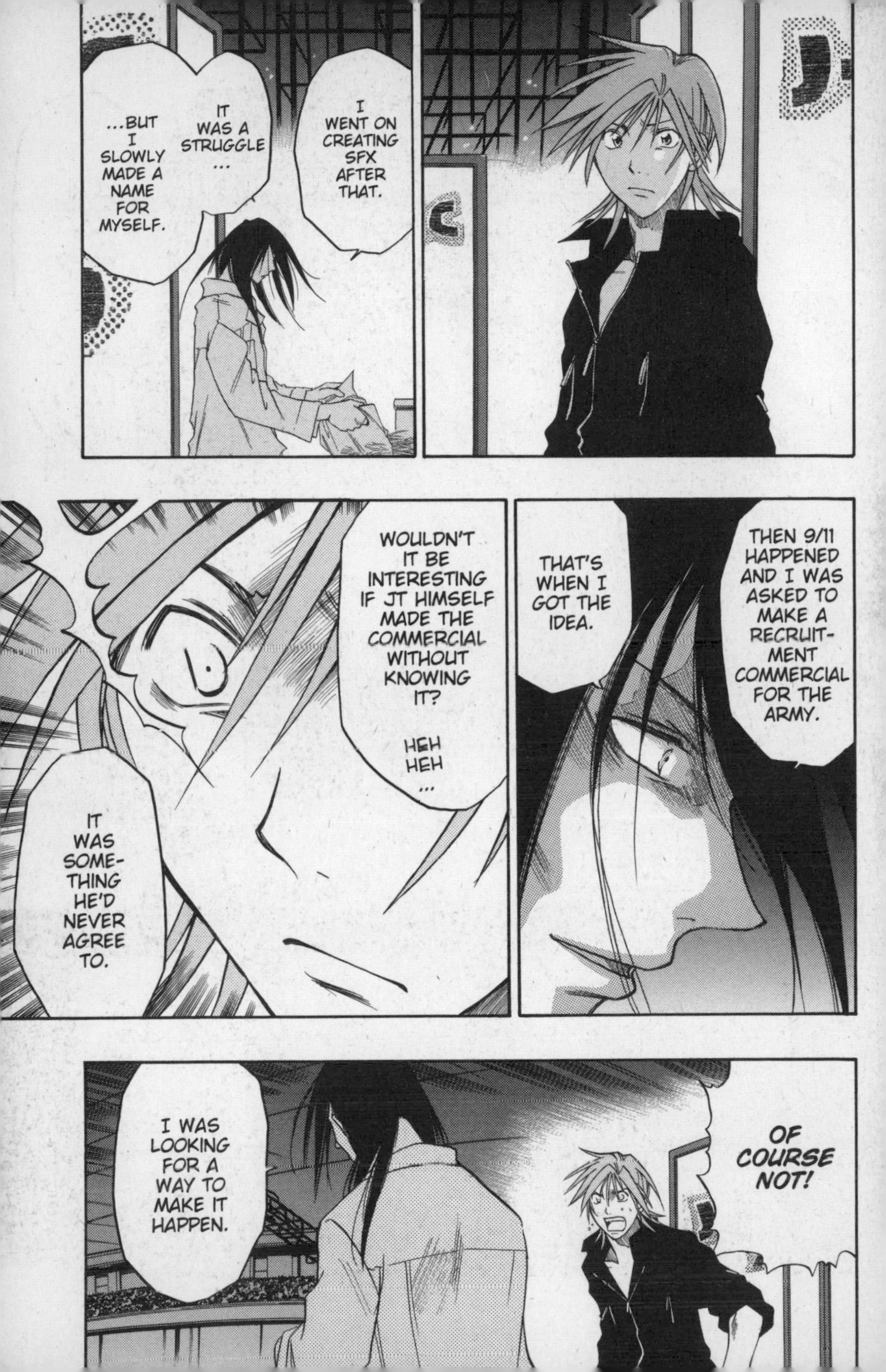

I WENT ON CREATING SFX AFTER THAT.
IT WAS A STRUGGLE...
...BUT I SLOWLY MADE A NAME FOR MYSELF.
THEN 9/11 HAPPENED AND I WAS ASKED TO MAKE A RECRUITMENT COMMERCIAL FOR THE ARMY.
THAT'S WHEN I GOT THE IDEA.
WOULDN'T IT BE INTERESTING IF JT HIMSELF MADE THE COMMERCIAL WITHOUT KNOWING IT?
HEH HEH...
IT WAS SOMETHING HE'D NEVER AGREE TO.
OF COURSE NOT!
I WAS LOOKING FOR A WAY TO MAKE IT HAPPEN.

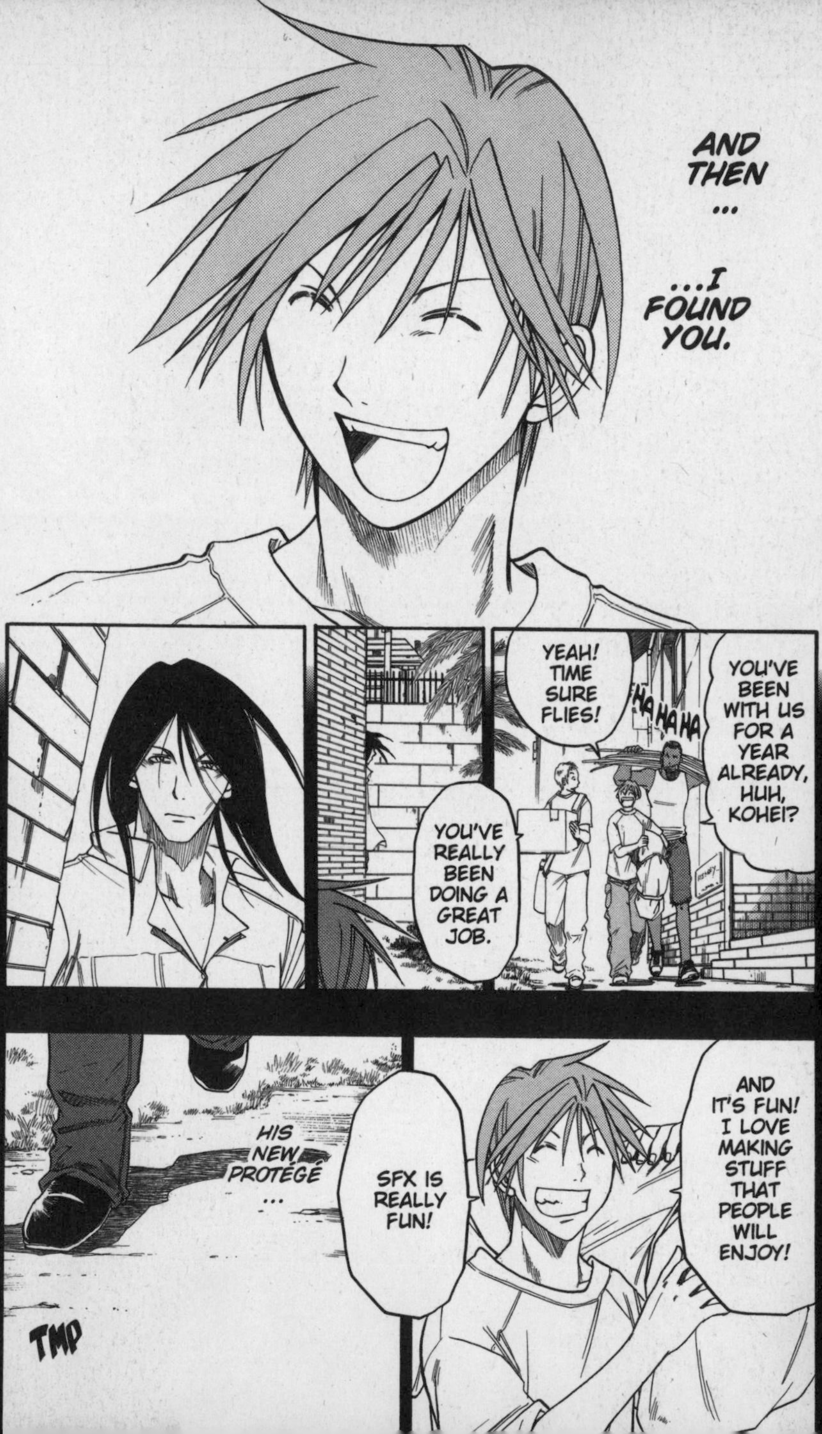
AND THEN ...
...I FOUND YOU.
YOU'VE BEEN WITH US FOR A YEAR ALREADY, HUH, KOHEI?
HA HA HA
YEAH! TIME SURE FLIES!
YOU'VE REALLY BEEN DOING A GREAT JOB.
SFX IS REALLY FUN!
AND IT'S FUN! I LOVE MAKING STUFF THAT PEOPLE WILL ENJOY!
HIS NEW PROTÉGÉ ...
TMP

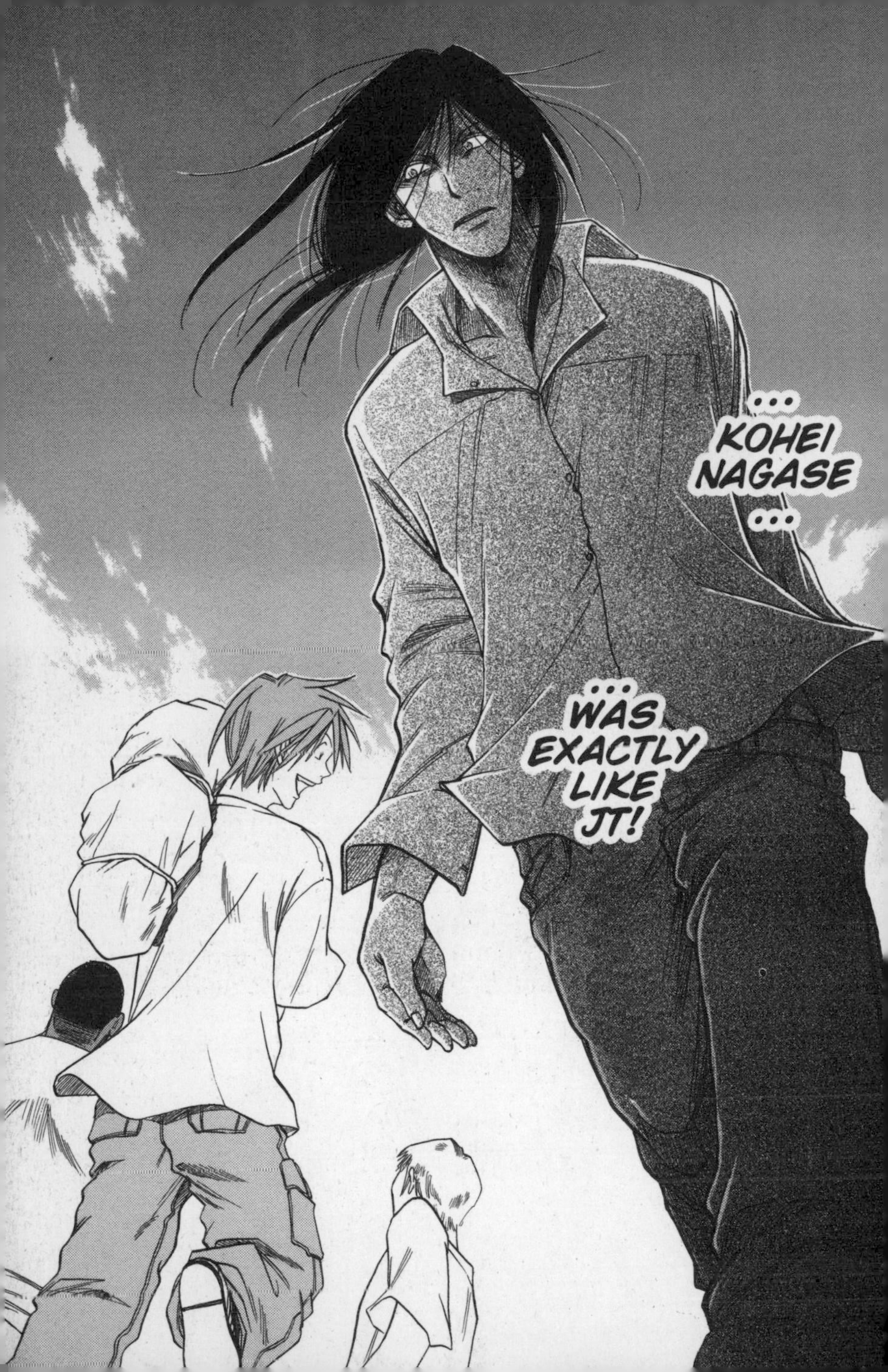
...KOHEI NAGASE ...
...WAS EXACTLY LIKE JT!

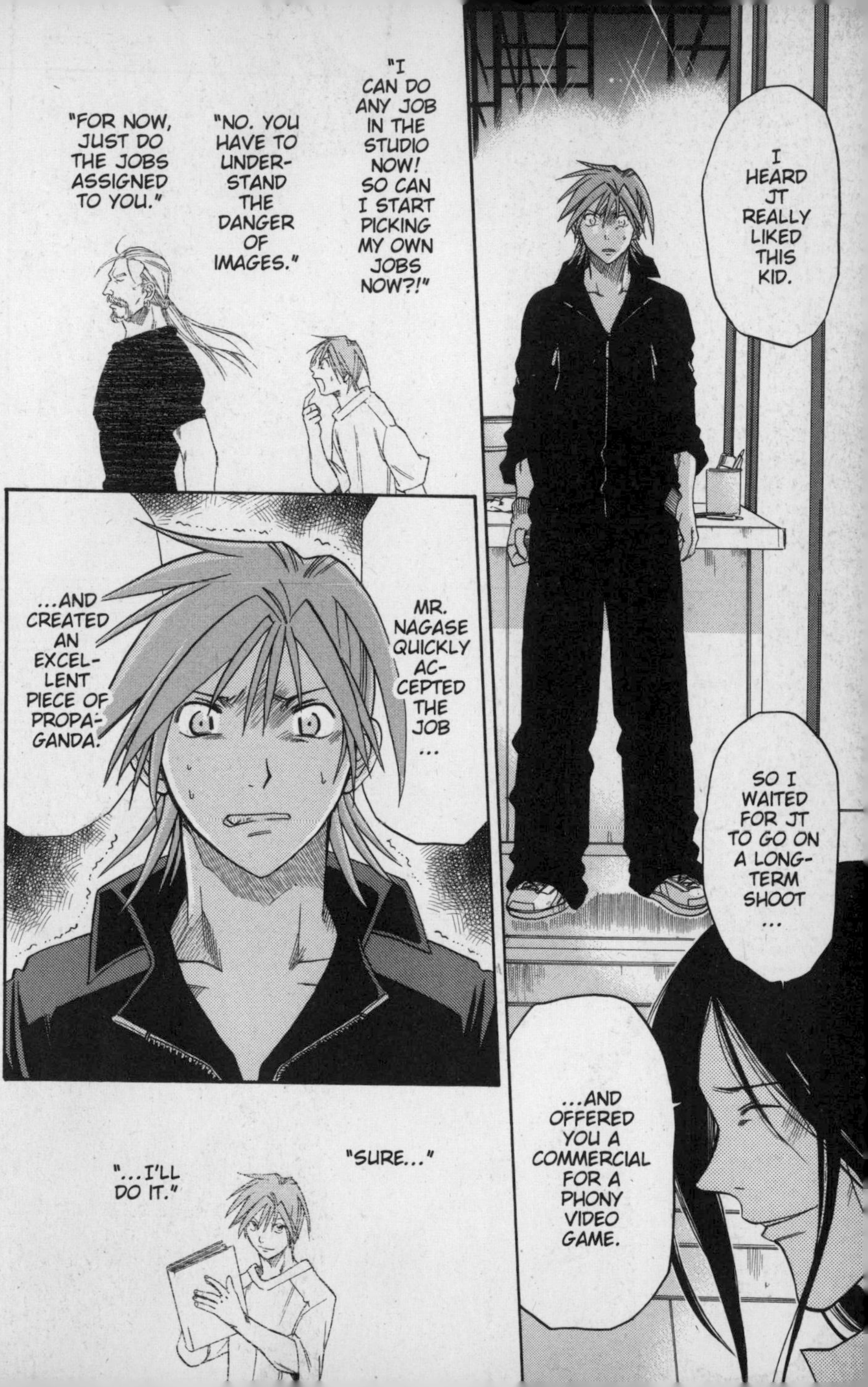
I HEARD JT REALLY LIKED THIS KID.
SO I WAITED FOR JT TO GO ON A LONG-TERM SHOOT...
"I CAN DO ANY JOB IN THE STUDIO NOW! SO CAN I START PICKING MY OWN JOBS NOW?!"
"NO. YOU HAVE TO UNDER-STAND THE DANGER OF IMAGES."
"FOR NOW, JUST DO THE JOBS ASSIGNED TO YOU."
MR. NAGASE QUICKLY AC-CEPTED THE JOB...
...AND CREATED AN EXCEL-LENT PIECE OF PROPA-GANDA.
...AND OFFERED YOU A COMMERCIAL FOR A PHONY VIDEO GAME.
"SURE..."
"...I'LL DO IT."

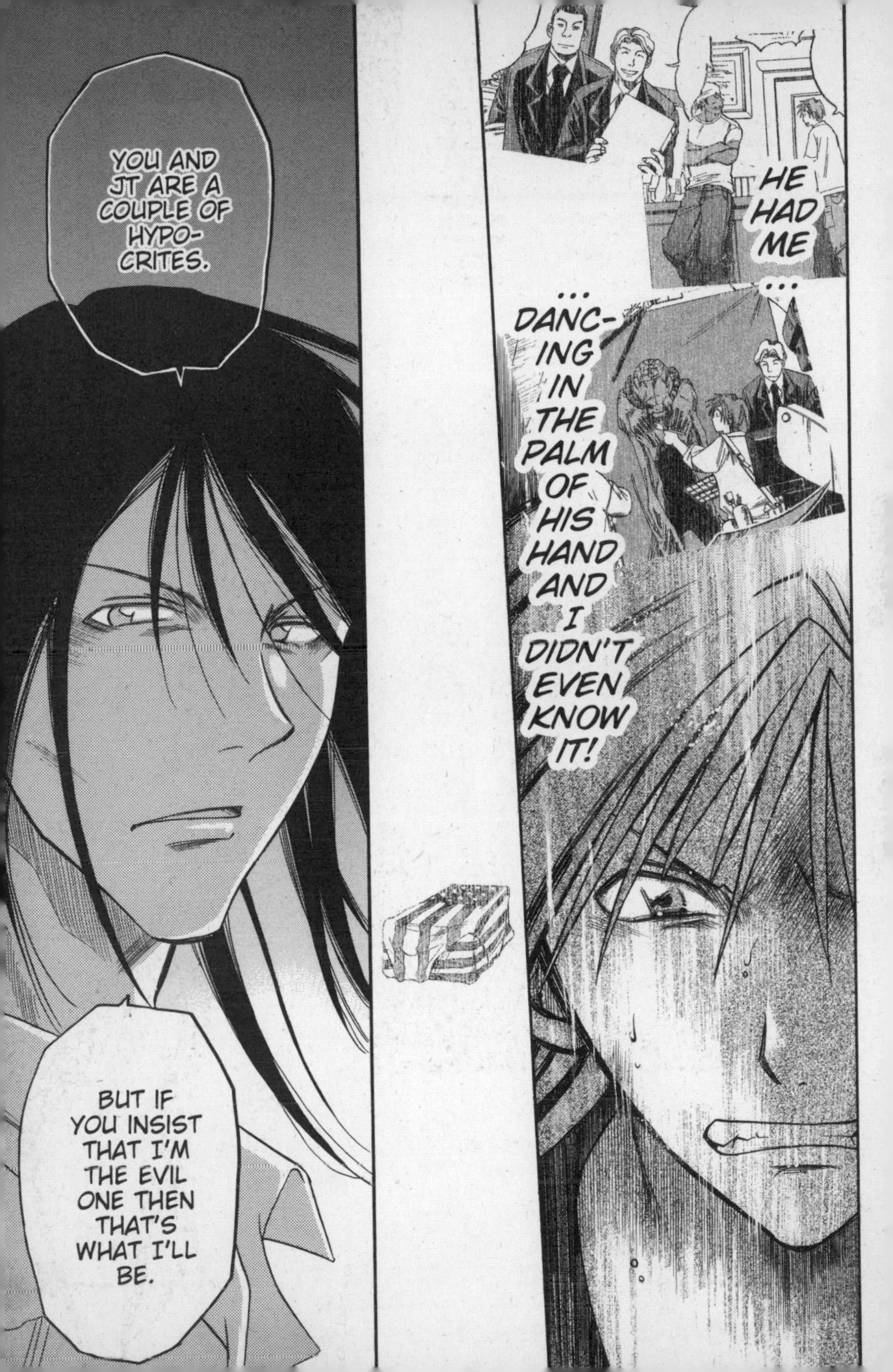
HE HAD ME ...
... DANCING IN THE PALM OF HIS HAND AND I DIDN'T EVEN KNOW IT!
YOU AND JT ARE A COUPLE OF HYPOCRITES.
BUT IF YOU INSIST THAT I'M THE EVIL ONE THEN THAT'S WHAT I'LL BE.

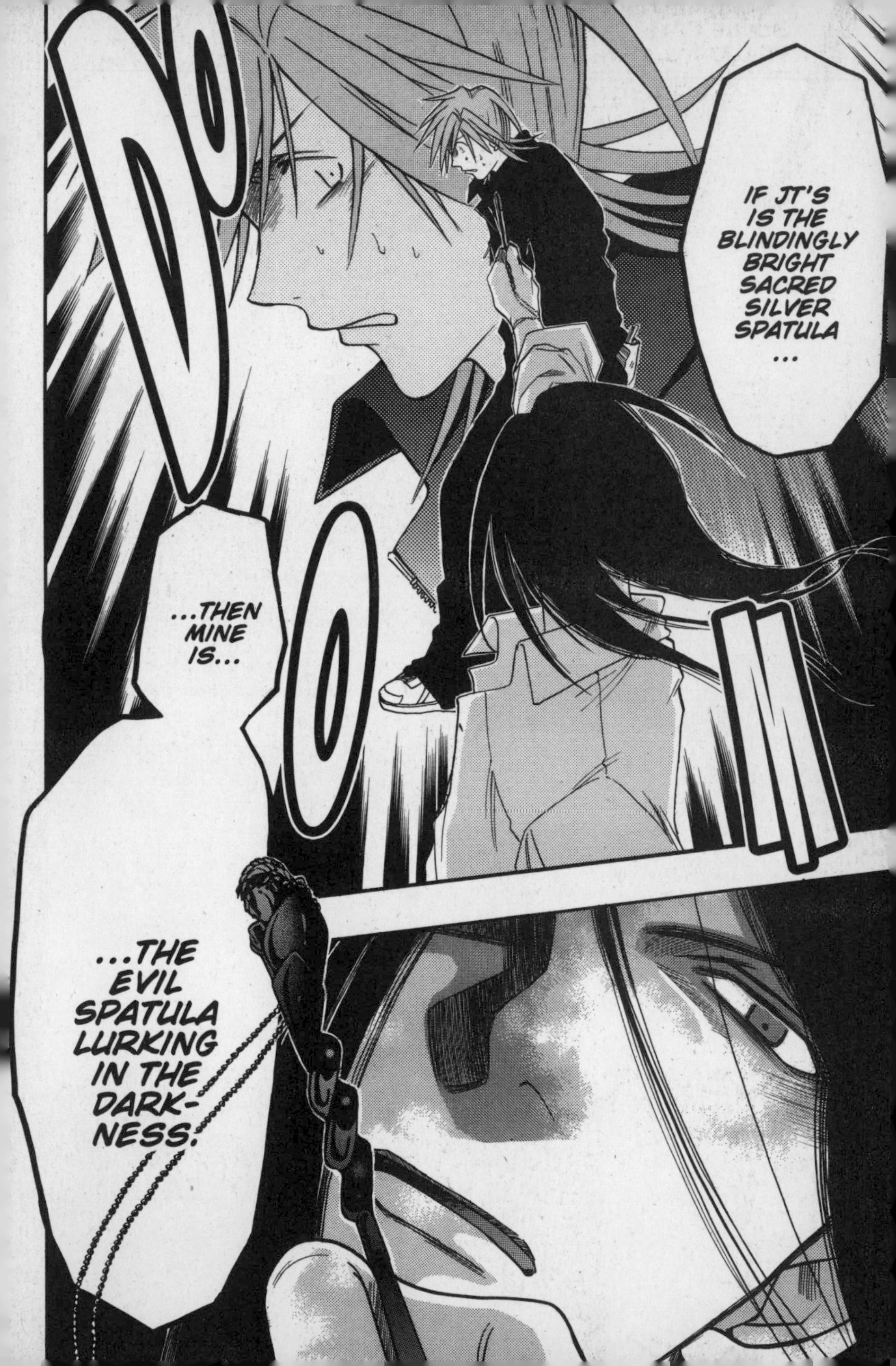
IF JT'S IS THE BLINDINGLY BRIGHT SACRED SILVER SPATULA ...
...THEN MINE IS...
...THE EVIL SPATULA LURKING IN THE DARK-NESS.

Scene 81: The Third Man (Part 4)

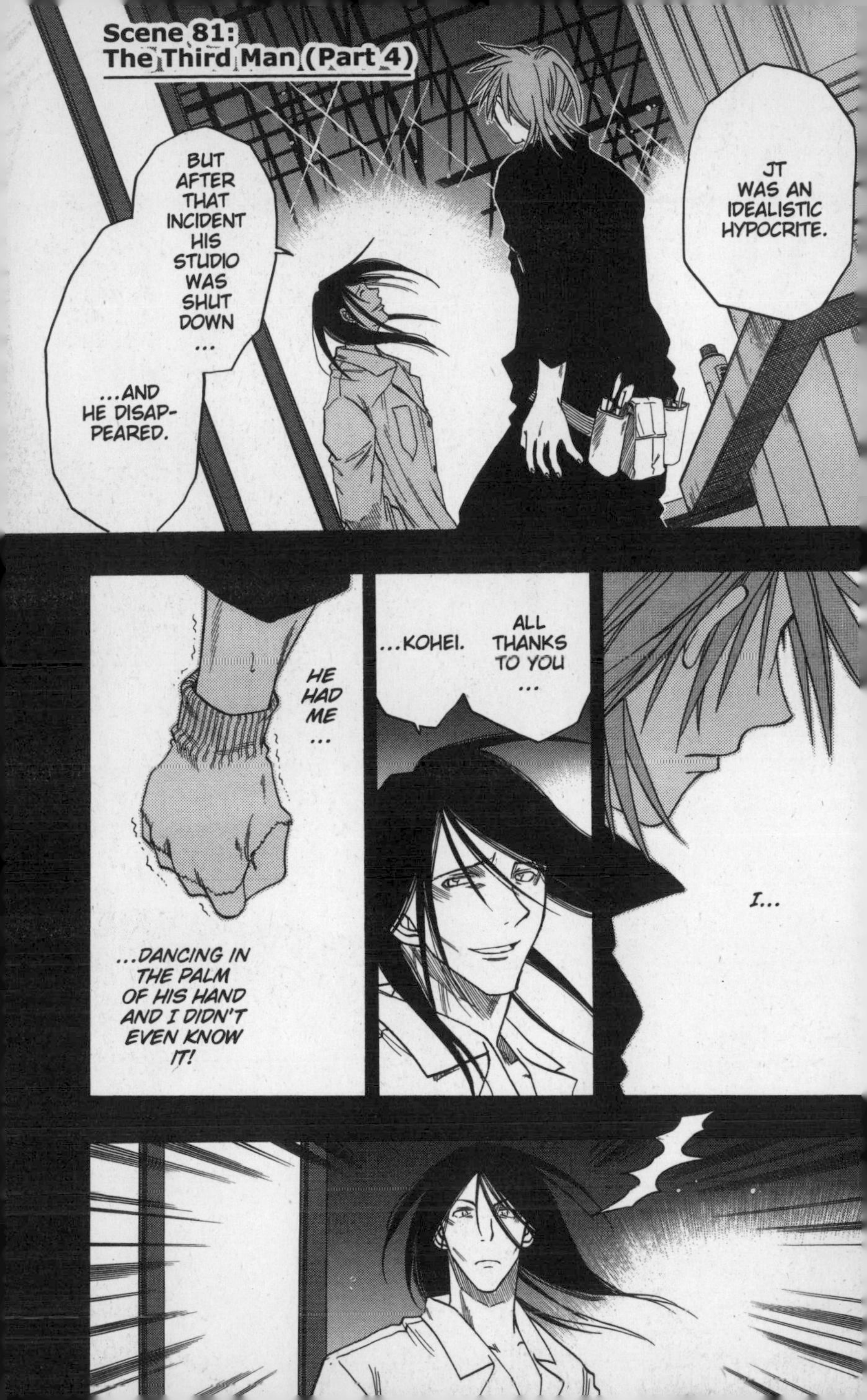
JT WAS AN IDEALISTIC HYPOCRITE.
BUT AFTER THAT INCIDENT HIS STUDIO WAS SHUT DOWN ...
...AND HE DISAPPEARED.
I...
ALL THANKS TO YOU ...
...KOHEI.
HE HAD ME ...
...DANCING IN THE PALM OF HIS HAND AND I DIDN'T EVEN KNOW IT!

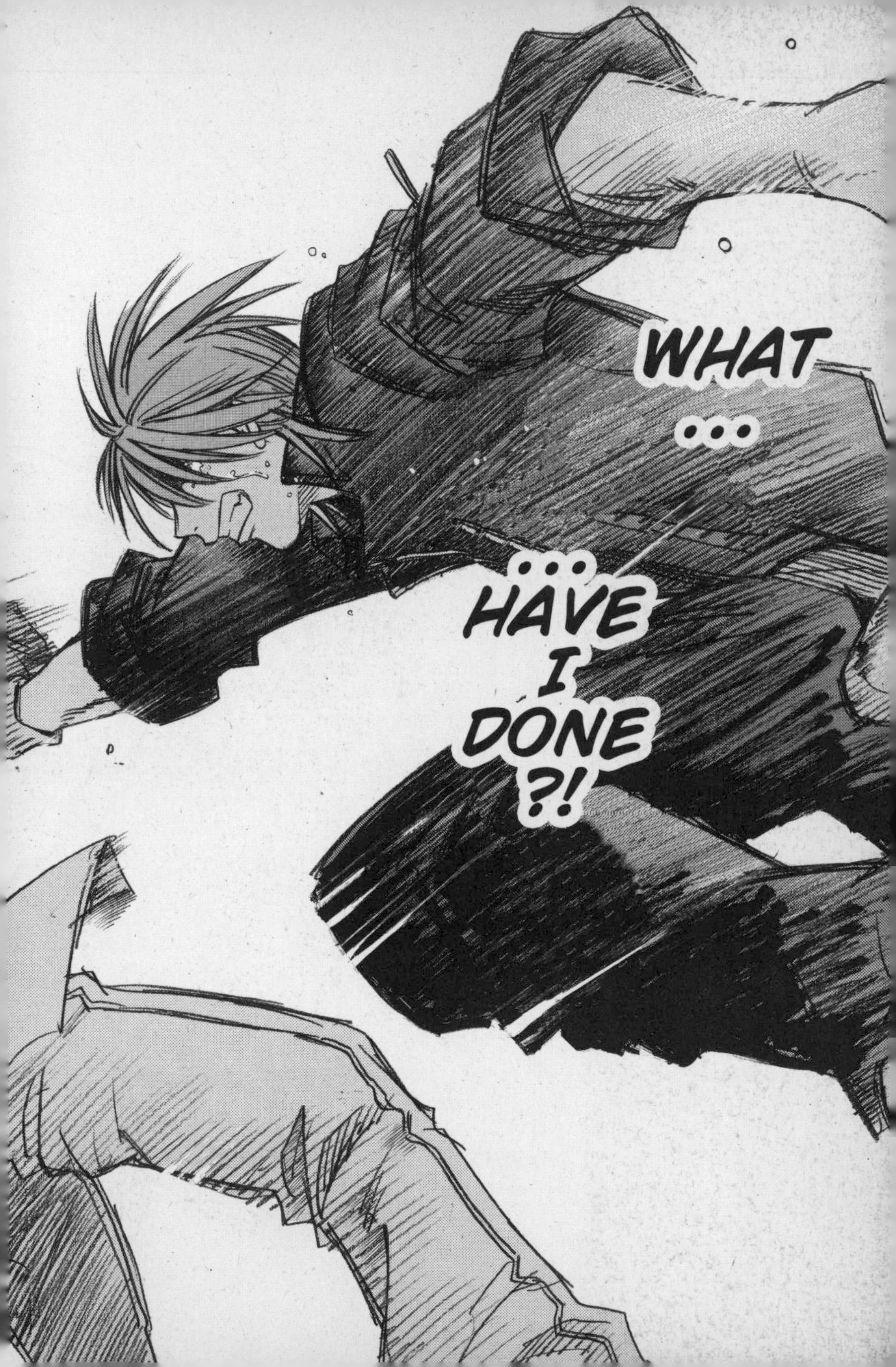
WHAT ...
... HAVE I DONE ?!

Scene 81: The Third Man (Part 4)

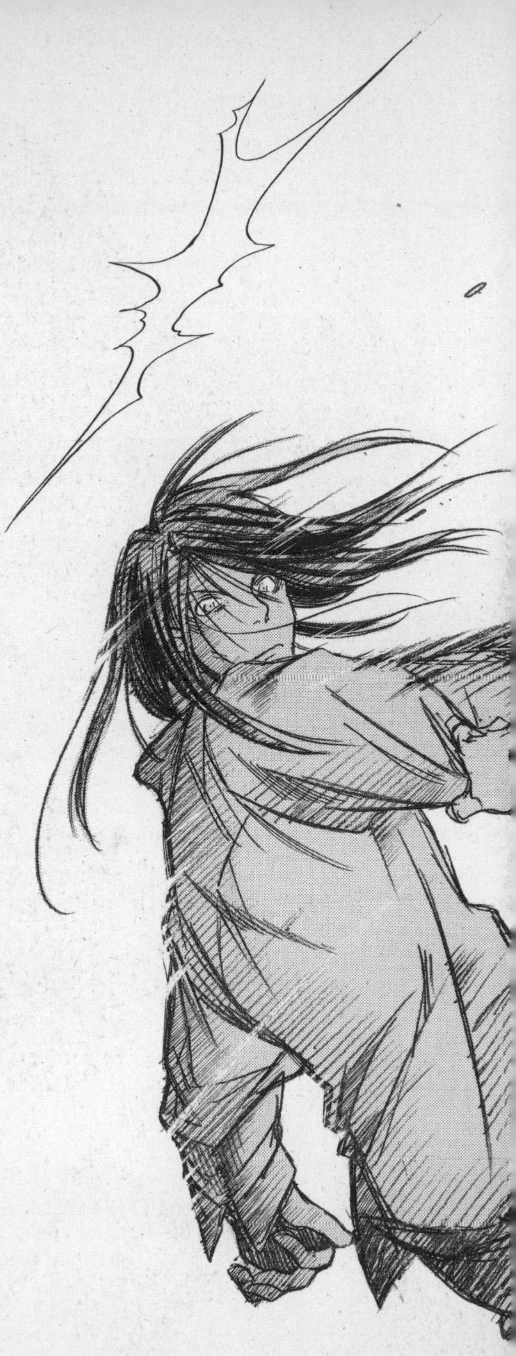

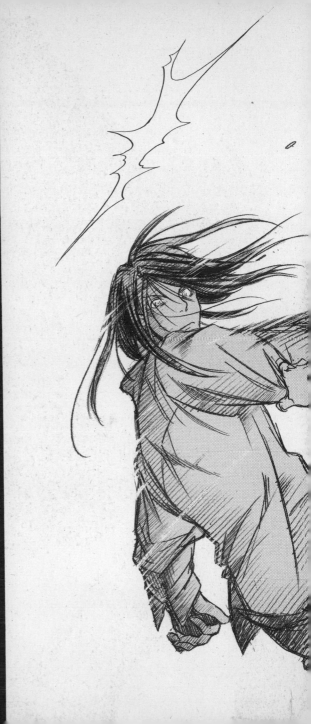

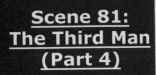

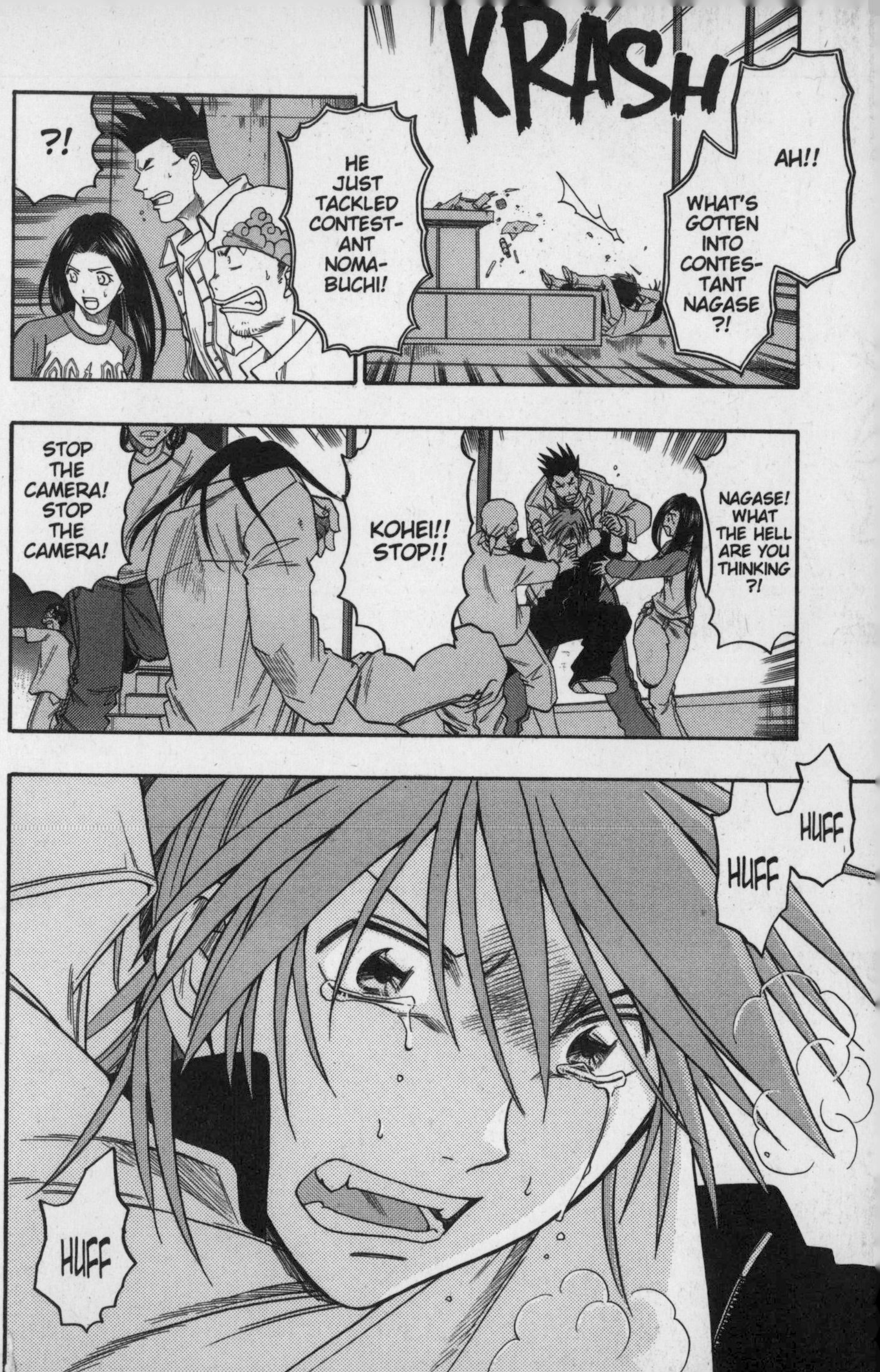
KRASH
AH!!
WHAT'S GOTTEN INTO CONTESTANT NAGASE ?!
HE JUST TACKLED CONTESTANT NOMABUCHI!
?!
NAGASE! WHAT THE HELL ARE YOU THINKING ?!
KOHEI!! STOP!!
STOP THE CAMERA! STOP THE CAMERA!
HUFF
HUFF
HUFF

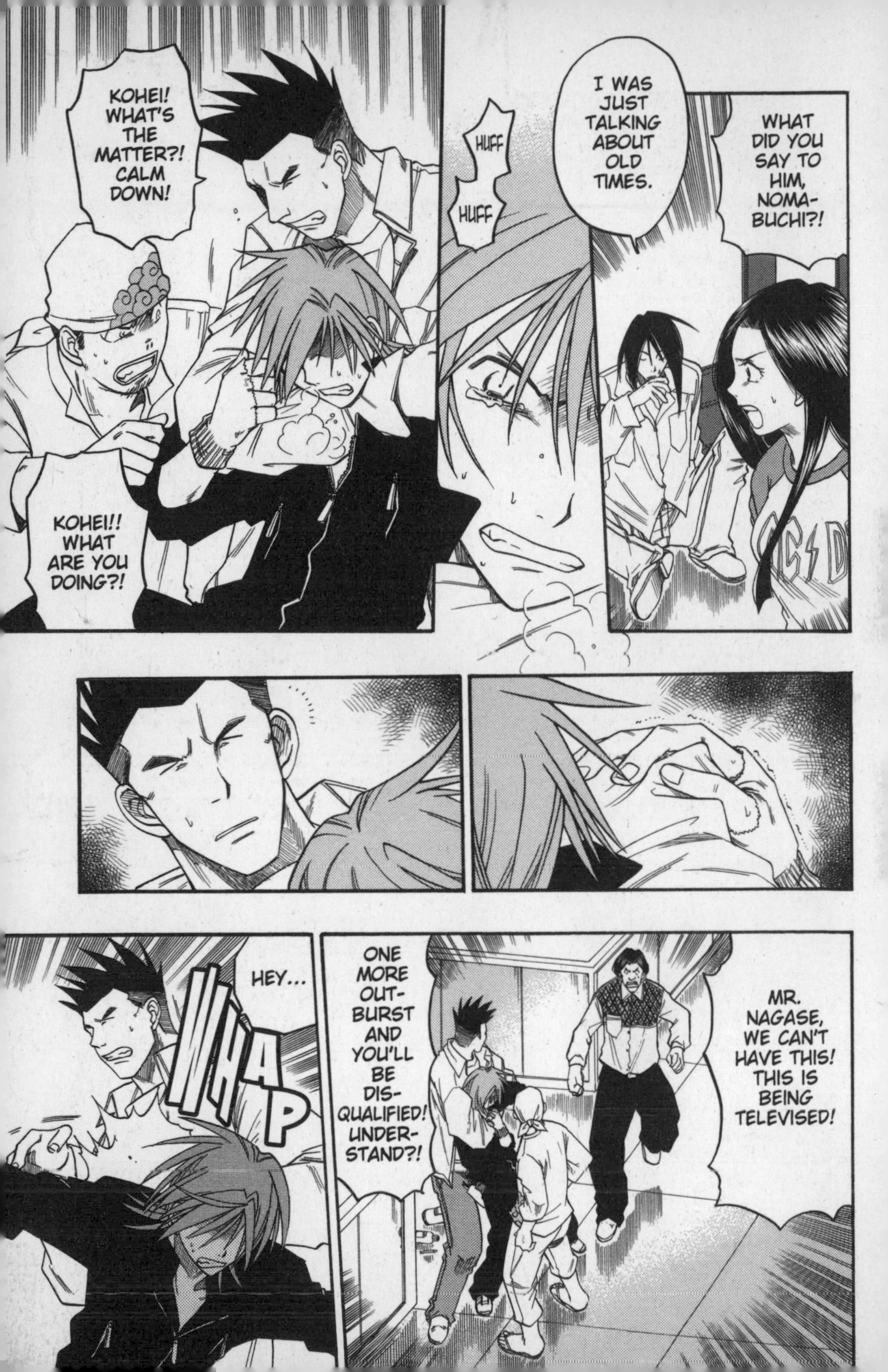
WHAT DID YOU SAY TO HIM, NOMA-BUCHI?!
I WAS JUST TALKING ABOUT OLD TIMES.
HUFF
HUFF
KOHEI! WHAT'S THE MATTER?! CALM DOWN!
KOHEI!! WHAT ARE YOU DOING?!
MR. NAGASE, WE CAN'T HAVE THIS! THIS IS BEING TELEVISED!
ONE MORE OUT-BURST AND YOU'LL BE DIS-QUALIFIED! UNDER-STAND?!
HEY...
WHAP

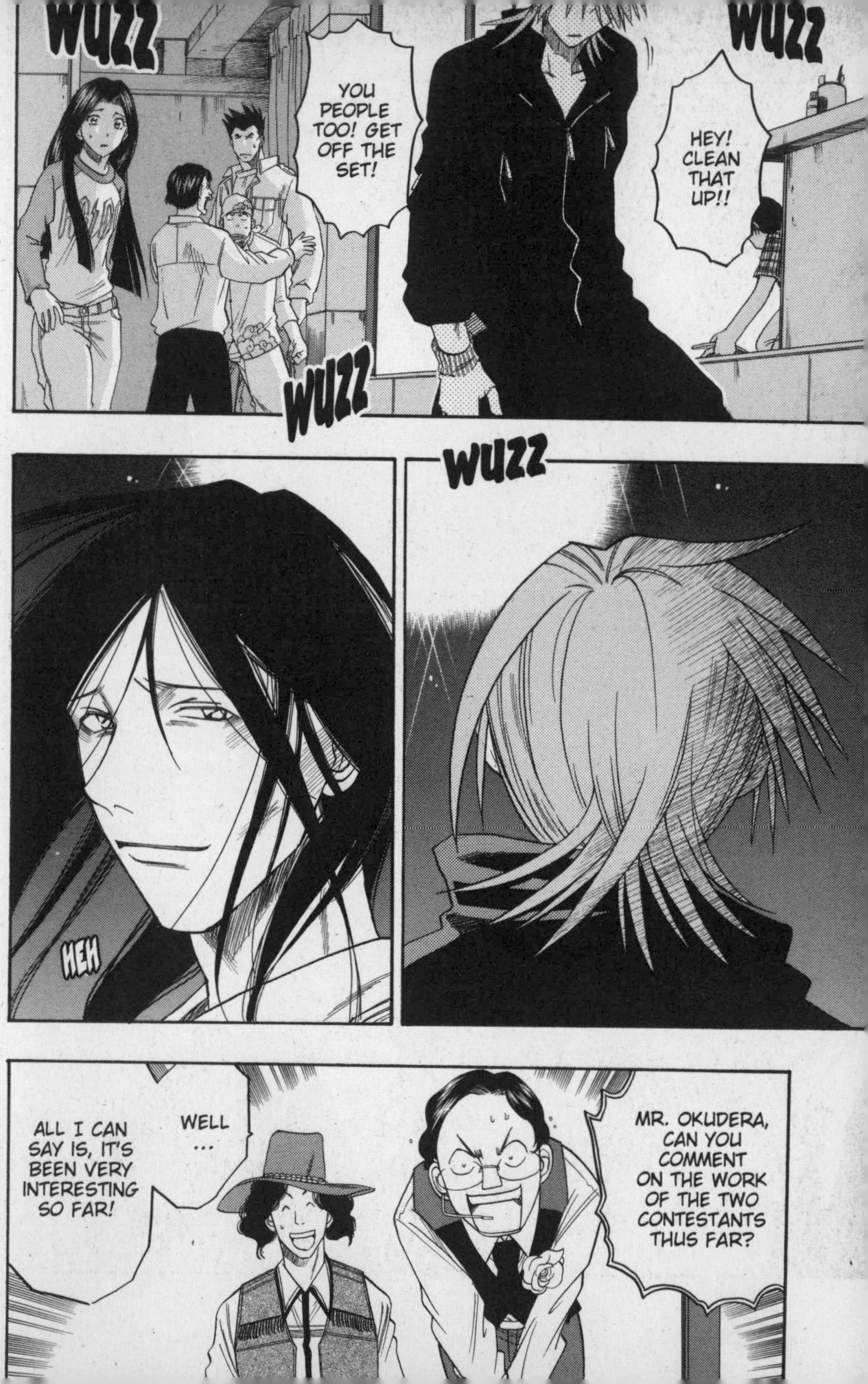
WUZZ
HEY! CLEAN THAT UP!!
YOU PEOPLE TOO! GET OFF THE SET!
WUZZ
WUZZ
WUZZ
HEH
MR. OKUDERA, CAN YOU COMMENT ON THE WORK OF THE TWO CONTESTANTS THUS FAR?
WELL ...
ALL I CAN SAY IS, IT'S BEEN VERY INTERESTING SO FAR!

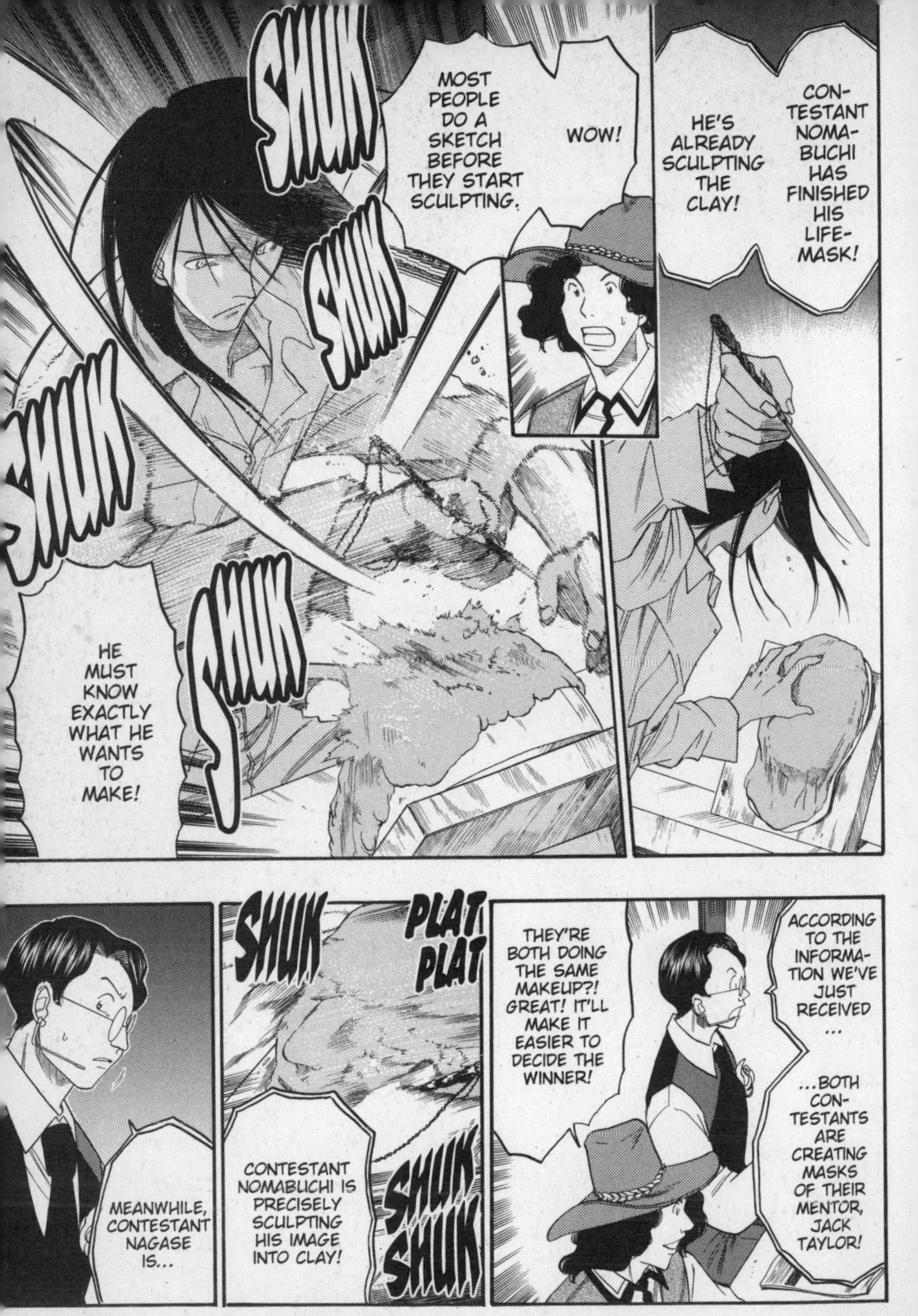
CON-TESTANT NOMA-BUCHI HAS FINISHED HIS LIFE-MASK!
HE'S ALREADY SCULPTING THE CLAY!
WOW!
MOST PEOPLE DO A SKETCH BEFORE THEY START SCULPTING.
SHUK
SHUK
SHUK
SHUK
SHUK
HE MUST KNOW EXACTLY WHAT HE WANTS TO MAKE!
ACCORDING TO THE INFORMATION WE'VE JUST RECEIVED...
...BOTH CONTESTANTS ARE CREATING MASKS OF THEIR MENTOR, JACK TAYLOR!
THEY'RE BOTH DOING THE SAME MAKEUP?! GREAT! IT'LL MAKE IT EASIER TO DECIDE THE WINNER!
PLAT PLAT
SHUK
SHUK SHUK
CONTESTANT NOMABUCHI IS PRECISELY SCULPTING HIS IMAGE INTO CLAY!
MEANWHILE, CONTESTANT NAGASE IS...

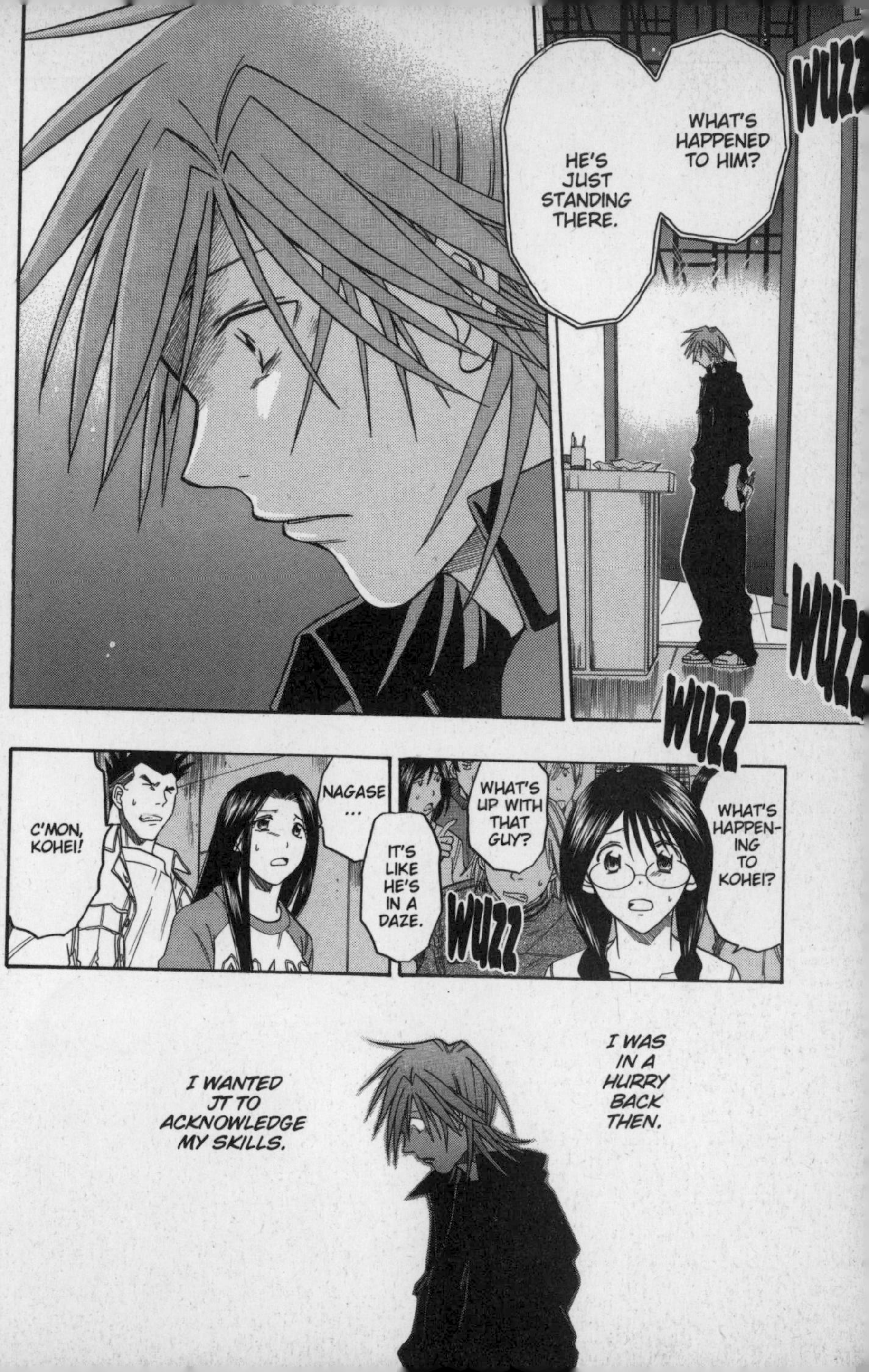
WHAT'S HAPPENED TO HIM?
HE'S JUST STANDING THERE.
WUZZ
WUZZ
WUZZ
WHAT'S HAPPENING TO KOHEI?
WHAT'S UP WITH THAT GUY?
IT'S LIKE HE'S IN A DAZE.
WUZZ
NAGASE ...
C'MON, KOHEI!
I WAS IN A HURRY BACK THEN.
I WANTED JT TO ACKNOWLEDGE MY SKILLS.

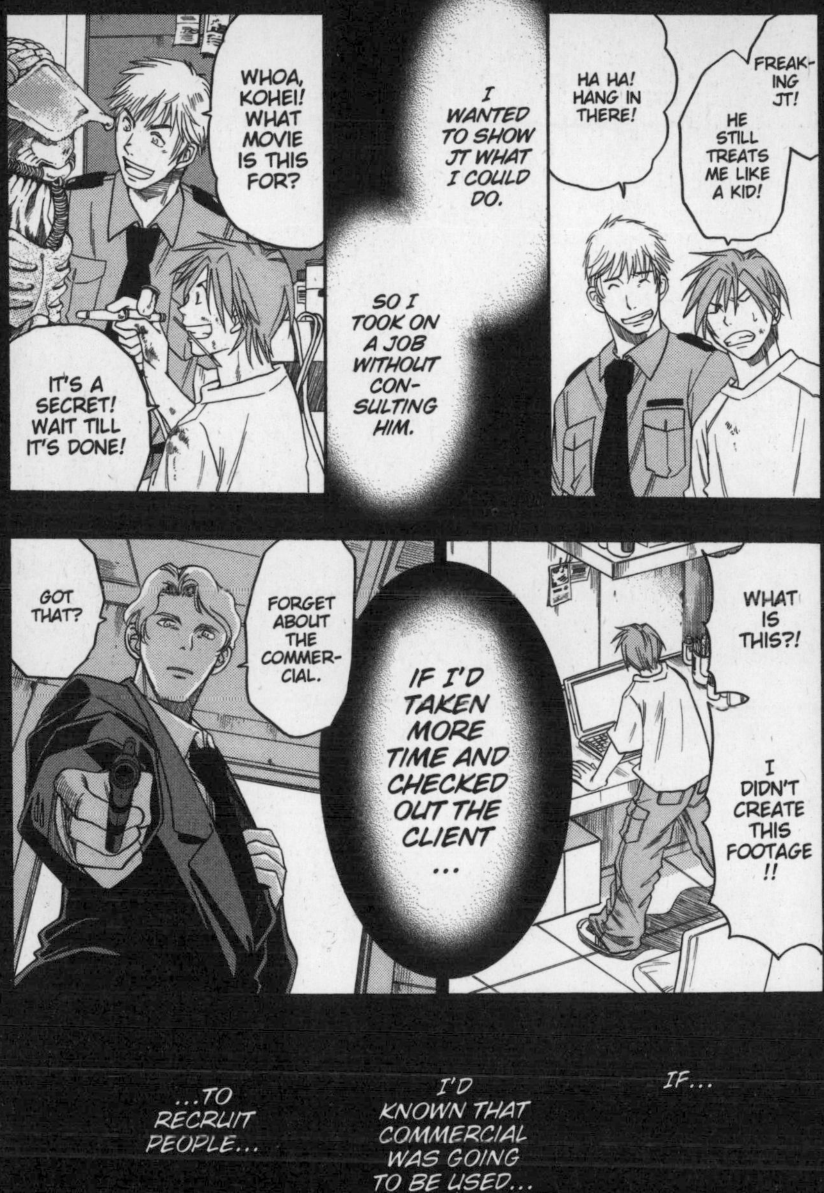
FREAKING JT!
HE STILL TREATS ME LIKE A KID!
HA HA! HANG IN THERE!
I WANTED TO SHOW JT WHAT I COULD DO.
SO I TOOK ON A JOB WITHOUT CONSULTING HIM.
WHOA, KOHEI! WHAT MOVIE IS THIS FOR?
IT'S A SECRET! WAIT TILL IT'S DONE!
WHAT IS THIS?!
I DIDN'T CREATE THIS FOOTAGE!!
IF I'D TAKEN MORE TIME AND CHECKED OUT THE CLIENT ...
FORGET ABOUT THE COMMERCIAL.
GOT THAT?
IF...
I'D KNOWN THAT COMMERCIAL WAS GOING TO BE USED...
...TO RECRUIT PEOPLE...

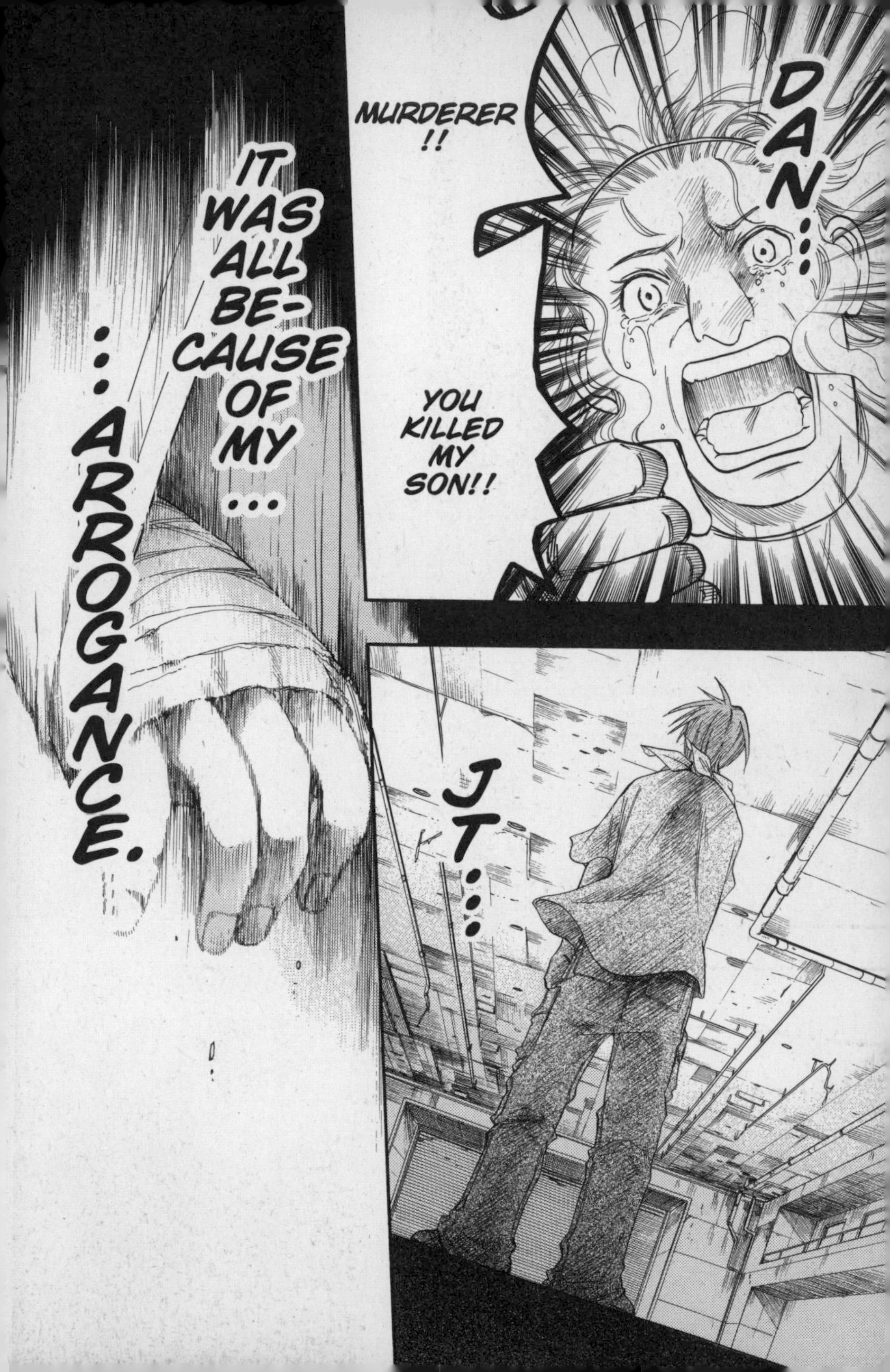
DAN...
MURDERER!!
YOU KILLED MY SON!!
JT...
IT WAS ALL BE-CAUSE OF MY...
...ARROGANCE.

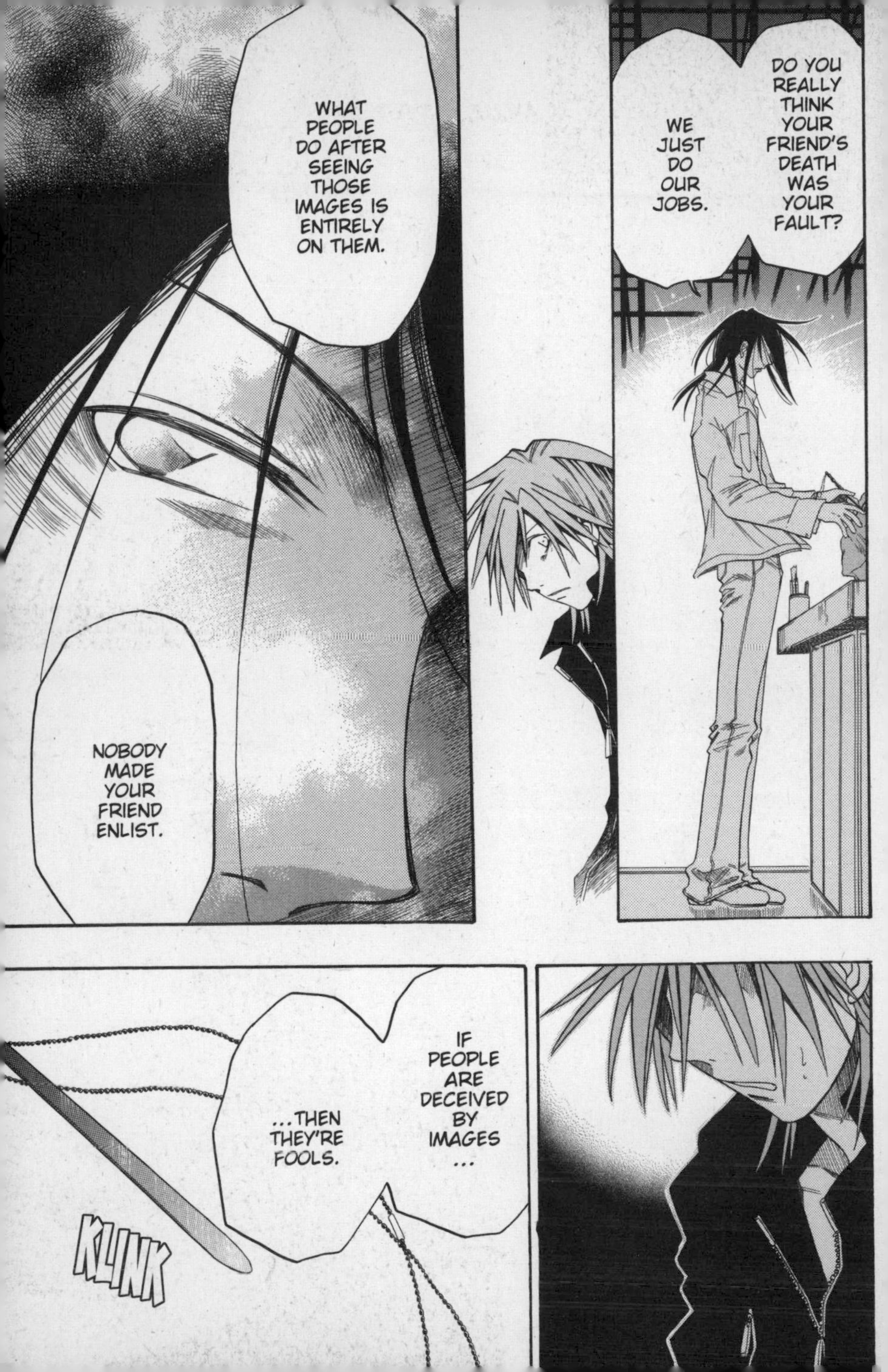
DO YOU REALLY THINK YOUR FRIEND'S DEATH WAS YOUR FAULT?
WE JUST DO OUR JOBS.
WHAT PEOPLE DO AFTER SEEING THOSE IMAGES IS ENTIRELY ON THEM.
NOBODY MADE YOUR FRIEND ENLIST.
IF PEOPLE ARE DECEIVED BY IMAGES...
...THEN THEY'RE FOOLS.
KLINK

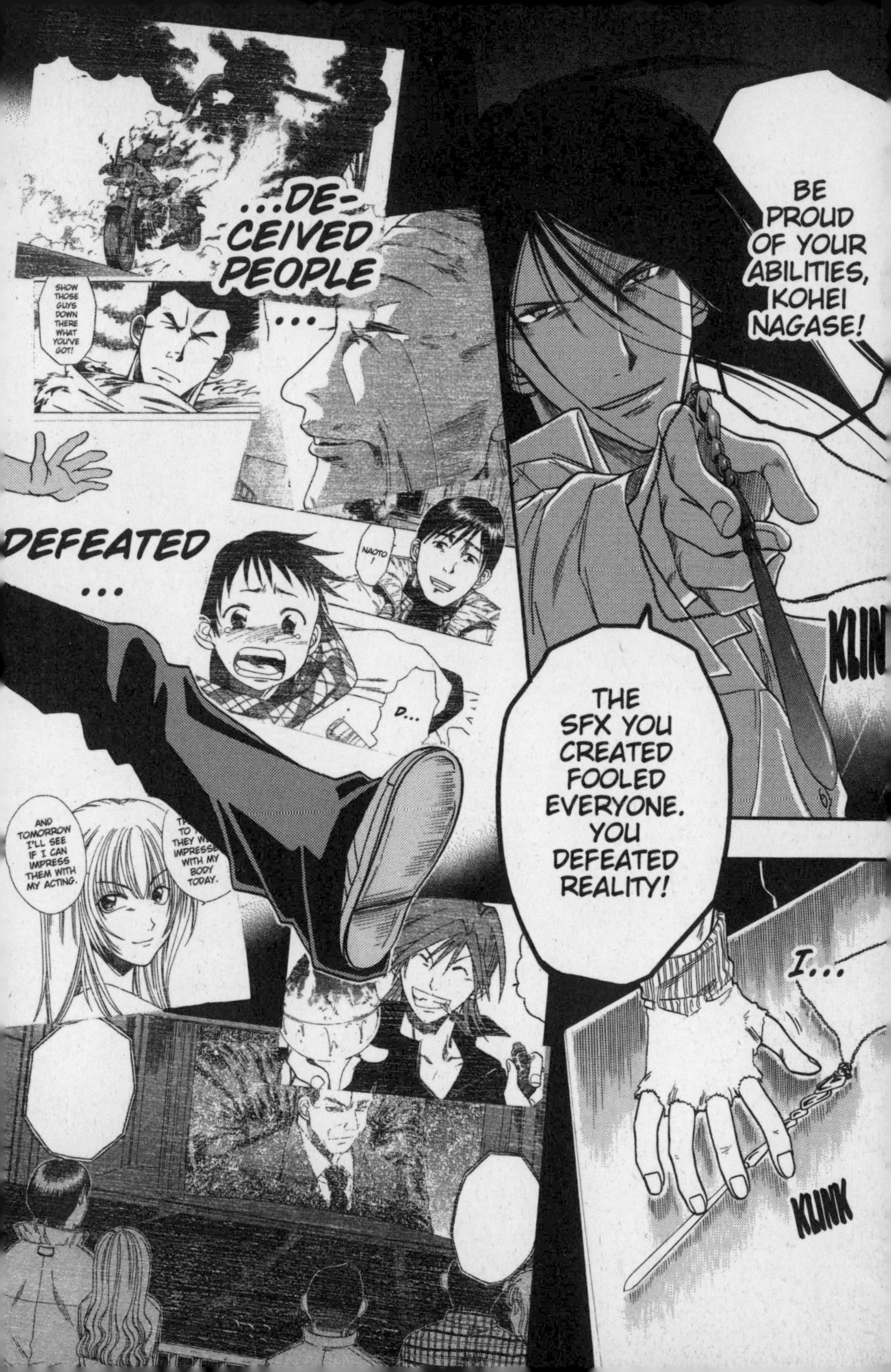

BE PROUD OF YOUR ABILITIES, KOHEI NAGASE!
KLIN
THE SFX YOU CREATED FOOLED EVERYONE. YOU DEFEATED REALITY!
I...
KLINK
...DE-CEIVED PEOPLE
...
SHOW THOSE GUYS DOWN THERE WHAT YOU'VE GOT!
DEFEATED ...
NAOTO!
D...
AND TOMORROW I'LL SEE IF I CAN IMPRESS THEM WITH MY ACTING.

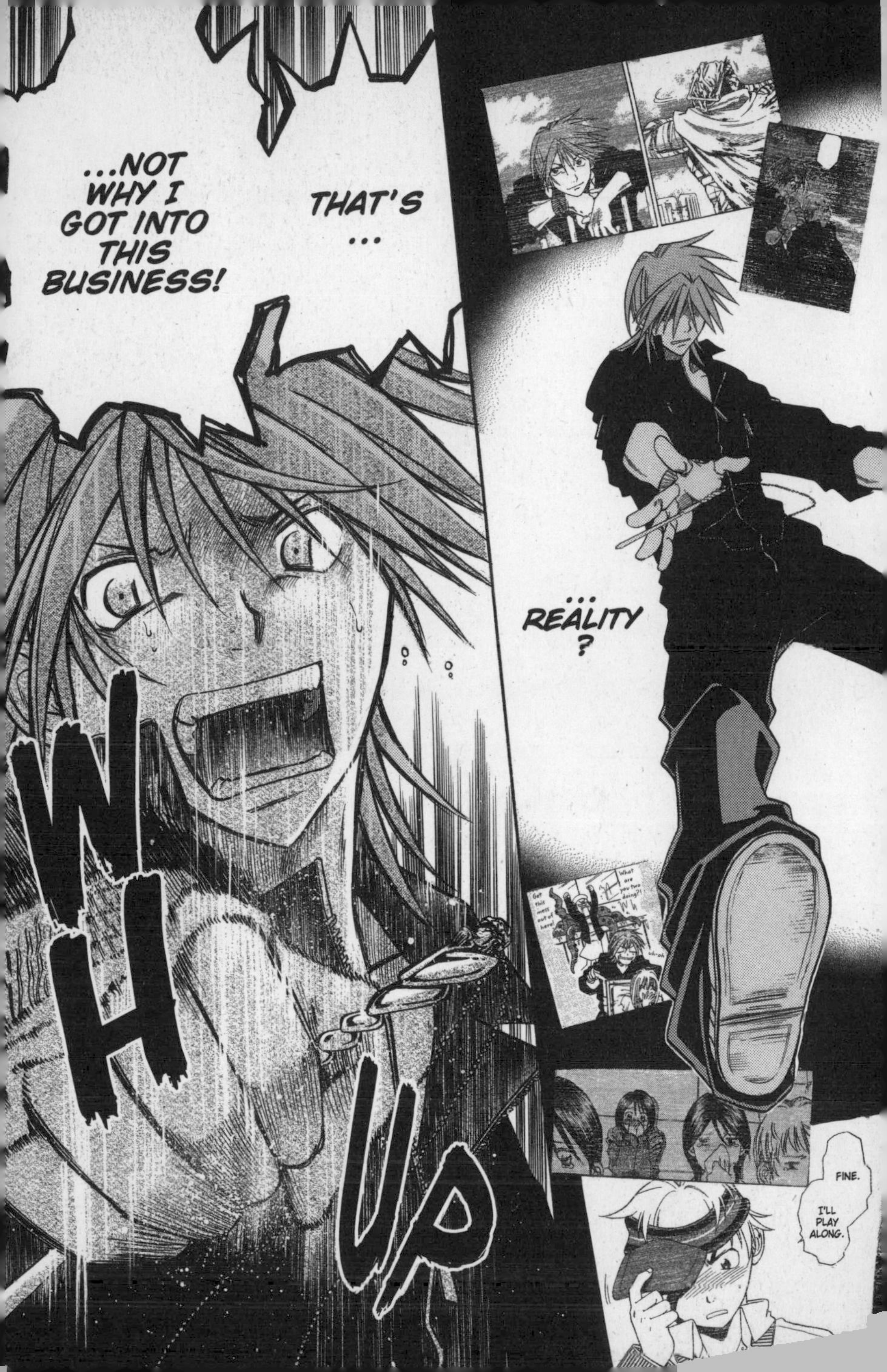
...REALITY?
What are you two doing?!
Wh
Get this mess out of here!
uh-oh
FINE.
I'LL PLAY ALONG.
THAT'S...
...NOT WHY I GOT INTO THIS BUSINESS!
WHUP

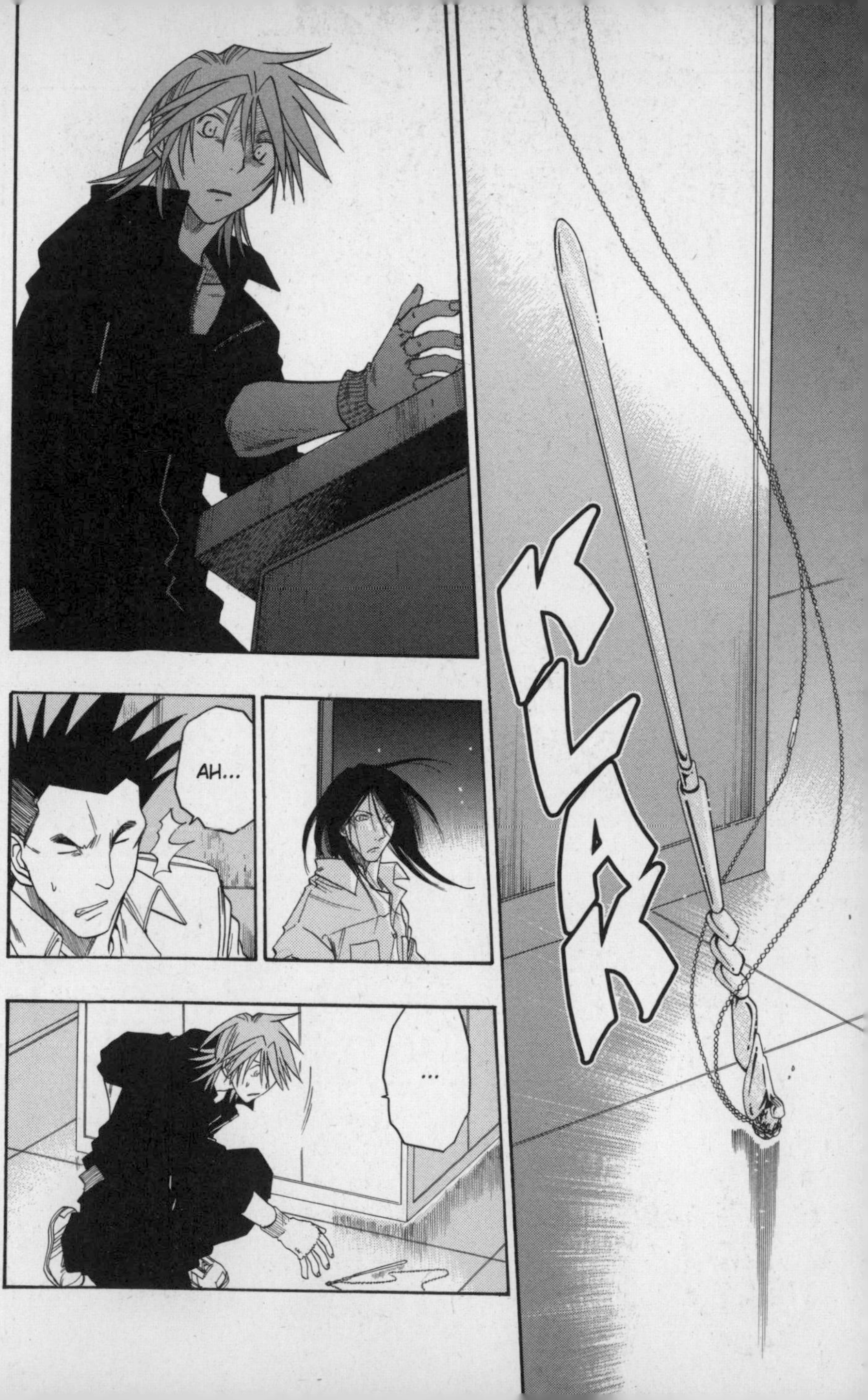
KLAK
AH...
...

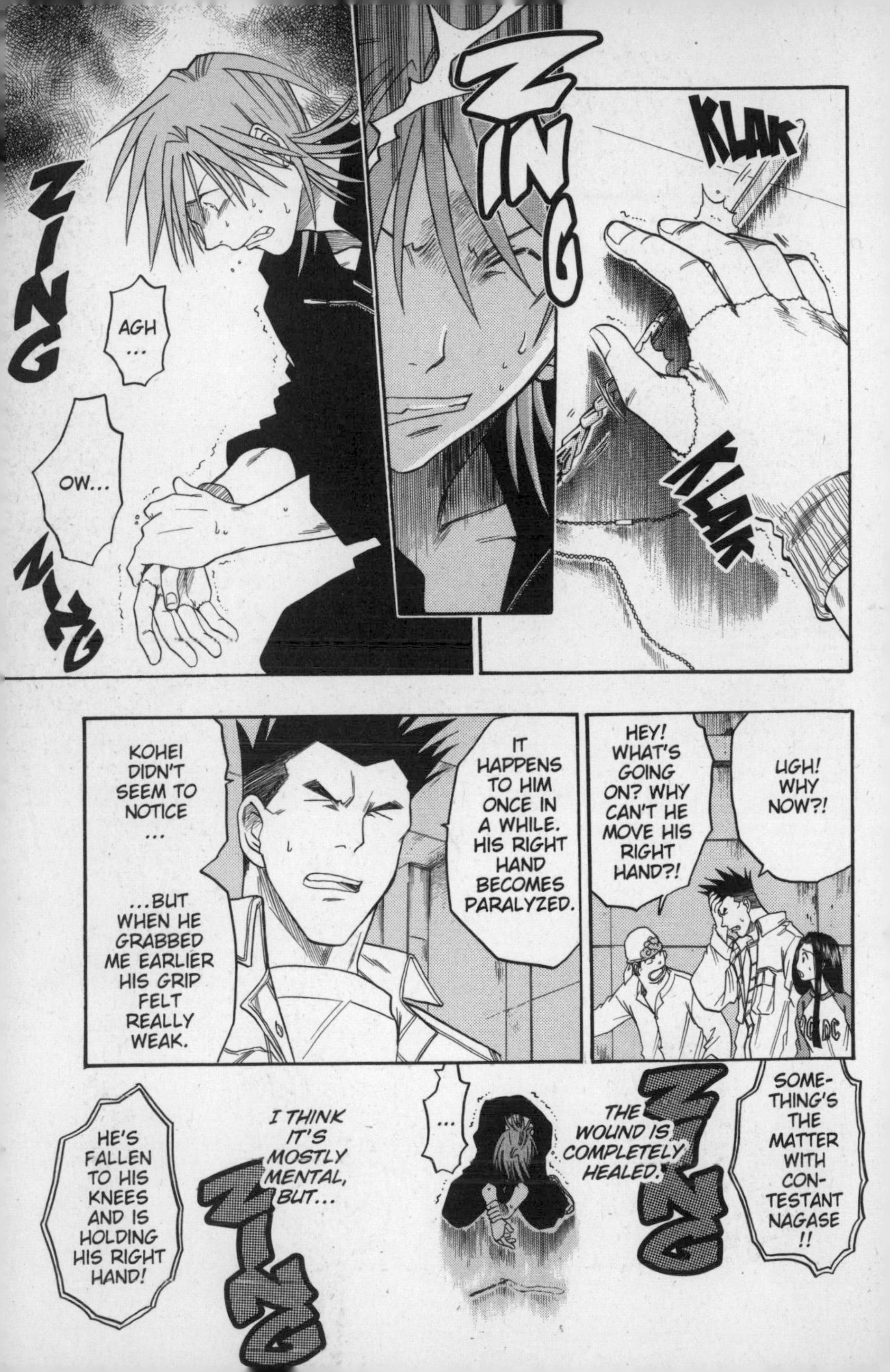
KLAK
KLAK
ZING
ZING
AGH...
OW...
ZING
UGH! WHY NOW?!
HEY! WHAT'S GOING ON? WHY CAN'T HE MOVE HIS RIGHT HAND?!
IT HAPPENS TO HIM ONCE IN A WHILE. HIS RIGHT HAND BECOMES PARALYZED.
KOHEI DIDN'T SEEM TO NOTICE...
...BUT WHEN HE GRABBED ME EARLIER HIS GRIP FELT REALLY WEAK.
SOMETHING'S THE MATTER WITH CONTESTANT NAGASE!!
ZING
THE WOUND IS COMPLETELY HEALED.
...
I THINK IT'S MOSTLY MENTAL, BUT...
ZING
HE'S FALLEN TO HIS KNEES AND IS HOLDING HIS RIGHT HAND!

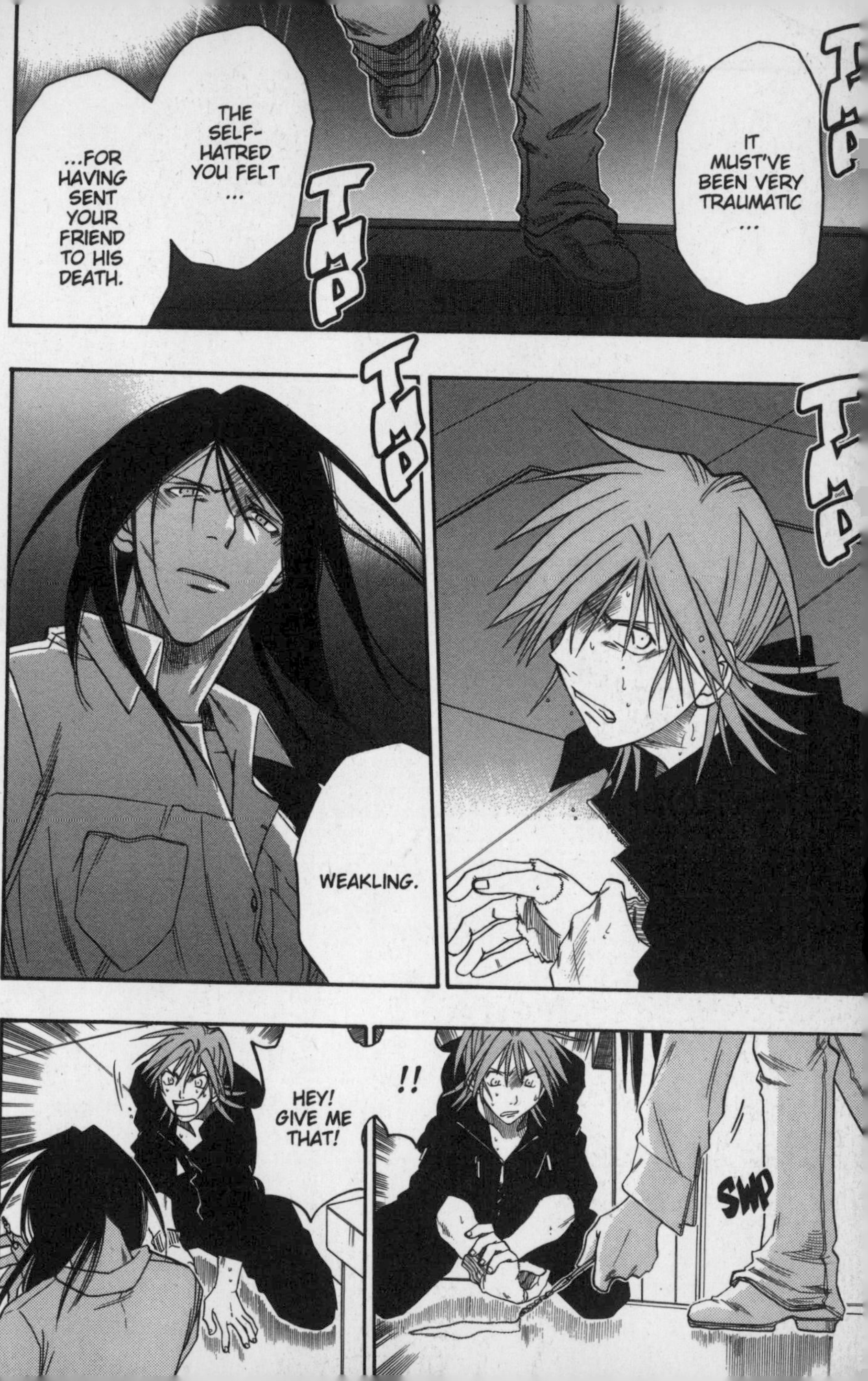
TMP
IT MUST'VE BEEN VERY TRAUMATIC ...
TMP
THE SELF-HATRED YOU FELT ...
...FOR HAVING SENT YOUR FRIEND TO HIS DEATH.
TMP
TMP
WEAKLING.
SWP
!!
HEY! GIVE ME THAT!

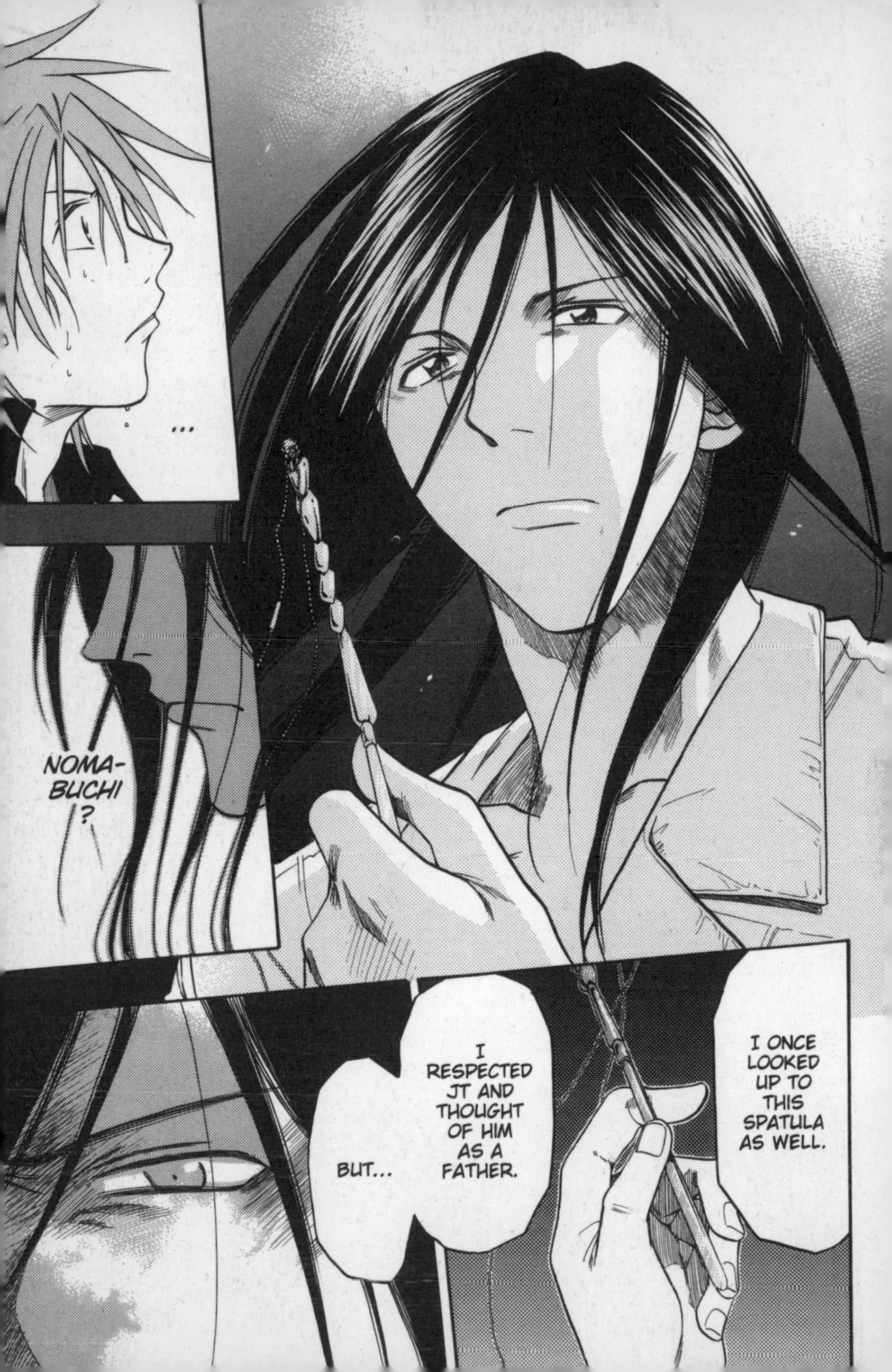
...
NOMA-BUCHI ?
I ONCE LOOKED UP TO THIS SPATULA AS WELL.
I RESPECTED JT AND THOUGHT OF HIM AS A FATHER.
BUT...

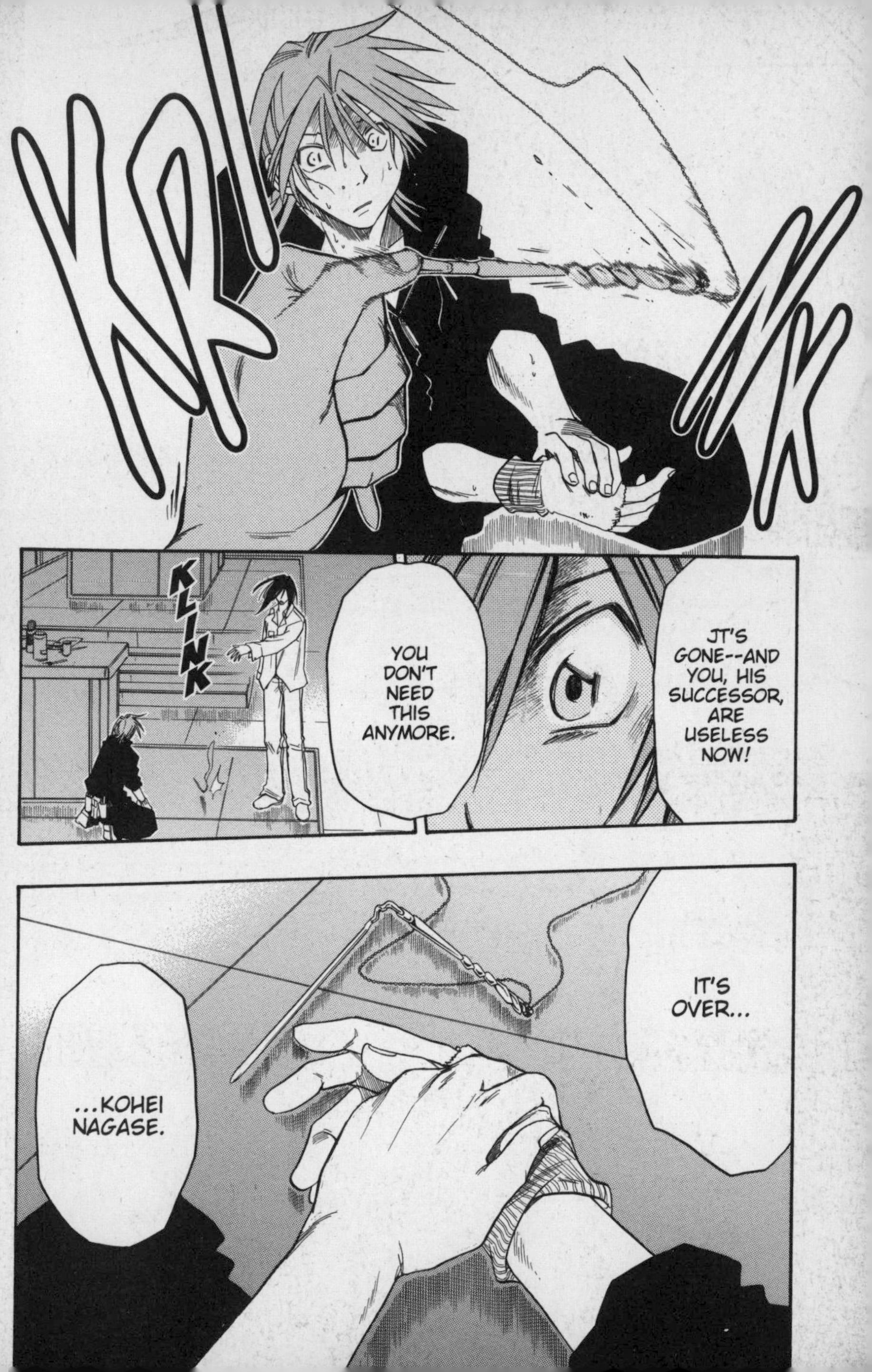
KRINNK
JT'S GONE--AND YOU, HIS SUCCESSOR, ARE USELESS NOW!
YOU DON'T NEED THIS ANYMORE.
KLINK
IT'S OVER...
...KOHEI NAGASE.

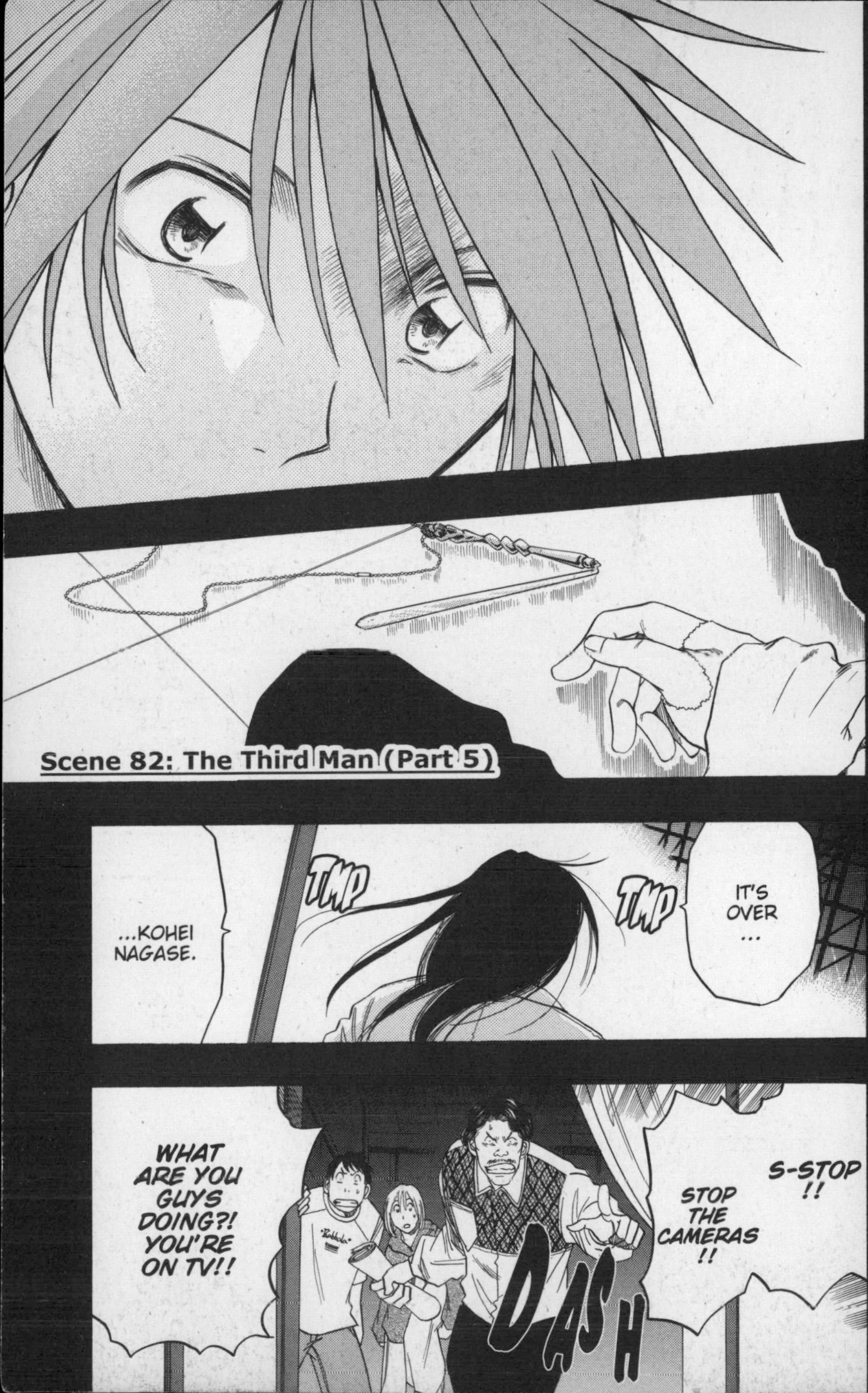
Scene 82: The Third Man (Part 5)
IT'S OVER ...
TMP
TMP
...KOHEI NAGASE.
S-STOP !!
STOP THE CAMERAS !!
DASH
WHAT ARE YOU GUYS DOING?! YOU'RE ON TV!!

Scene 82: The Third Man (Part 5)

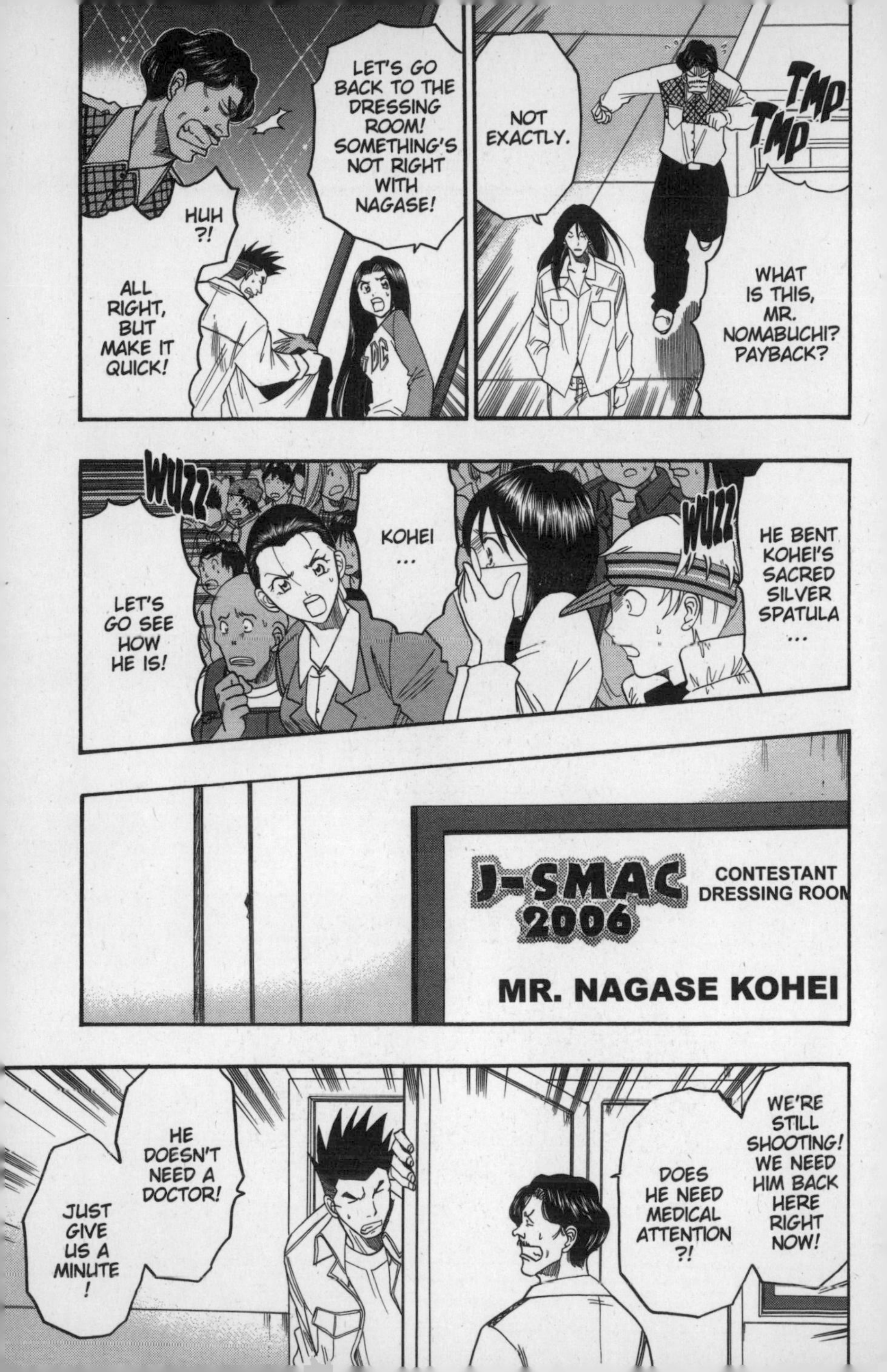
TMP TMP
WHAT IS THIS, MR. NOMABUCHI? PAYBACK?
NOT EXACTLY.
LET'S GO BACK TO THE DRESSING ROOM! SOMETHING'S NOT RIGHT WITH NAGASE!
HUH ?!
ALL RIGHT, BUT MAKE IT QUICK!
WUZZ
HE BENT KOHEI'S SACRED SILVER SPATULA ...
KOHEI ...
WUZZ
LET'S GO SEE HOW HE IS!
J-SMAC 2006
CONTESTANT DRESSING ROOM
MR. NAGASE KOHEI
WE'RE STILL SHOOTING! WE NEED HIM BACK HERE RIGHT NOW!
DOES HE NEED MEDICAL ATTENTION ?!
HE DOESN'T NEED A DOCTOR!
JUST GIVE US A MINUTE !

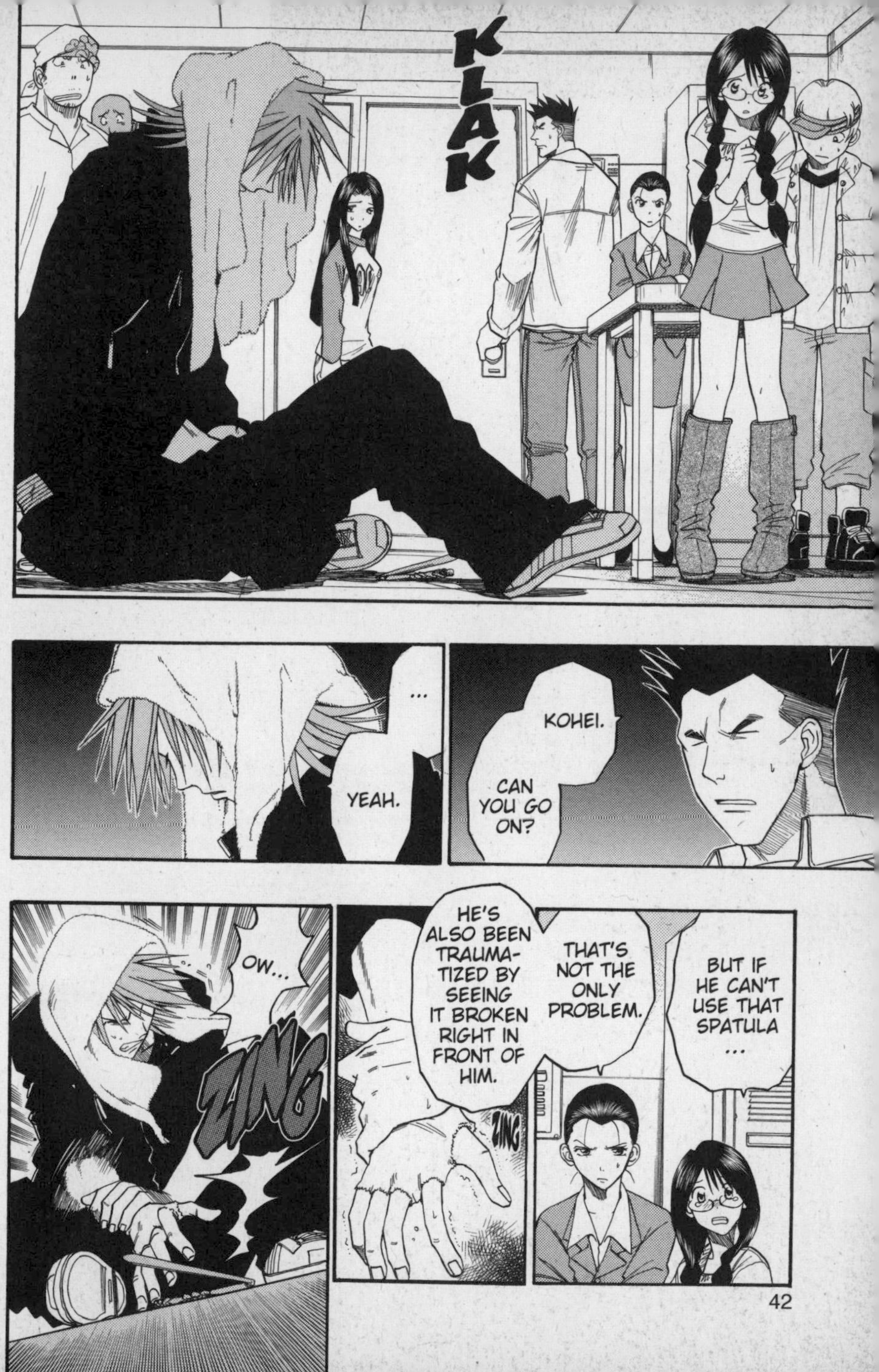
KLAK
KOHEI.
CAN YOU GO ON?
...
YEAH.
BUT IF HE CAN'T USE THAT SPATULA ...
THAT'S NOT THE ONLY PROBLEM.
HE'S ALSO BEEN TRAUMATIZED BY SEEING IT BROKEN RIGHT IN FRONT OF HIM.
ZING
OW...
ZING

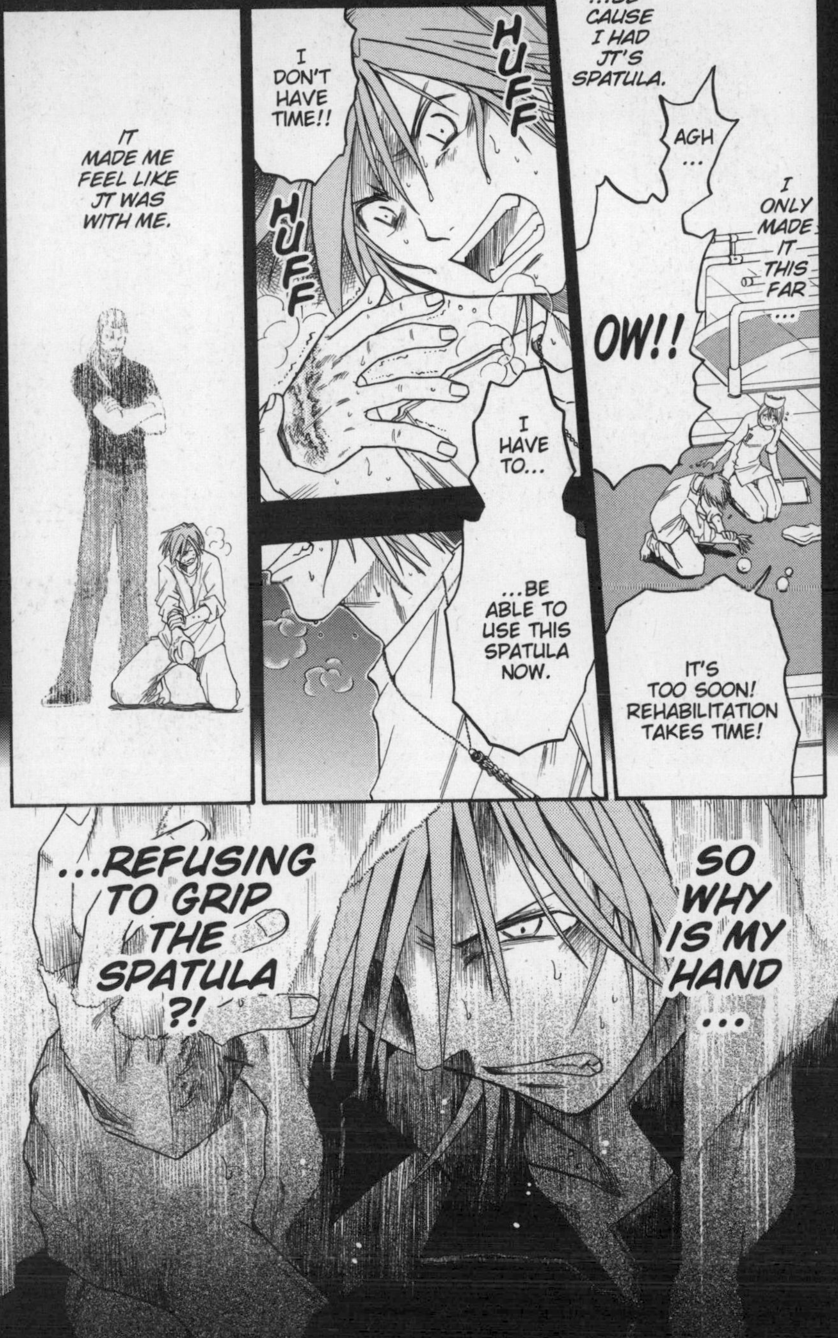
I ONLY MADE IT THIS FAR...
...BECAUSE I HAD JT'S SPATULA.
AGH...
OW!!
IT'S TOO SOON! REHABILITATION TAKES TIME!
I DON'T HAVE TIME!!
HUFF
HUFF
I HAVE TO...
...BE ABLE TO USE THIS SPATULA NOW.
IT MADE ME FEEL LIKE JT WAS WITH ME.
SO WHY IS MY HAND...
...REFUSING TO GRIP THE SPATULA?!

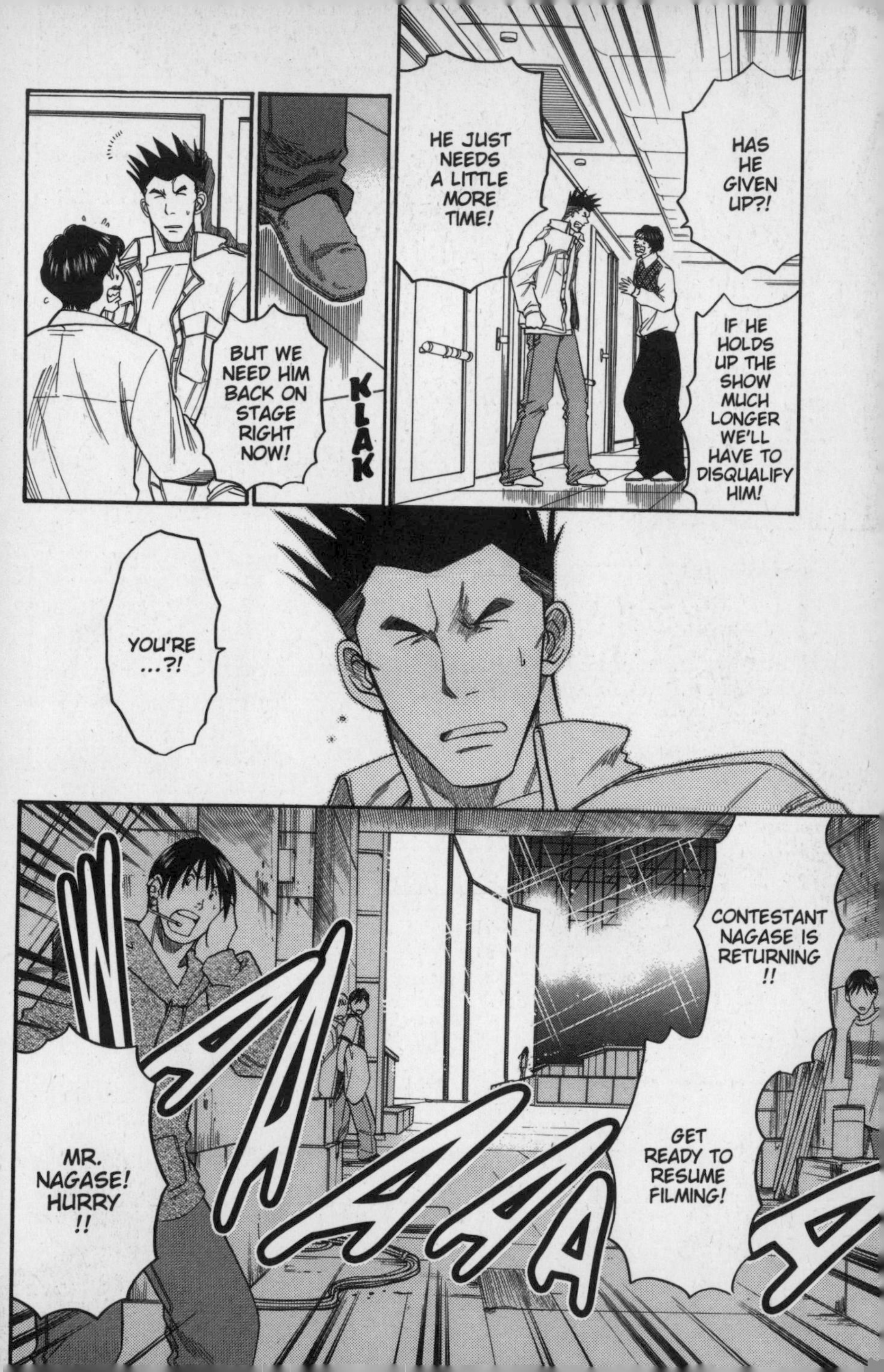
HAS HE GIVEN UP?!
HE JUST NEEDS A LITTLE MORE TIME!
IF HE HOLDS UP THE SHOW MUCH LONGER WE'LL HAVE TO DISQUALIFY HIM!
KLAK
BUT WE NEED HIM BACK ON STAGE RIGHT NOW!
YOU'RE ...?!
CONTESTANT NAGASE IS RETURNING!!
GET READY TO RESUME FILMING!
WAAAAAA
MR. NAGASE! HURRY!!

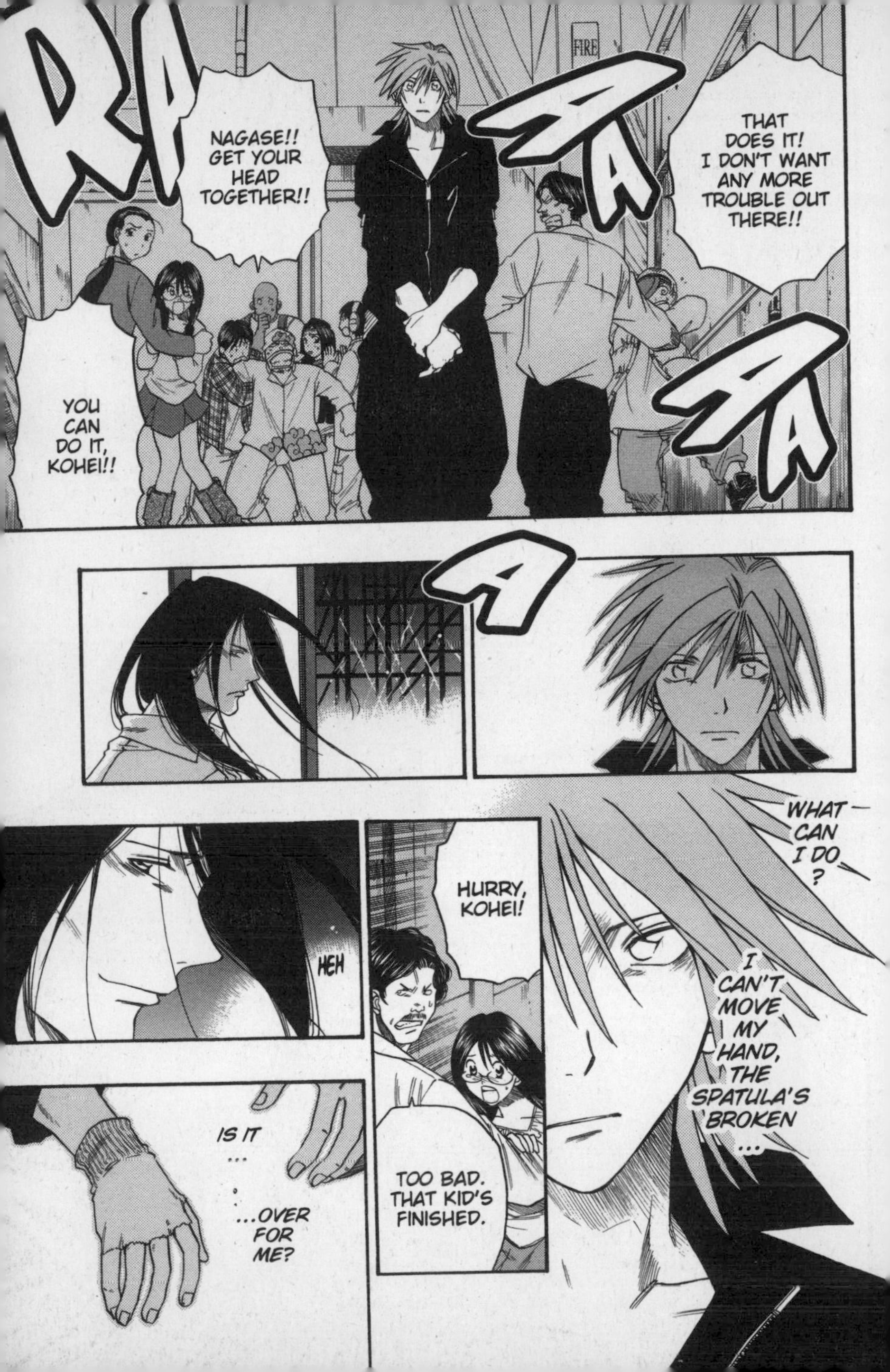
THAT DOES IT! I DON'T WANT ANY MORE TROUBLE OUT THERE!!
RAAAAA
NAGASE!! GET YOUR HEAD TOGETHER!!
YOU CAN DO IT, KOHEI!!
WHAT CAN I DO?
I CAN'T MOVE MY HAND, THE SPATULA'S BROKEN...
HURRY, KOHEI!
TOO BAD. THAT KID'S FINISHED.
HEH
IS IT...
...OVER FOR ME?

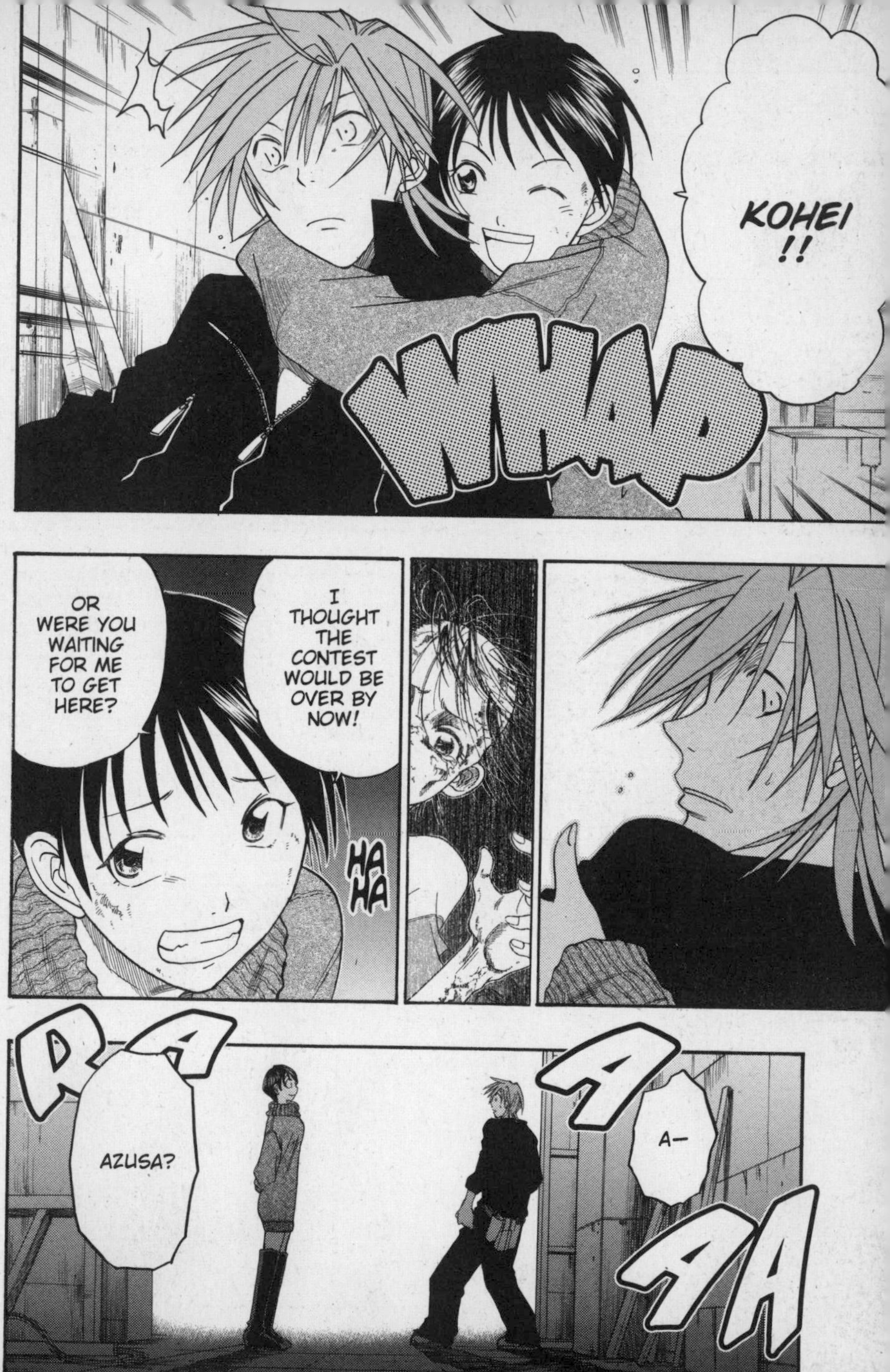

KOHEI !!
WHAP
I THOUGHT THE CONTEST WOULD BE OVER BY NOW!
OR WERE YOU WAITING FOR ME TO GET HERE?
HA HA
A—
AZUSA?
R-A A A A A

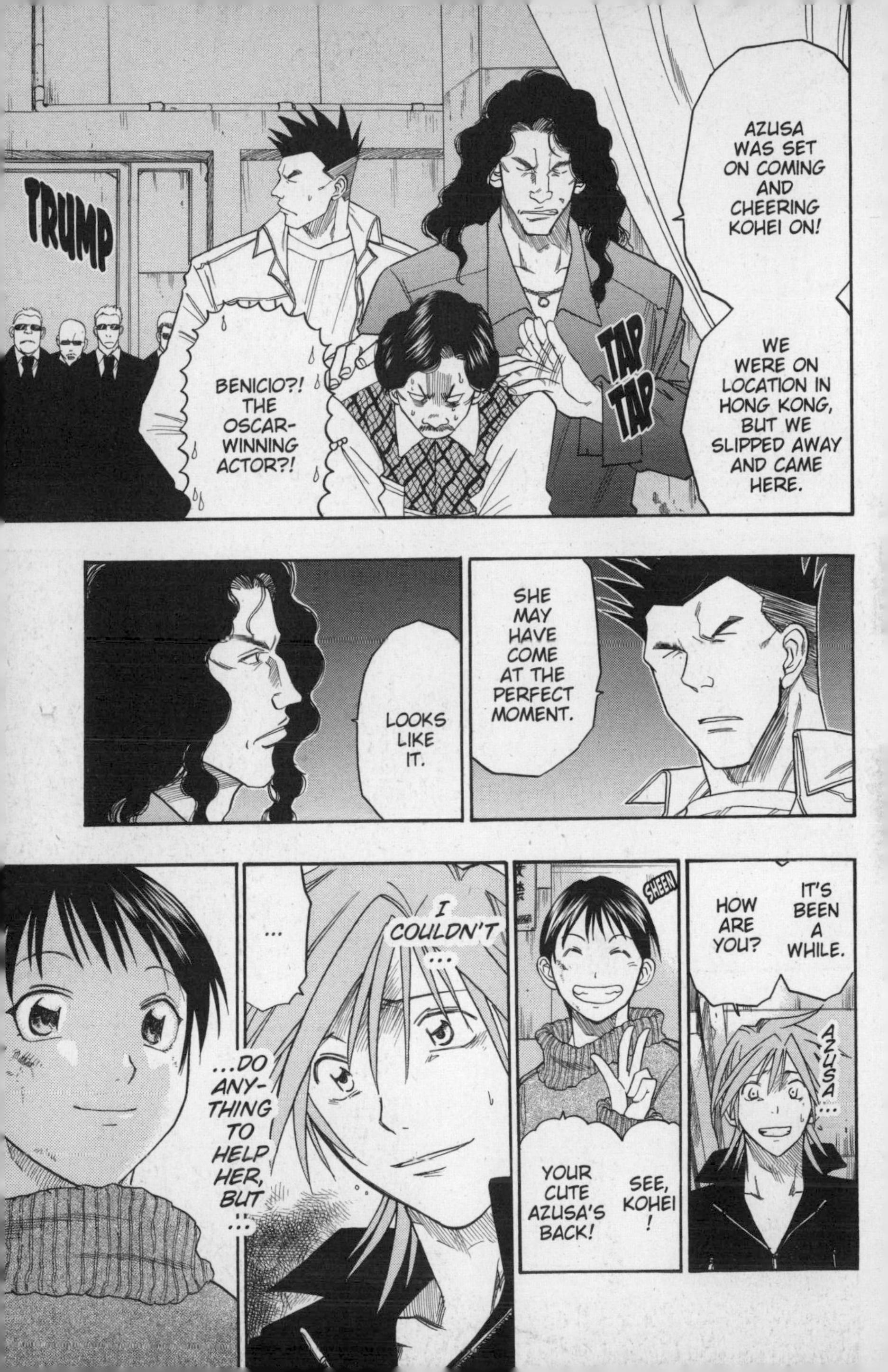
AZUSA WAS SET ON COMING AND CHEERING KOHEI ON!
WE WERE ON LOCATION IN HONG KONG, BUT WE SLIPPED AWAY AND CAME HERE.
TAP TAP
BENICIO?! THE OSCAR-WINNING ACTOR?!
TRUMP
SHE MAY HAVE COME AT THE PERFECT MOMENT.
LOOKS LIKE IT.
IT'S BEEN A WHILE.
HOW ARE YOU?
AZUSA...
SHEEN
SEE, KOHEI!
YOUR CUTE AZUSA'S BACK!
I COULDN'T...
...
...DO ANYTHING TO HELP HER, BUT...

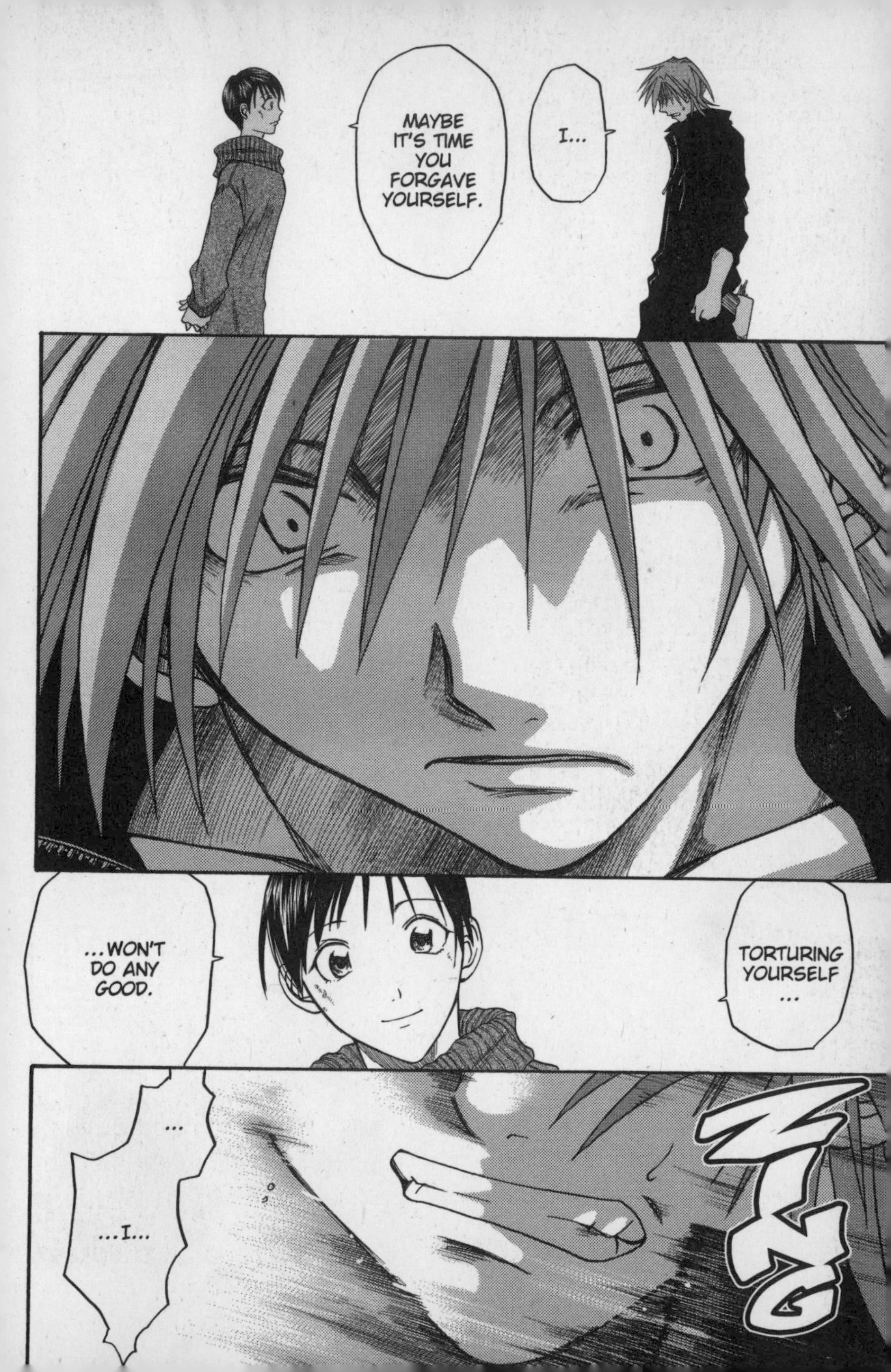
I...
MAYBE IT'S TIME YOU FORGAVE YOURSELF.
TORTURING YOURSELF ...
...WON'T DO ANY GOOD.
...
...I...

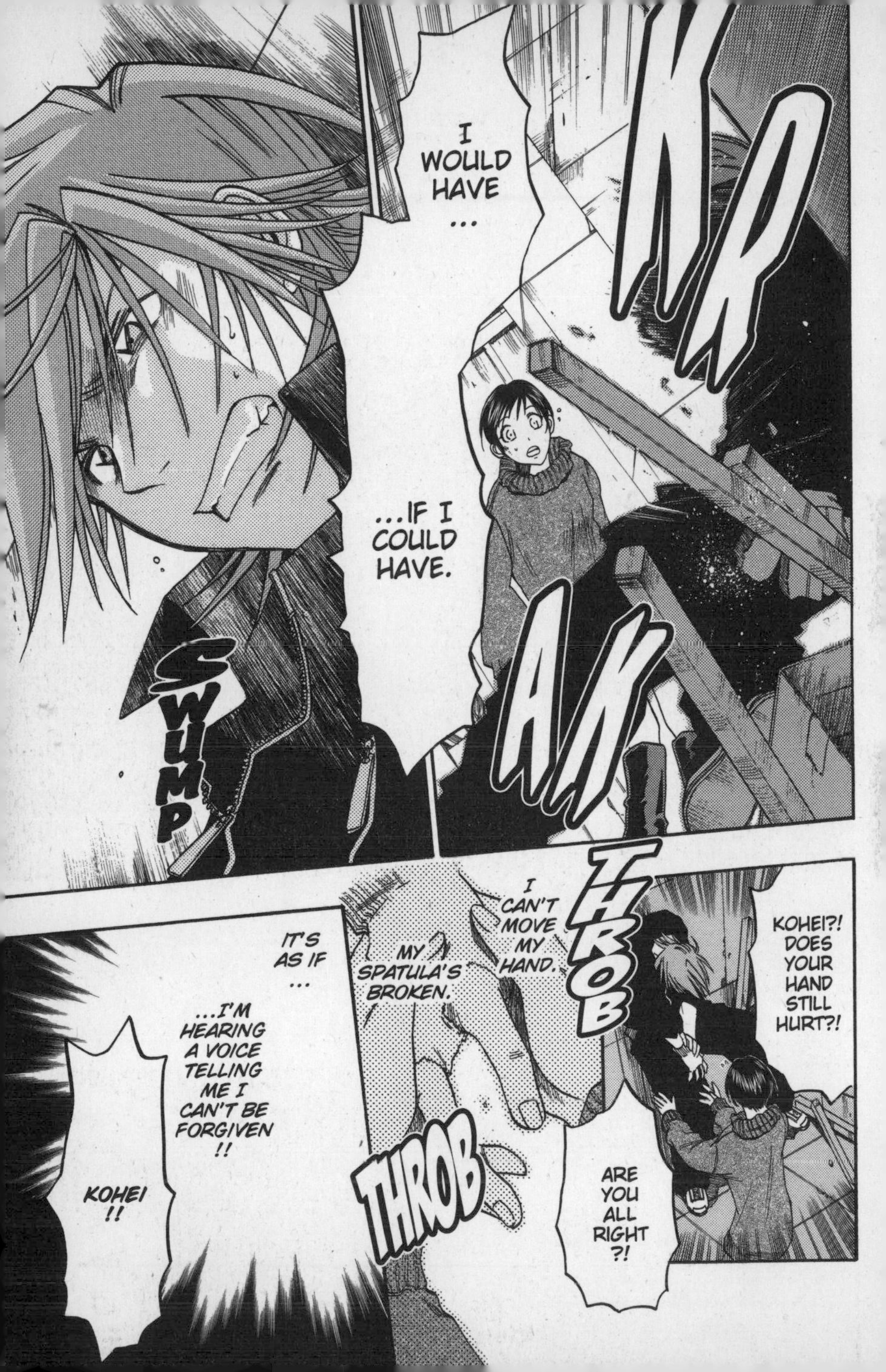
KRAK
I WOULD HAVE ...
...IF I COULD HAVE.
SWUMP
KOHEI?! DOES YOUR HAND STILL HURT?!
THROB
ARE YOU ALL RIGHT?!
I CAN'T MOVE MY HAND.
MY SPATULA'S BROKEN.
THROB
IT'S AS IF ...
...I'M HEARING A VOICE TELLING ME I CAN'T BE FORGIVEN!!
KOHEI!!

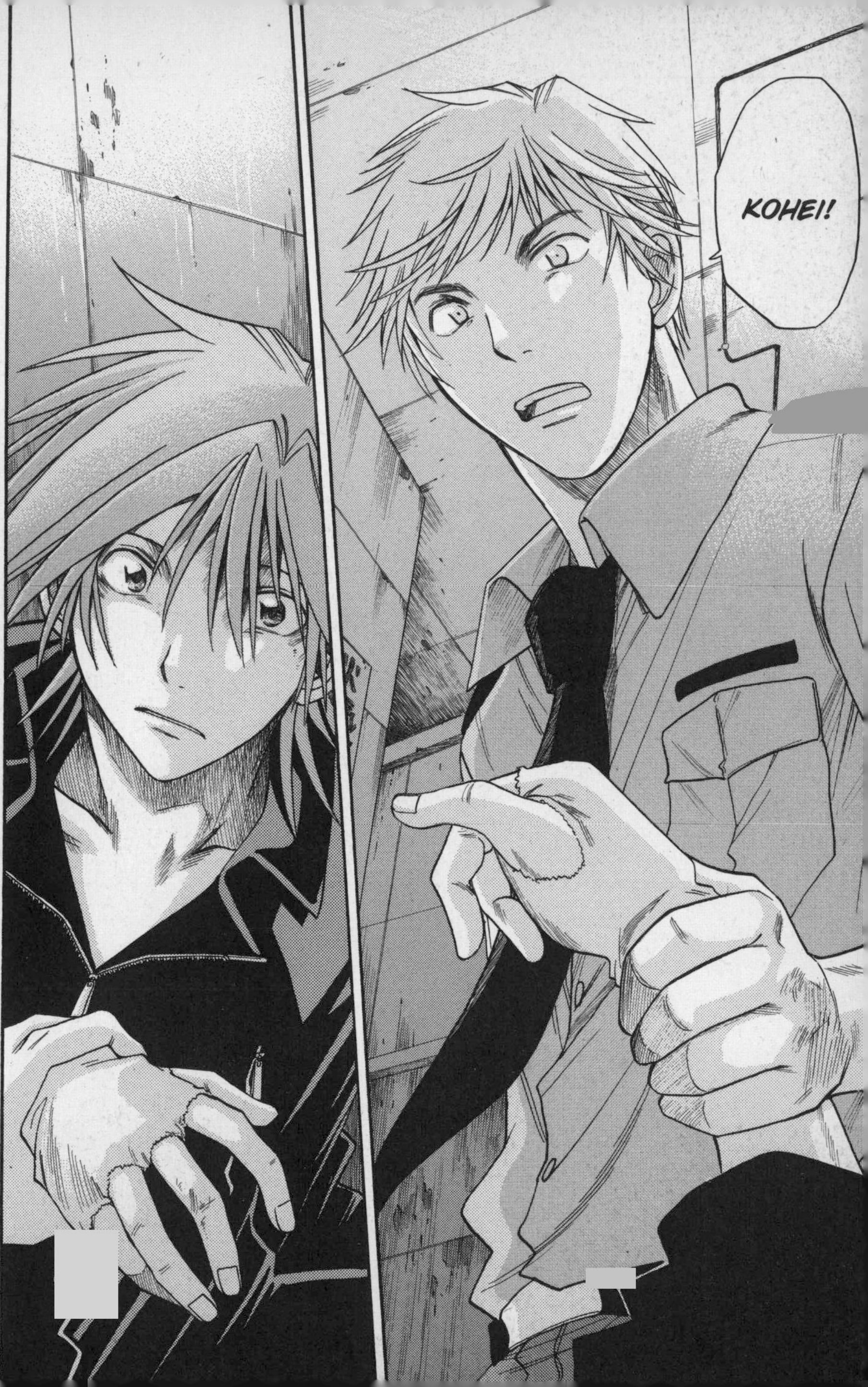
KOHEI!

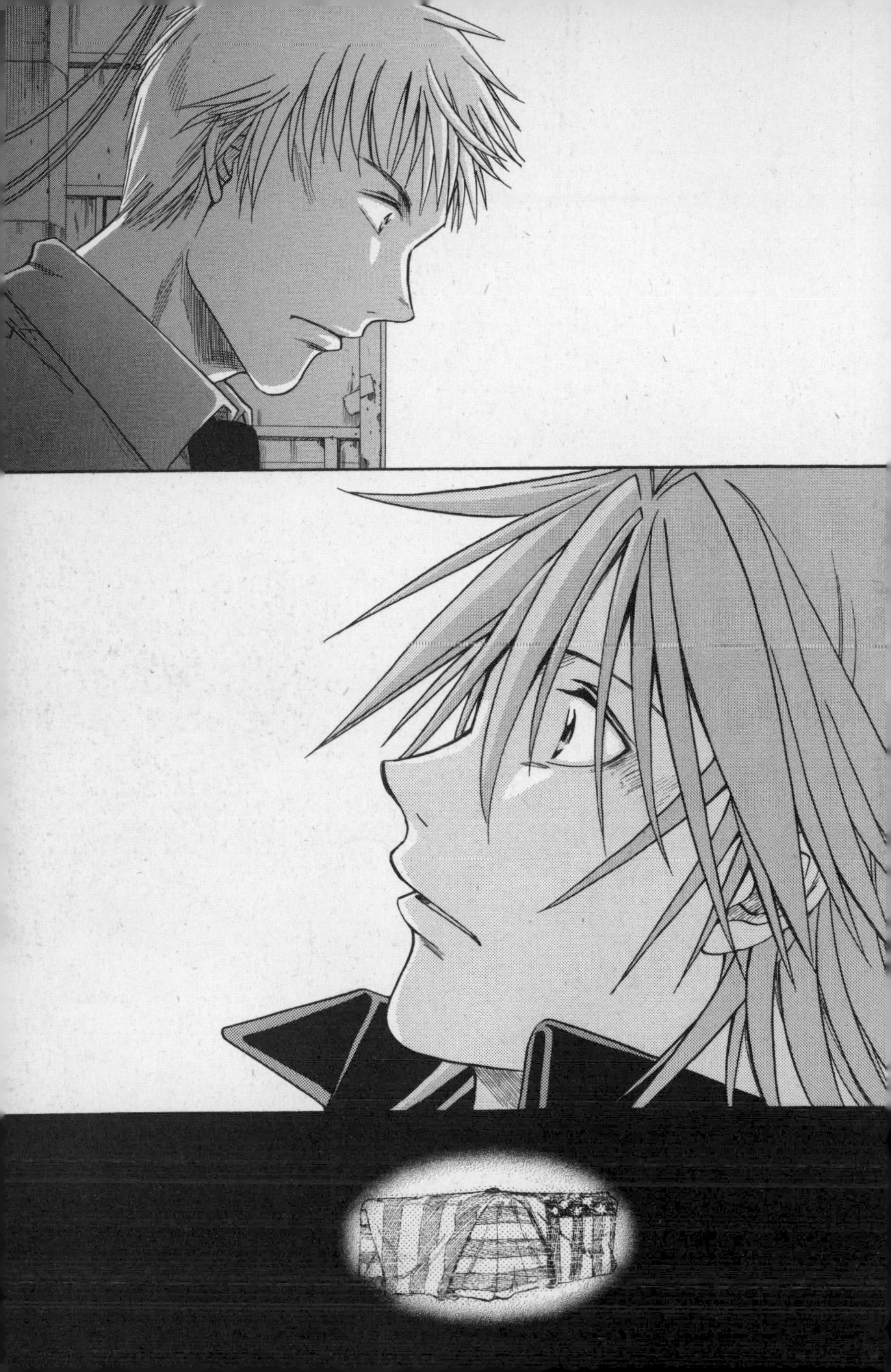

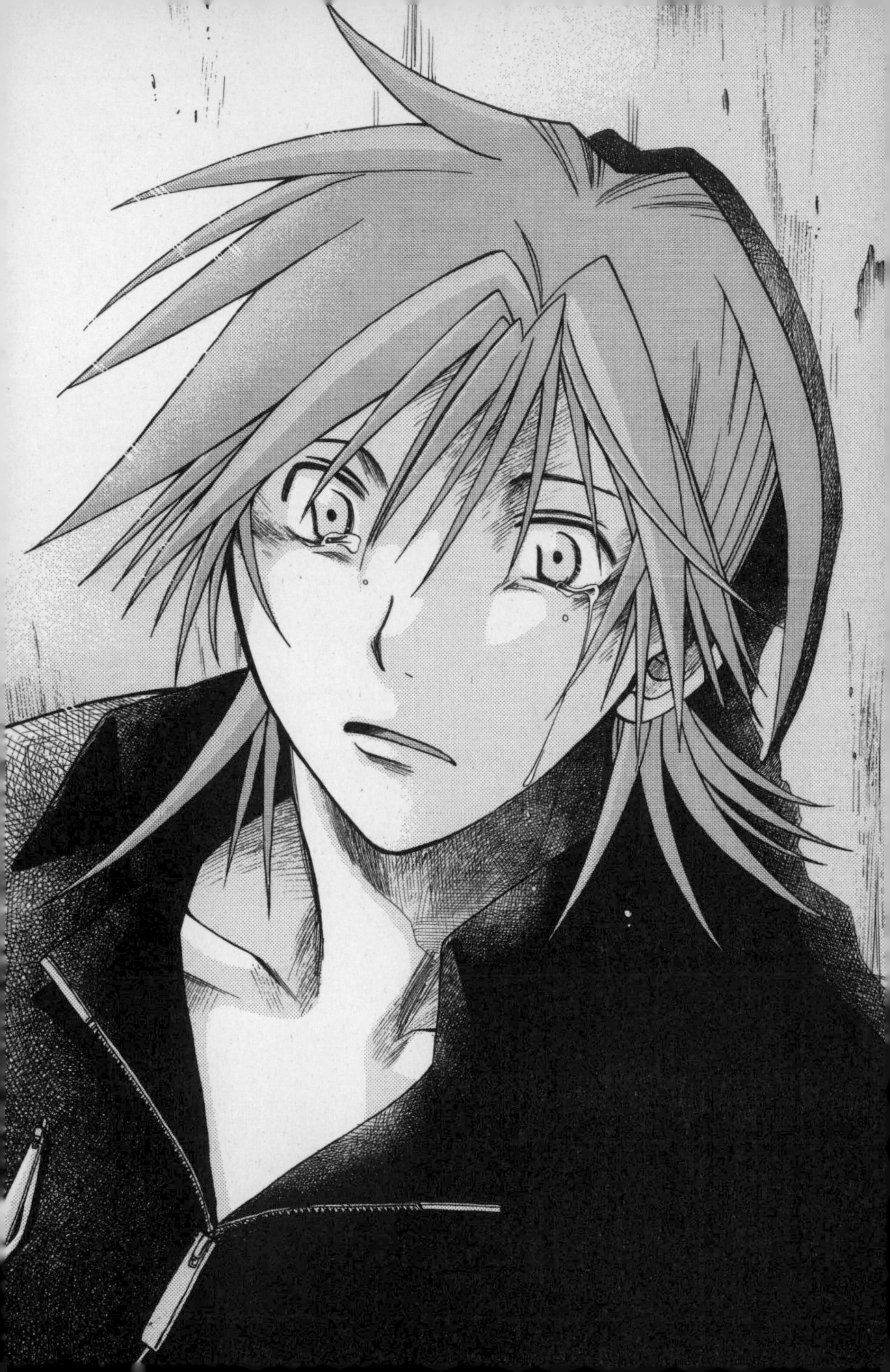

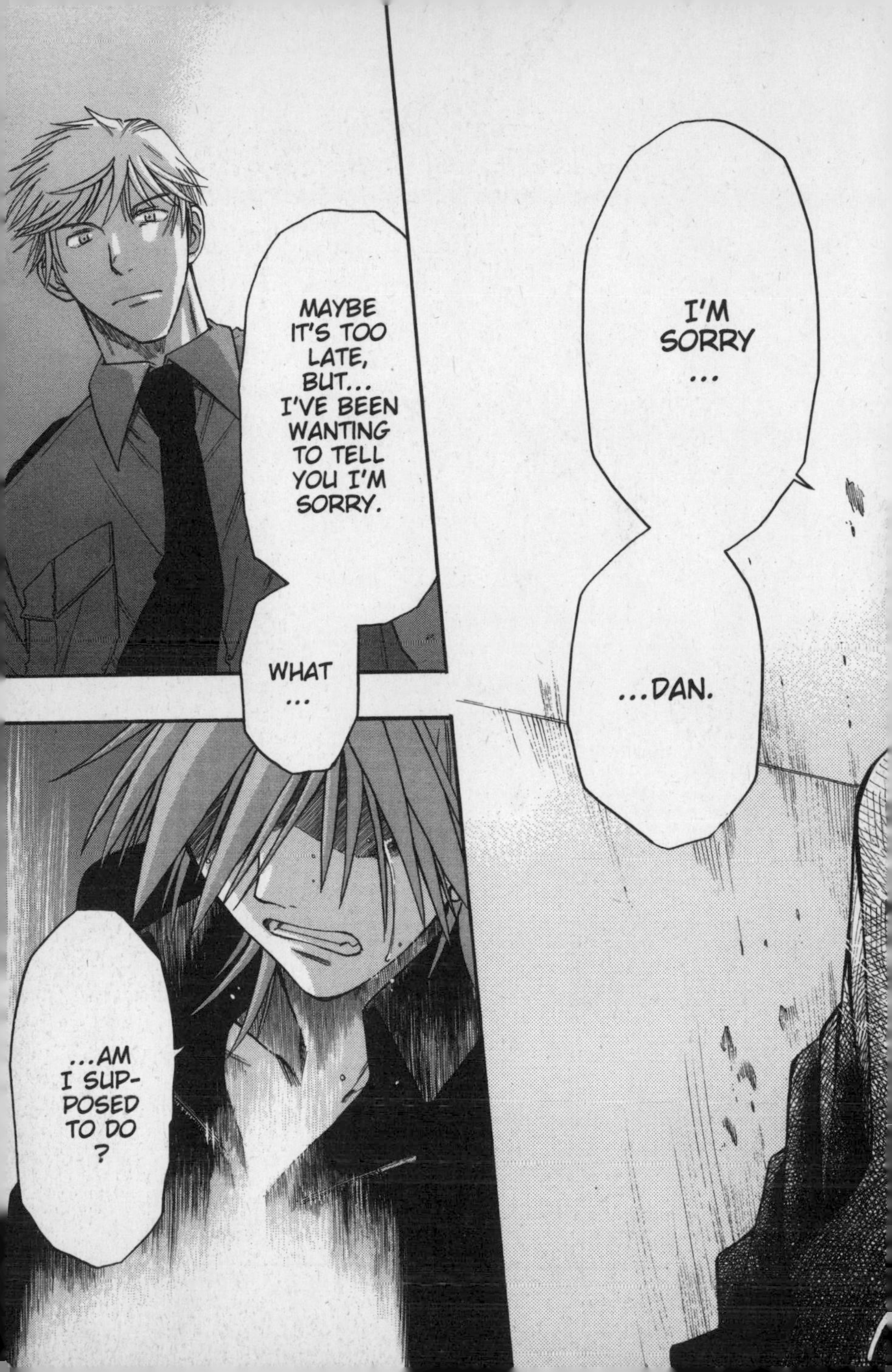
I'M SORRY ...
...DAN.
MAYBE IT'S TOO LATE, BUT... I'VE BEEN WANTING TO TELL YOU I'M SORRY.
WHAT ...
...AM I SUP-POSED TO DO ?

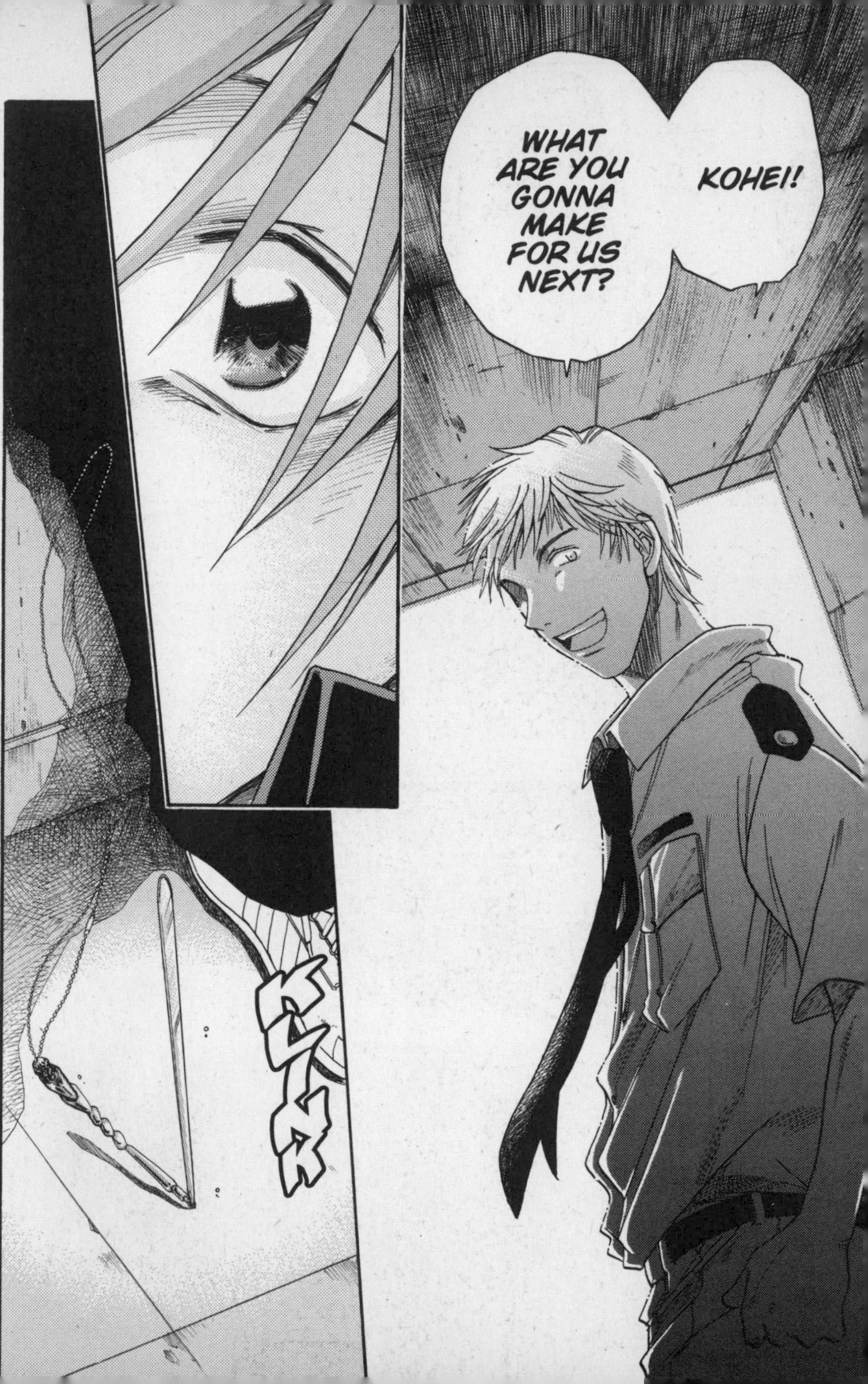
KOHEI!
WHAT ARE YOU GONNA MAKE FOR US NEXT?
CLK

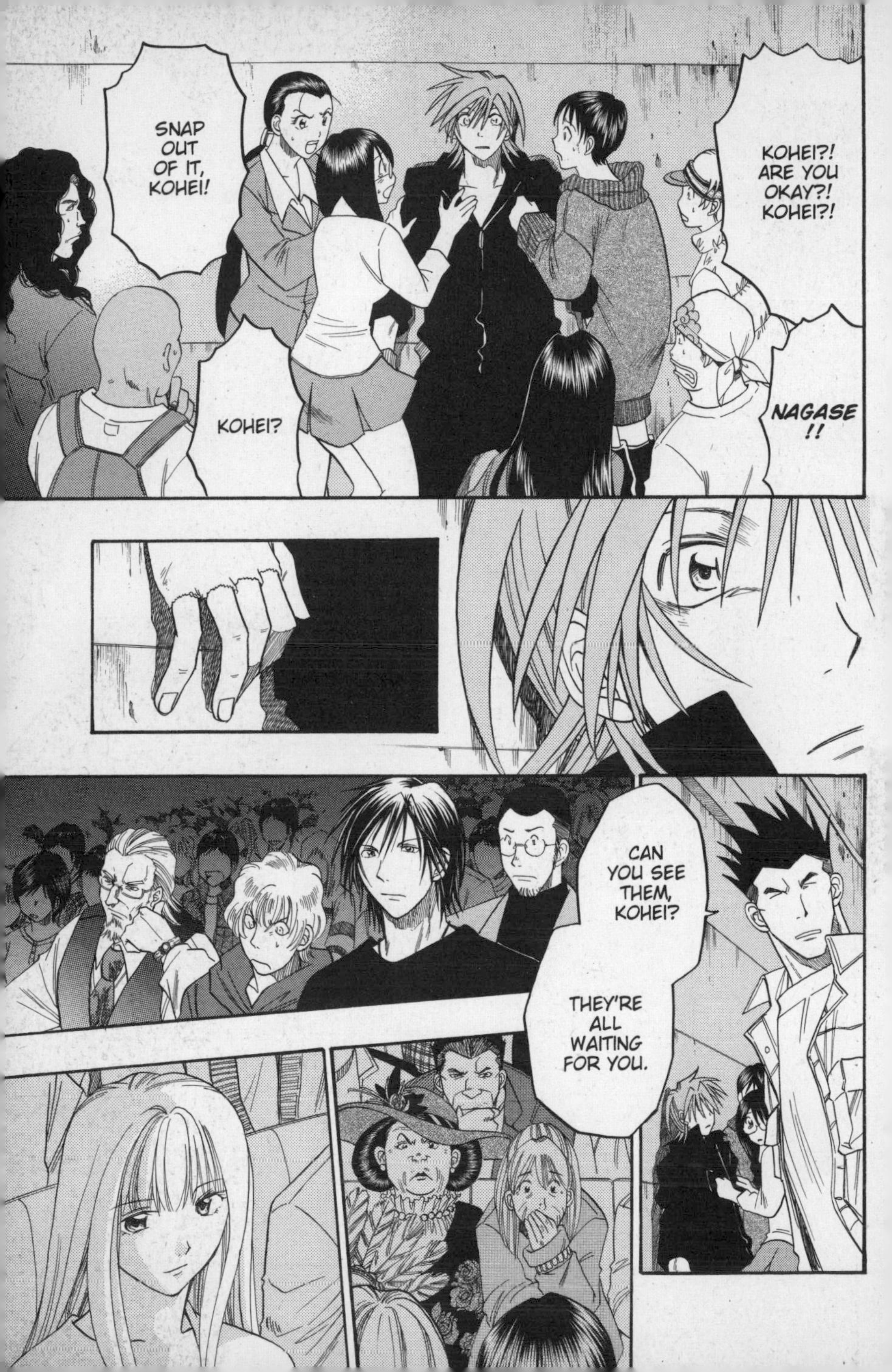
KOHEI?! ARE YOU OKAY?! KOHEI?!
NAGASE !!
SNAP OUT OF IT, KOHEI!
KOHEI?
CAN YOU SEE THEM, KOHEI?
THEY'RE ALL WAITING FOR YOU.

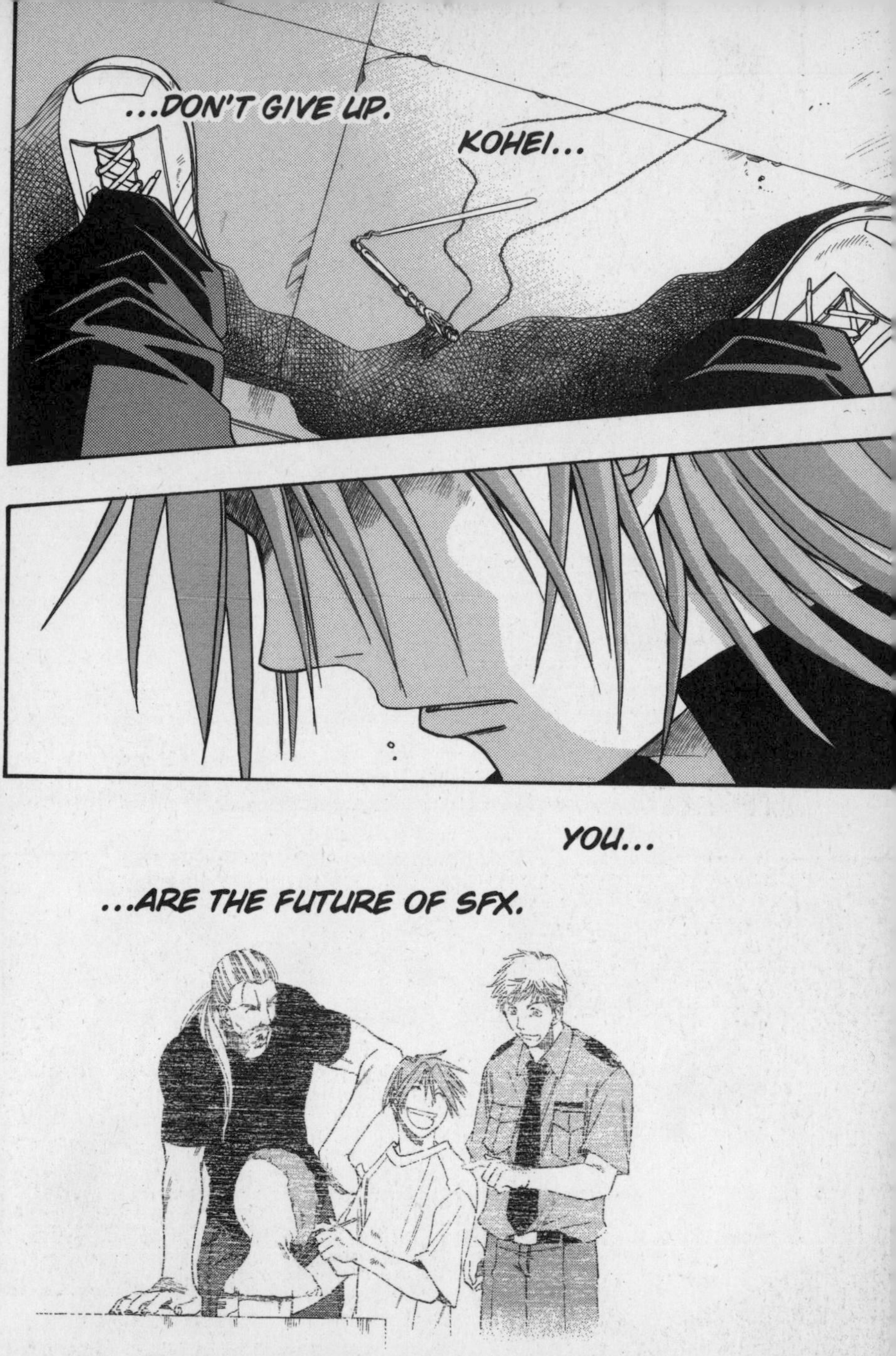
...
KOHEI...
...DON'T GIVE UP.
YOU...
...ARE THE FUTURE OF SFX.

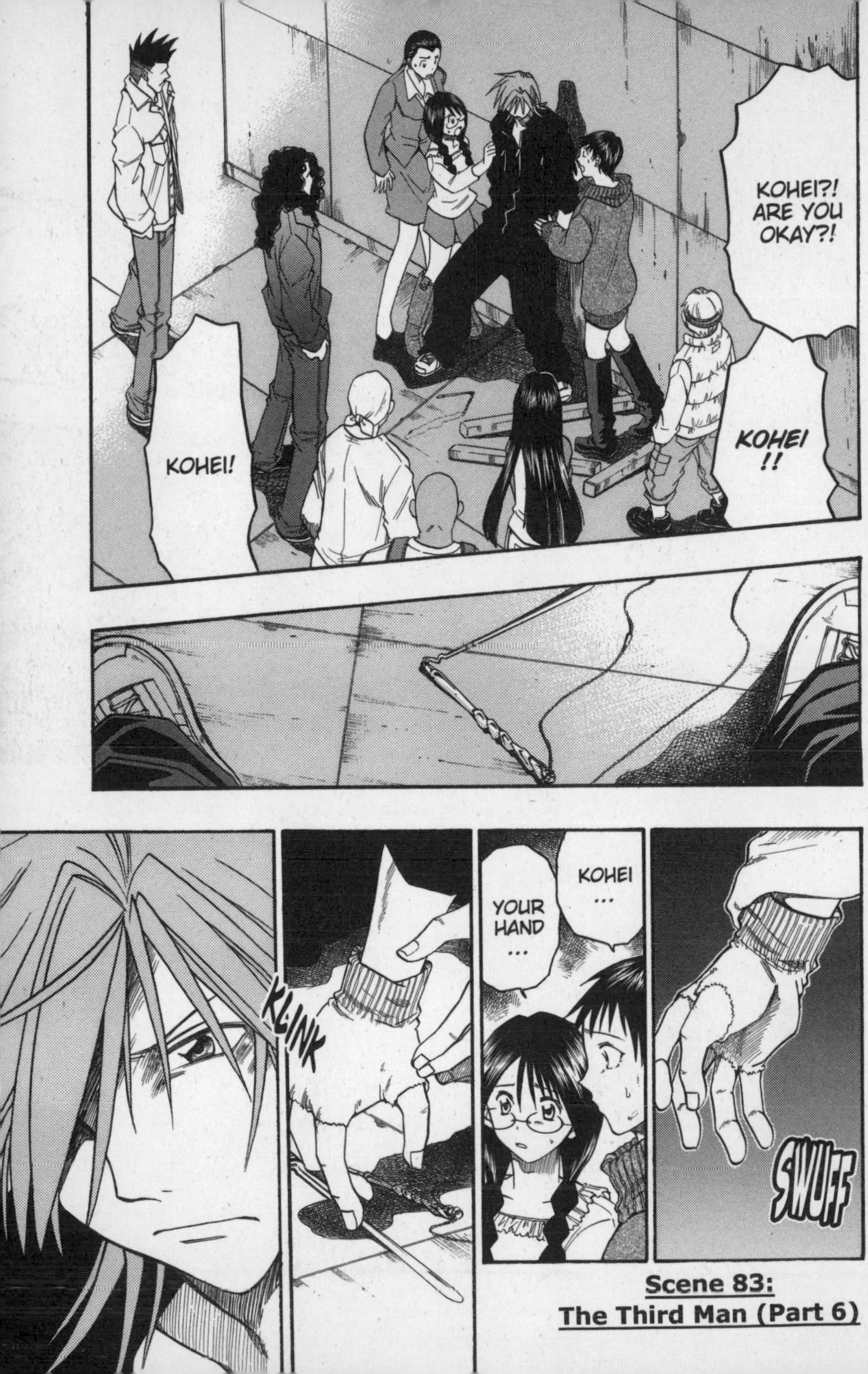
KOHEI?! ARE YOU OKAY?!
KOHEI !!
KOHEI!
SWUFF
KOHEI ...
YOUR HAND ...
KLINK

Scene 83:
The Third Man (Part 6)

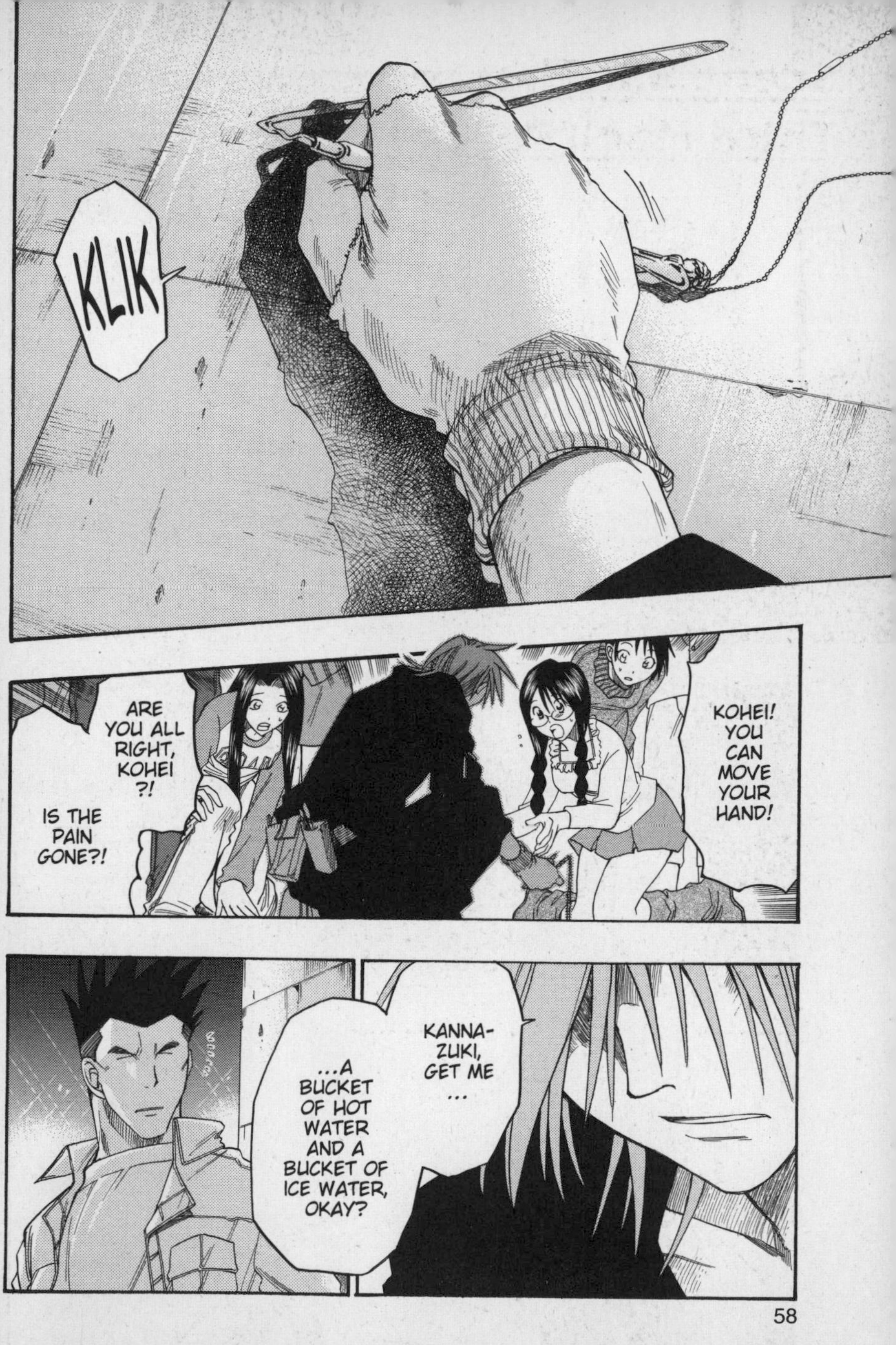
KLIK
KOHEI! YOU CAN MOVE YOUR HAND!
ARE YOU ALL RIGHT, KOHEI?!
IS THE PAIN GONE?!
KANNA-ZUKI, GET ME ...
...A BUCKET OF HOT WATER AND A BUCKET OF ICE WATER, OKAY?

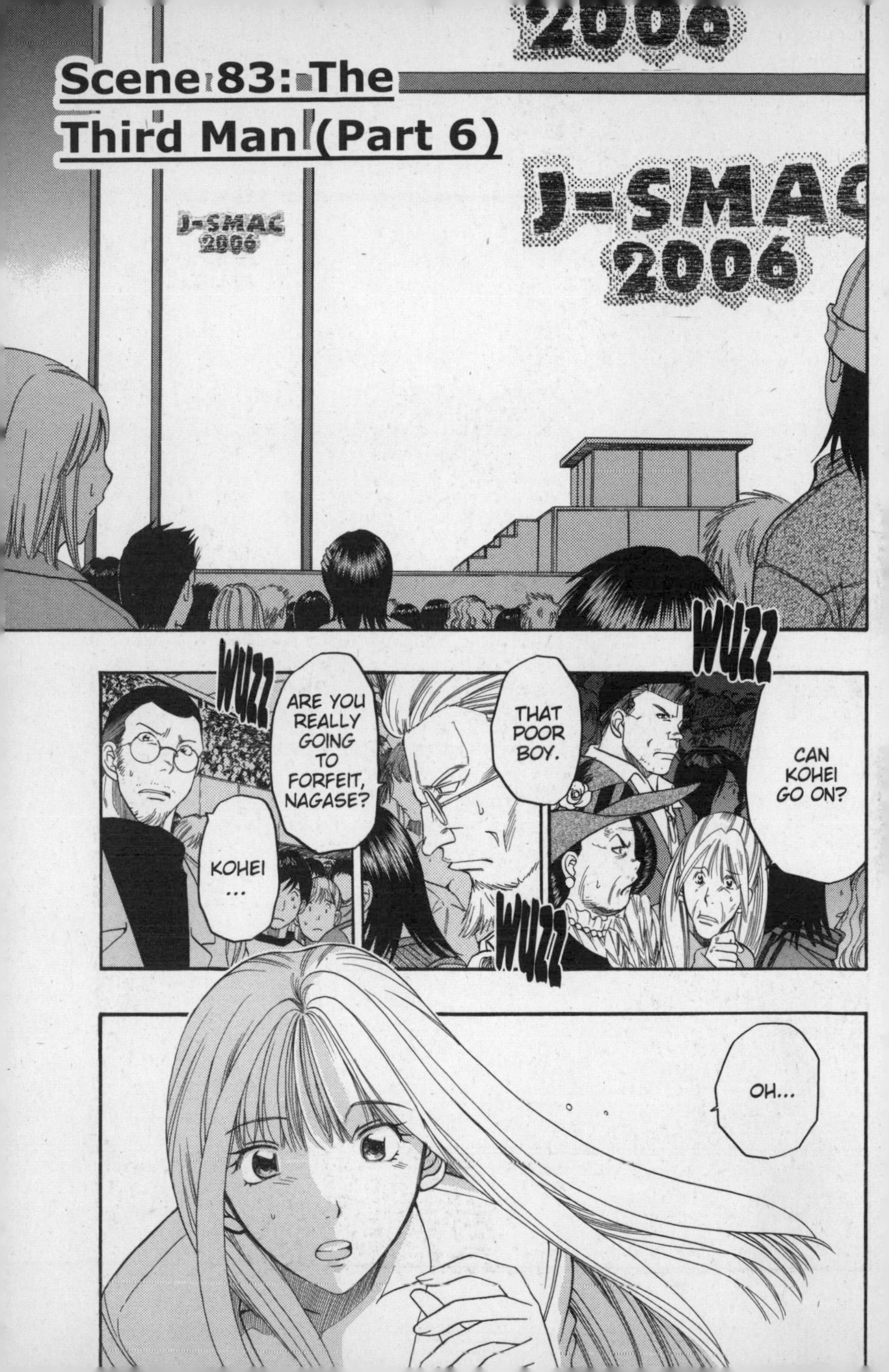
Scene 83: The Third Man (Part 6)
2006
J-SMAC 2006
J-SMAC 2006
WUZZ
CAN KOHEI GO ON?
THAT POOR BOY.
WUZZ
ARE YOU REALLY GOING TO FORFEIT, NAGASE?
WUZZ
KOHEI ...
OH...

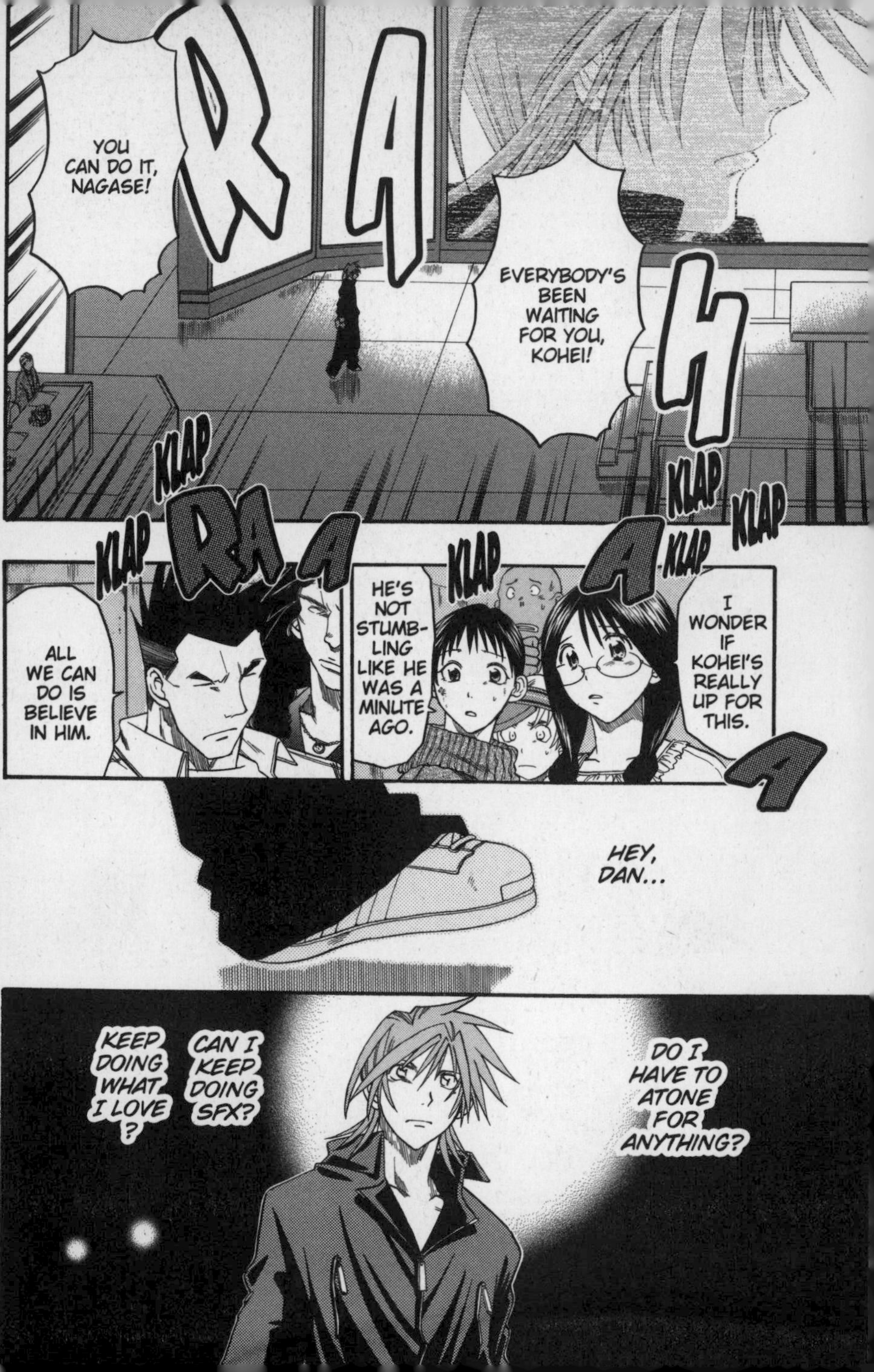

EVERYBODY'S BEEN WAITING FOR YOU, KOHEI!
YOU CAN DO IT, NAGASE!
R A H
KLAP KLAP KLAP KLAP KLAP KLAP
RA A A A
I WONDER IF KOHEI'S REALLY UP FOR THIS.
HE'S NOT STUMBLING LIKE HE WAS A MINUTE AGO.
ALL WE CAN DO IS BELIEVE IN HIM.
HEY, DAN...
DO I HAVE TO ATONE FOR ANYTHING?
CAN I KEEP DOING SFX?
KEEP DOING WHAT I LOVE?

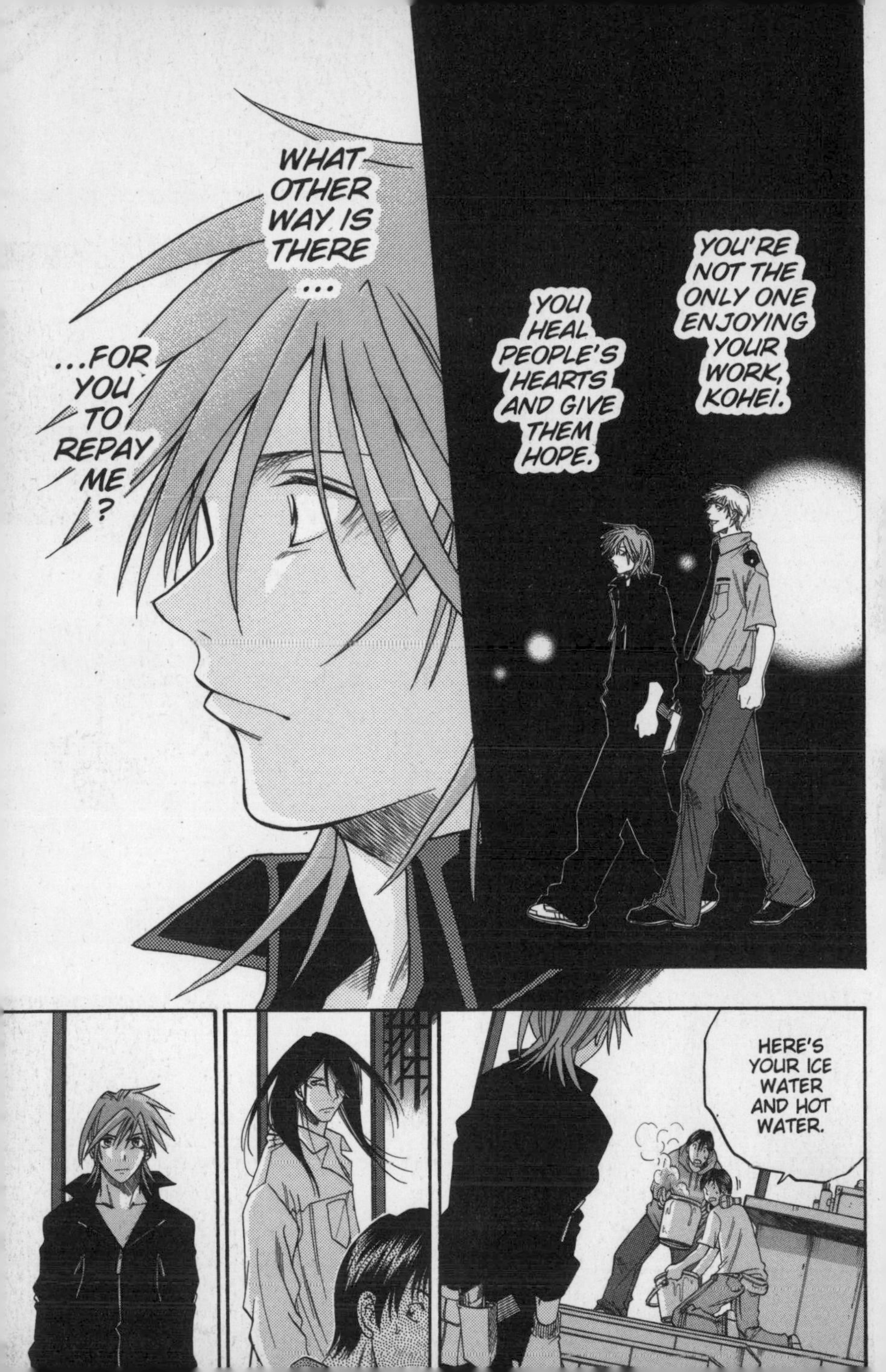
YOU'RE NOT THE ONLY ONE ENJOYING YOUR WORK, KOHEI.
YOU HEAL PEOPLE'S HEARTS AND GIVE THEM HOPE.
WHAT OTHER WAY IS THERE...
...FOR YOU TO REPAY ME?
HERE'S YOUR ICE WATER AND HOT WATER.

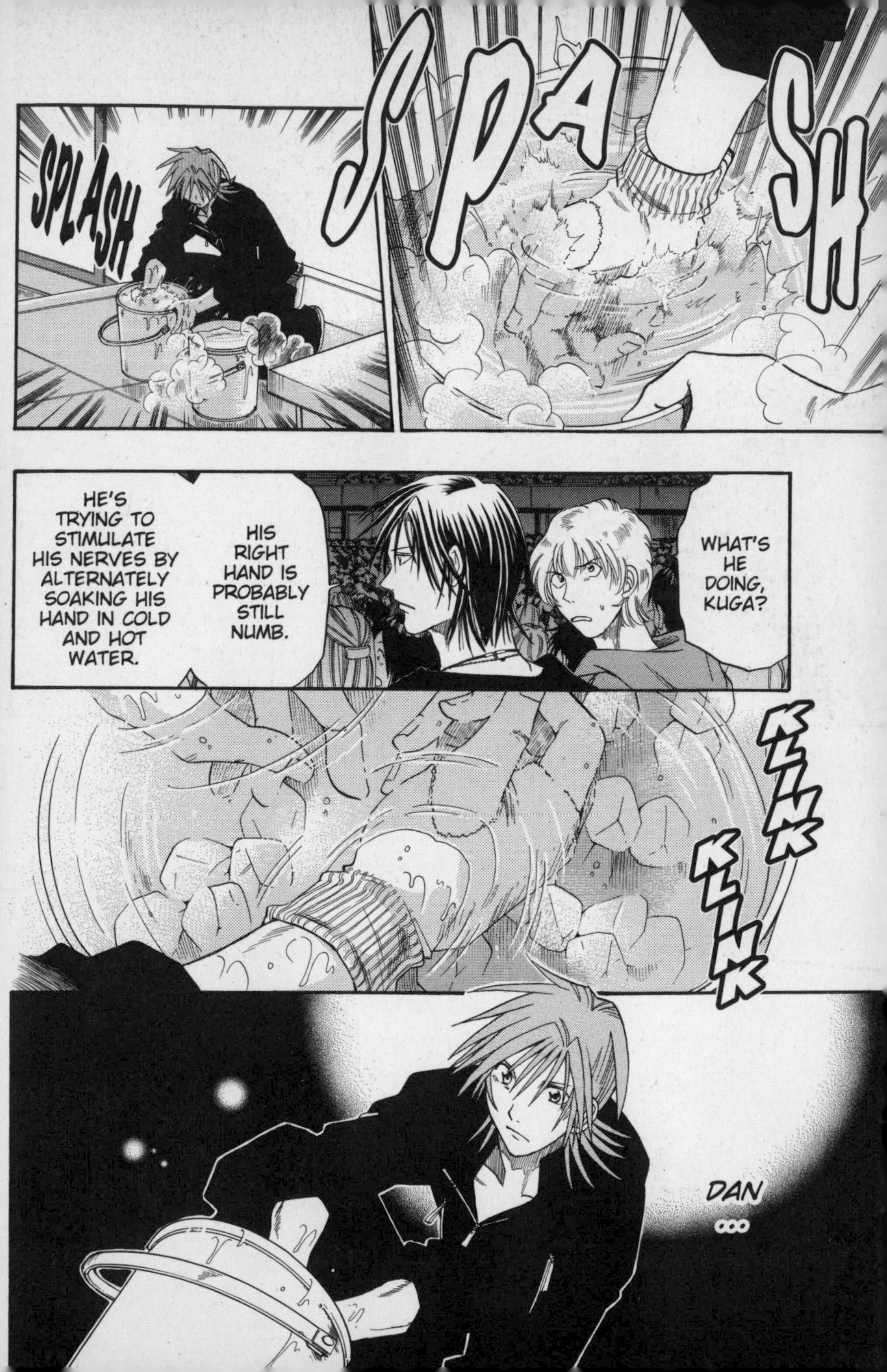
SPASH
SPLASH
WHAT'S HE DOING, KUGA?
HIS RIGHT HAND IS PROBABLY STILL NUMB.
HE'S TRYING TO STIMULATE HIS NERVES BY ALTERNATELY SOAKING HIS HAND IN COLD AND HOT WATER.
KLINK
KLINK
DAN...

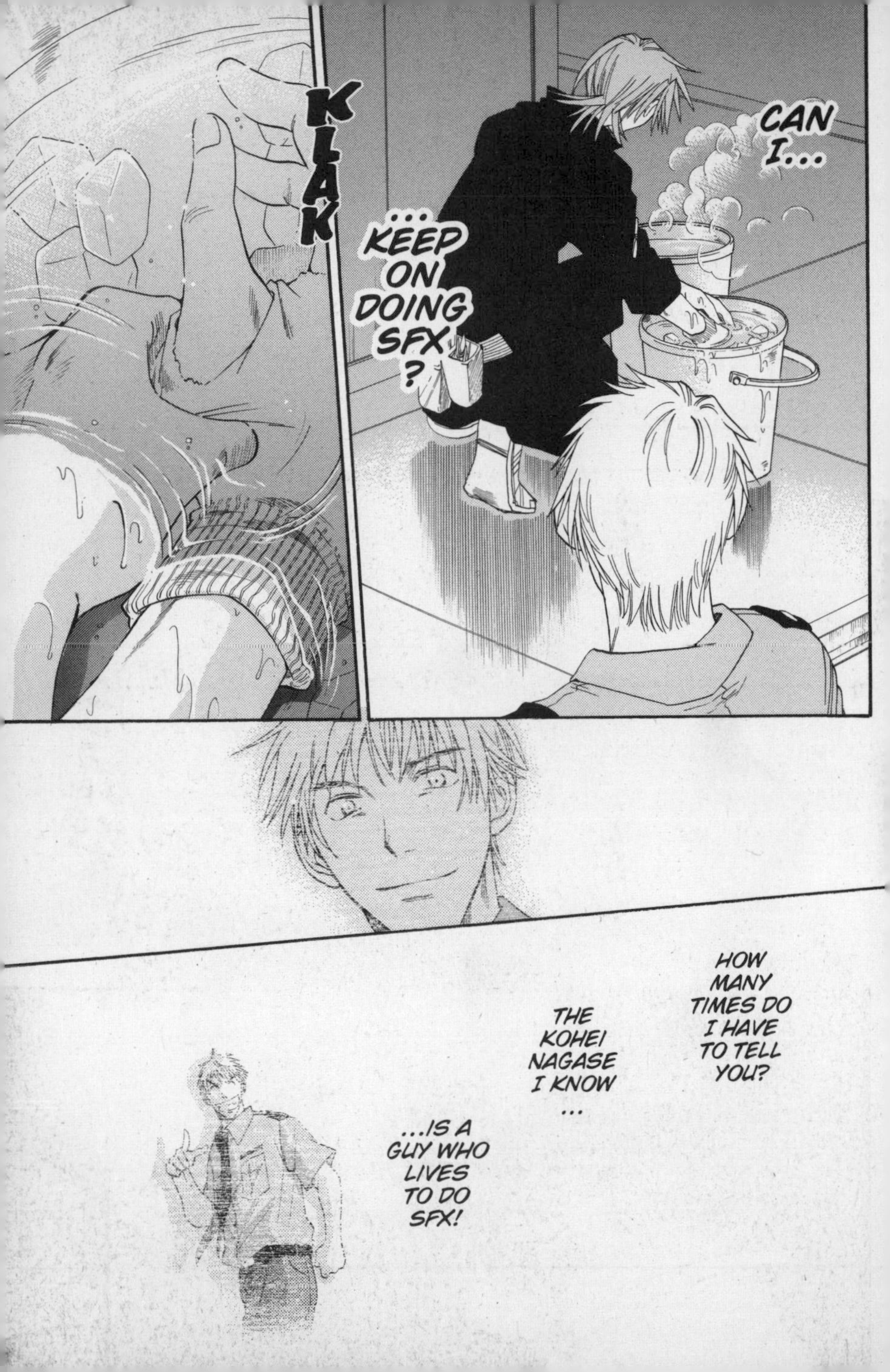
CAN I...
...KEEP ON DOING SFX?
KLAK
HOW MANY TIMES DO I HAVE TO TELL YOU?
THE KOHEI NAGASE I KNOW...
...IS A GUY WHO LIVES TO DO SFX!

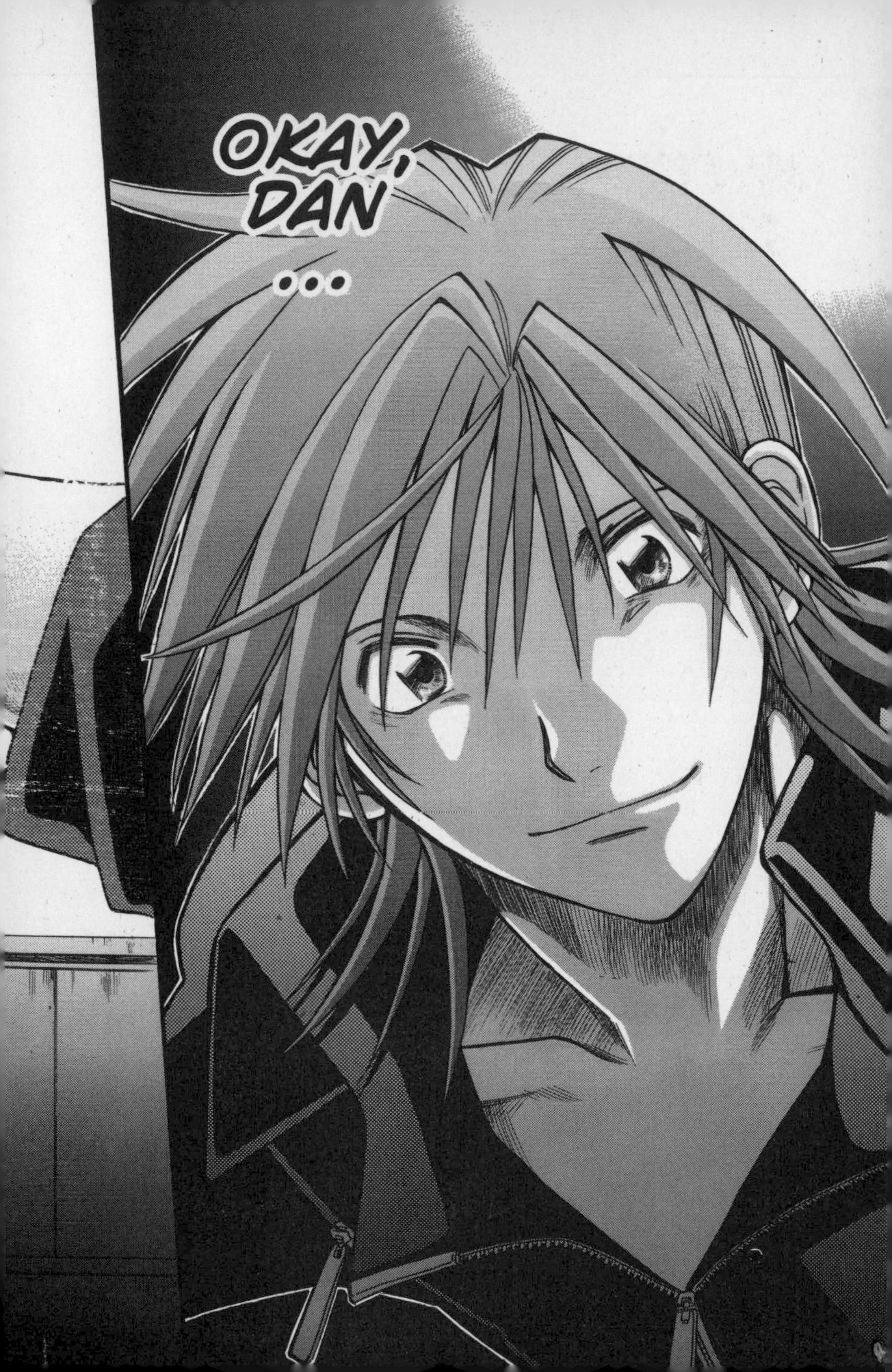
OKAY, DAN
...

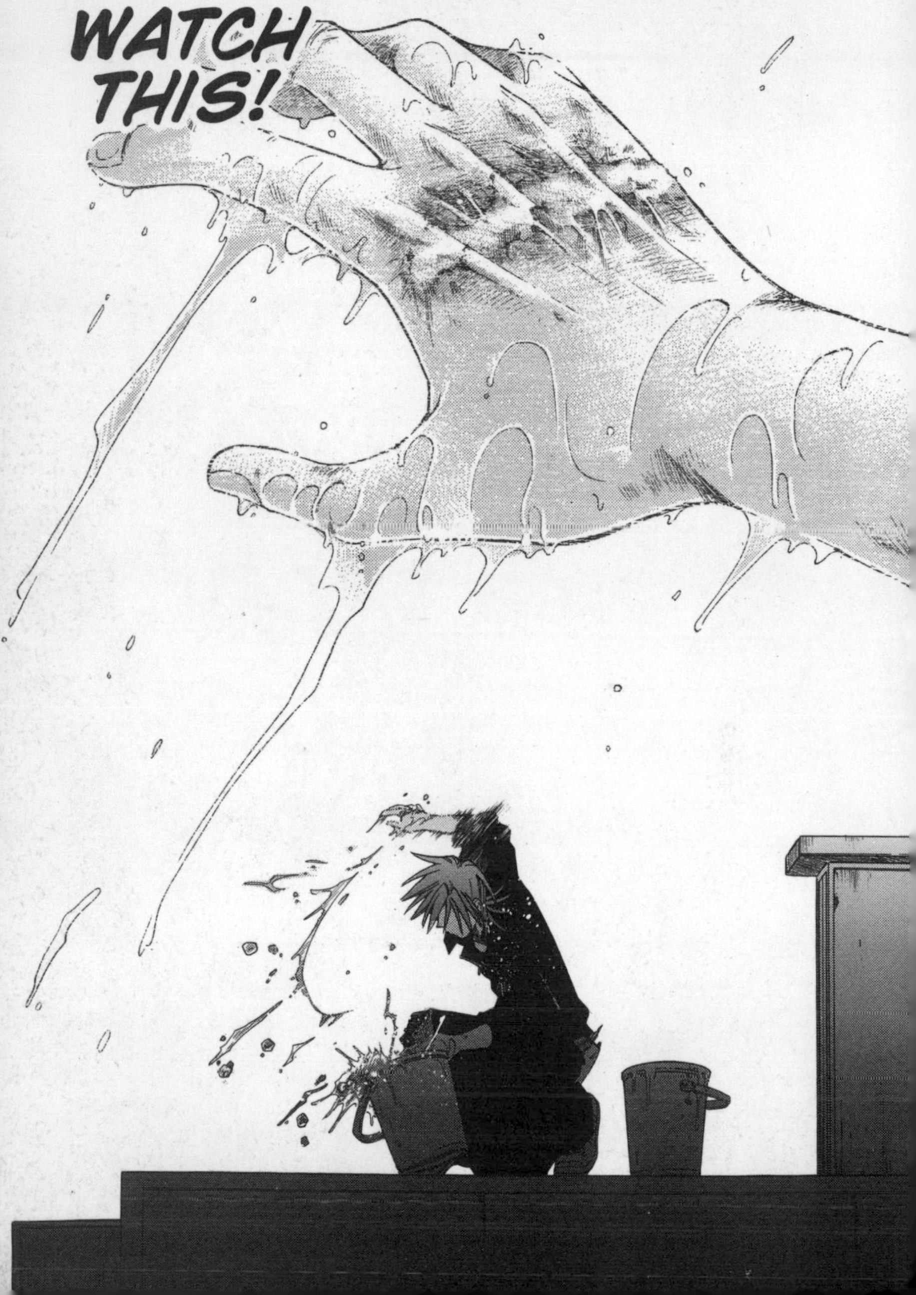
WATCH THIS!

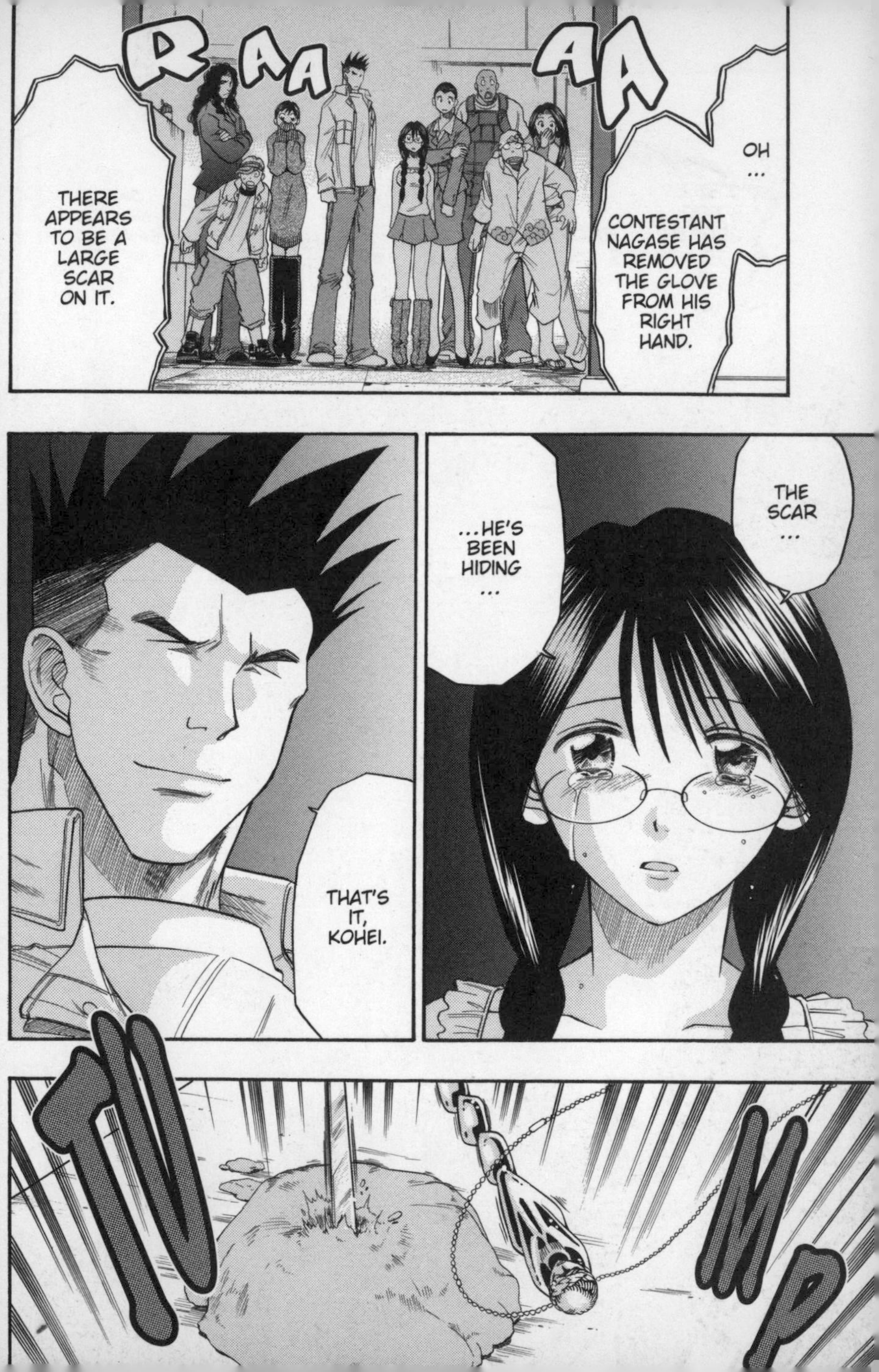
RAAAA
OH ...
CONTESTANT NAGASE HAS REMOVED THE GLOVE FROM HIS RIGHT HAND.
THERE APPEARS TO BE A LARGE SCAR ON IT.
THE SCAR ...
...HE'S BEEN HIDING ...
THAT'S IT, KOHEI.
THUMP

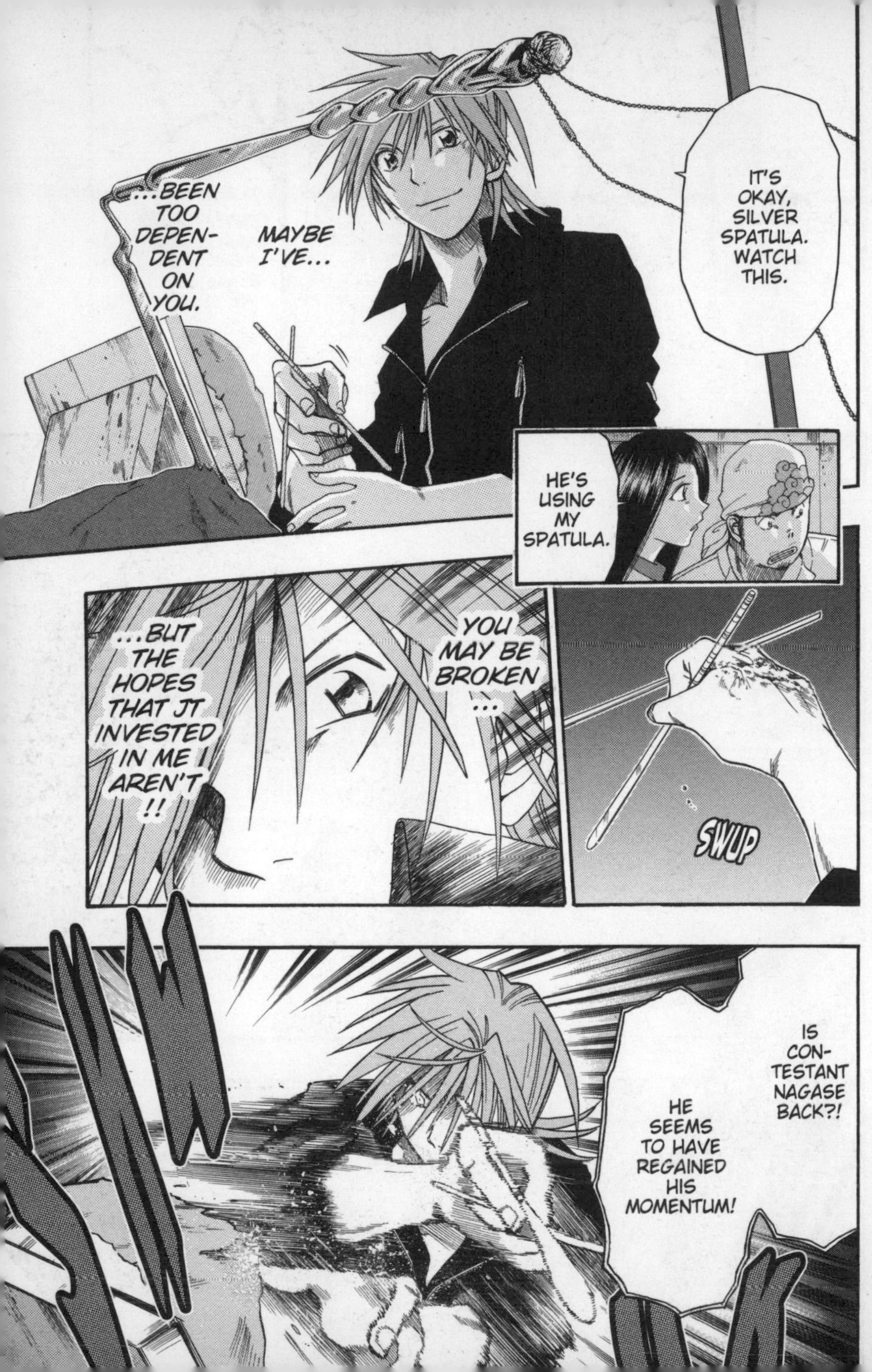
IT'S OKAY, SILVER SPATULA. WATCH THIS.
MAYBE I'VE...
...BEEN TOO DEPENDENT ON YOU.
HE'S USING MY SPATULA.
SWUP
YOU MAY BE BROKEN...
...BUT THE HOPES THAT JT INVESTED IN ME AREN'T!!
IS CONTESTANT NAGASE BACK?!
HE SEEMS TO HAVE REGAINED HIS MOMENTUM!

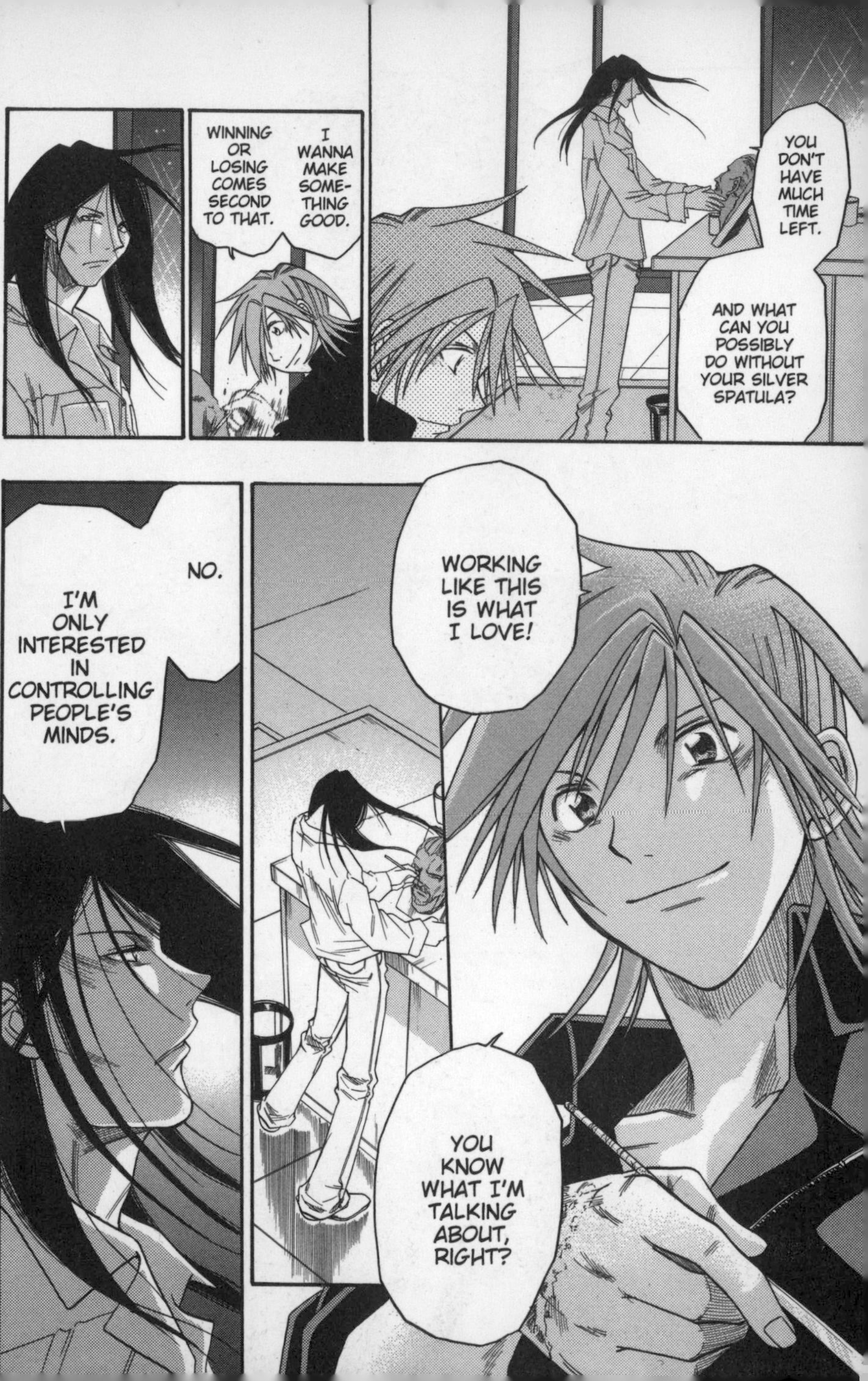
YOU DON'T HAVE MUCH TIME LEFT.
AND WHAT CAN YOU POSSIBLY DO WITHOUT YOUR SILVER SPATULA?
I WANNA MAKE SOME-THING GOOD.
WINNING OR LOSING COMES SECOND TO THAT.
WORKING LIKE THIS IS WHAT I LOVE!
YOU KNOW WHAT I'M TALKING ABOUT, RIGHT?
NO.
I'M ONLY INTERESTED IN CONTROLLING PEOPLE'S MINDS.

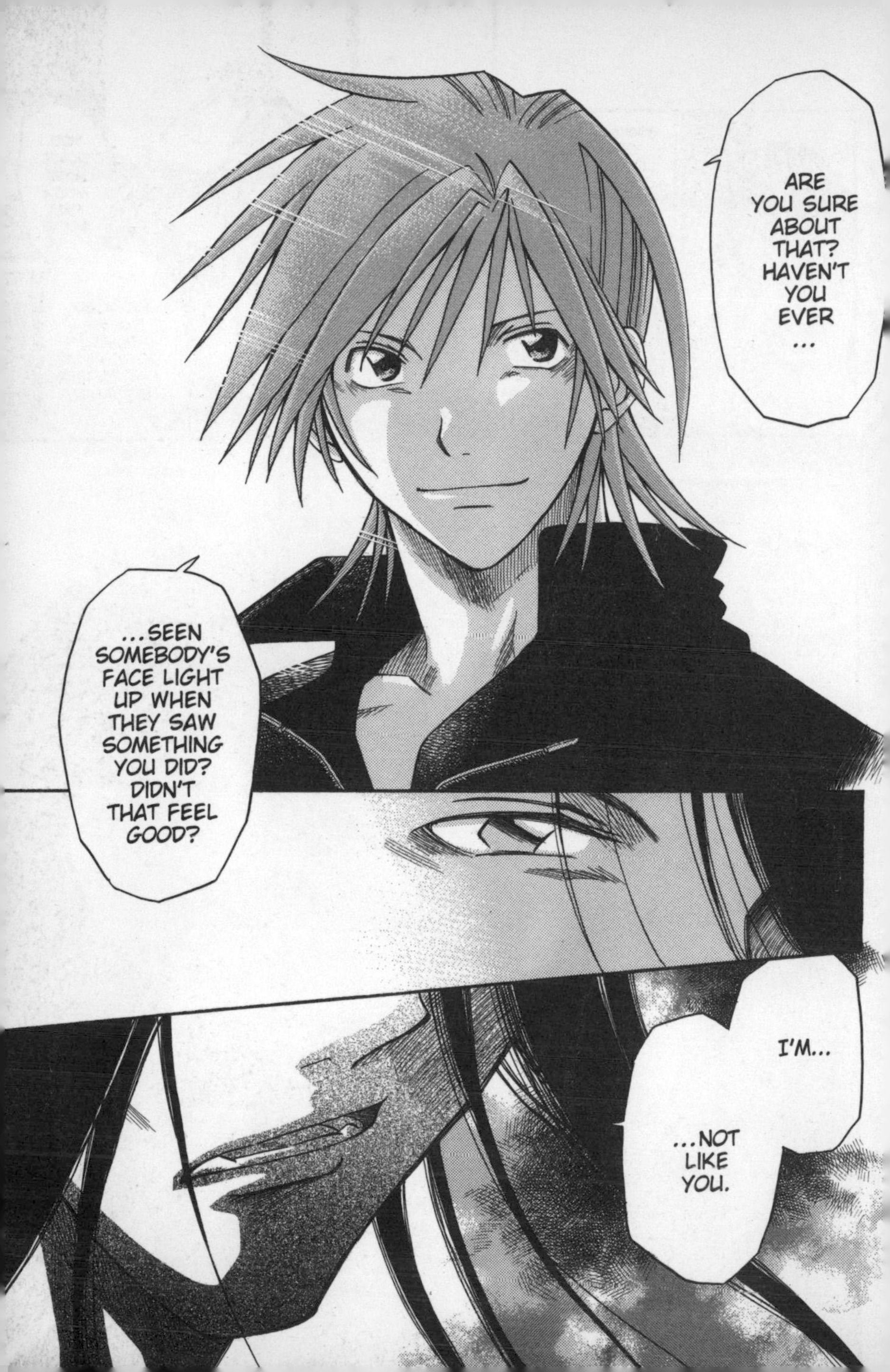
ARE YOU SURE ABOUT THAT? HAVEN'T YOU EVER ...
...SEEN SOMEBODY'S FACE LIGHT UP WHEN THEY SAW SOMETHING YOU DID? DIDN'T THAT FEEL GOOD?
I'M...
...NOT LIKE YOU.

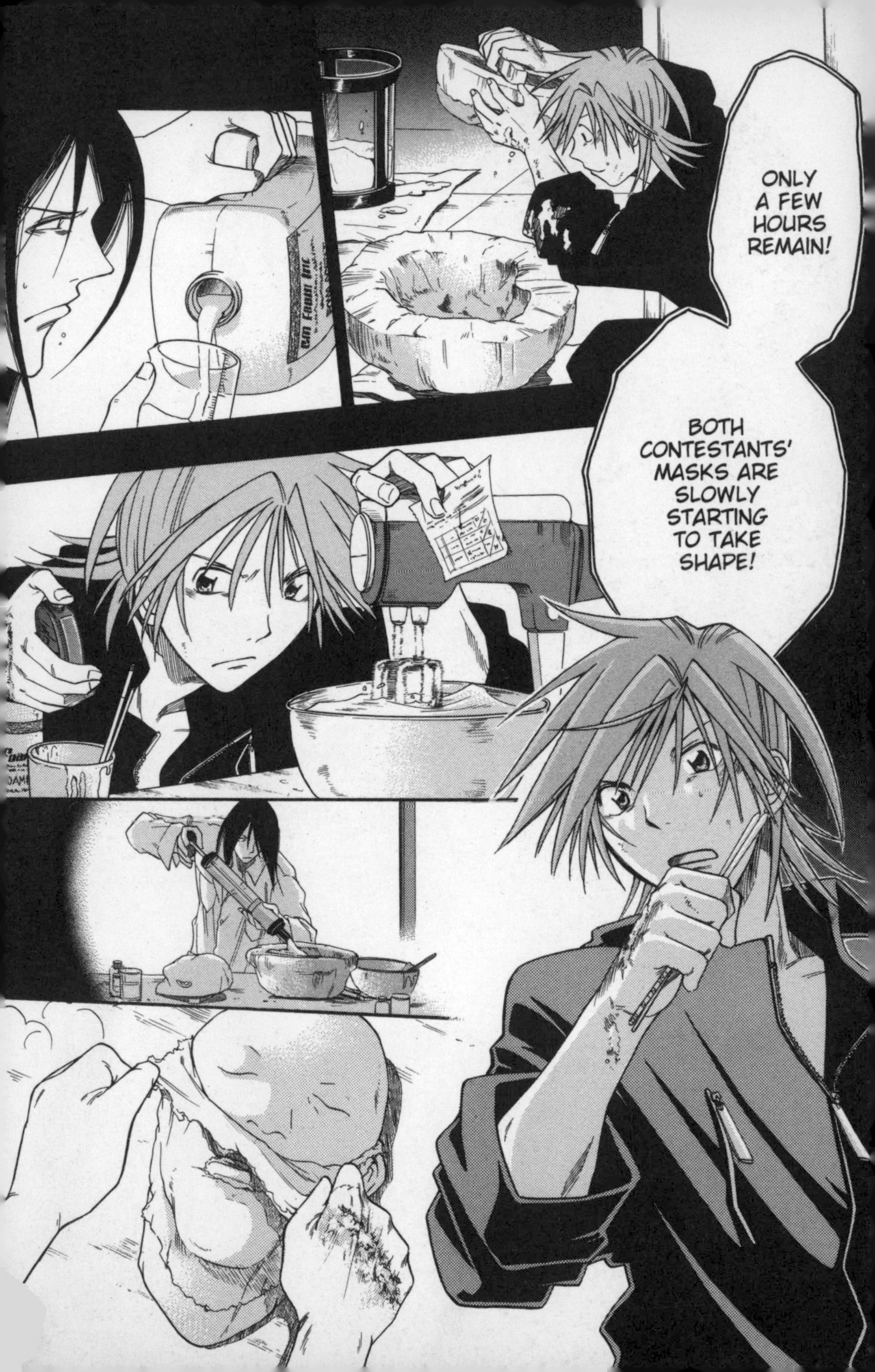
ONLY A FEW HOURS REMAIN!
BOTH CONTESTANTS' MASKS ARE SLOWLY STARTING TO TAKE SHAPE!

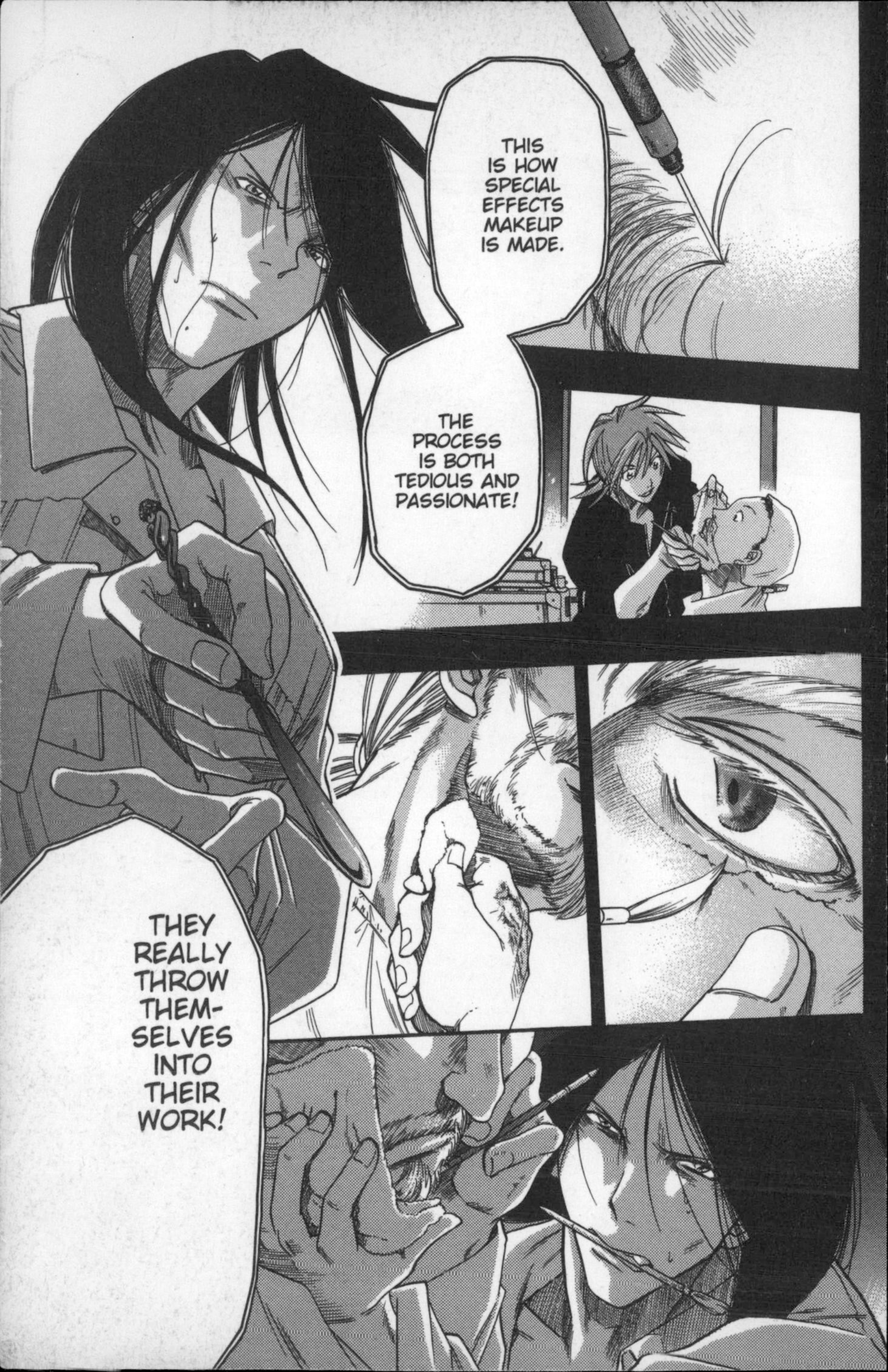
THIS IS HOW SPECIAL EFFECTS MAKEUP IS MADE.
THE PROCESS IS BOTH TEDIOUS AND PASSIONATE!
THEY REALLY THROW THEM-SELVES INTO THEIR WORK!

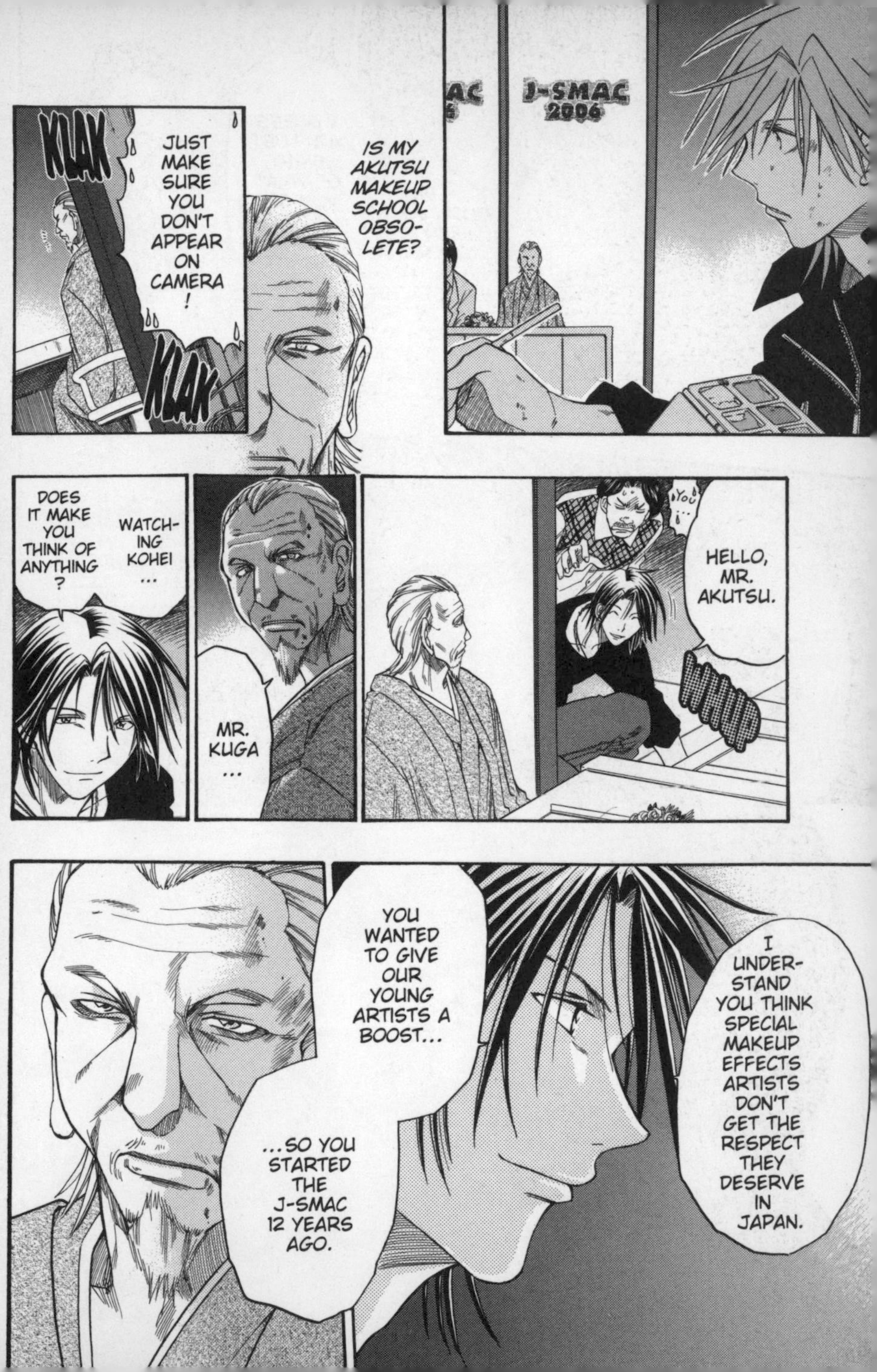
J-SMAC 2006
IS MY AKUTSU MAKEUP SCHOOL OBSOLETE?
KLAK
JUST MAKE SURE YOU DON'T APPEAR ON CAMERA!
KLAK
YOU...
HELLO, MR. AKUTSU.
WHAP
MR. KUGA...
WATCHING KOHEI...
DOES IT MAKE YOU THINK OF ANYTHING?
I UNDERSTAND YOU THINK SPECIAL MAKEUP EFFECTS ARTISTS DON'T GET THE RESPECT THEY DESERVE IN JAPAN.
YOU WANTED TO GIVE OUR YOUNG ARTISTS A BOOST...
...SO YOU STARTED THE J-SMAC 12 YEARS AGO.

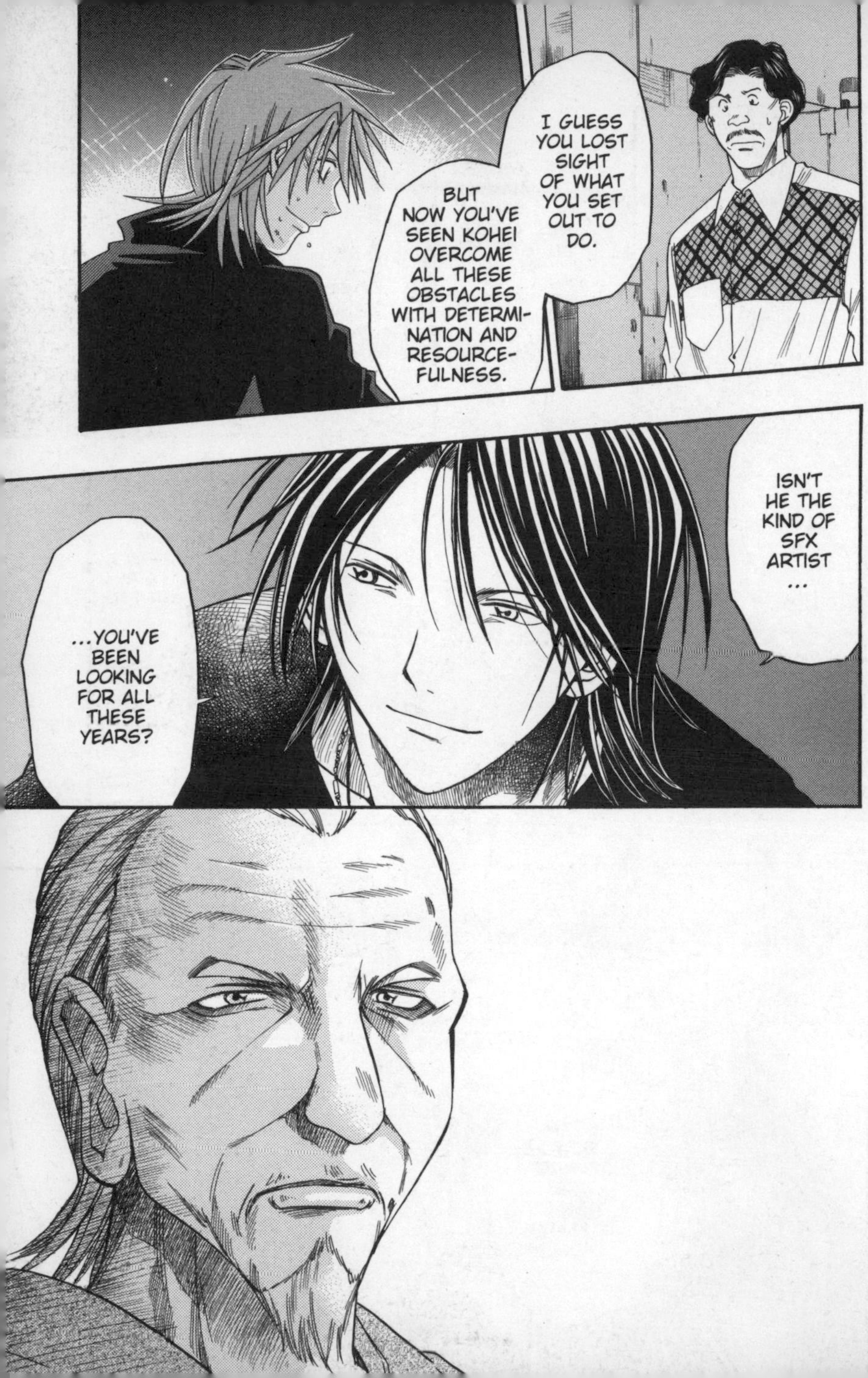
I GUESS YOU LOST SIGHT OF WHAT YOU SET OUT TO DO.
BUT NOW YOU'VE SEEN KOHEI OVERCOME ALL THESE OBSTACLES WITH DETERMINATION AND RESOURCEFULNESS.
ISN'T HE THE KIND OF SFX ARTIST ...
...YOU'VE BEEN LOOKING FOR ALL THESE YEARS?

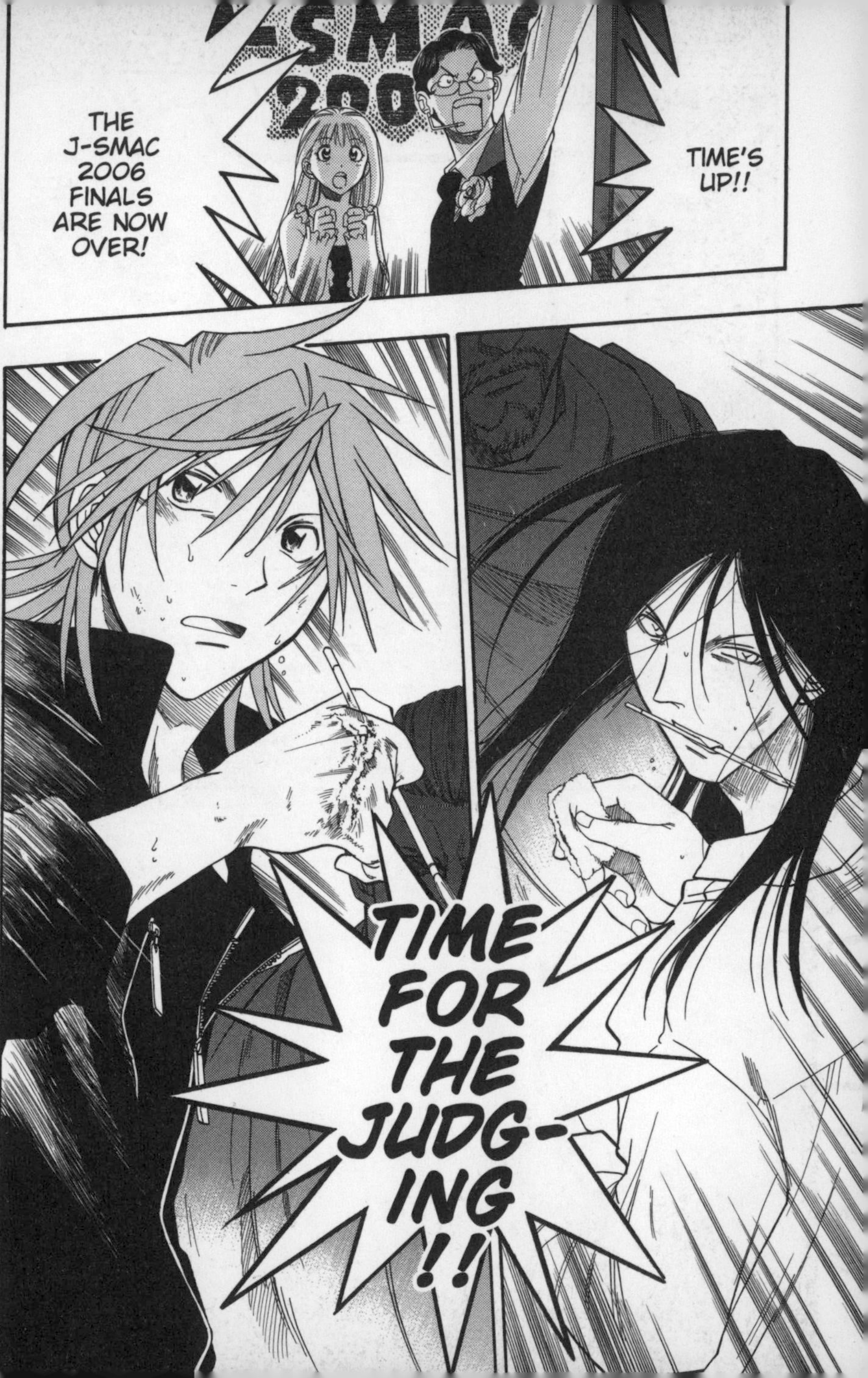
TIME'S UP!!
THE J-SMAC 2006 FINALS ARE NOW OVER!
TIME FOR THE JUDG-ING!!

Scene 84: The Third Man (Part 7)

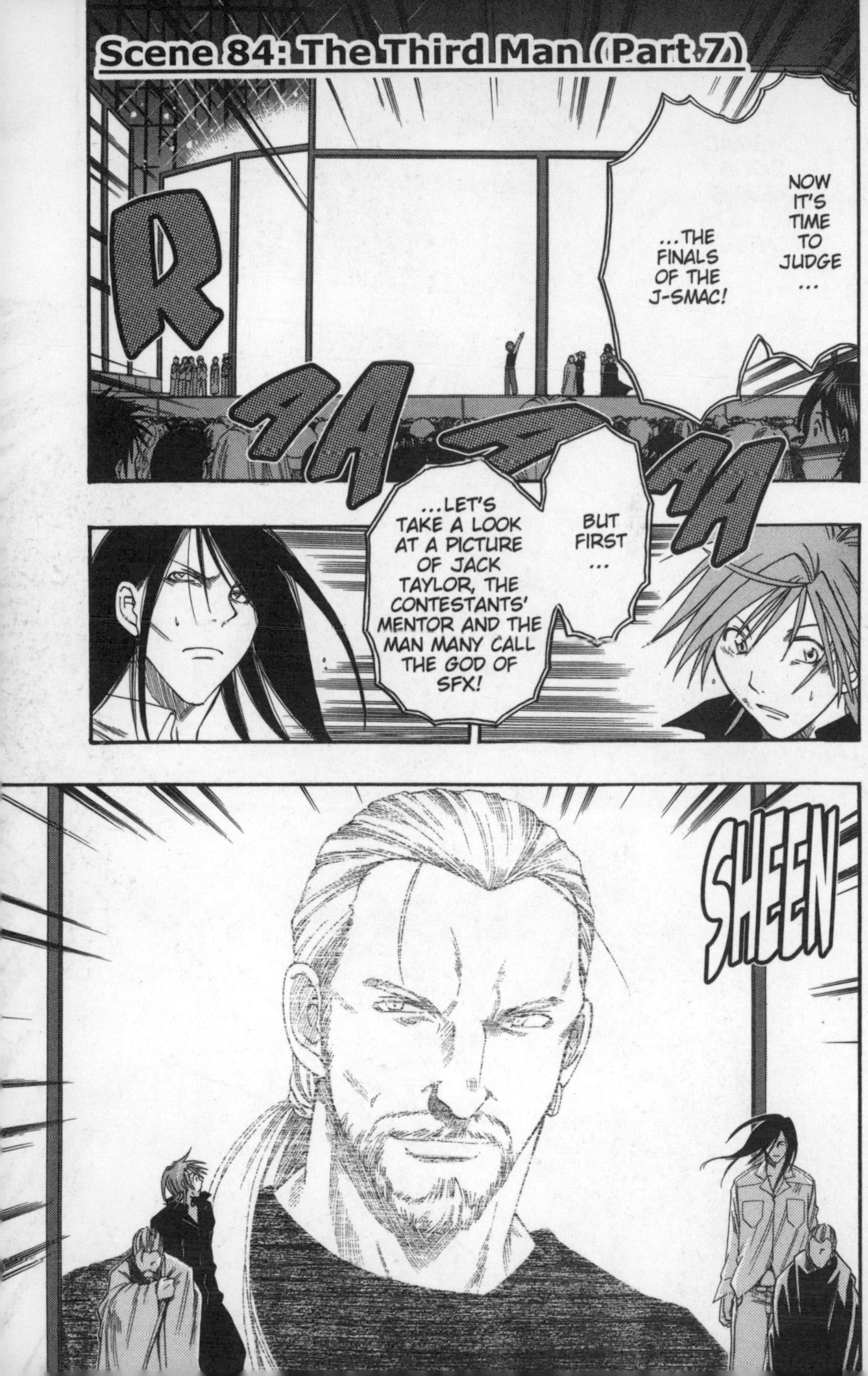

NOW IT'S TIME TO JUDGE ...
...THE FINALS OF THE J-SMAC!
RAAAAA
BUT FIRST ...
...LET'S TAKE A LOOK AT A PICTURE OF JACK TAYLOR, THE CONTESTANTS' MENTOR AND THE MAN MANY CALL THE GOD OF SFX!
SHEEN

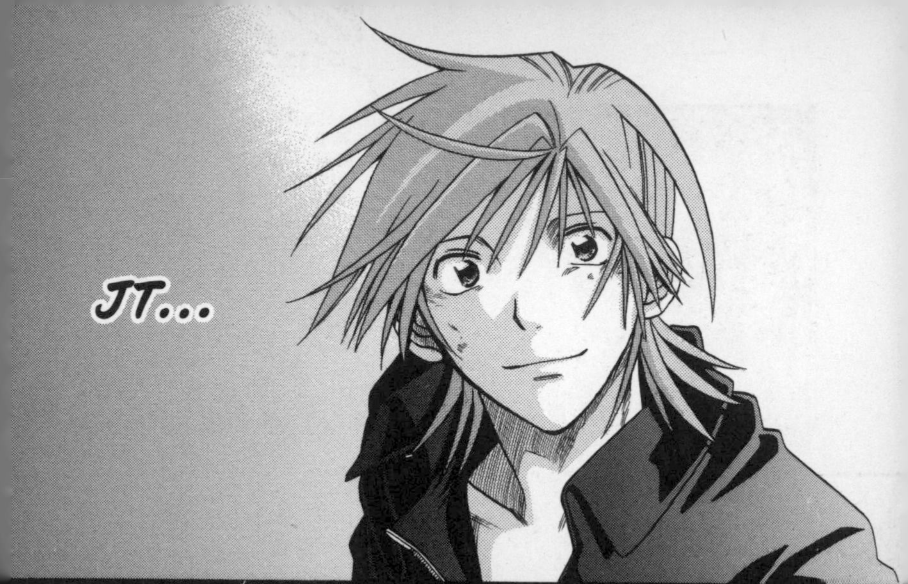
JT...

Scene 84: The Third Man (Part 7)

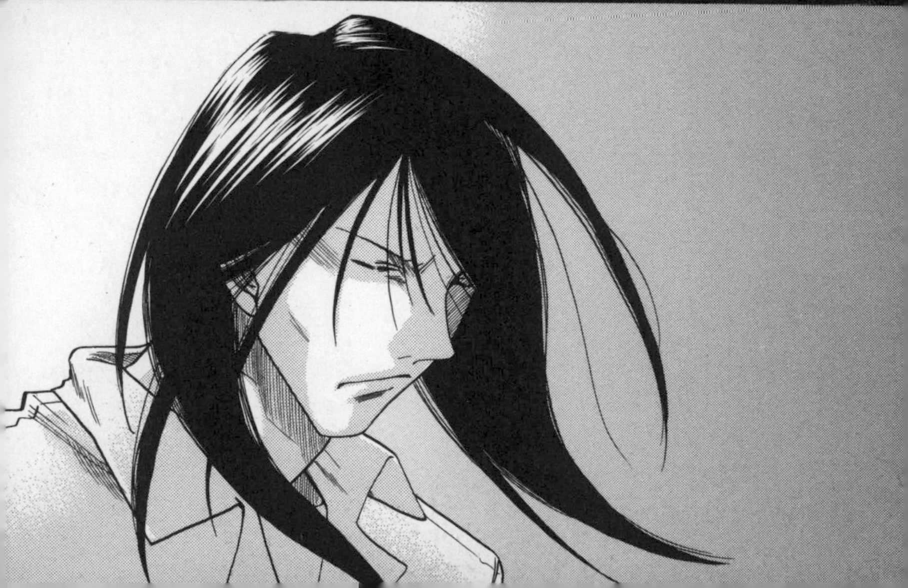

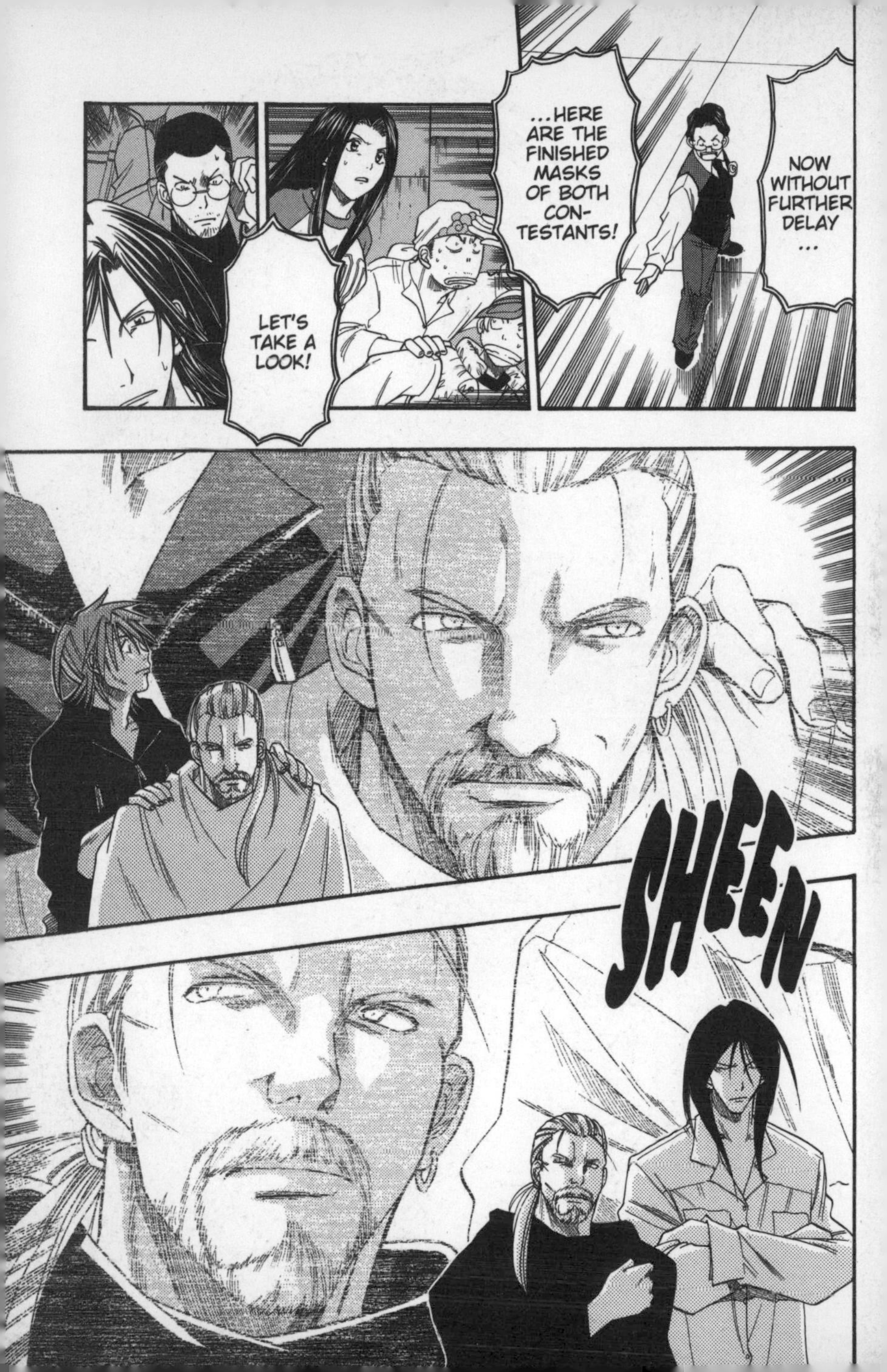
NOW WITHOUT FURTHER DELAY ...
...HERE ARE THE FINISHED MASKS OF BOTH CON-TESTANTS!
LET'S TAKE A LOOK!
SHEEN

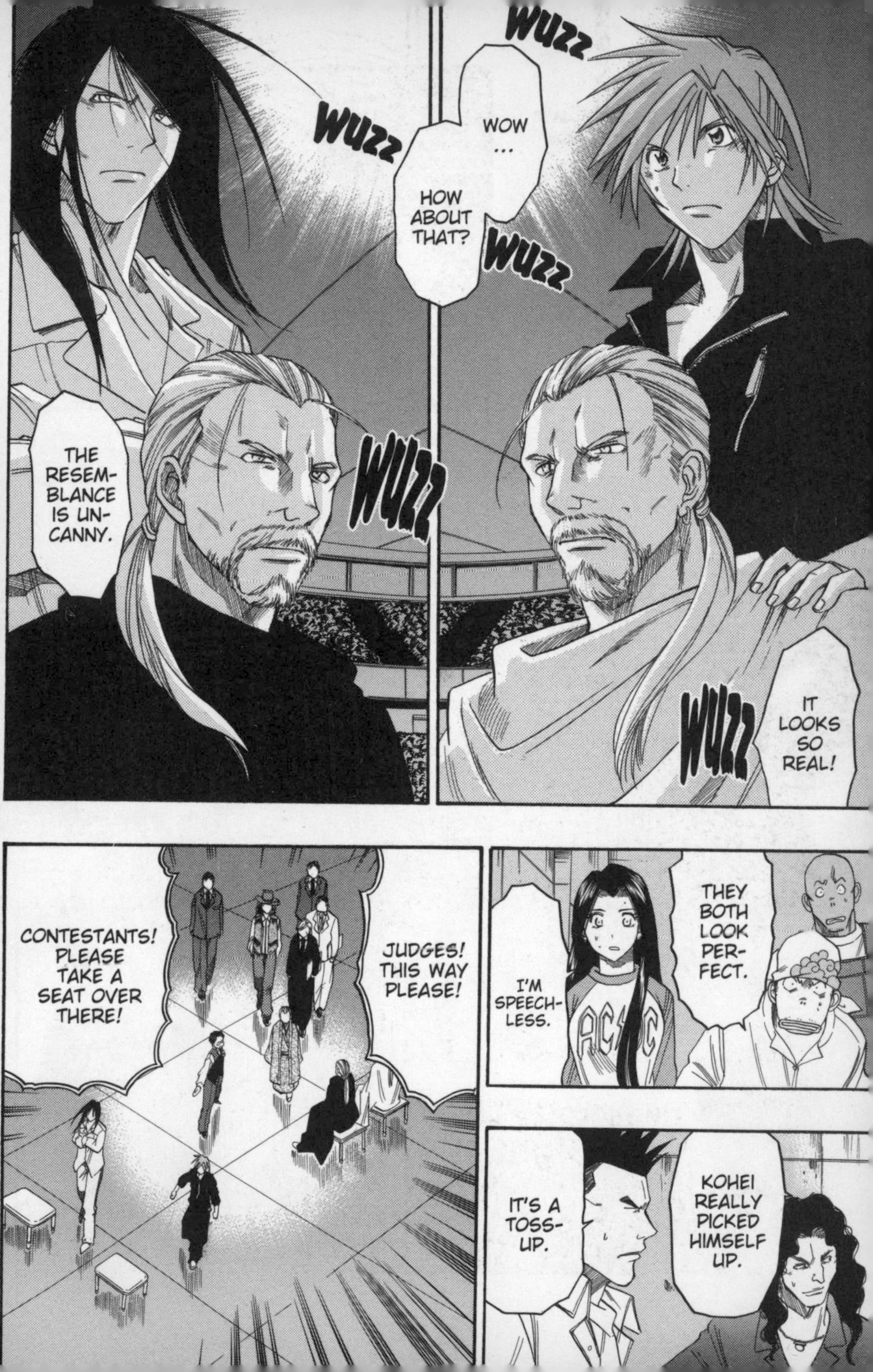
WUZZ
WOW ... HOW ABOUT THAT?
WUZZ
WUZZ
WUZZ
IT LOOKS SO REAL!
WUZZ
THE RESEMBLANCE IS UNCANNY.
THEY BOTH LOOK PERFECT.
I'M SPEECHLESS.
KOHEI REALLY PICKED HIMSELF UP.
IT'S A TOSS-UP.
JUDGES! THIS WAY PLEASE!
CONTESTANTS! PLEASE TAKE A SEAT OVER THERE!

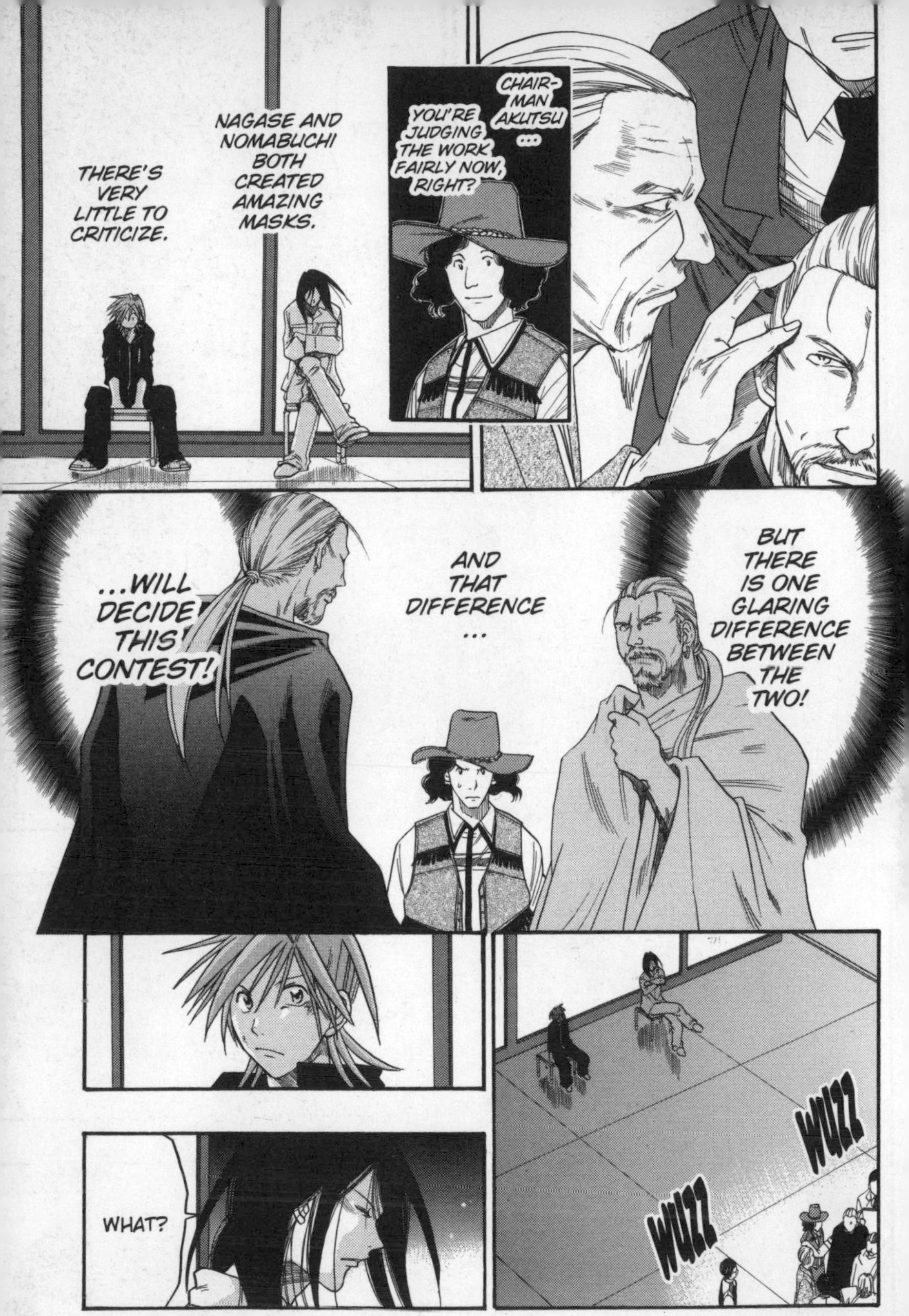
CHAIR-MAN AKUTSU...
YOU'RE JUDGING THE WORK FAIRLY NOW, RIGHT?
NAGASE AND NOMABUCHI BOTH CREATED AMAZING MASKS.
THERE'S VERY LITTLE TO CRITICIZE.
BUT THERE IS ONE GLARING DIFFERENCE BETWEEN THE TWO!
AND THAT DIFFERENCE...
...WILL DECIDE THIS CONTEST!
WUZZ
WUZZ
WHAT?

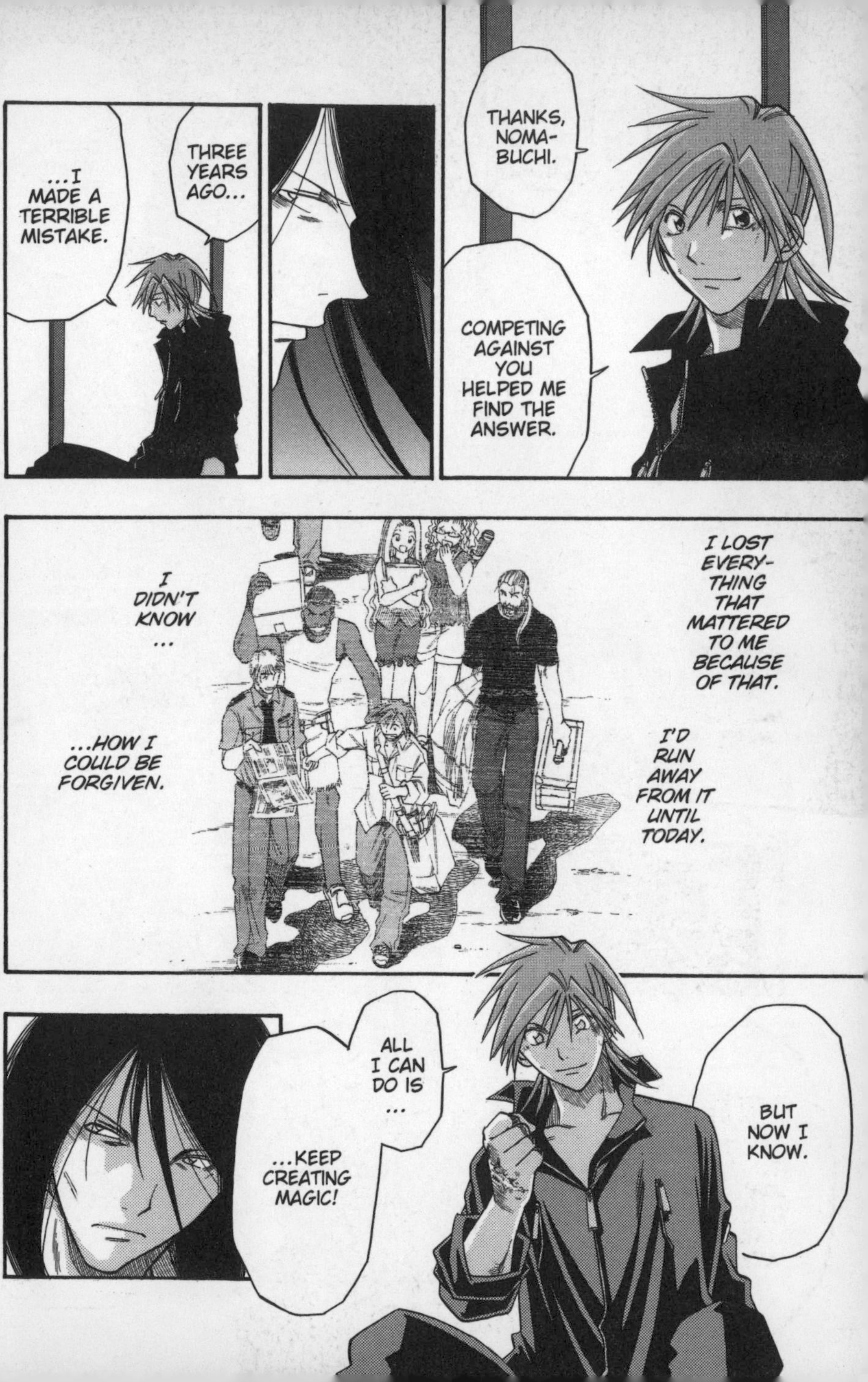
THANKS, NOMA-BUCHI.
COMPETING AGAINST YOU HELPED ME FIND THE ANSWER.
THREE YEARS AGO...
...I MADE A TERRIBLE MISTAKE.
I LOST EVERY-THING THAT MATTERED TO ME BECAUSE OF THAT.
I'D RUN AWAY FROM IT UNTIL TODAY.
I DIDN'T KNOW ...
...HOW I COULD BE FORGIVEN.
BUT NOW I KNOW.
ALL I CAN DO IS ...
...KEEP CREATING MAGIC!

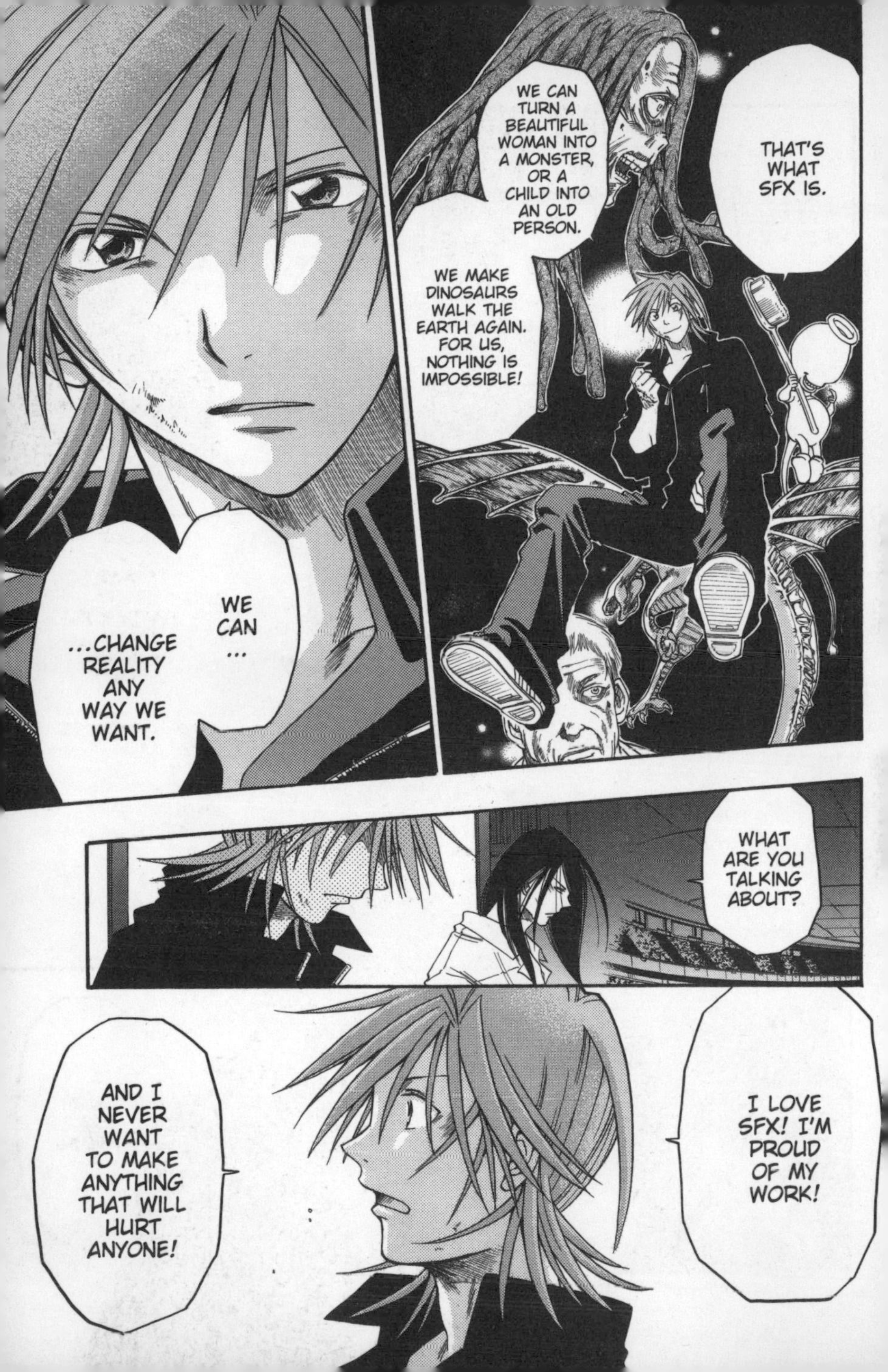
THAT'S WHAT SFX IS.
WE CAN TURN A BEAUTIFUL WOMAN INTO A MONSTER, OR A CHILD INTO AN OLD PERSON.
WE MAKE DINOSAURS WALK THE EARTH AGAIN. FOR US, NOTHING IS IMPOSSIBLE!
WE CAN...
...CHANGE REALITY ANY WAY WE WANT.
WHAT ARE YOU TALKING ABOUT?
I LOVE SFX! I'M PROUD OF MY WORK!
AND I NEVER WANT TO MAKE ANYTHING THAT WILL HURT ANYONE!

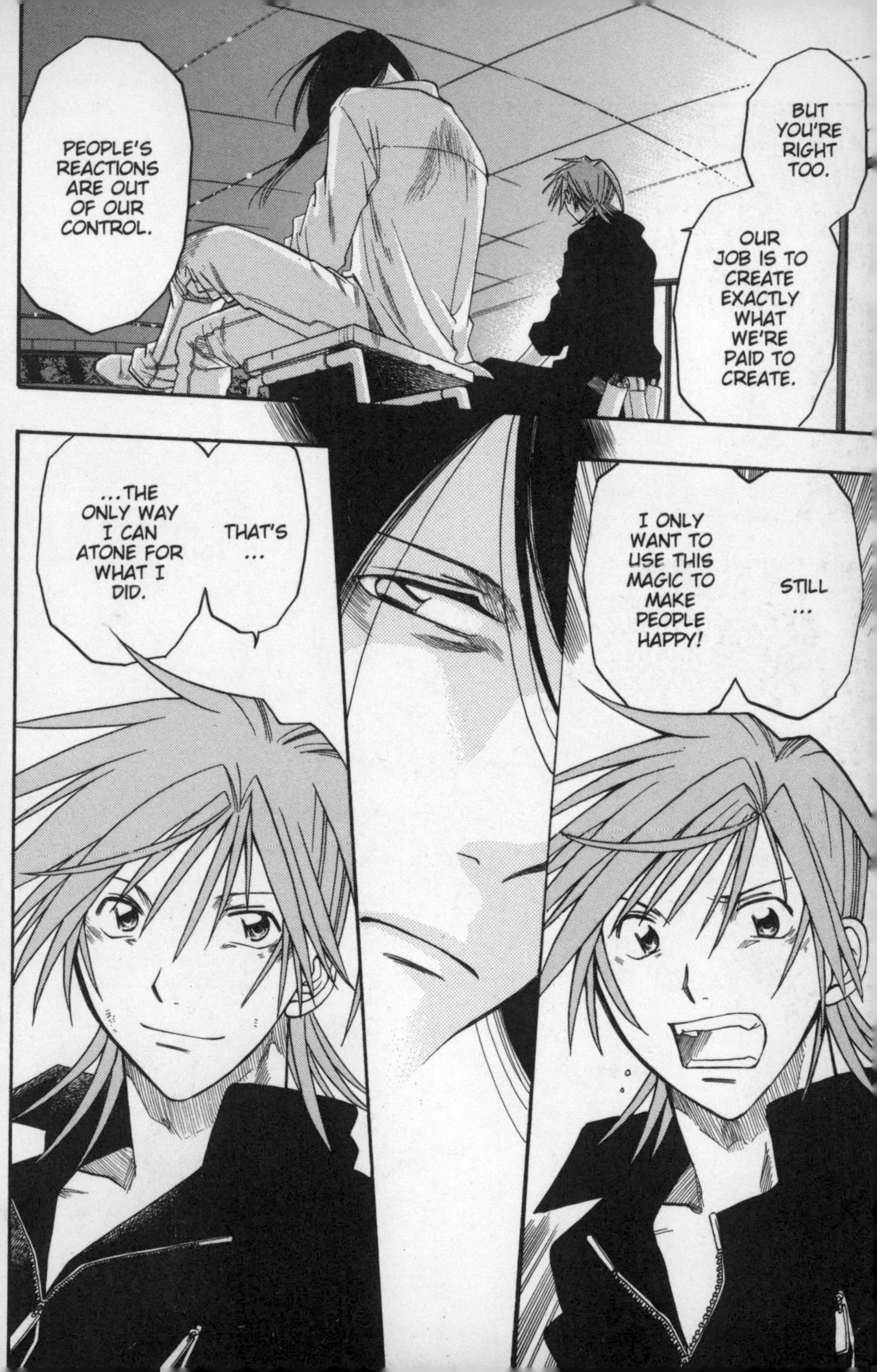
BUT YOU'RE RIGHT TOO.
OUR JOB IS TO CREATE EXACTLY WHAT WE'RE PAID TO CREATE.
PEOPLE'S REACTIONS ARE OUT OF OUR CONTROL.
STILL ...
I ONLY WANT TO USE THIS MAGIC TO MAKE PEOPLE HAPPY!
THAT'S ...
...THE ONLY WAY I CAN ATONE FOR WHAT I DID.

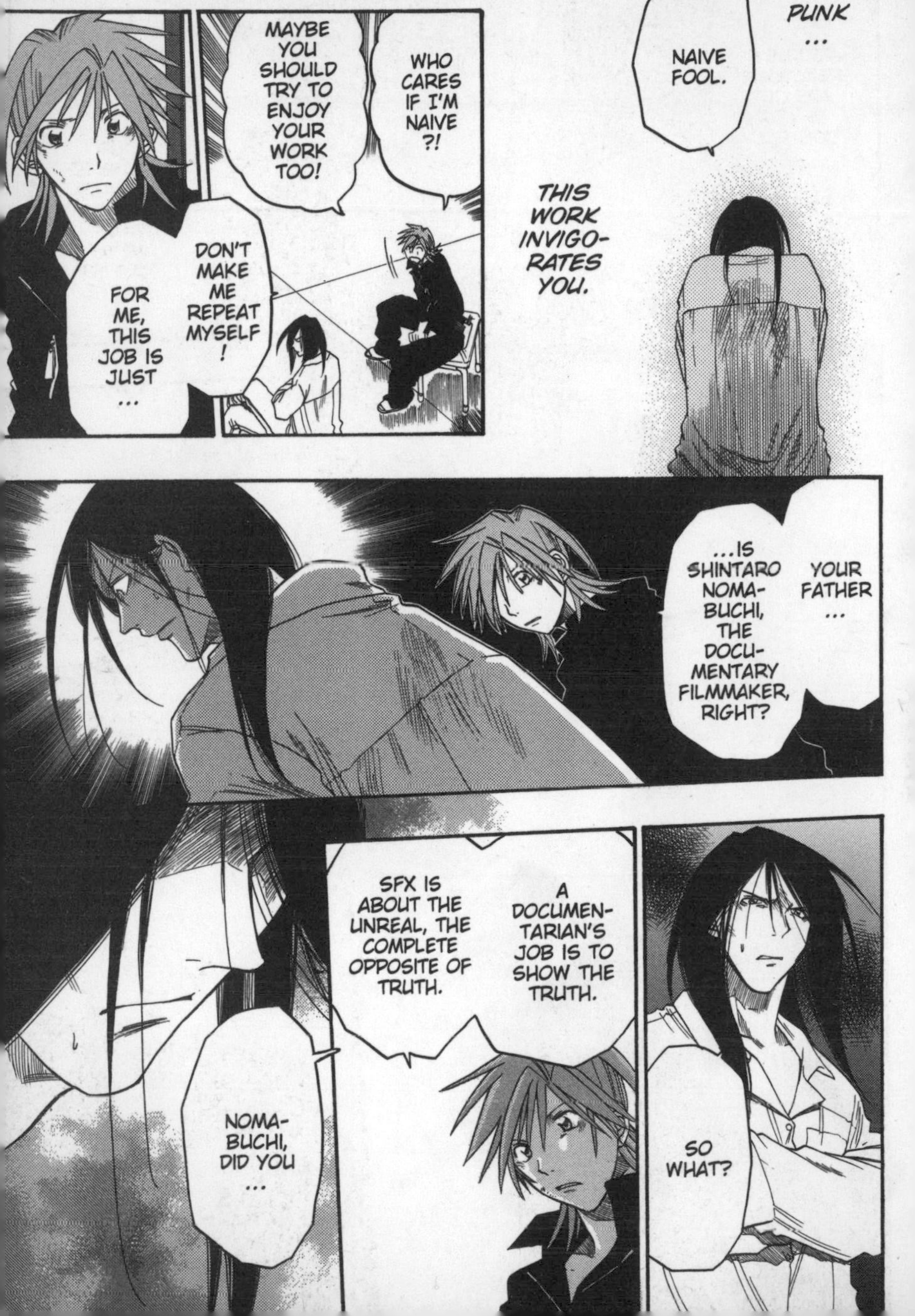
PUNK ...
NAIVE FOOL.
THIS WORK INVIGORATES YOU.
WHO CARES IF I'M NAIVE?!
MAYBE YOU SHOULD TRY TO ENJOY YOUR WORK TOO!
DON'T MAKE ME REPEAT MYSELF!
FOR ME, THIS JOB IS JUST ...
YOUR FATHER ...
...IS SHINTARO NOMABUCHI, THE DOCUMENTARY FILMMAKER, RIGHT?
SO WHAT?
A DOCUMENTARIAN'S JOB IS TO SHOW THE TRUTH.
SFX IS ABOUT THE UNREAL, THE COMPLETE OPPOSITE OF TRUTH.
NOMABUCHI, DID YOU ...

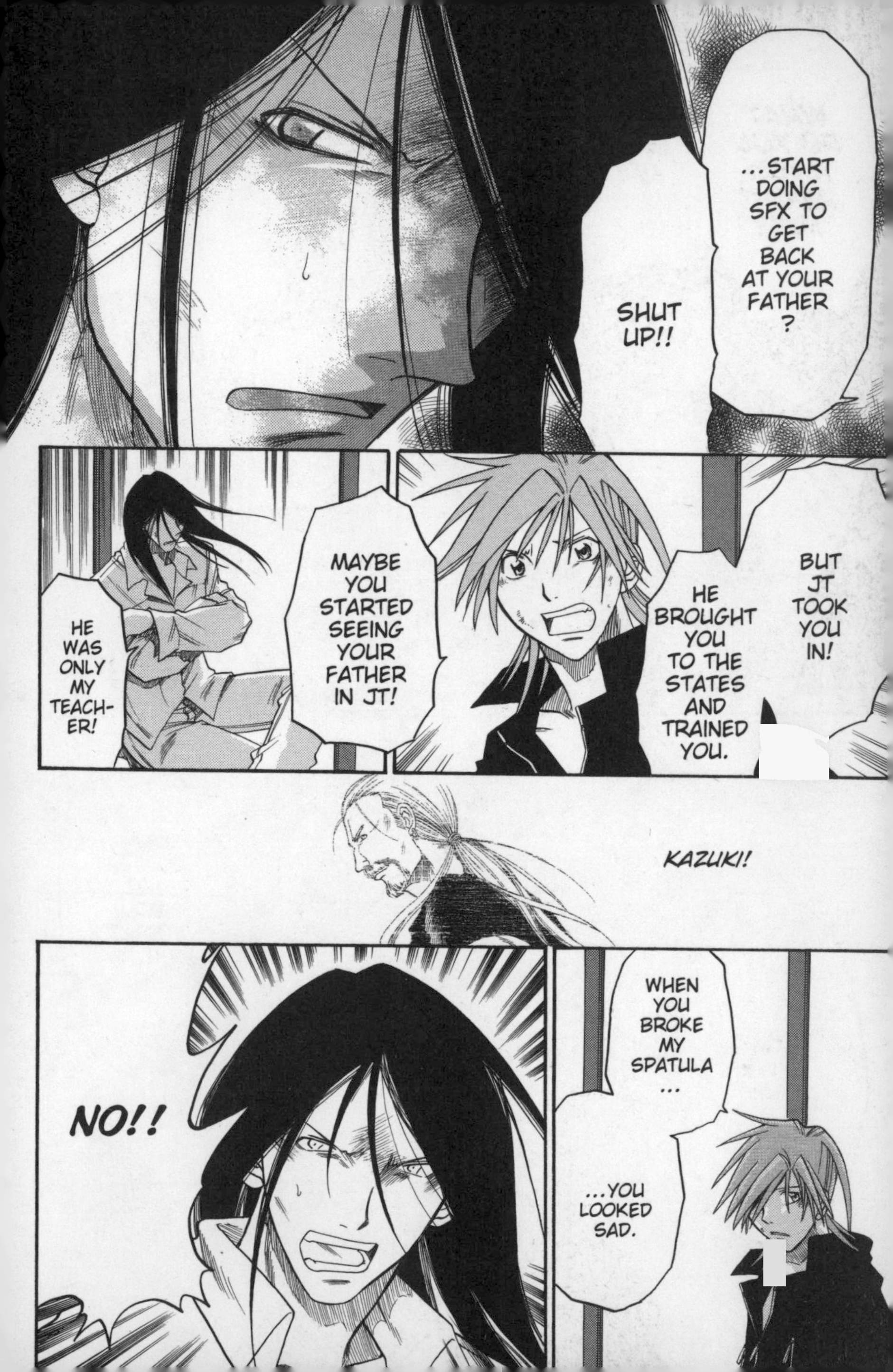
...START DOING SFX TO GET BACK AT YOUR FATHER?
SHUT UP!!
BUT JT TOOK YOU IN!
HE BROUGHT YOU TO THE STATES AND TRAINED YOU.
MAYBE YOU STARTED SEEING YOUR FATHER IN JT!
HE WAS ONLY MY TEACHER!
KAZUKI!
WHEN YOU BROKE MY SPATULA...
...YOU LOOKED SAD.
NO!!

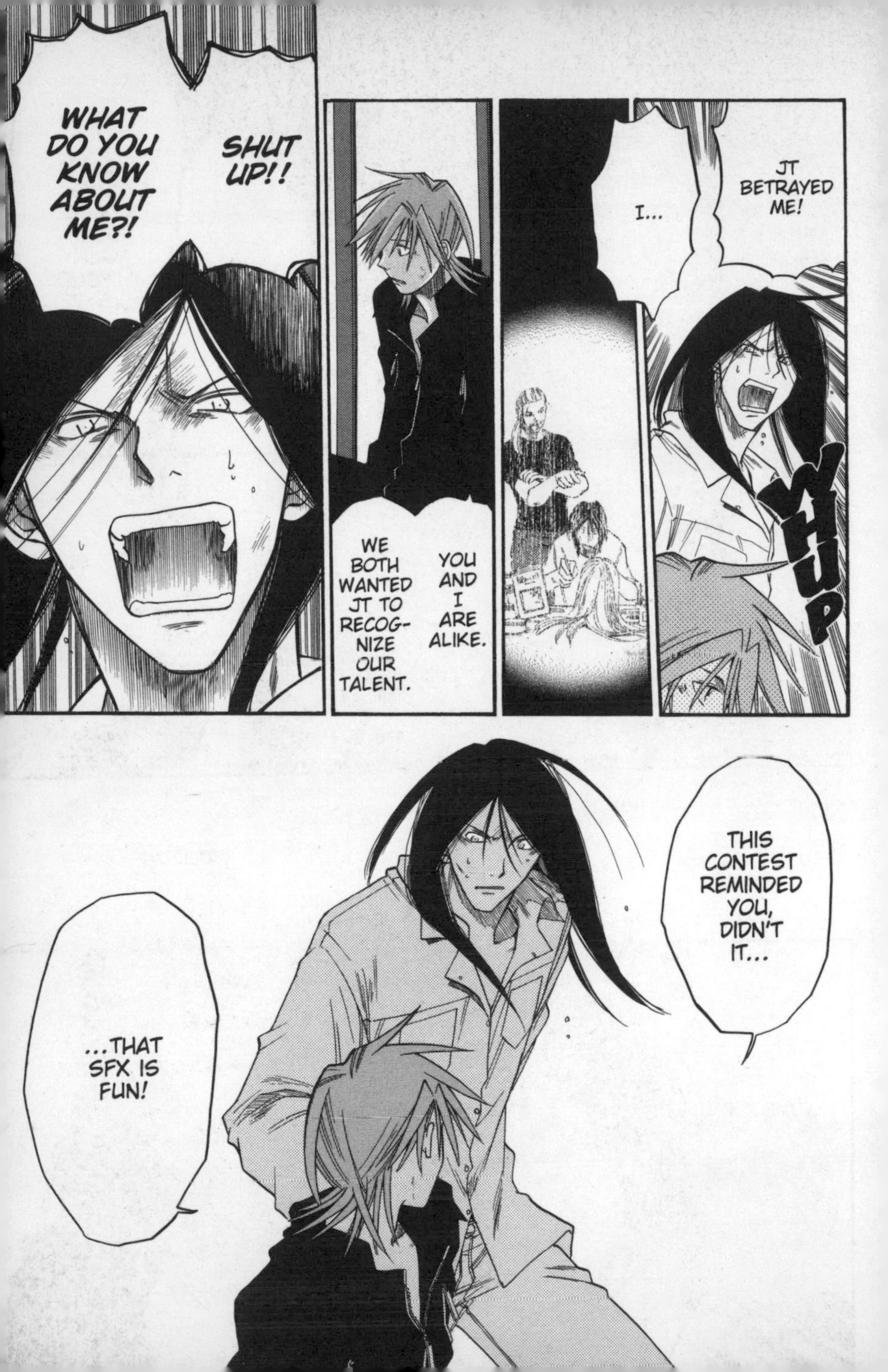
JT BETRAYED ME!
I...
WHUP
YOU AND I ARE ALIKE.
WE BOTH WANTED JT TO RECOGNIZE OUR TALENT.
SHUT UP!!
WHAT DO YOU KNOW ABOUT ME?!
THIS CONTEST REMINDED YOU, DIDN'T IT...
...THAT SFX IS FUN!

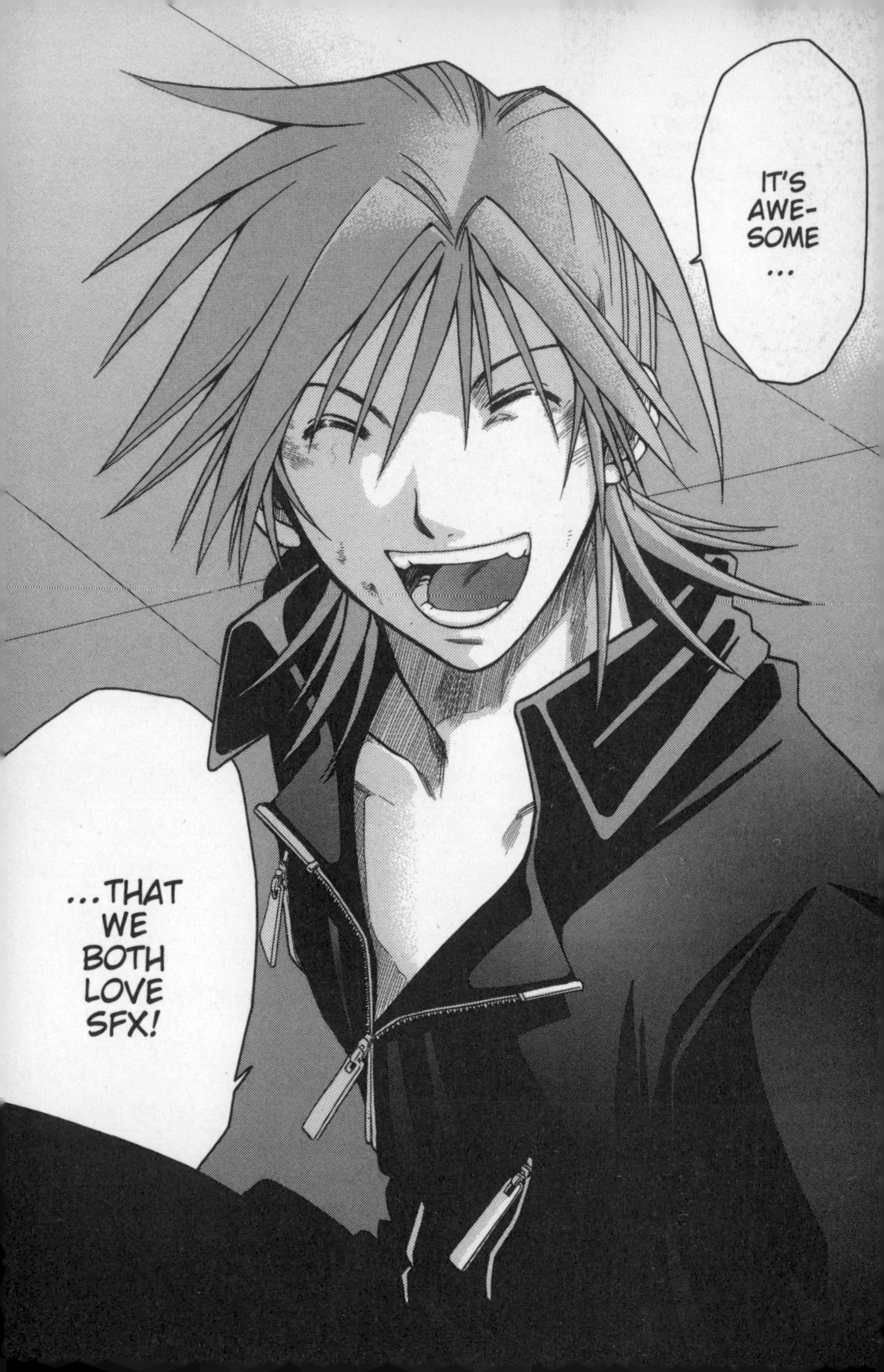
IT'S AWE-SOME ...
...THAT WE BOTH LOVE SFX!

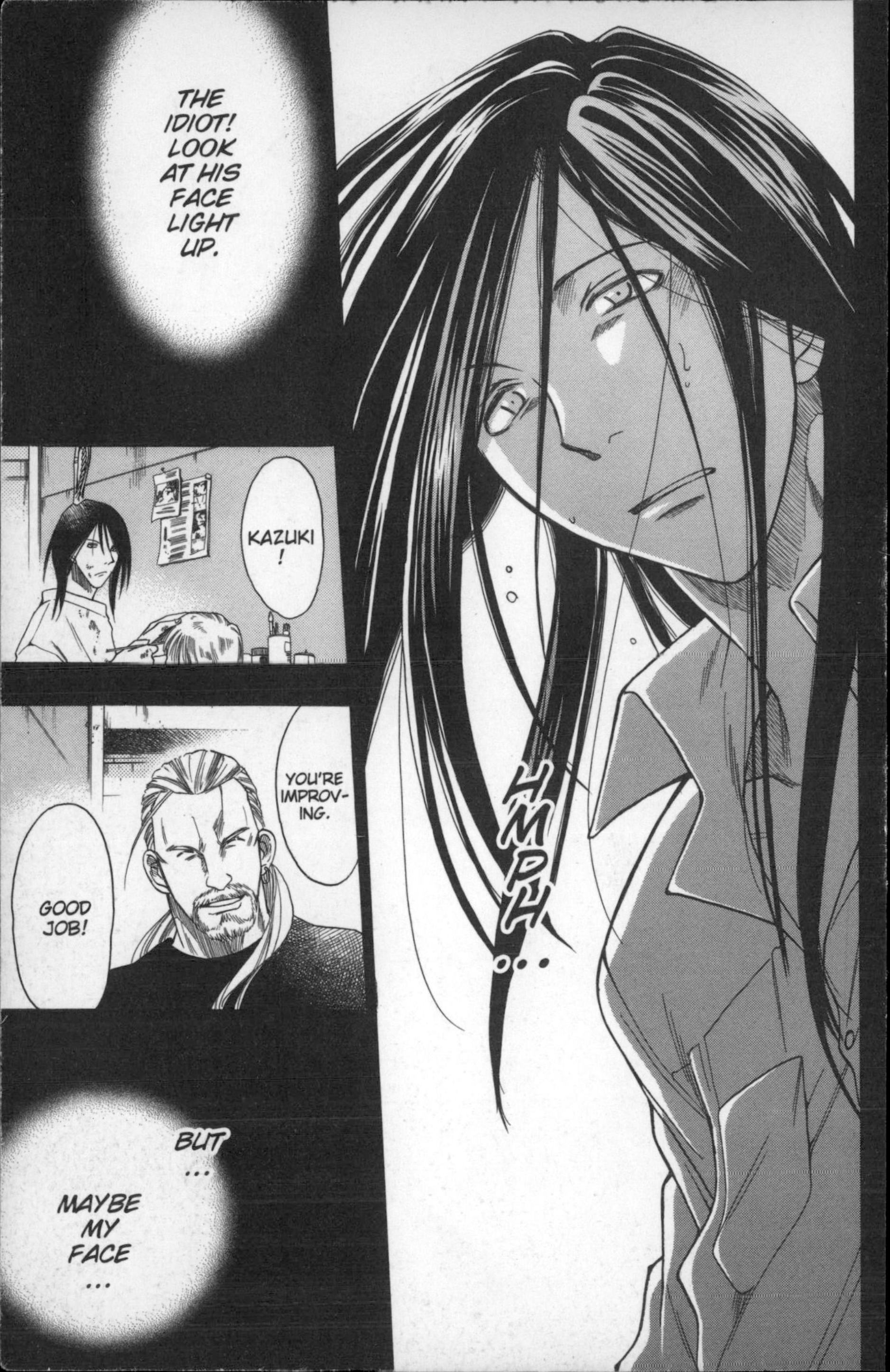
HMPH...
THE IDIOT! LOOK AT HIS FACE LIGHT UP.
KAZUKI!
YOU'RE IMPROVING.
GOOD JOB!
BUT... MAYBE MY FACE...

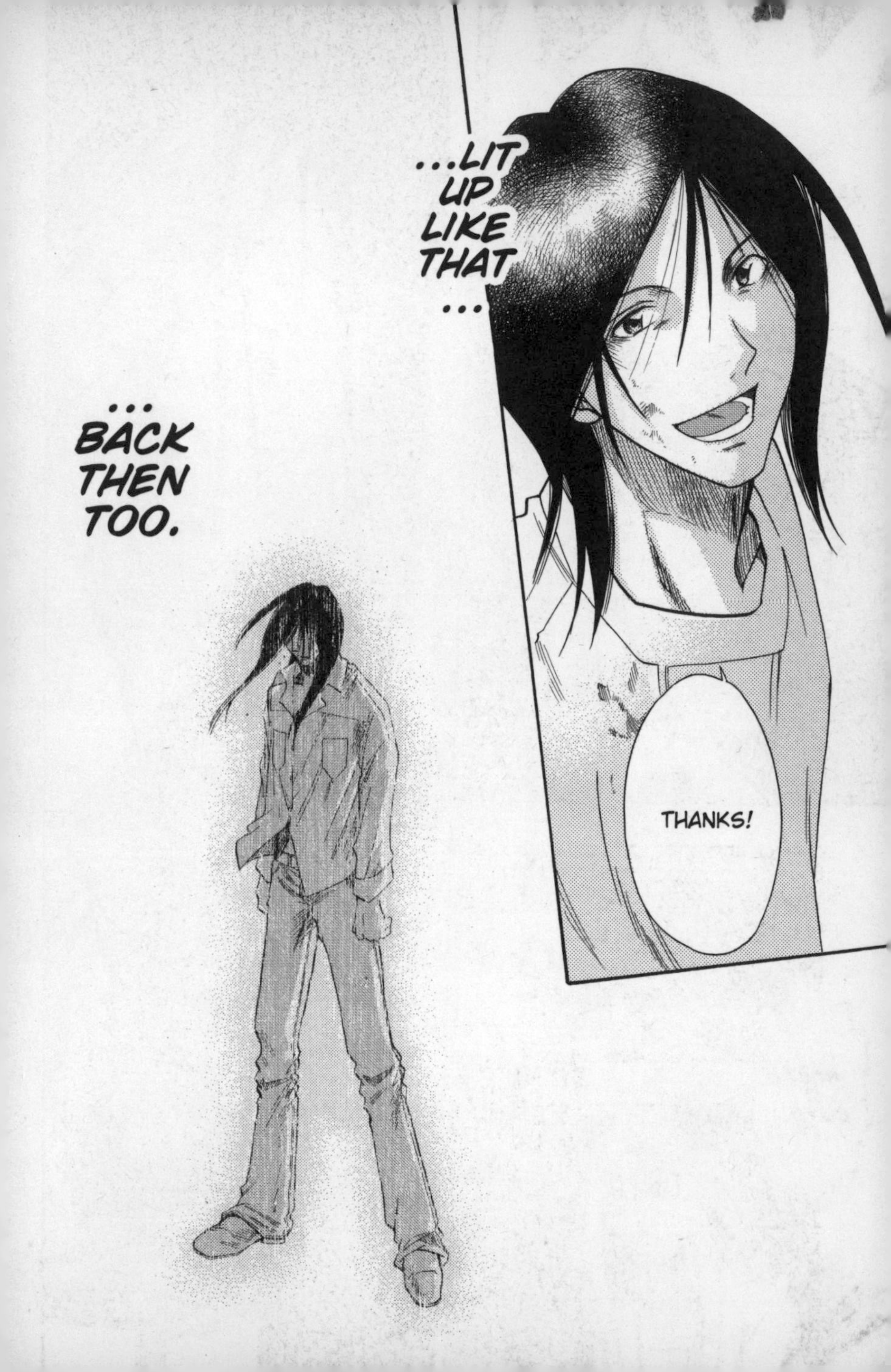
...LIT UP LIKE THAT...
THANKS!
...BACK THEN TOO.

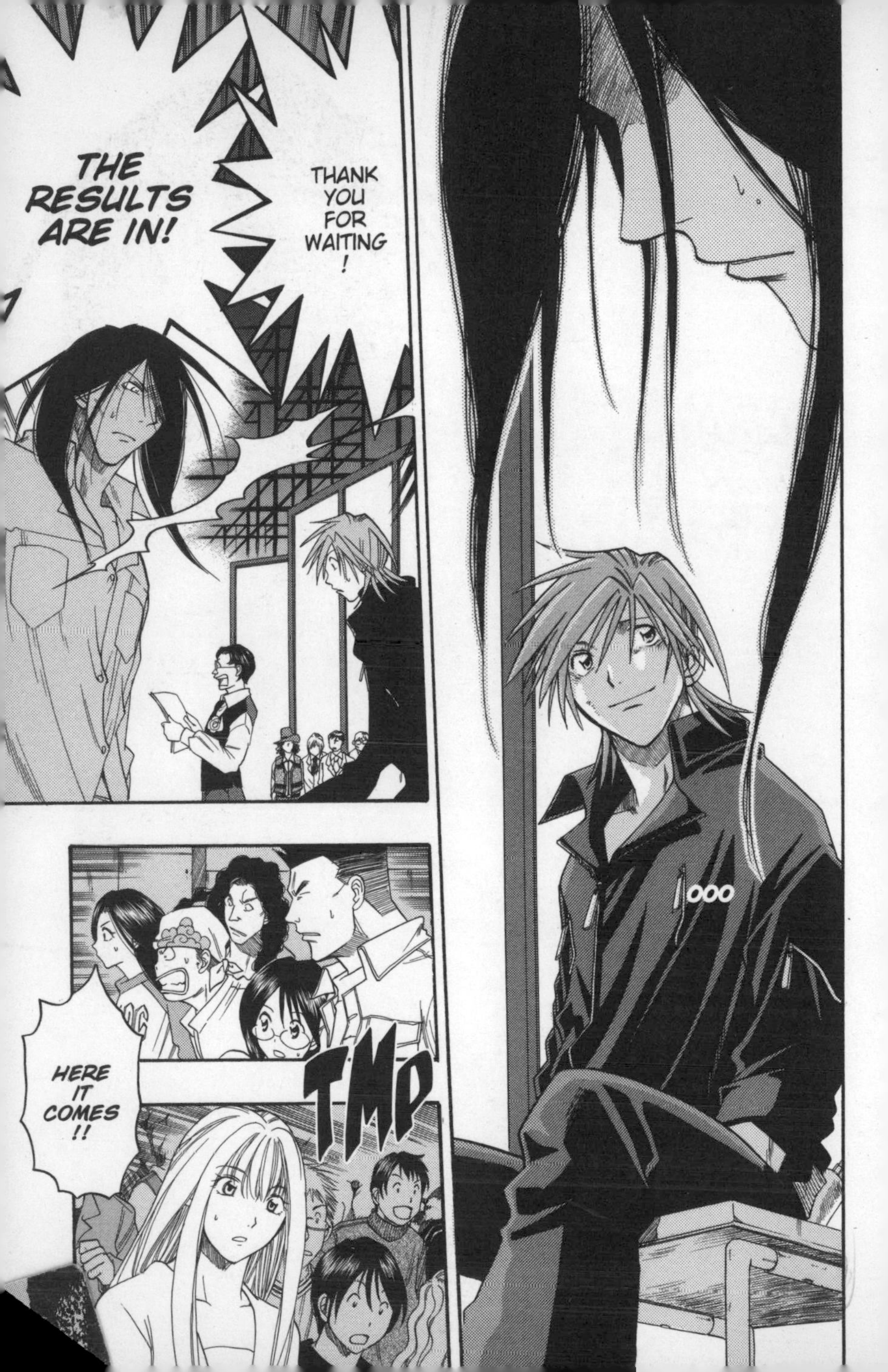
OOO
THANK YOU FOR WAITING!
THE RESULTS ARE IN!
HERE IT COMES!!
TMP

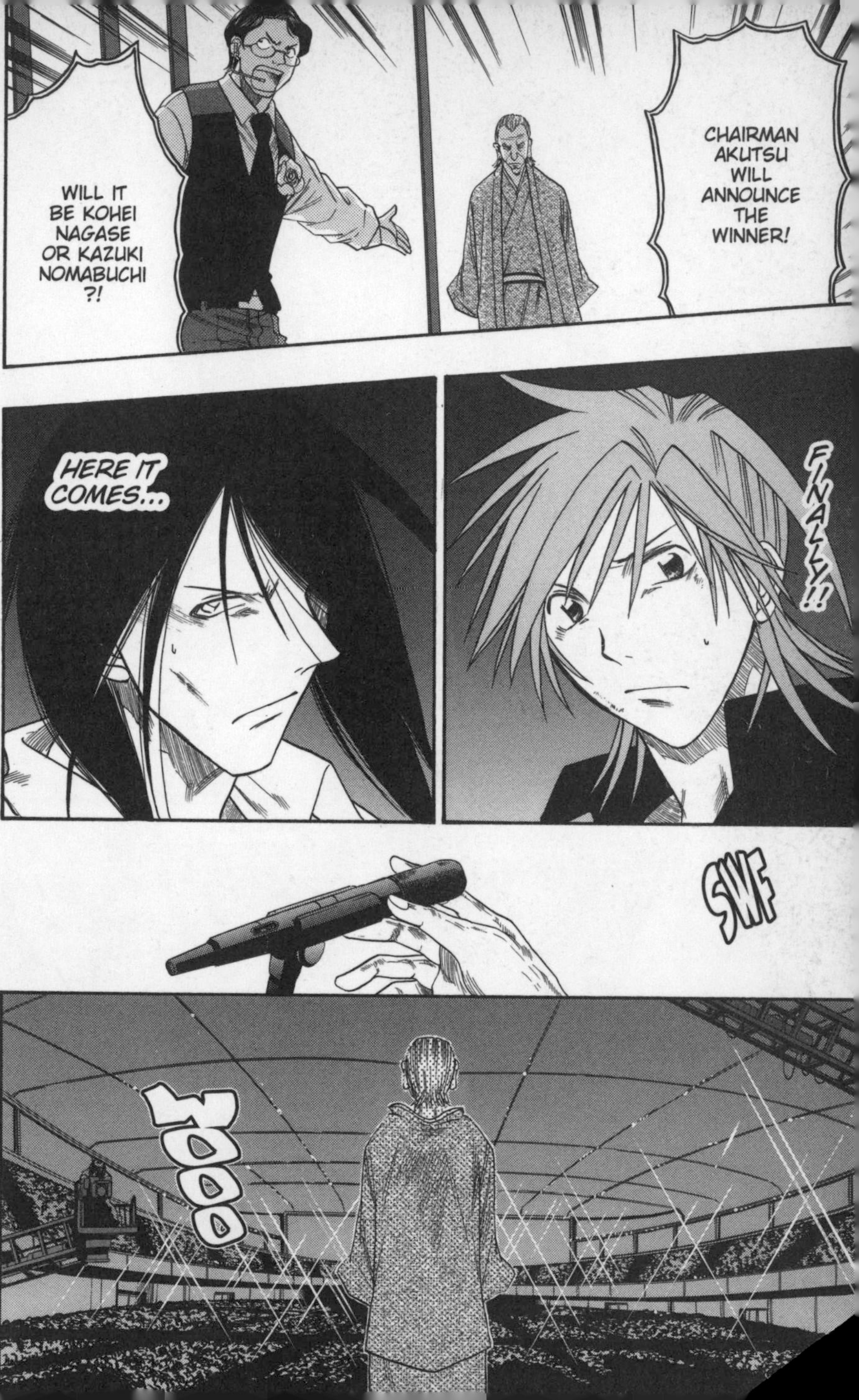
CHAIRMAN AKUTSU WILL ANNOUNCE THE WINNER!
WILL IT BE KOHEI NAGASE OR KAZUKI NOMABUCHI ?!
FINALLY!!
HERE IT COMES...
SWF
WOOO

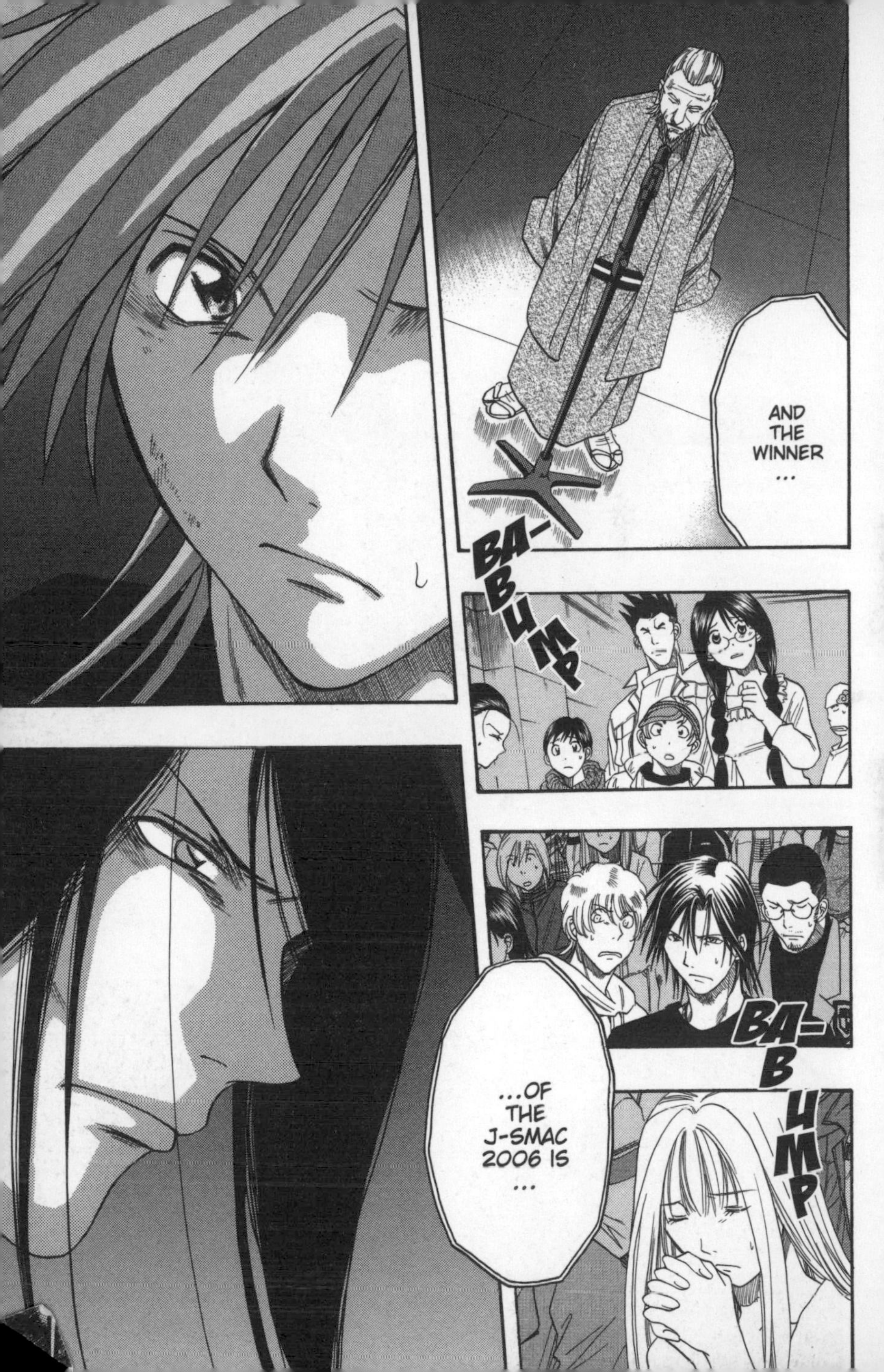
AND THE WINNER ...
BA-BUMP
...OF THE J-SMAC 2006 IS ...
BA-BUMP

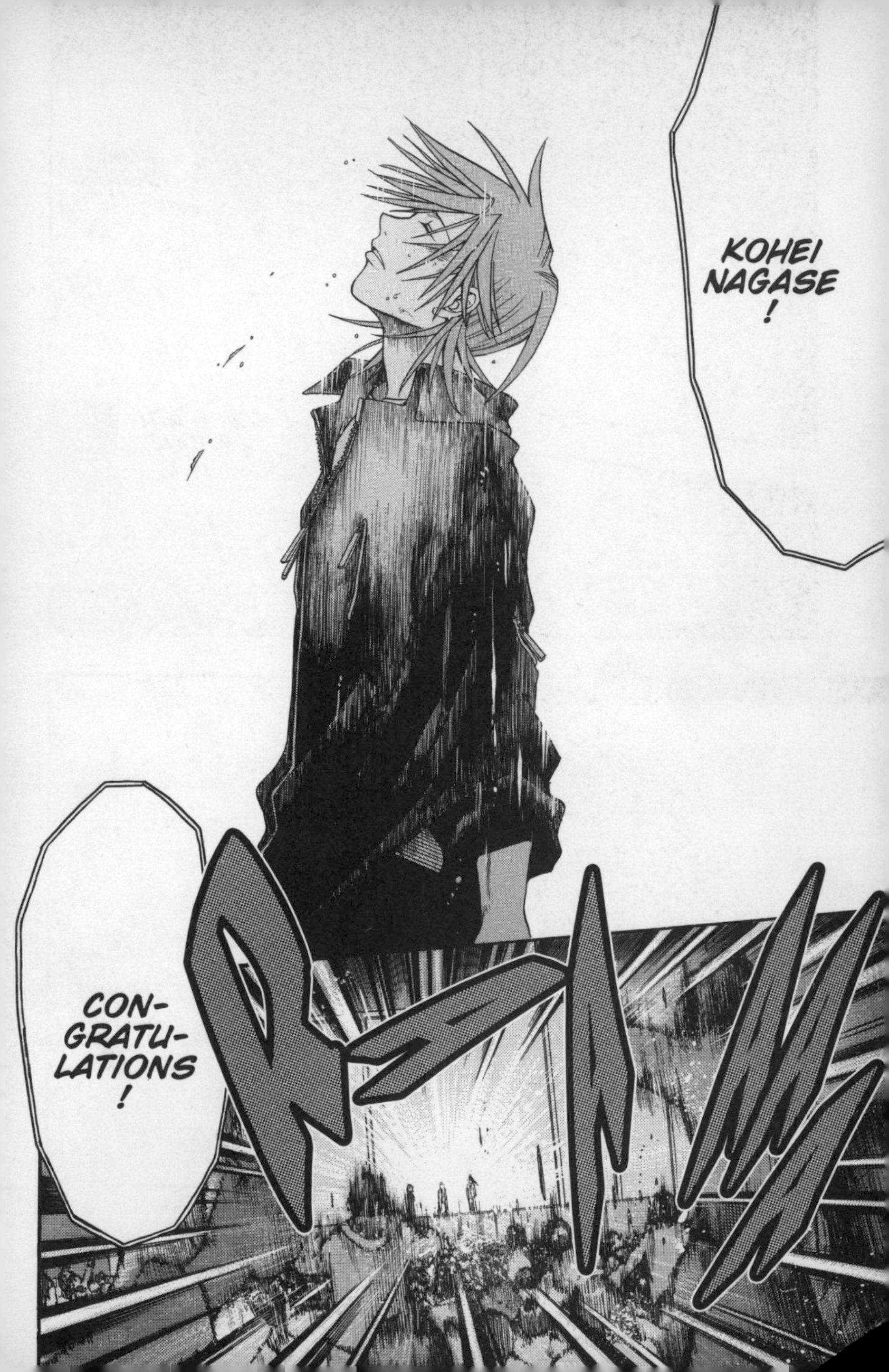
KOHEI NAGASE!
CON-GRATU-LATIONS!

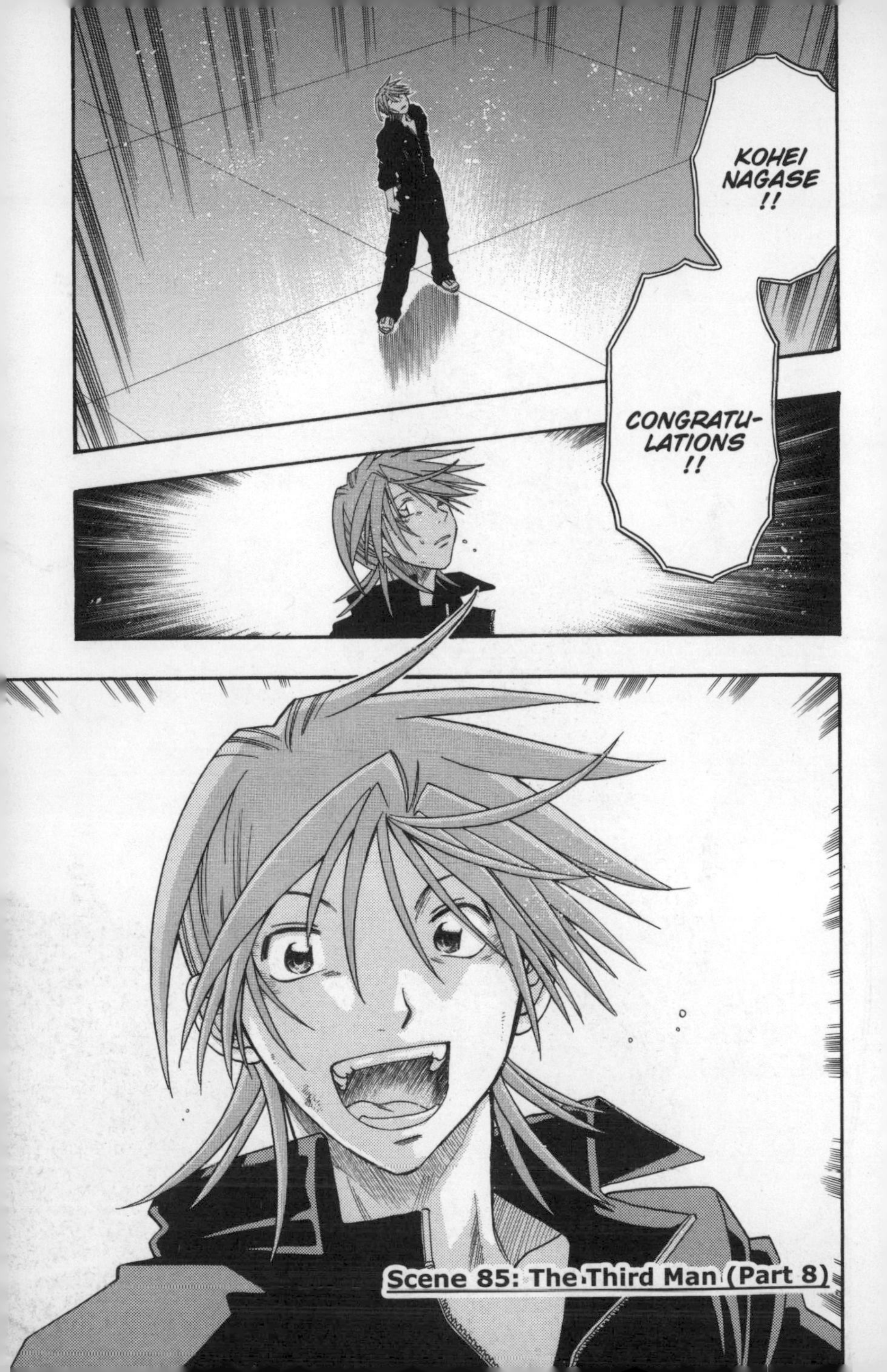
KOHEI NAGASE !!
CONGRATU-LATIONS !!
Scene 85: The Third Man (Part 8)

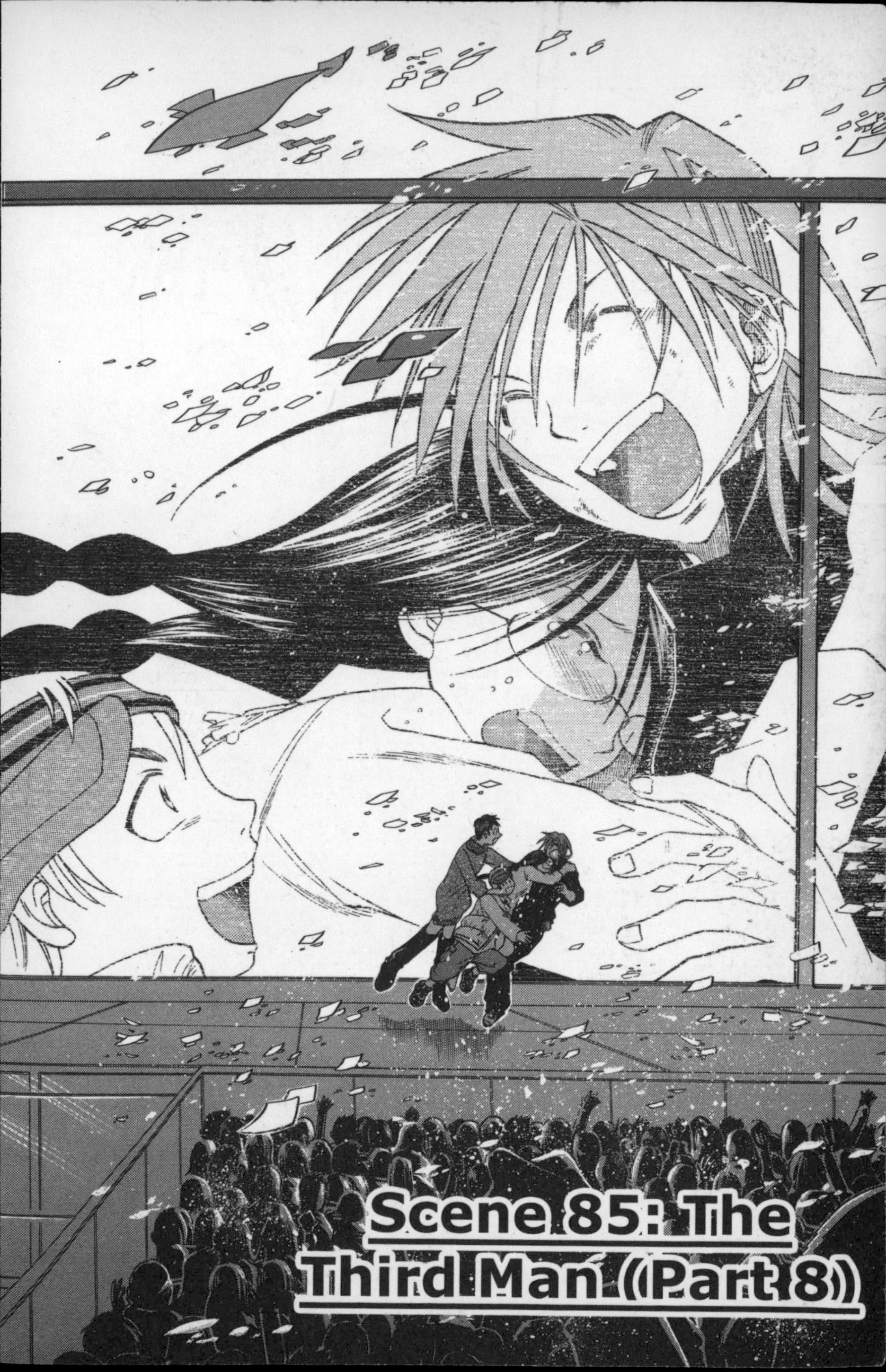
Scene 85: The
Third Man (Part 8)

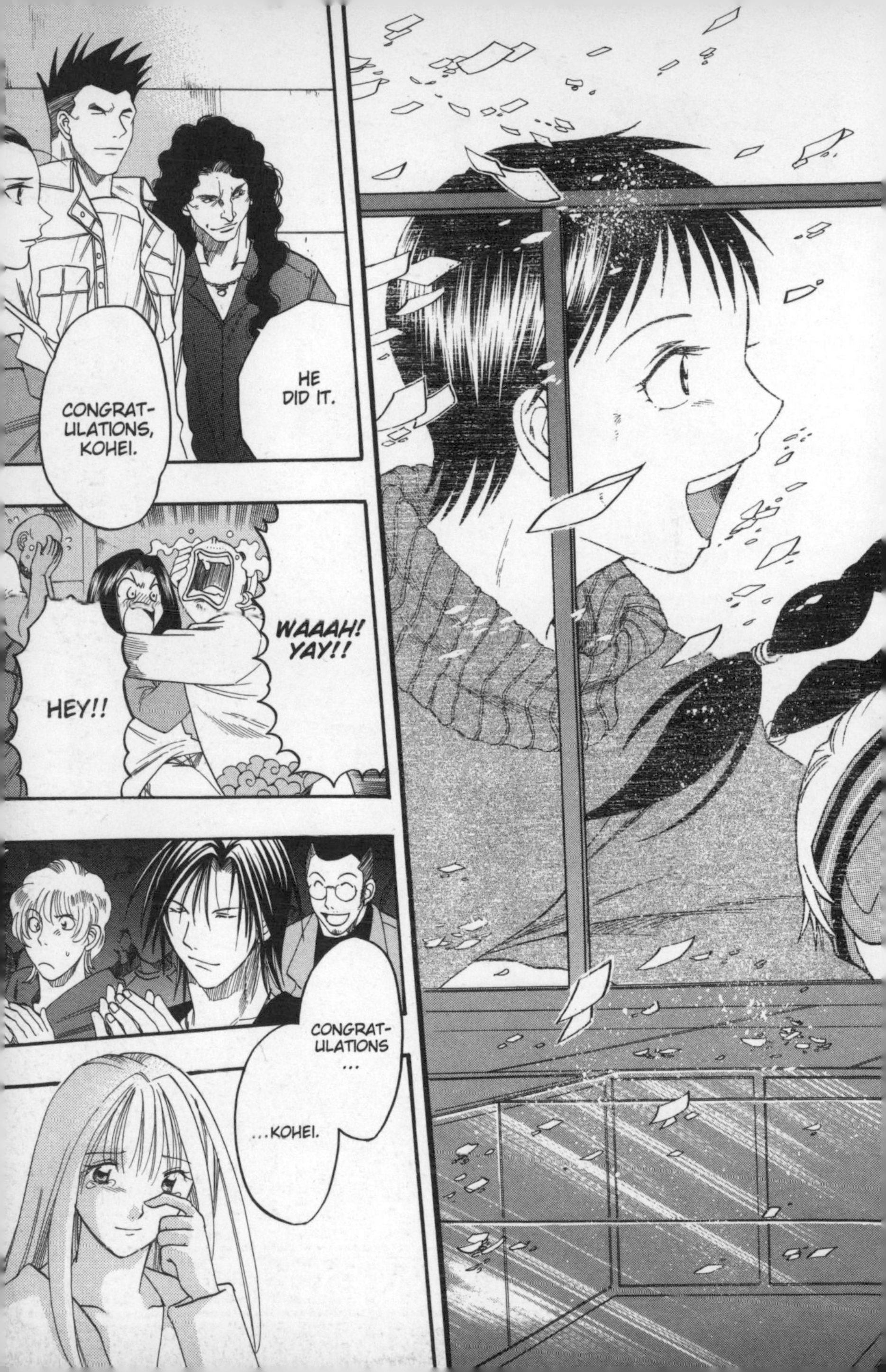
HE DID IT.
CONGRAT-ULATIONS, KOHEI.
WAAAH! YAY!!
HEY!!
CONGRAT-ULATIONS ...
...KOHEI.

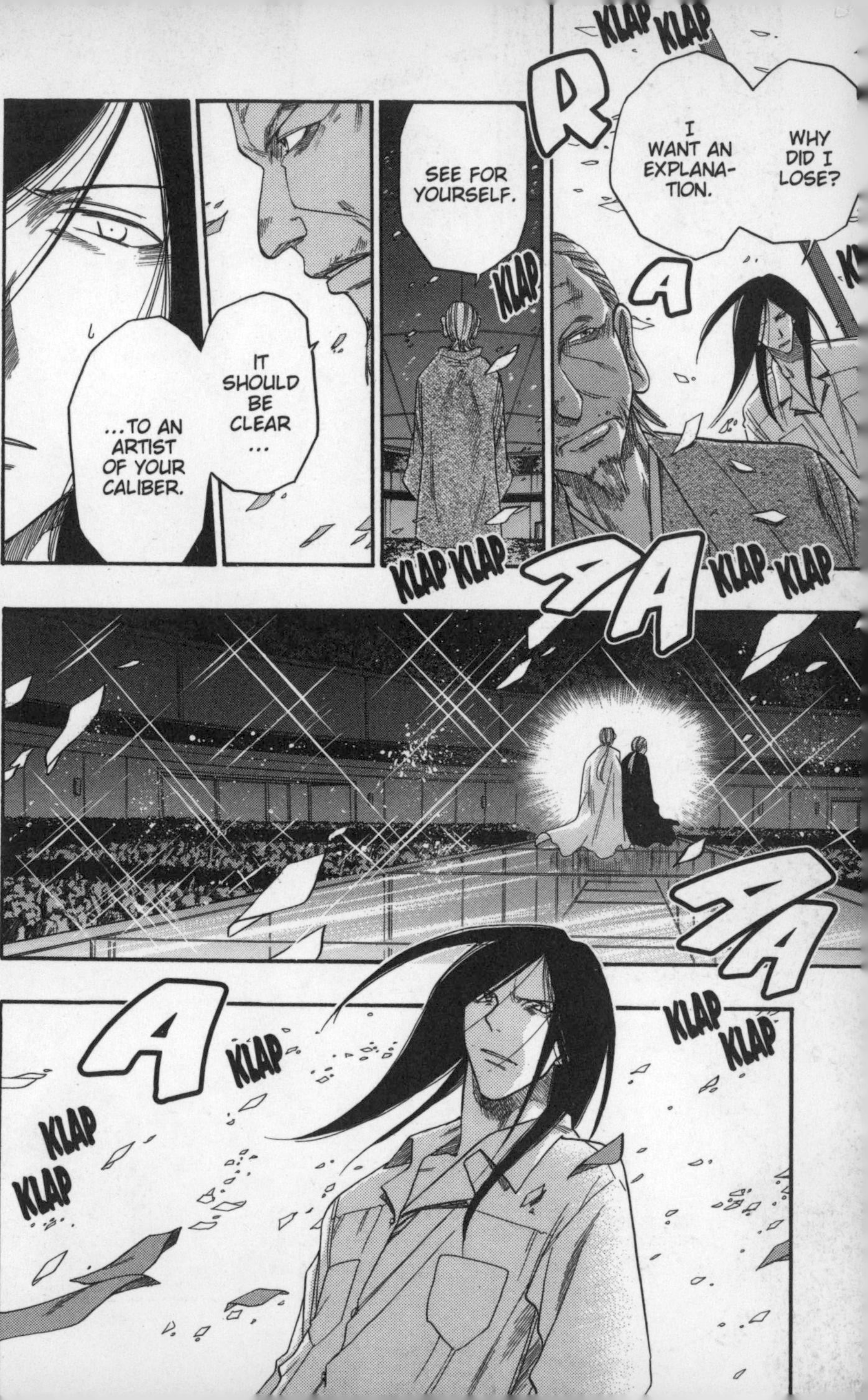
KLAP KLAP
R
WHY DID I LOSE?
I WANT AN EXPLANATION.
A
KLAP
SEE FOR YOURSELF.
KLAP
IT SHOULD BE CLEAR...
...TO AN ARTIST OF YOUR CALIBER.
KLAP KLAP
AA
KLAP KLAP
KLAP KLAP
AA
KLAP KLAP
A
KLAP
KLAP
KLAP

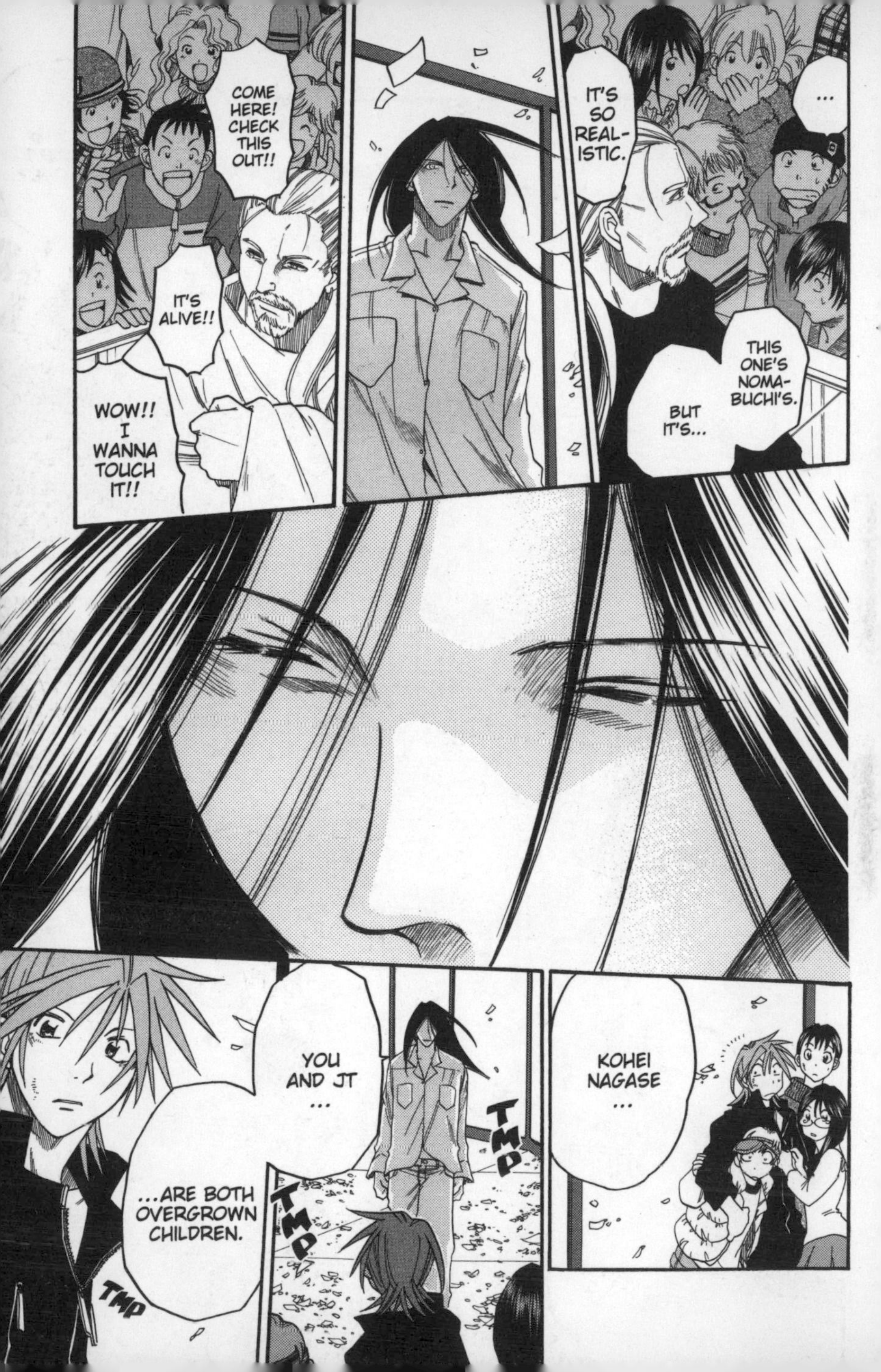
...
IT'S SO REAL-ISTIC.
THIS ONE'S NOMA-BUCHI'S.
BUT IT'S...
COME HERE! CHECK THIS OUT!!
IT'S ALIVE!!
WOW!! I WANNA TOUCH IT!!
KOHEI NAGASE ...
TMP
TMP
YOU AND JT ...
...ARE BOTH OVERGROWN CHILDREN.
TMP

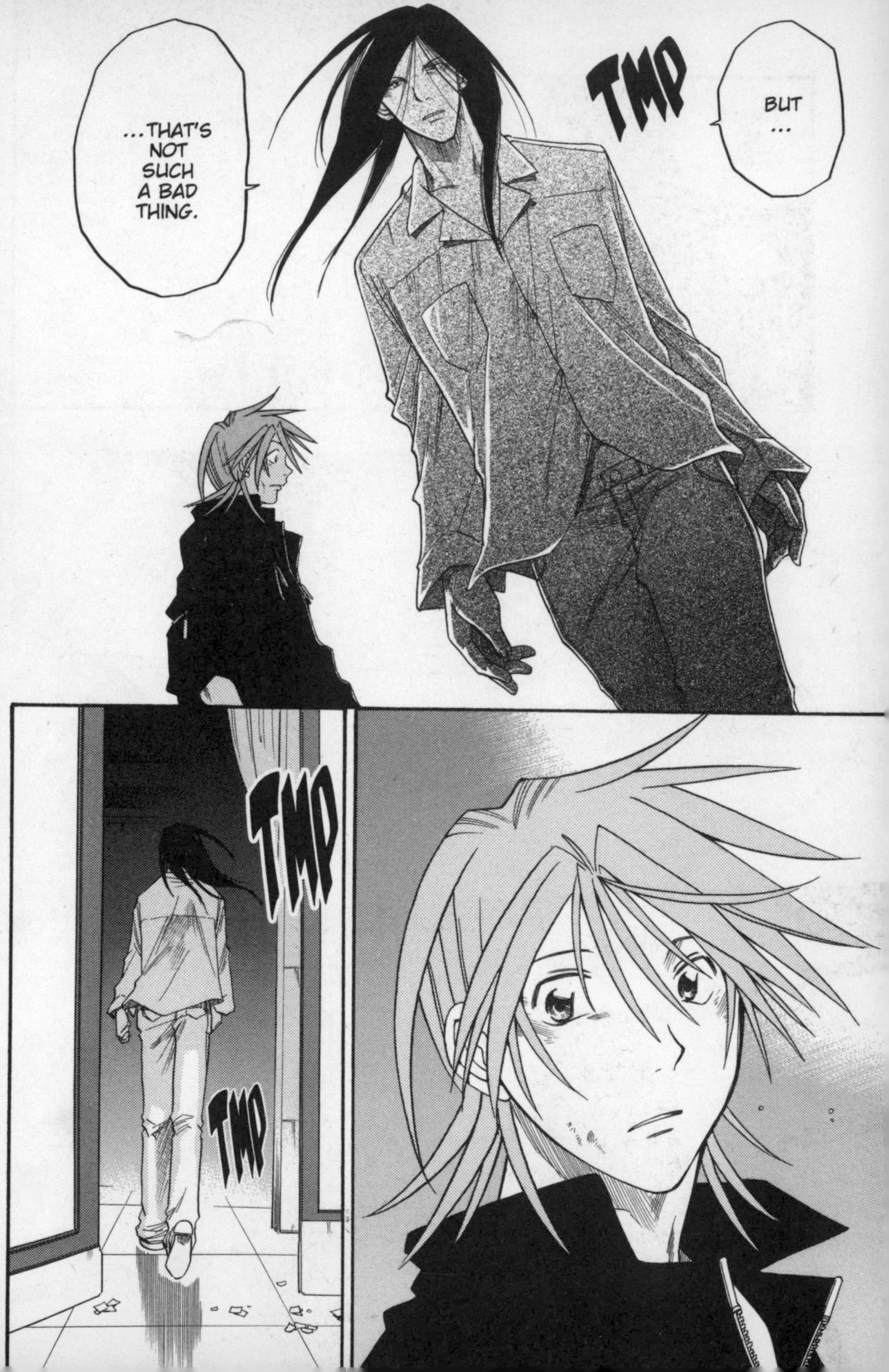
BUT ...
TMP
...THAT'S NOT SUCH A BAD THING.
TMP
TMP

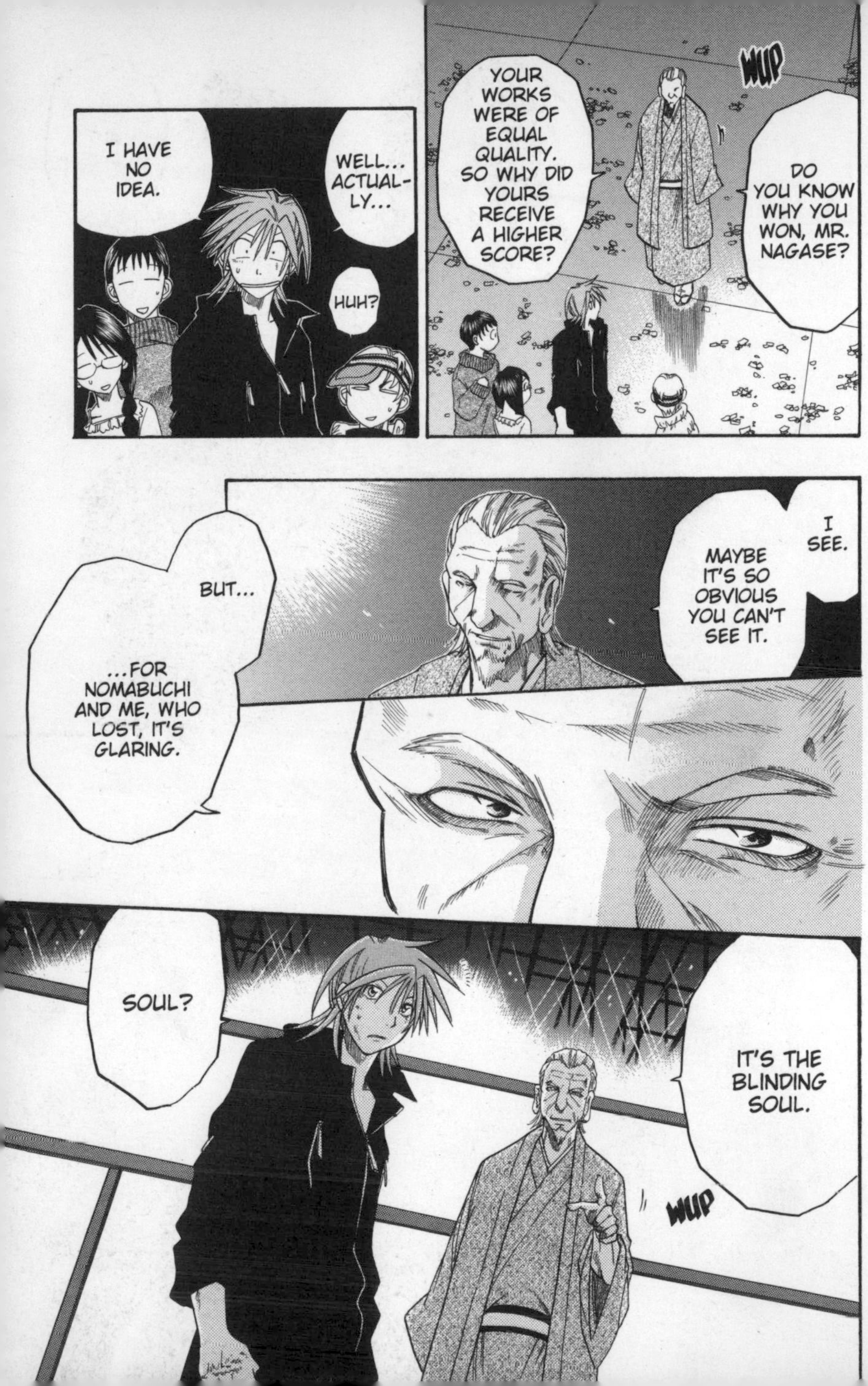
WUP
DO YOU KNOW WHY YOU WON, MR. NAGASE?
YOUR WORKS WERE OF EQUAL QUALITY. SO WHY DID YOURS RECEIVE A HIGHER SCORE?
WELL... ACTUAL-LY...
HUH?
I HAVE NO IDEA.
I SEE.
MAYBE IT'S SO OBVIOUS YOU CAN'T SEE IT.
BUT...
...FOR NOMABUCHI AND ME, WHO LOST, IT'S GLARING.
IT'S THE BLINDING SOUL.
WUP
SOUL?

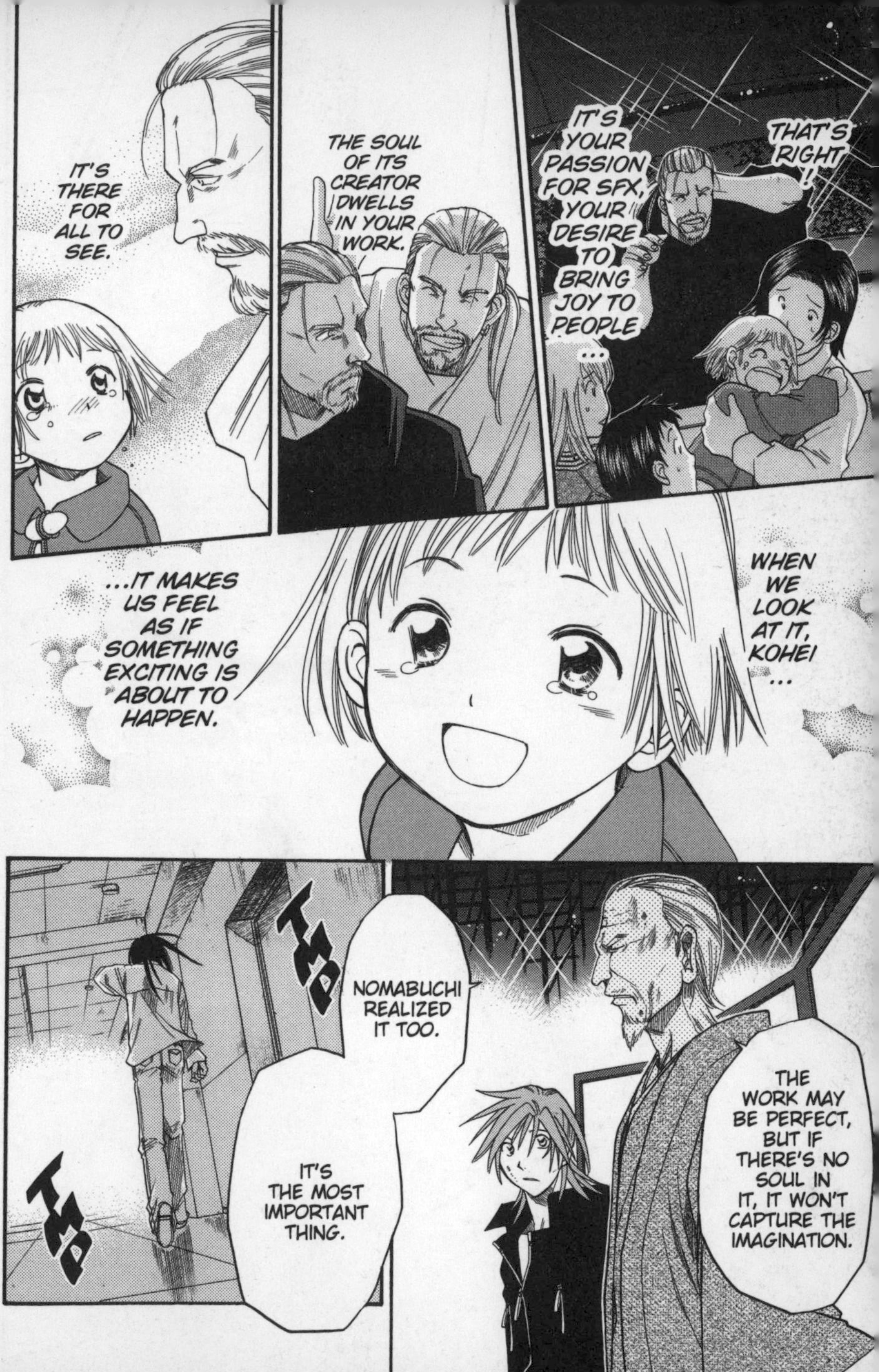
THAT'S RIGHT!
IT'S YOUR PASSION FOR SFX, YOUR DESIRE TO BRING JOY TO PEOPLE...
THE SOUL OF ITS CREATOR DWELLS IN YOUR WORK.
IT'S THERE FOR ALL TO SEE.
WHEN WE LOOK AT IT, KOHEI...
...IT MAKES US FEEL AS IF SOMETHING EXCITING IS ABOUT TO HAPPEN.
THE WORK MAY BE PERFECT, BUT IF THERE'S NO SOUL IN IT, IT WON'T CAPTURE THE IMAGINATION.
NOMABUCHI REALIZED IT TOO.
IT'S THE MOST IMPORTANT THING.
TMP
TMP

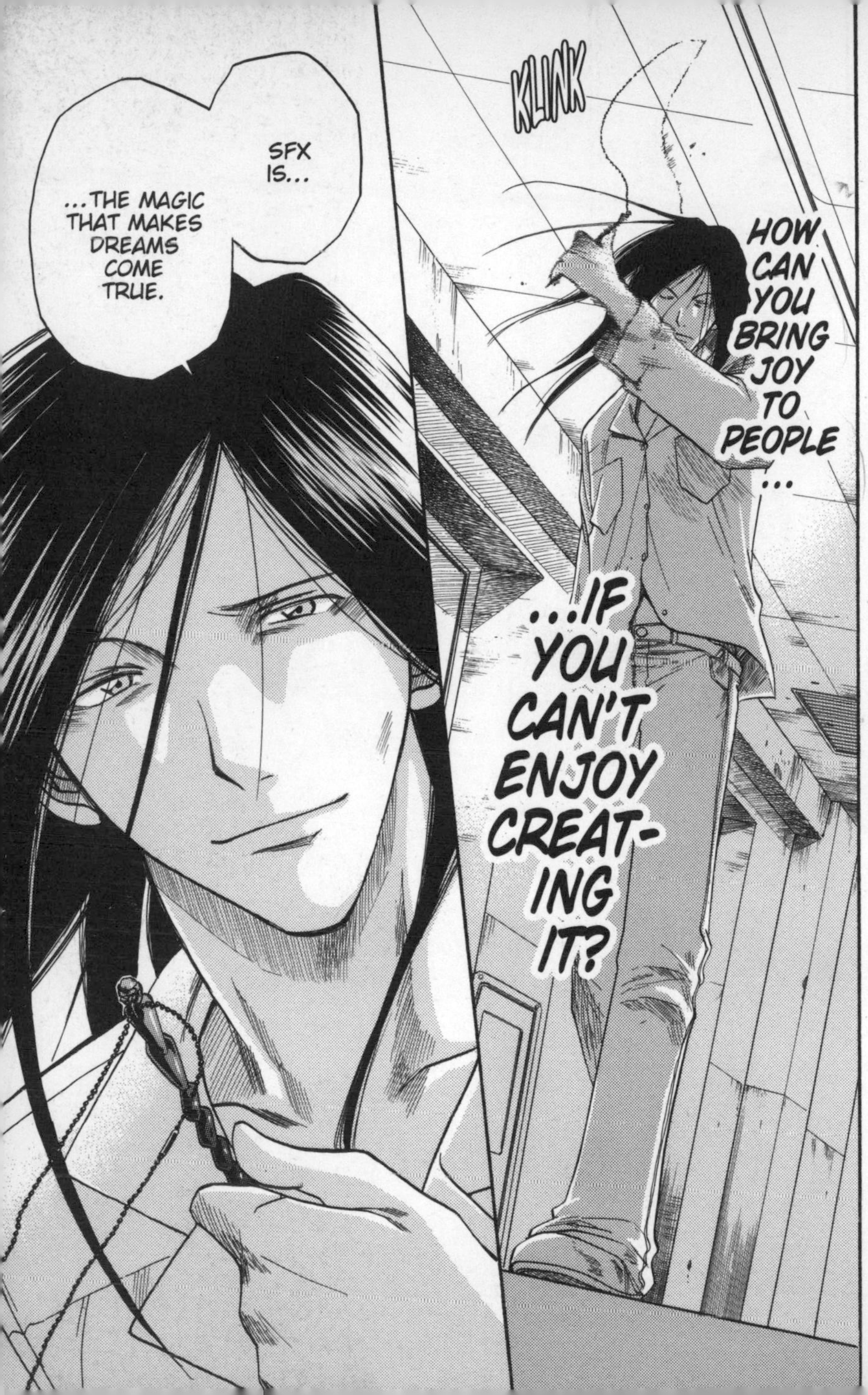
KLINK
HOW CAN YOU BRING JOY TO PEOPLE...
...IF YOU CAN'T ENJOY CREATING IT?
SFX IS...
...THE MAGIC THAT MAKES DREAMS COME TRUE.

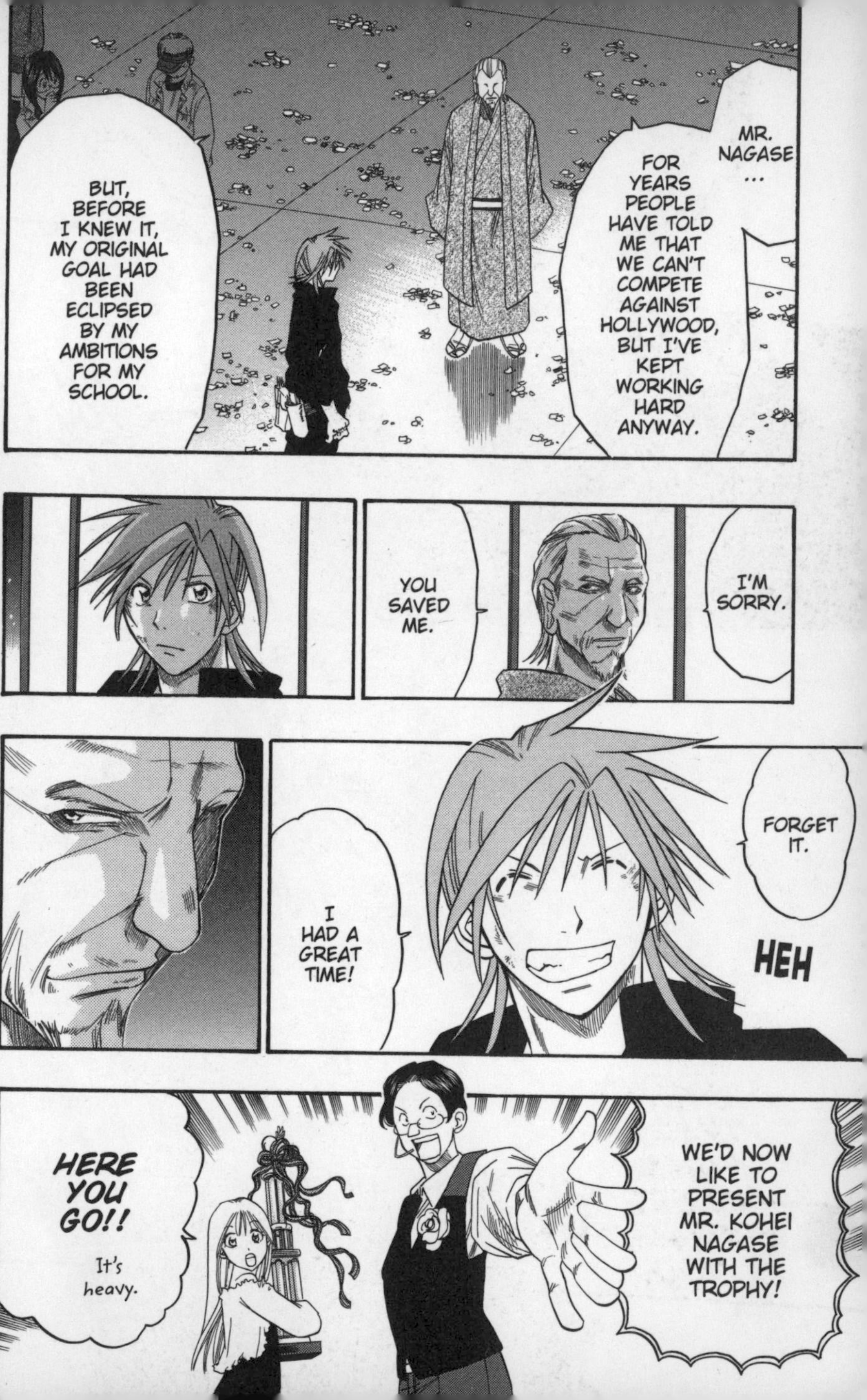
MR. NAGASE...
FOR YEARS PEOPLE HAVE TOLD ME THAT WE CAN'T COMPETE AGAINST HOLLYWOOD, BUT I'VE KEPT WORKING HARD ANYWAY.
BUT, BEFORE I KNEW IT, MY ORIGINAL GOAL HAD BEEN ECLIPSED BY MY AMBITIONS FOR MY SCHOOL.
I'M SORRY.
YOU SAVED ME.
FORGET IT.
HEH
I HAD A GREAT TIME!
WE'D NOW LIKE TO PRESENT MR. KOHEI NAGASE WITH THE TROPHY!
HERE YOU GO!!
It's heavy.

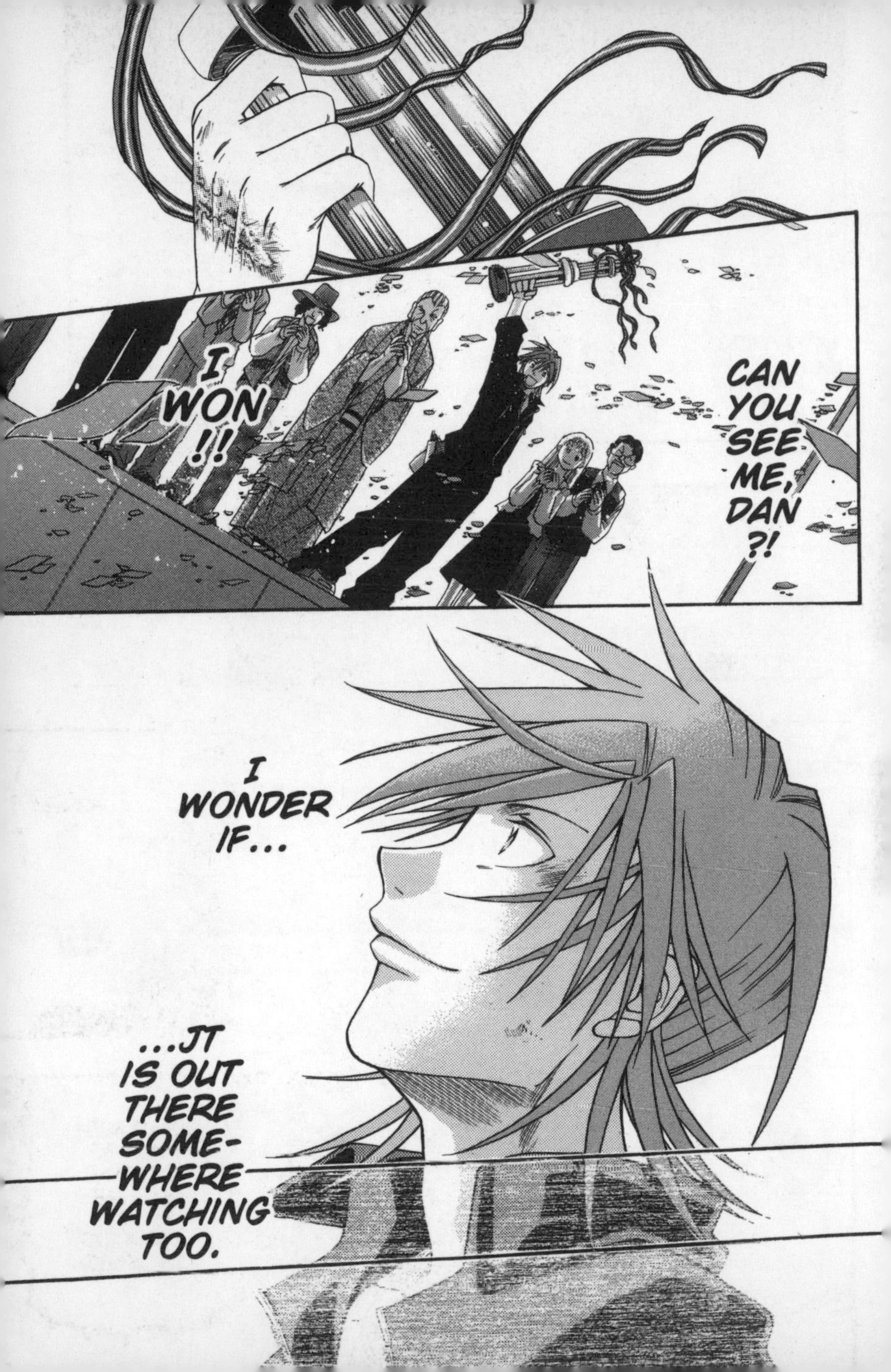
CAN YOU SEE ME, DAN?!
I WON!!
I WONDER IF...
...JT IS OUT THERE SOME-WHERE WATCHING TOO.

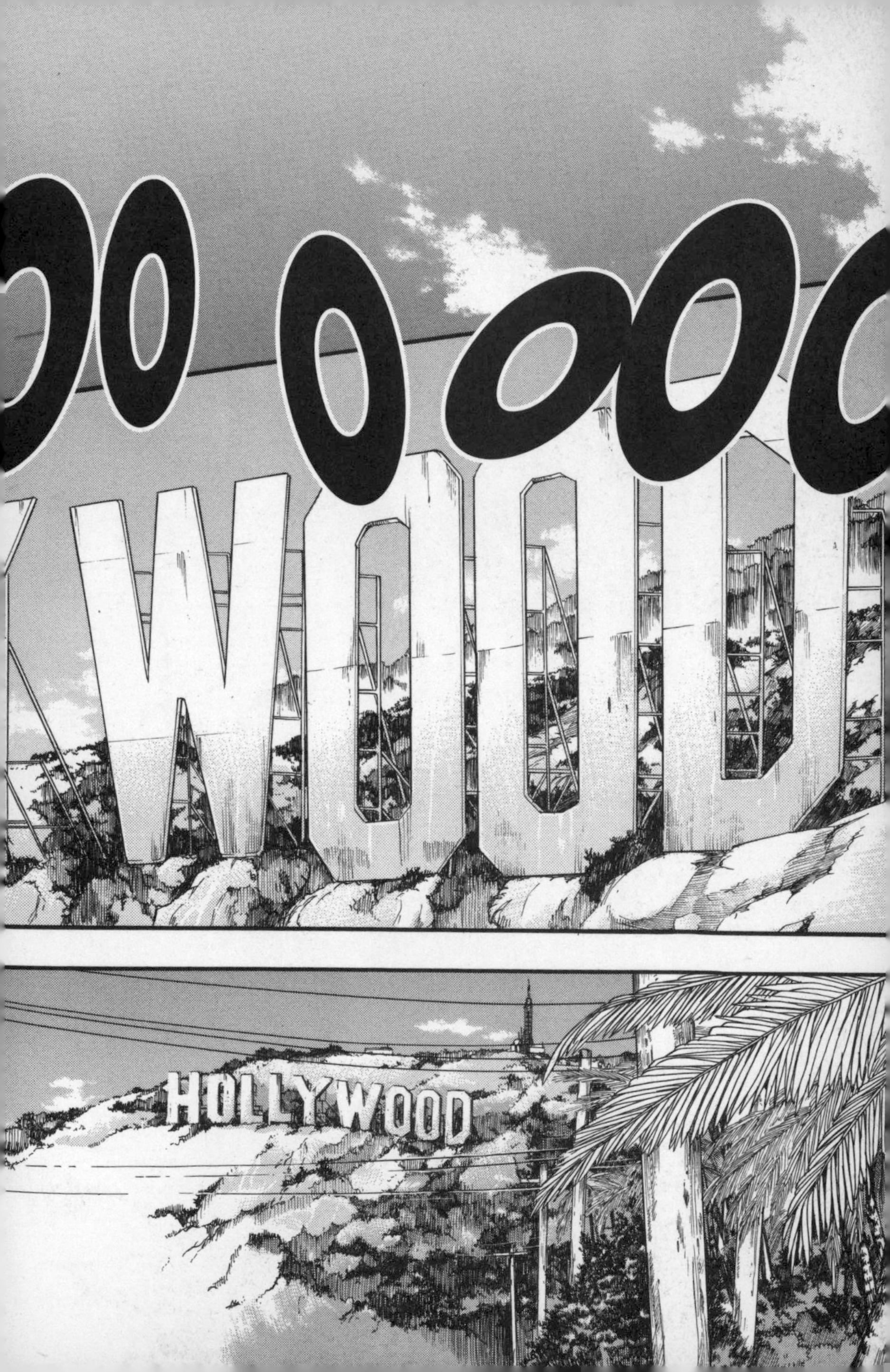

OOOOOO
HOLLYWOOD

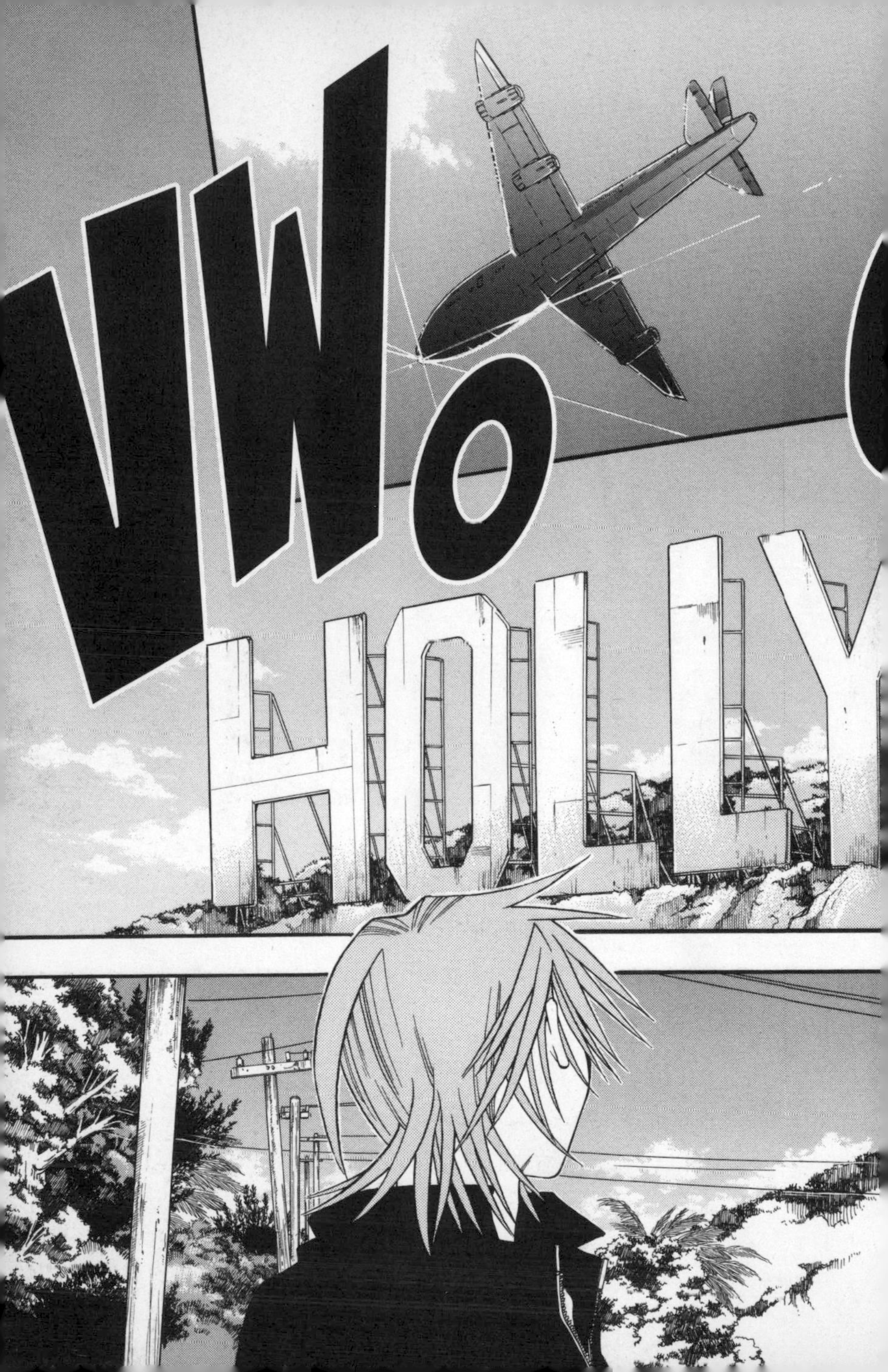
VWO
HOLLY

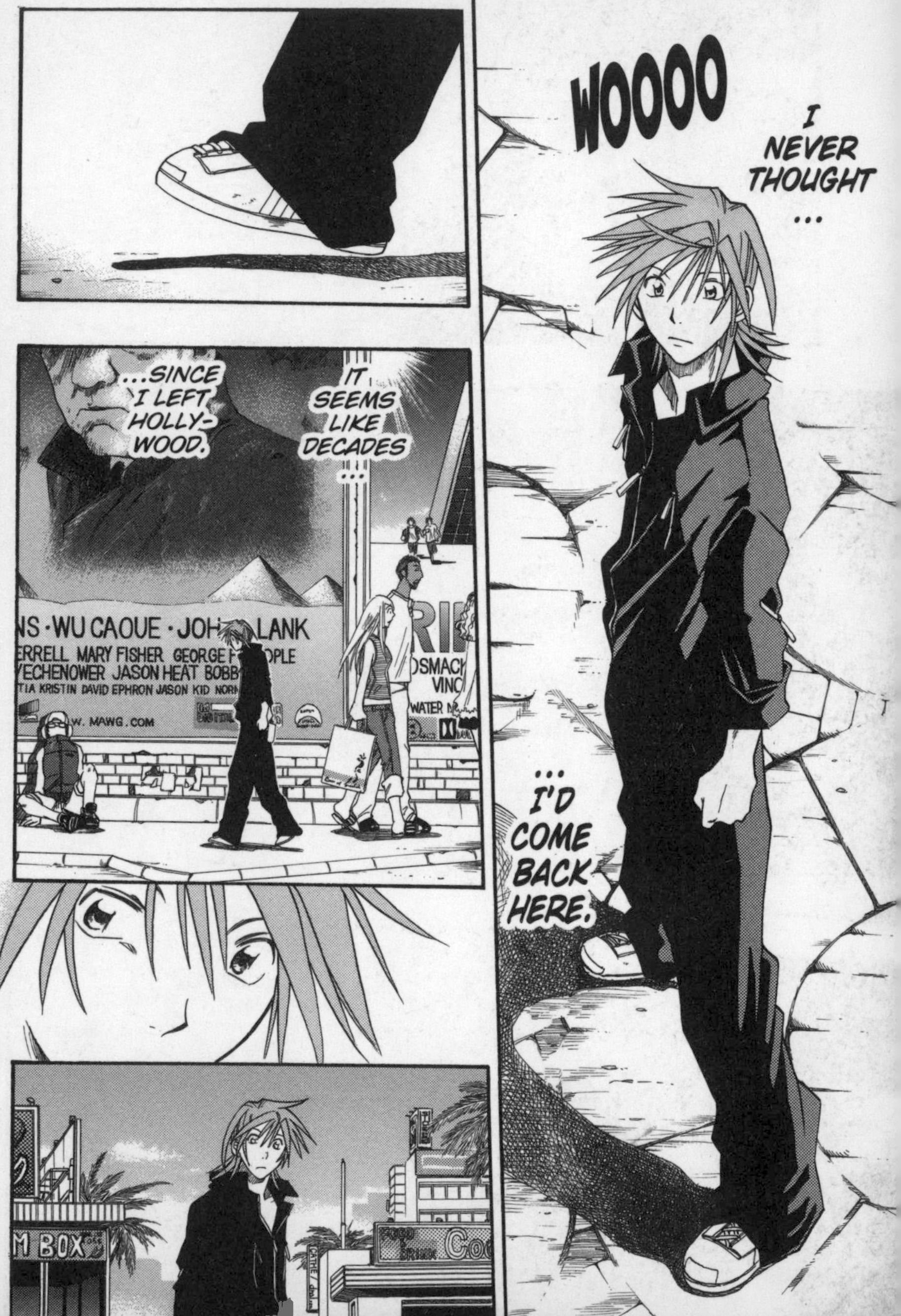
WOOOO
I NEVER THOUGHT ...
... I'D COME BACK HERE.
IT SEEMS LIKE DECADES ...
...SINCE I LEFT HOLLY-WOOD.
NS · WU CAOUE · JOH LANK
W. MAWG. COM
M BOX
FOOD DRINK

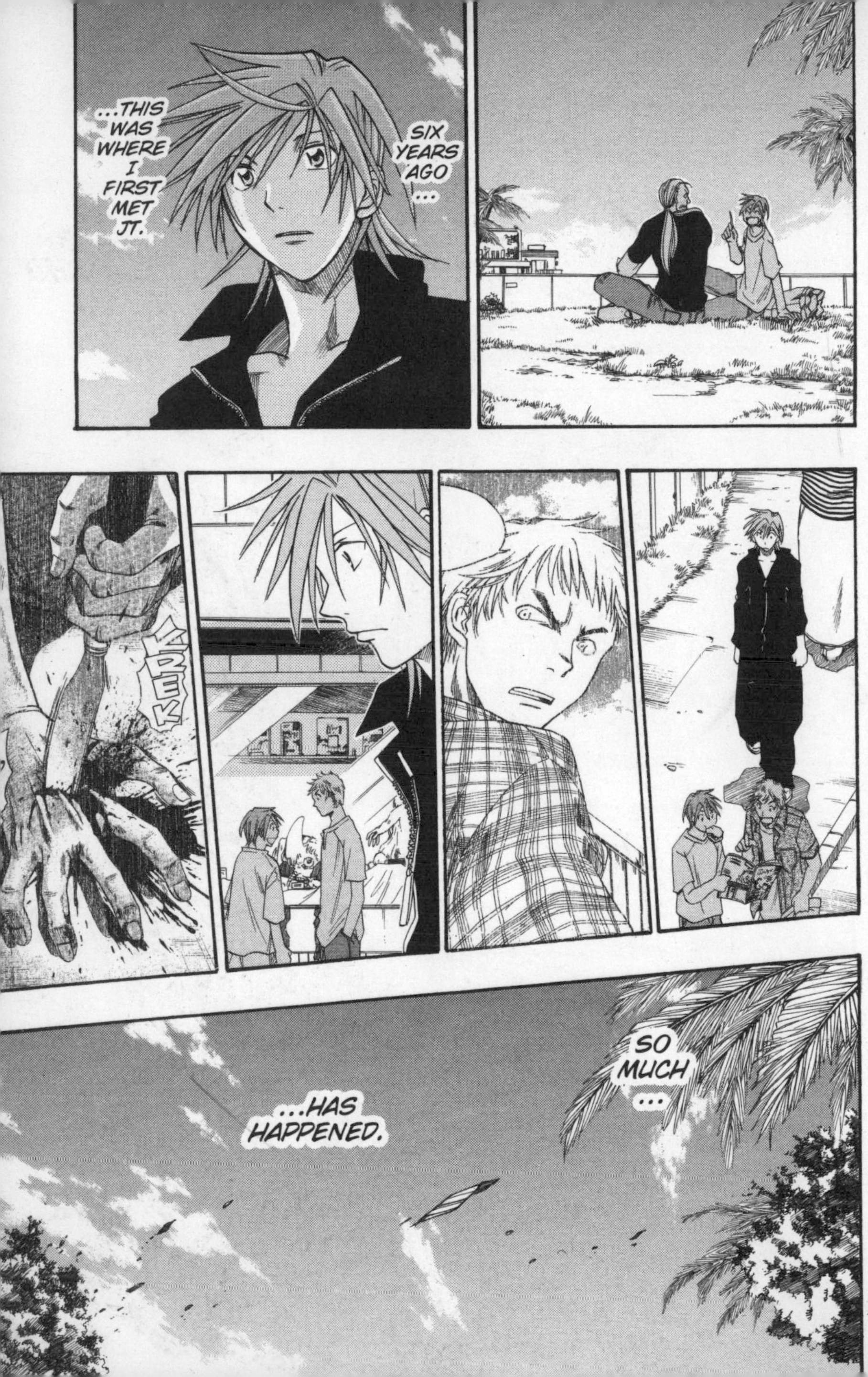
SIX YEARS AGO...
...THIS WAS WHERE I FIRST MET JT.
KREK
SO MUCH...
...HAS HAPPENED.

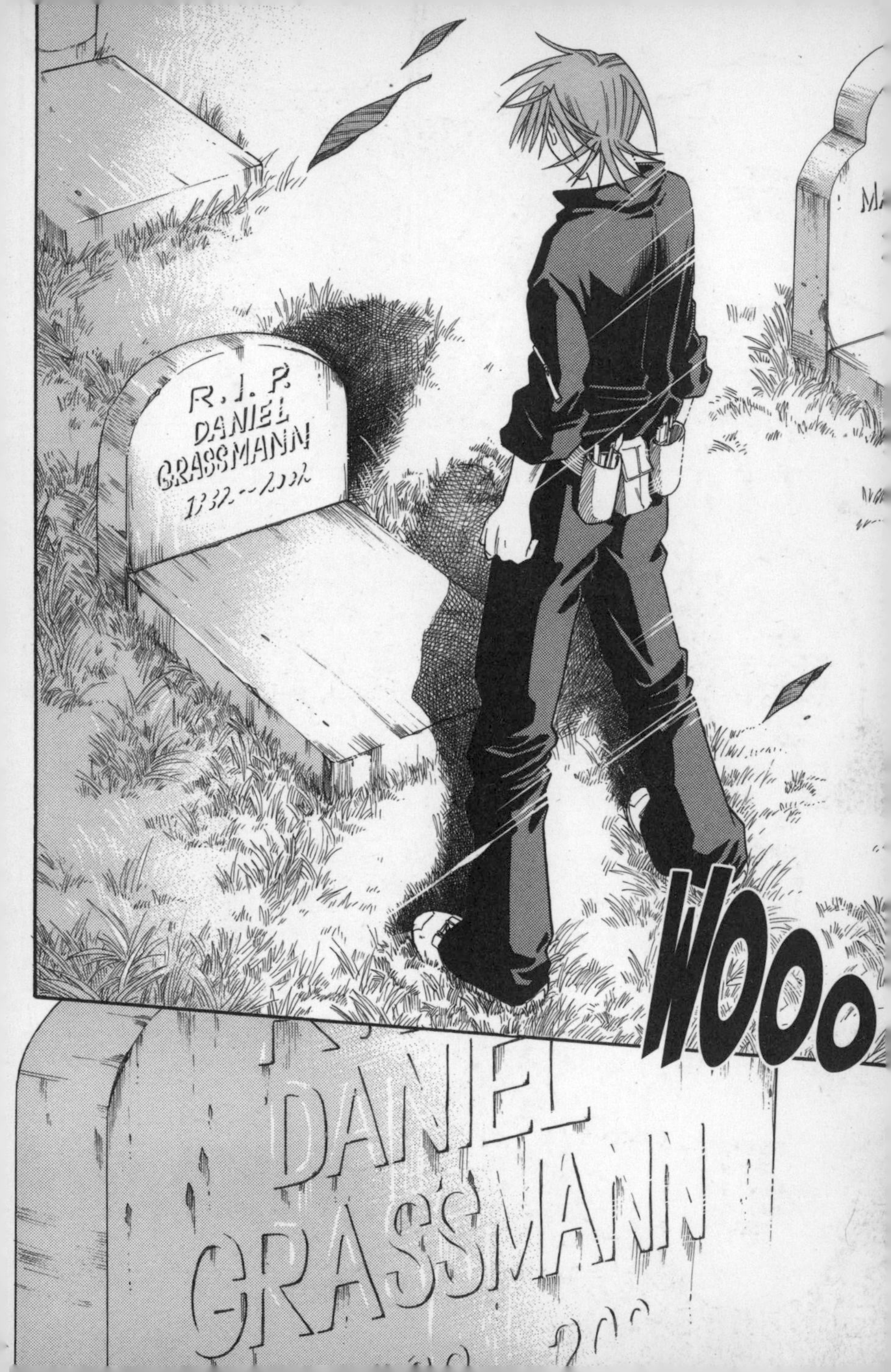
R.I.P.
DANIEL
GRASSMANN
WOOO
DANIEL
GRASSMANN

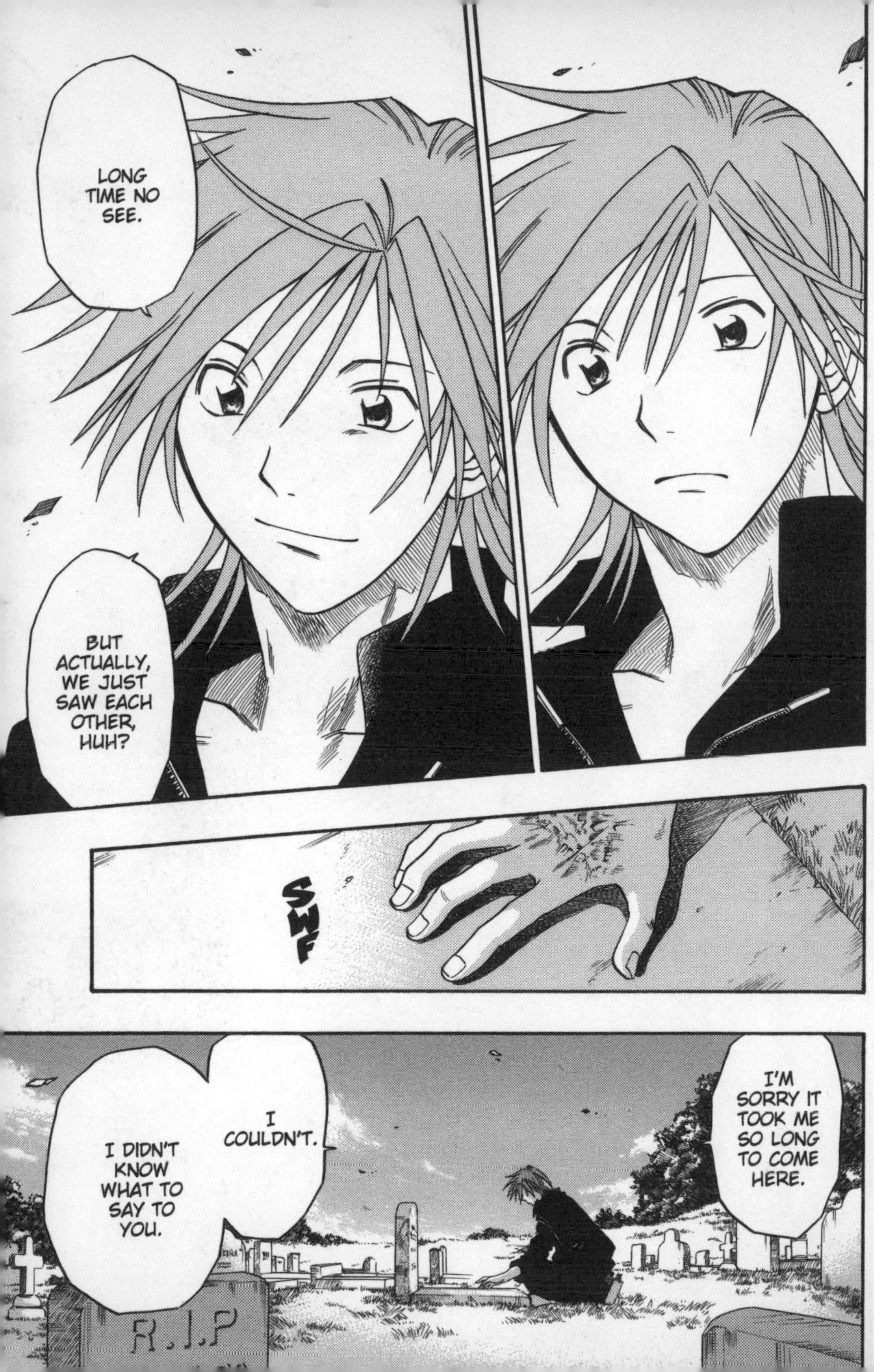
LONG TIME NO SEE.
BUT ACTUALLY, WE JUST SAW EACH OTHER, HUH?
SWF
I'M SORRY IT TOOK ME SO LONG TO COME HERE.
I COULDN'T.
I DIDN'T KNOW WHAT TO SAY TO YOU.
R.I.P

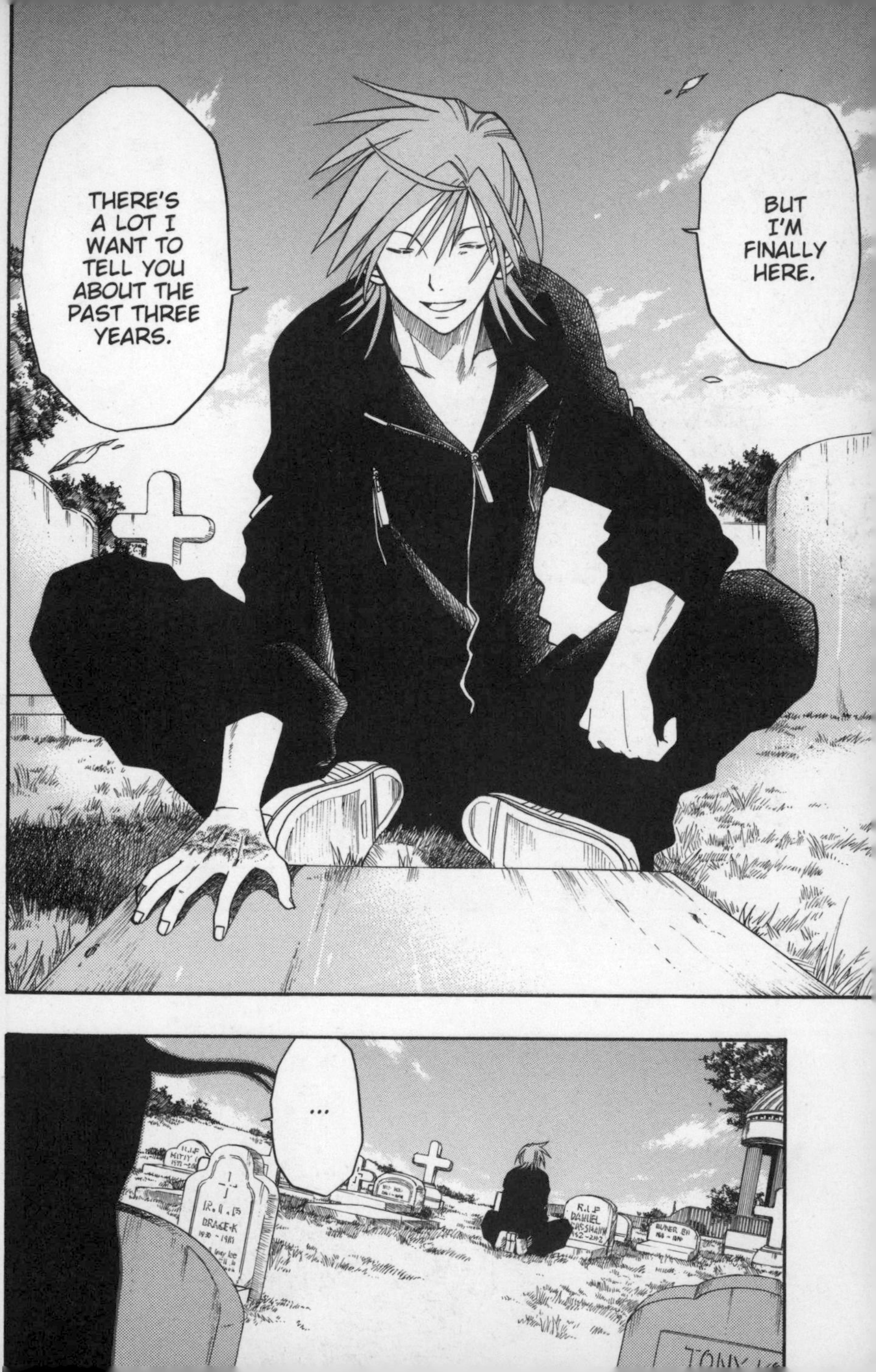
BUT I'M FINALLY HERE.
THERE'S A LOT I WANT TO TELL YOU ABOUT THE PAST THREE YEARS.
...

Scene 86: Field of Dreams Redux (Part 1)

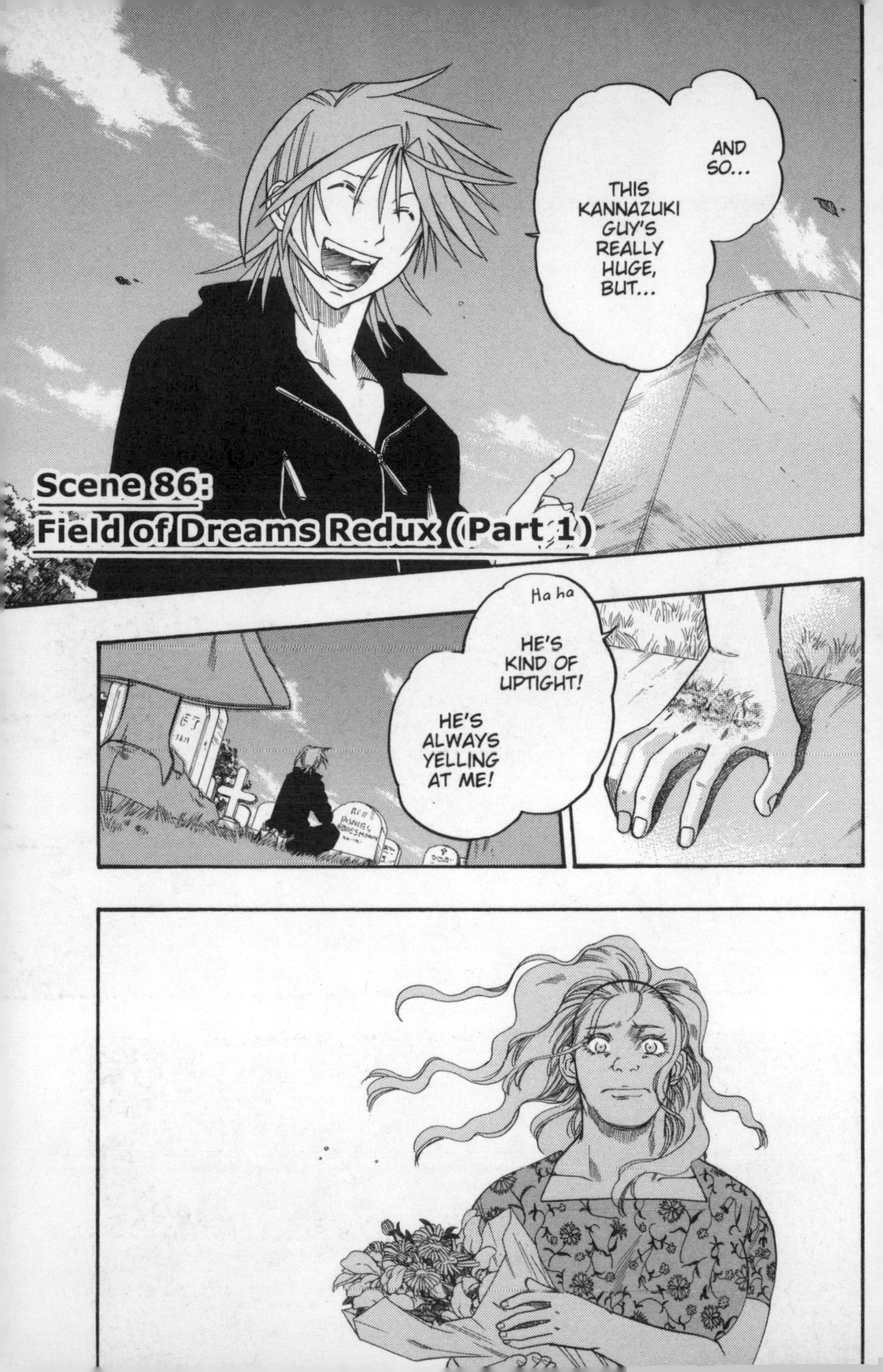
AND SO...
THIS KANNAZUKI GUY'S REALLY HUGE, BUT...
Ha ha
HE'S KIND OF UPTIGHT!
HE'S ALWAYS YELLING AT ME!

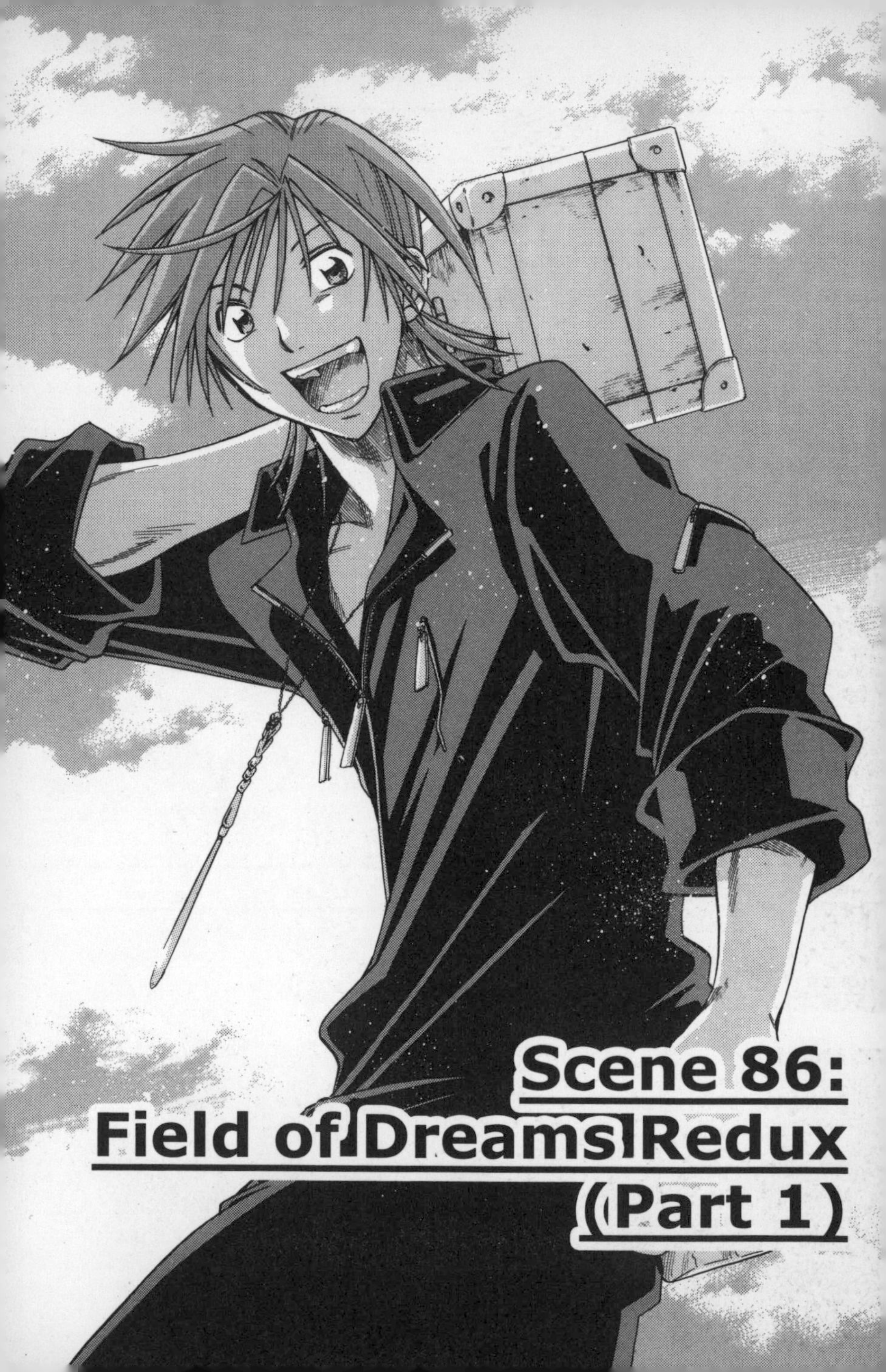
Scene 86:
Field of Dreams Redux
(Part 1)

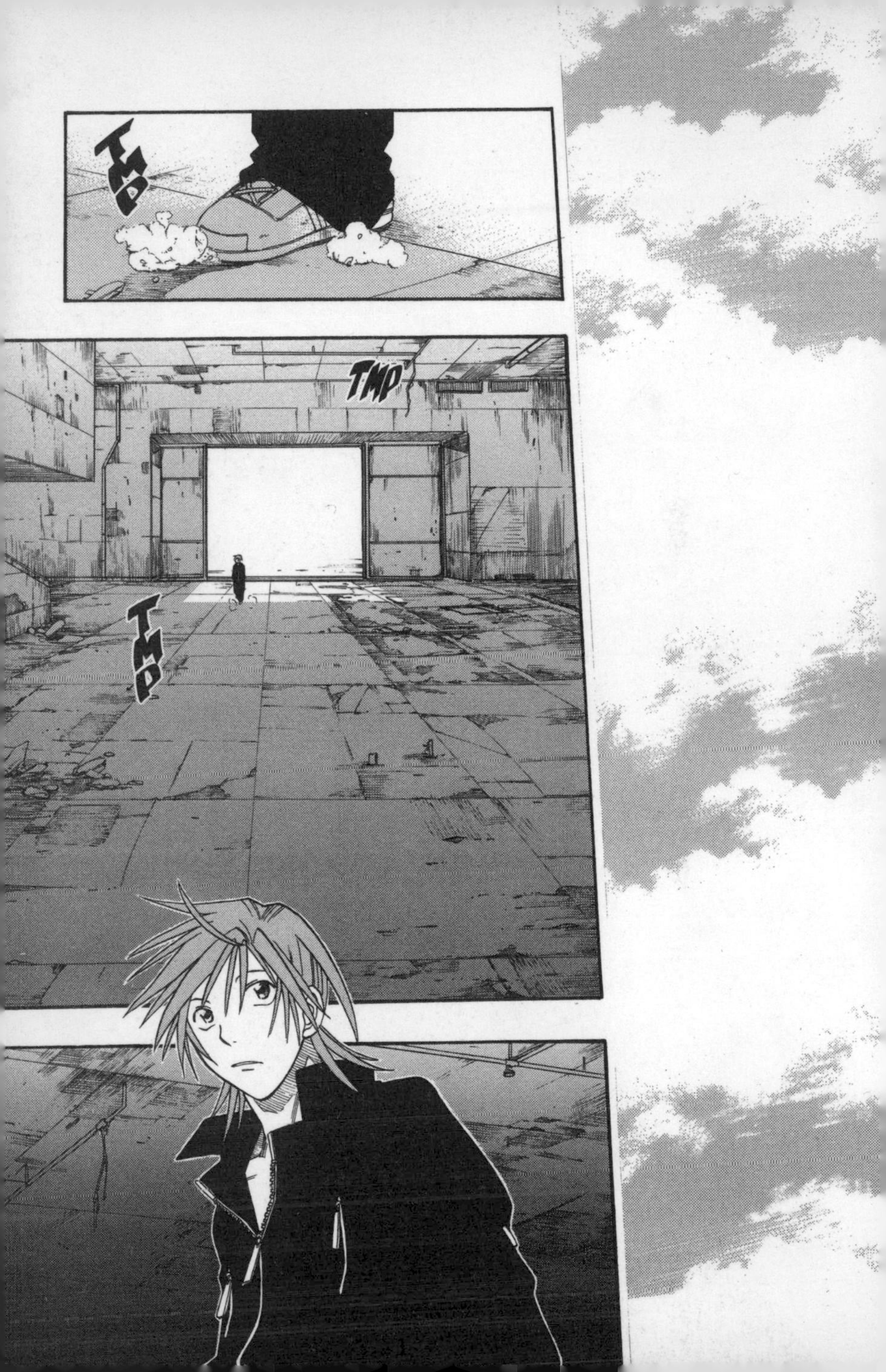
TMP
TMP
TMP

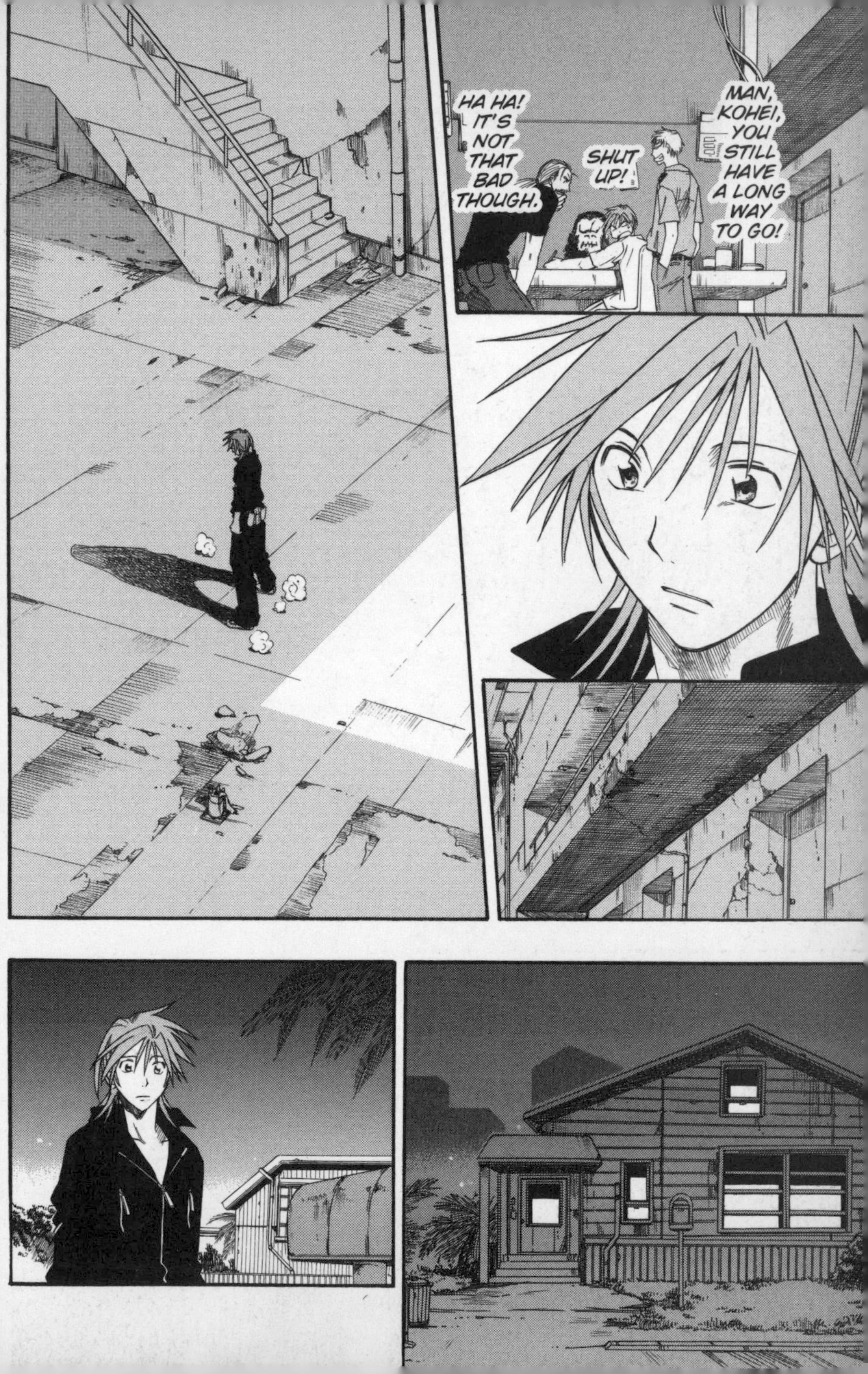
MAN, KOHEI, YOU STILL HAVE A LONG WAY TO GO!
SHUT UP!
HA HA! IT'S NOT THAT BAD THOUGH.

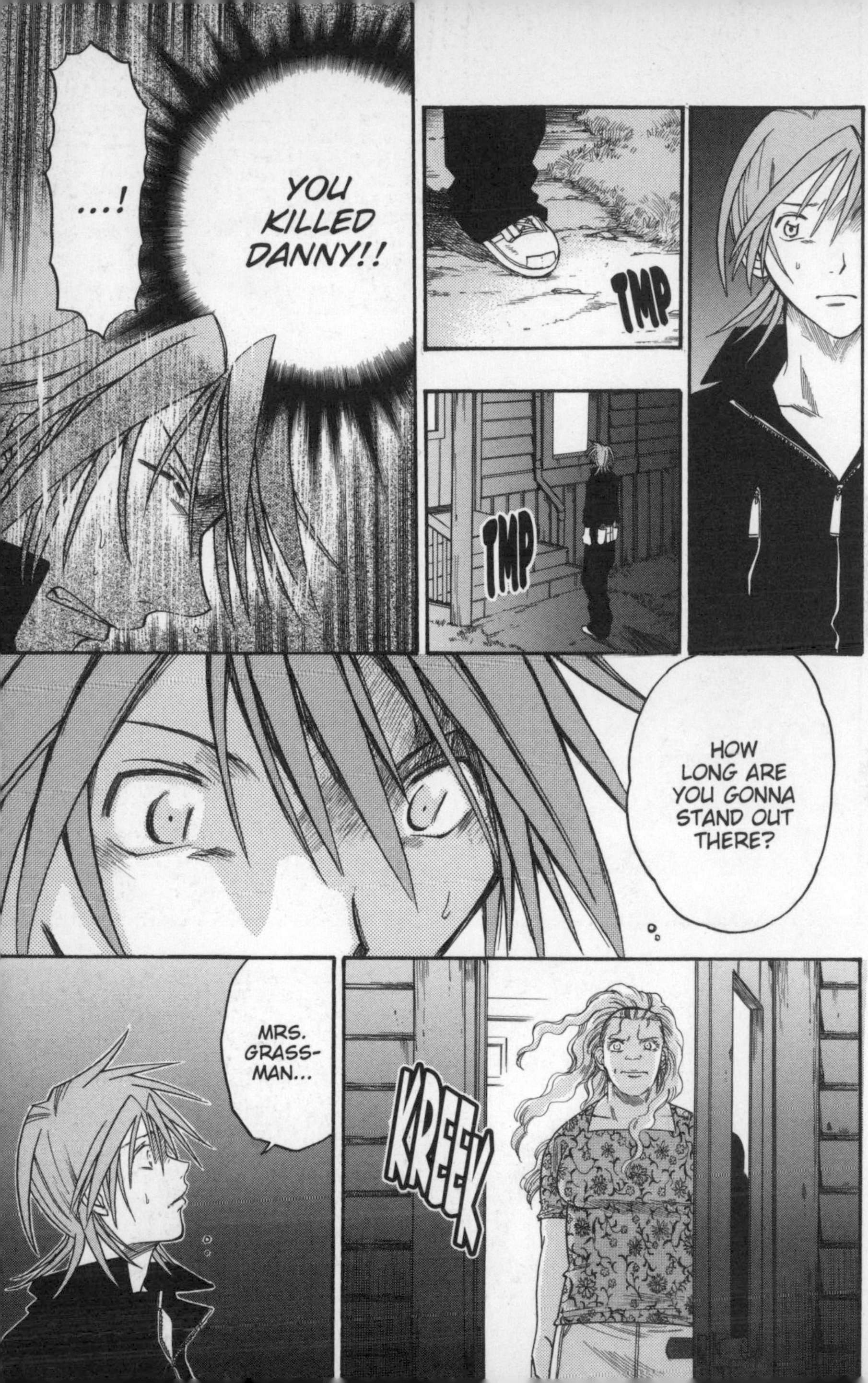
TMP
TMP
YOU KILLED DANNY!!
...!
HOW LONG ARE YOU GONNA STAND OUT THERE?
KREEK
MRS. GRASS-MAN...

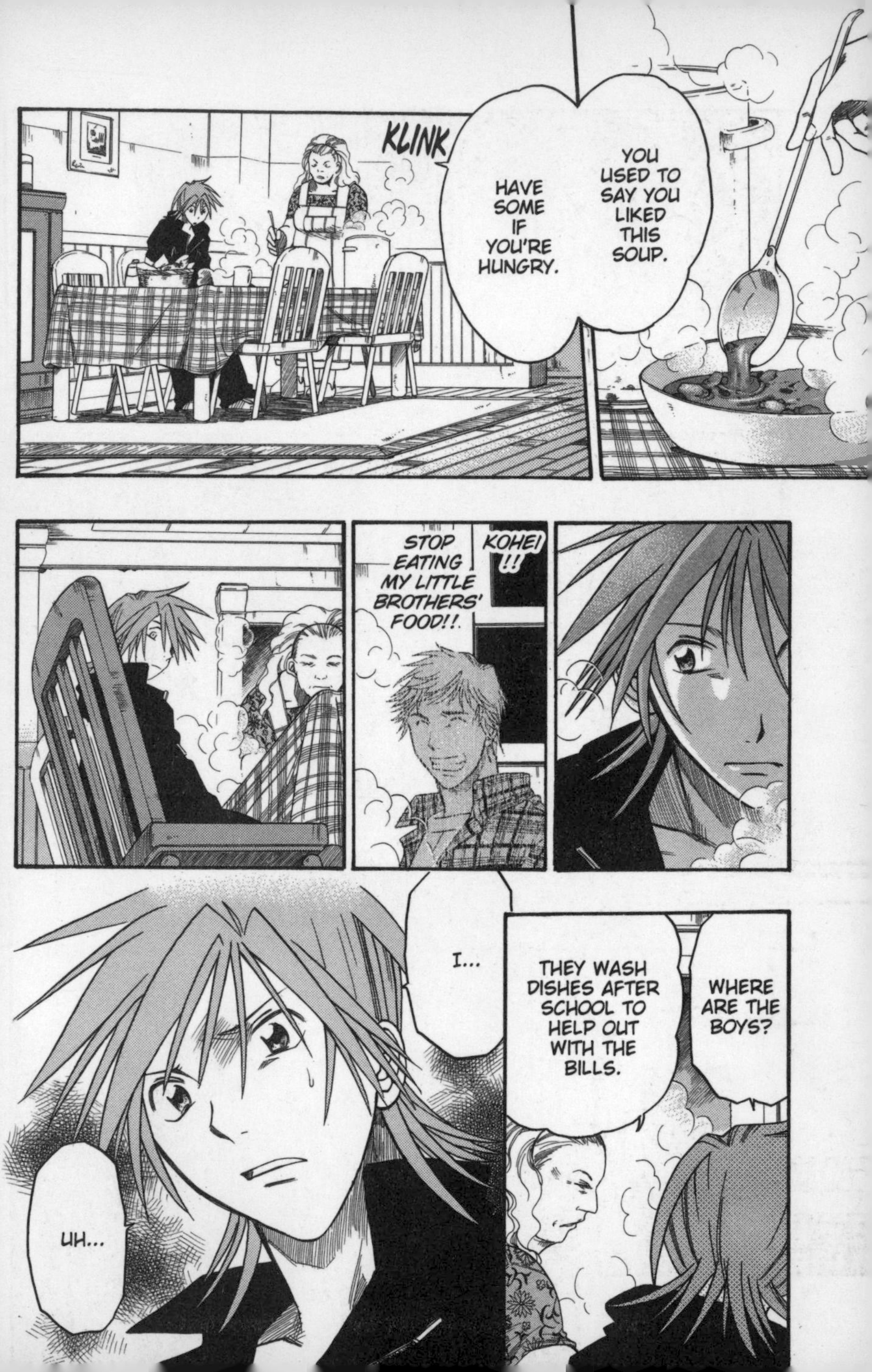
YOU USED TO SAY YOU LIKED THIS SOUP.
HAVE SOME IF YOU'RE HUNGRY.
KLINK
KOHEI!!
STOP EATING MY LITTLE BROTHERS' FOOD!!
WHERE ARE THE BOYS?
THEY WASH DISHES AFTER SCHOOL TO HELP OUT WITH THE BILLS.
I...
UH...

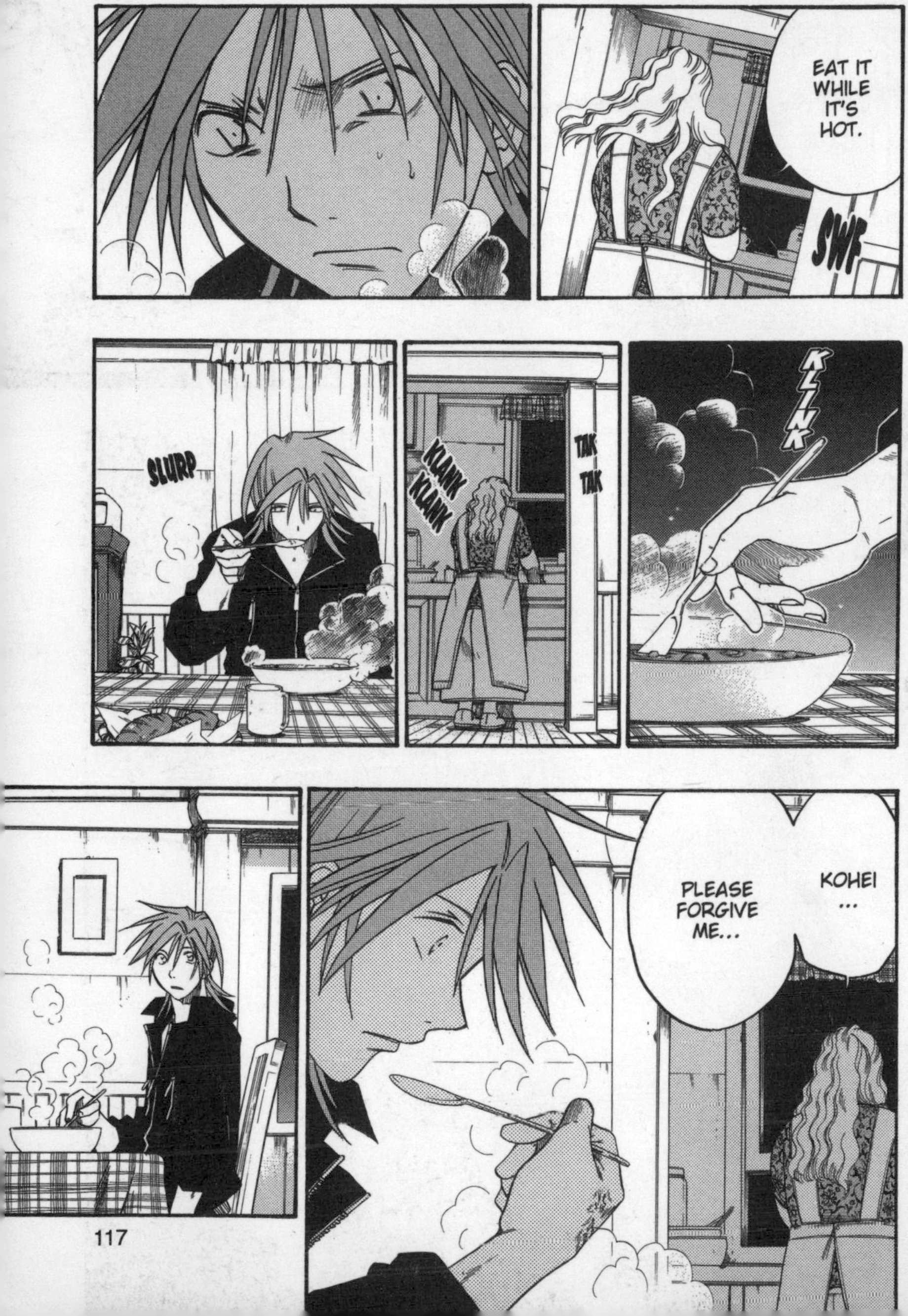
EAT IT WHILE IT'S HOT.
SWF
KLINK
TAK TAK
KLANK KLANK
SLURP
KOHEI ...
PLEASE FORGIVE ME...

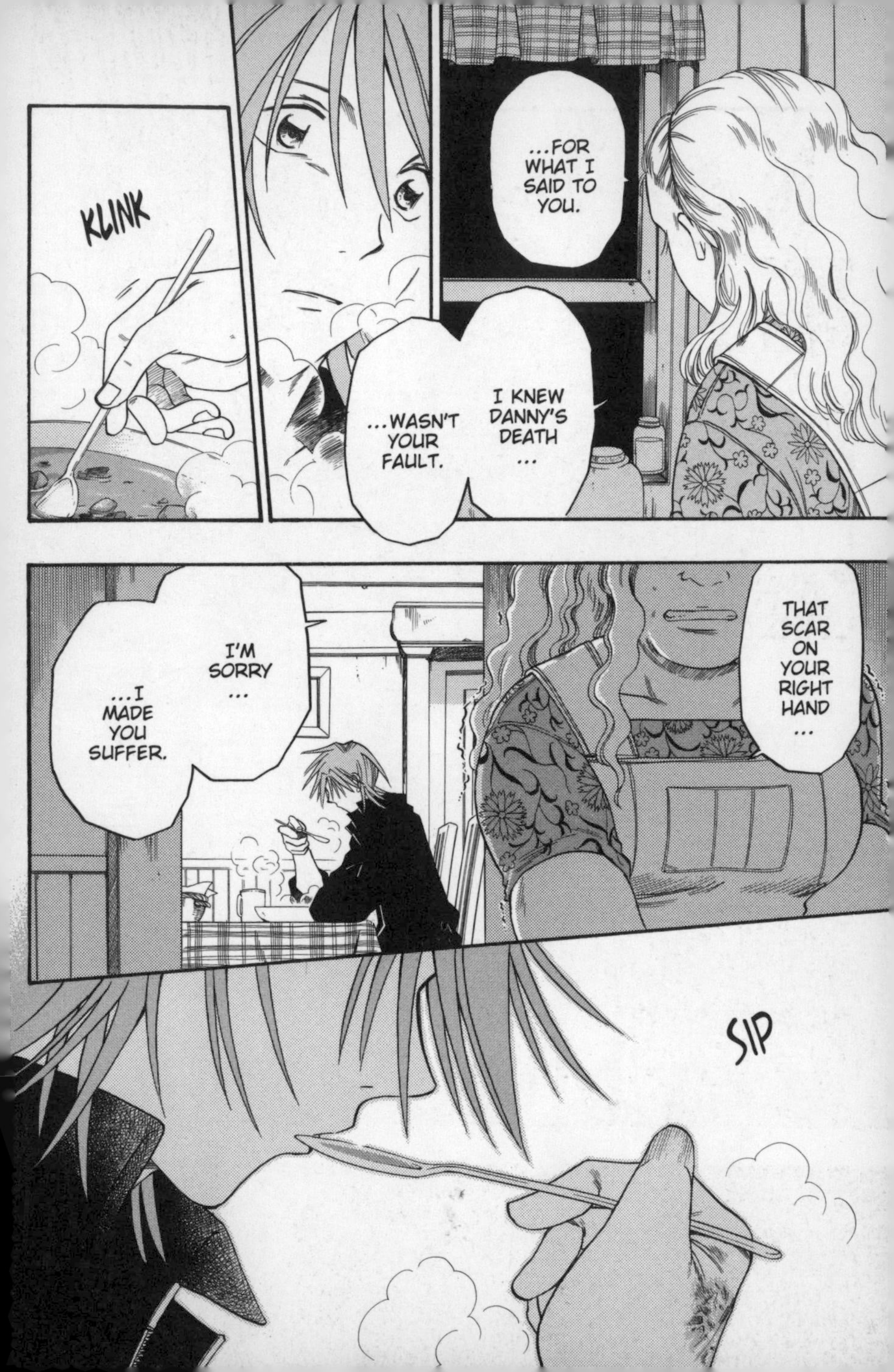
...FOR WHAT I SAID TO YOU.
I KNEW DANNY'S DEATH ...
...WASN'T YOUR FAULT.
KLINK
THAT SCAR ON YOUR RIGHT HAND ...
I'M SORRY ...
...I MADE YOU SUFFER.
SIP

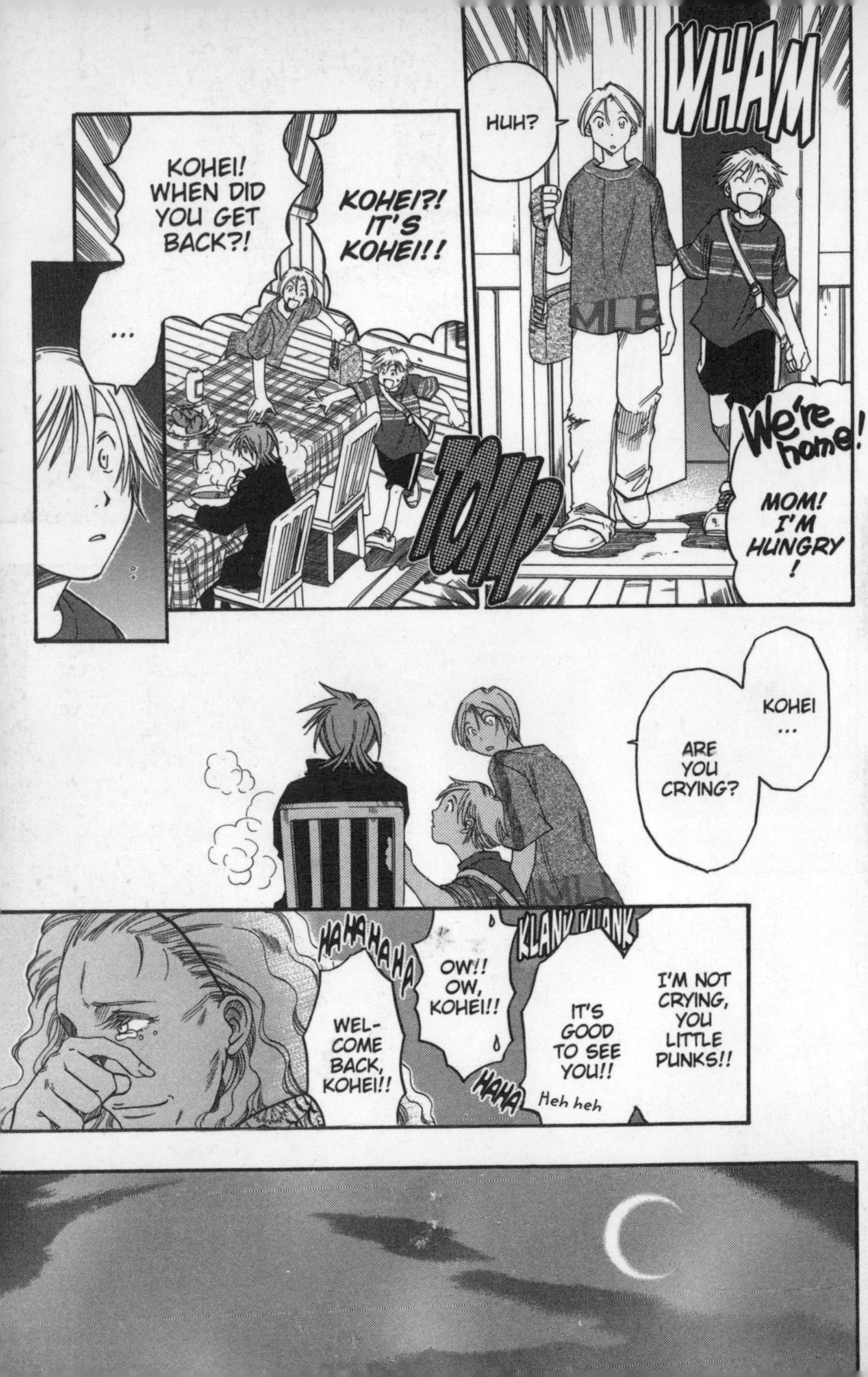
WHAM
HUH?
We're home!
MOM! I'M HUNGRY!
KOHEI?! IT'S KOHEI!!
KOHEI! WHEN DID YOU GET BACK?!
TOMP
...
KOHEI ...
ARE YOU CRYING?
I'M NOT CRYING, YOU LITTLE PUNKS!!
IT'S GOOD TO SEE YOU!!
OW!! OW, KOHEI!!
HAHA
Heh heh
WEL-COME BACK, KOHEI!!
HA HA HA HA HA

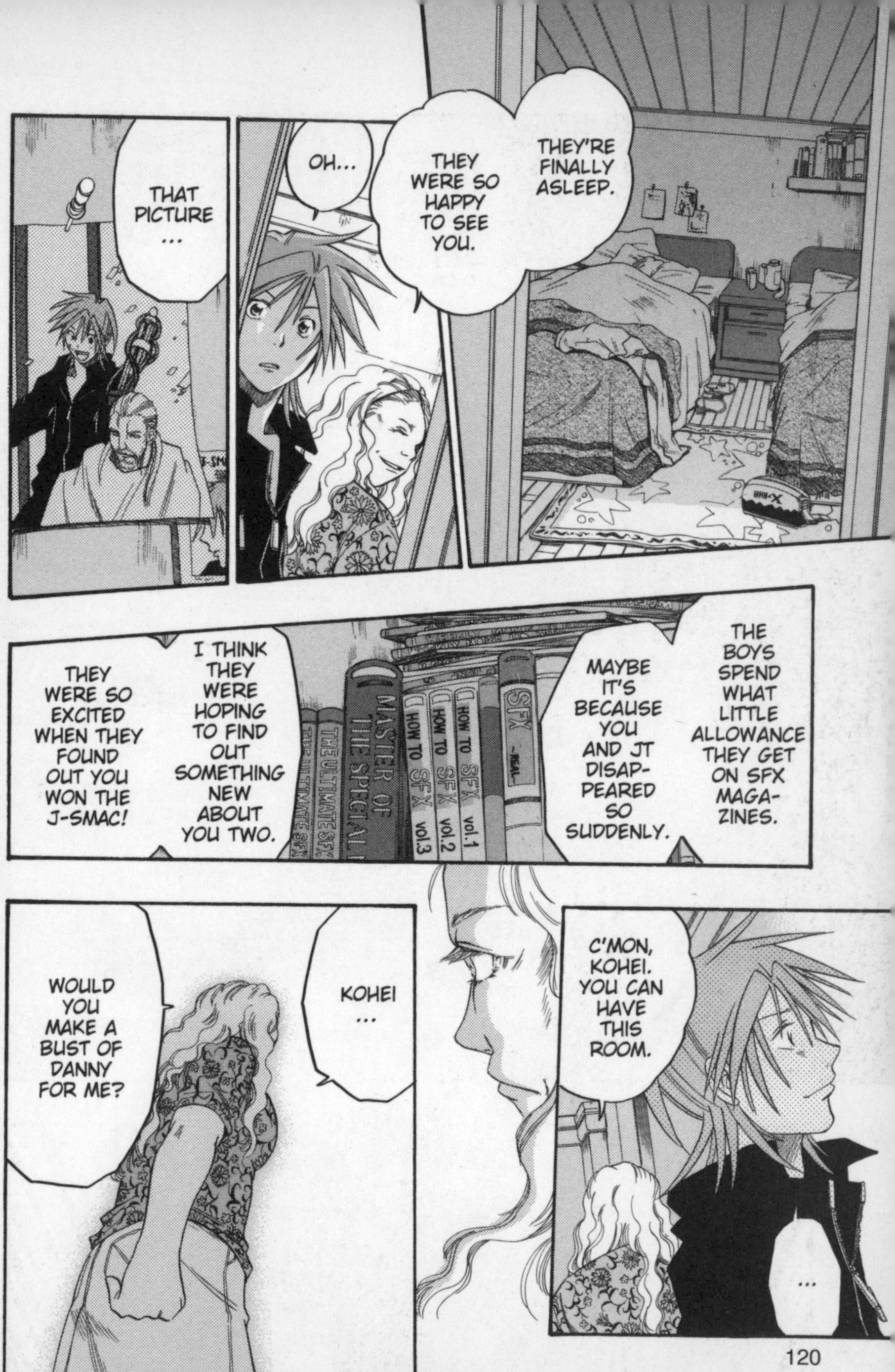
THEY'RE FINALLY ASLEEP.
THEY WERE SO HAPPY TO SEE YOU.
OH...
THAT PICTURE ...
THE BOYS SPEND WHAT LITTLE ALLOWANCE THEY GET ON SFX MAGAZINES.
MAYBE IT'S BECAUSE YOU AND JT DISAPPEARED SO SUDDENLY.
SFX -REAL-
HOW TO SFX vol.1
HOW TO SFX vol.2
HOW TO SFX vol.3
MASTER OF THE SPECIAL
THE ULTIMATE SFX
I THINK THEY WERE HOPING TO FIND OUT SOMETHING NEW ABOUT YOU TWO.
THEY WERE SO EXCITED WHEN THEY FOUND OUT YOU WON THE J-SMAC!
C'MON, KOHEI. YOU CAN HAVE THIS ROOM.
...
KOHEI ...
WOULD YOU MAKE A BUST OF DANNY FOR ME?

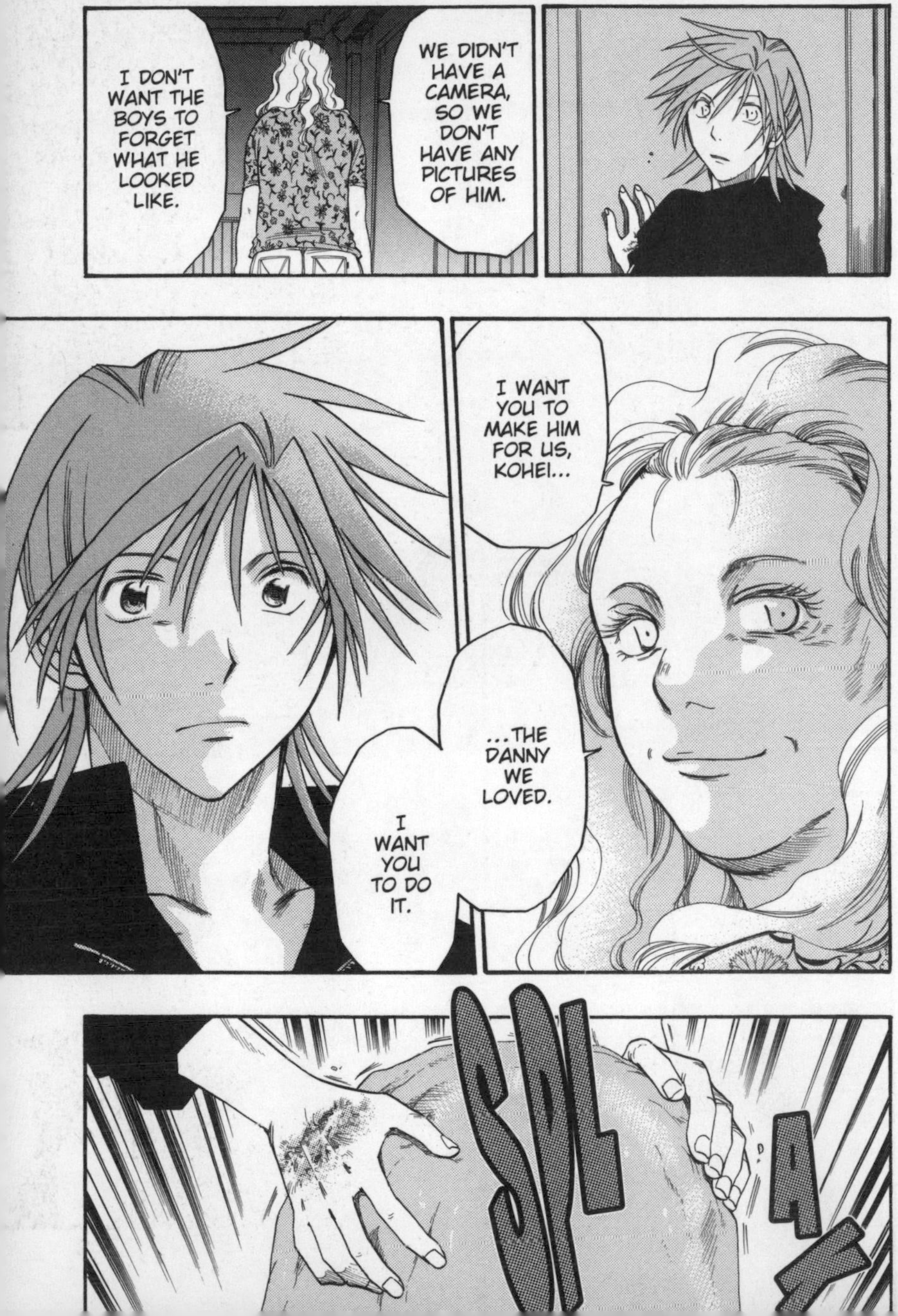
WE DIDN'T HAVE A CAMERA, SO WE DON'T HAVE ANY PICTURES OF HIM.
I DON'T WANT THE BOYS TO FORGET WHAT HE LOOKED LIKE.
I WANT YOU TO MAKE HIM FOR US, KOHEI...
...THE DANNY WE LOVED.
I WANT YOU TO DO IT.
SPLA

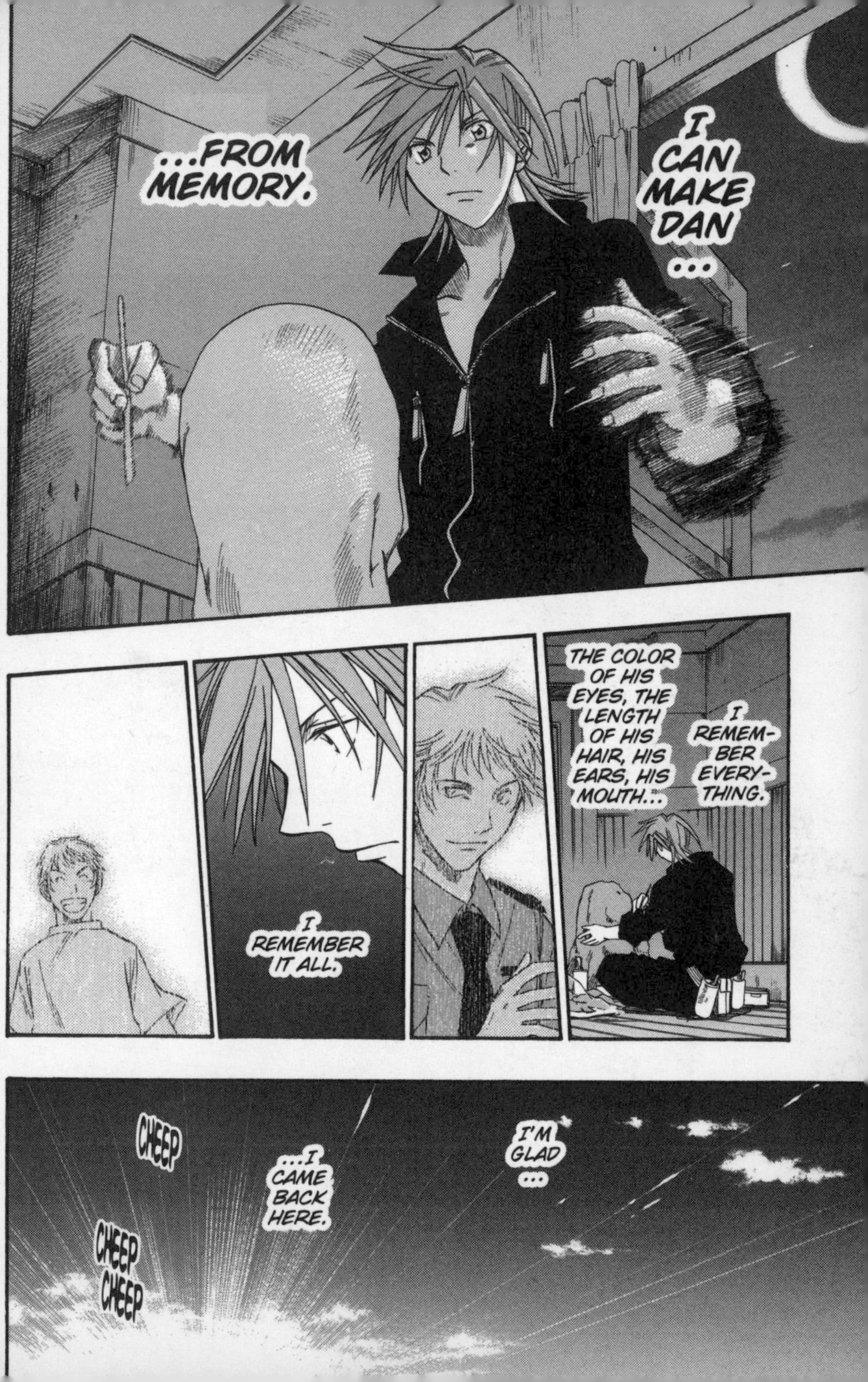
I CAN MAKE DAN ...
...FROM MEMORY.
THE COLOR OF HIS EYES, THE LENGTH OF HIS HAIR, HIS EARS, HIS MOUTH...
I REMEMBER EVERYTHING.
I REMEMBER IT ALL.
I'M GLAD ...
...I CAME BACK HERE.
CHEEP
CHEEP CHEEP

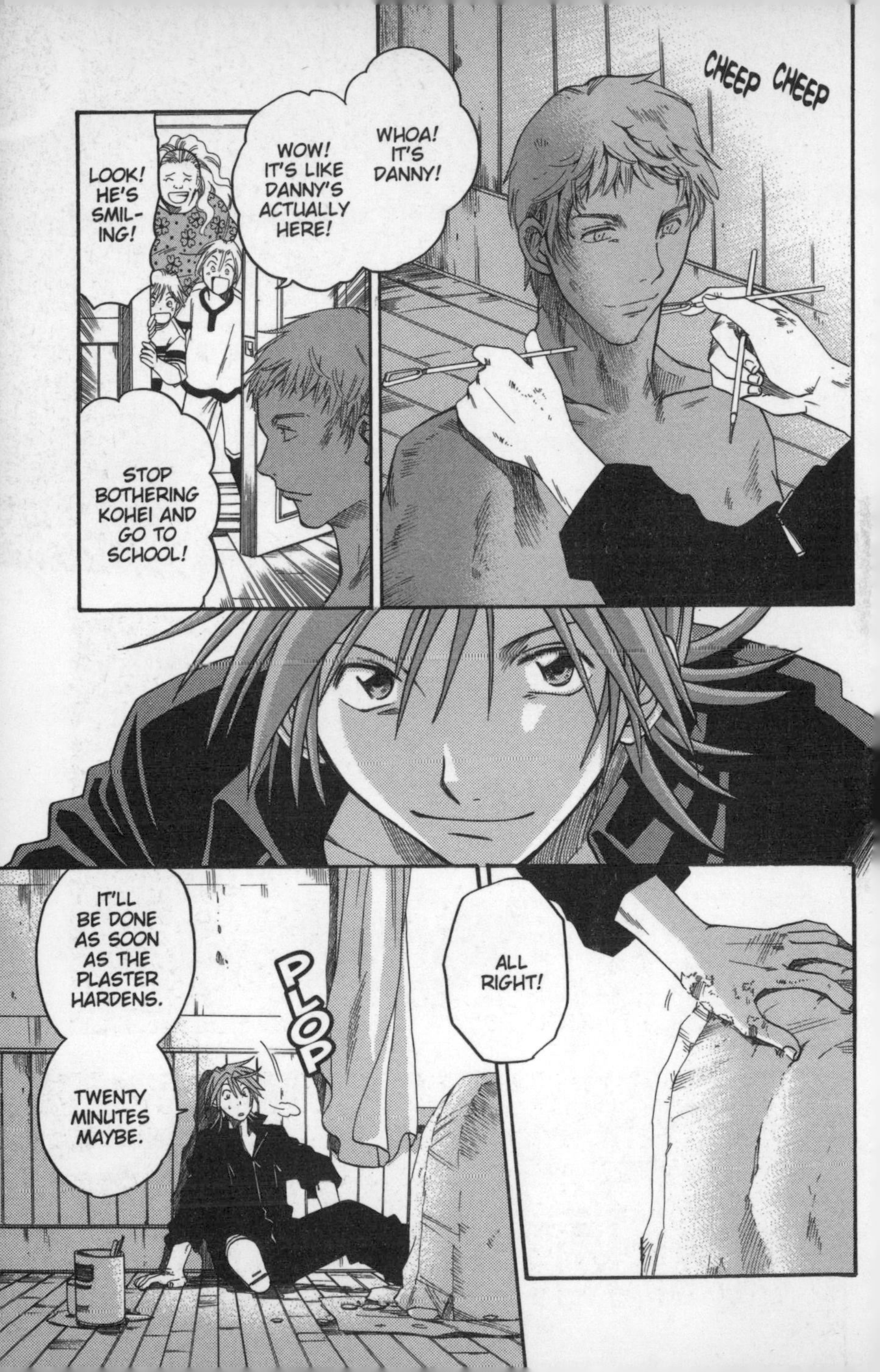
CHEEP CHEEP
WHOA! IT'S DANNY!
WOW! IT'S LIKE DANNY'S ACTUALLY HERE!
LOOK! HE'S SMIL-ING!
STOP BOTHERING KOHEI AND GO TO SCHOOL!
ALL RIGHT!
PLOP
IT'LL BE DONE AS SOON AS THE PLASTER HARDENS.
TWENTY MINUTES MAYBE.

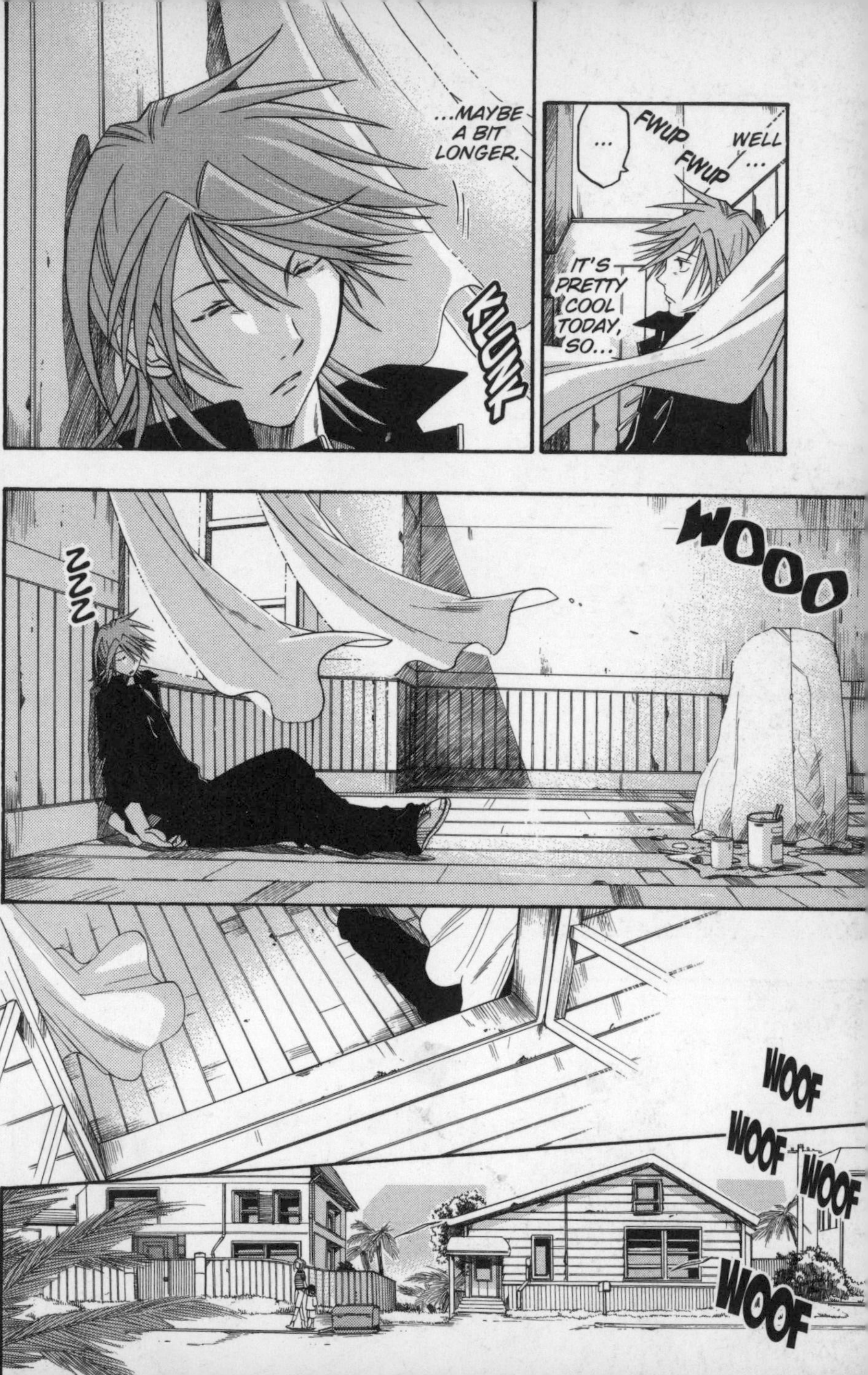
WELL...
FWUP FWUP
...
IT'S PRETTY COOL TODAY, SO...
...MAYBE A BIT LONGER.
KLUNK
WOOO
ZZZ
WOOF
WOOF
WOOF
WOOF

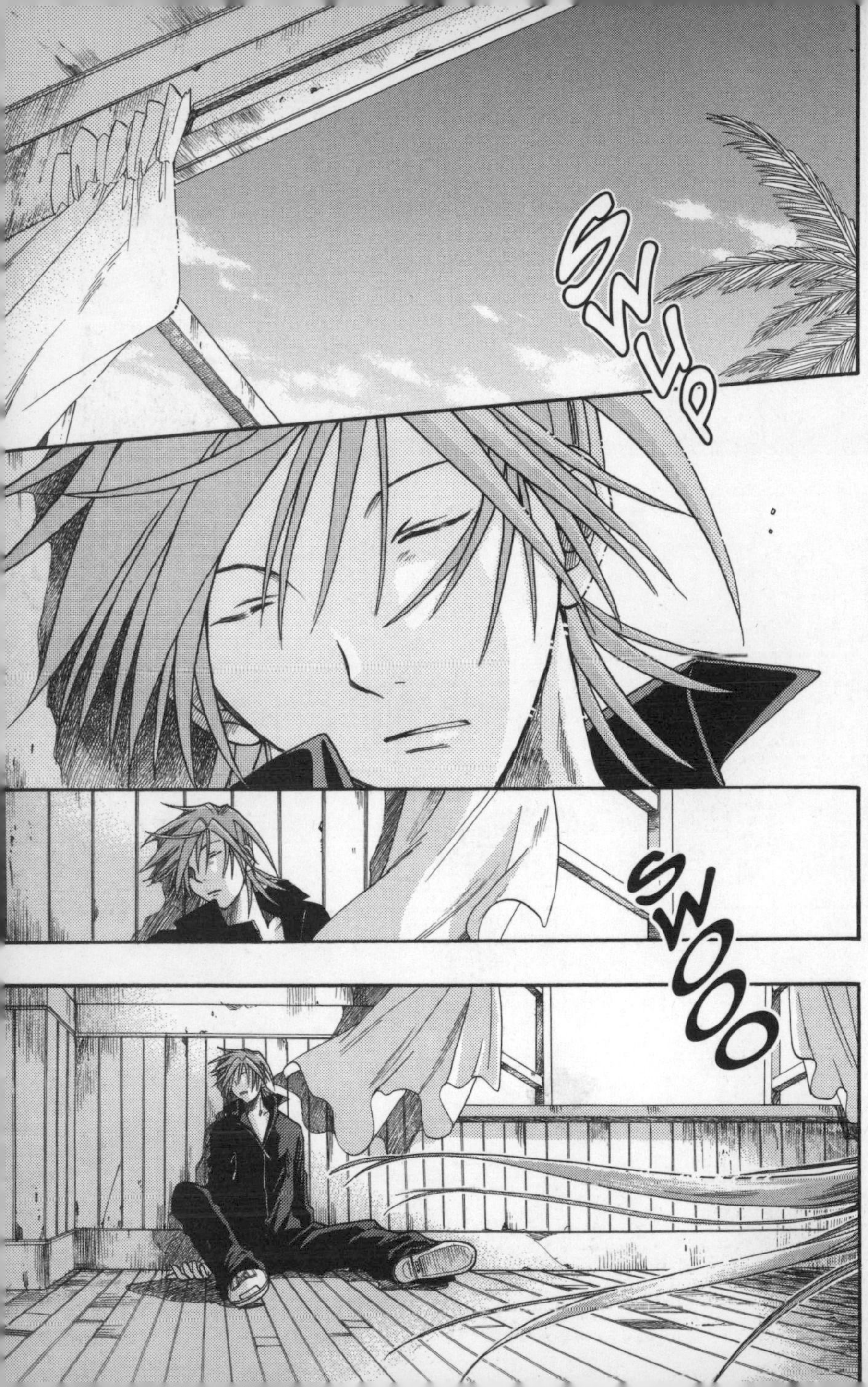
SWUP
SWOOO

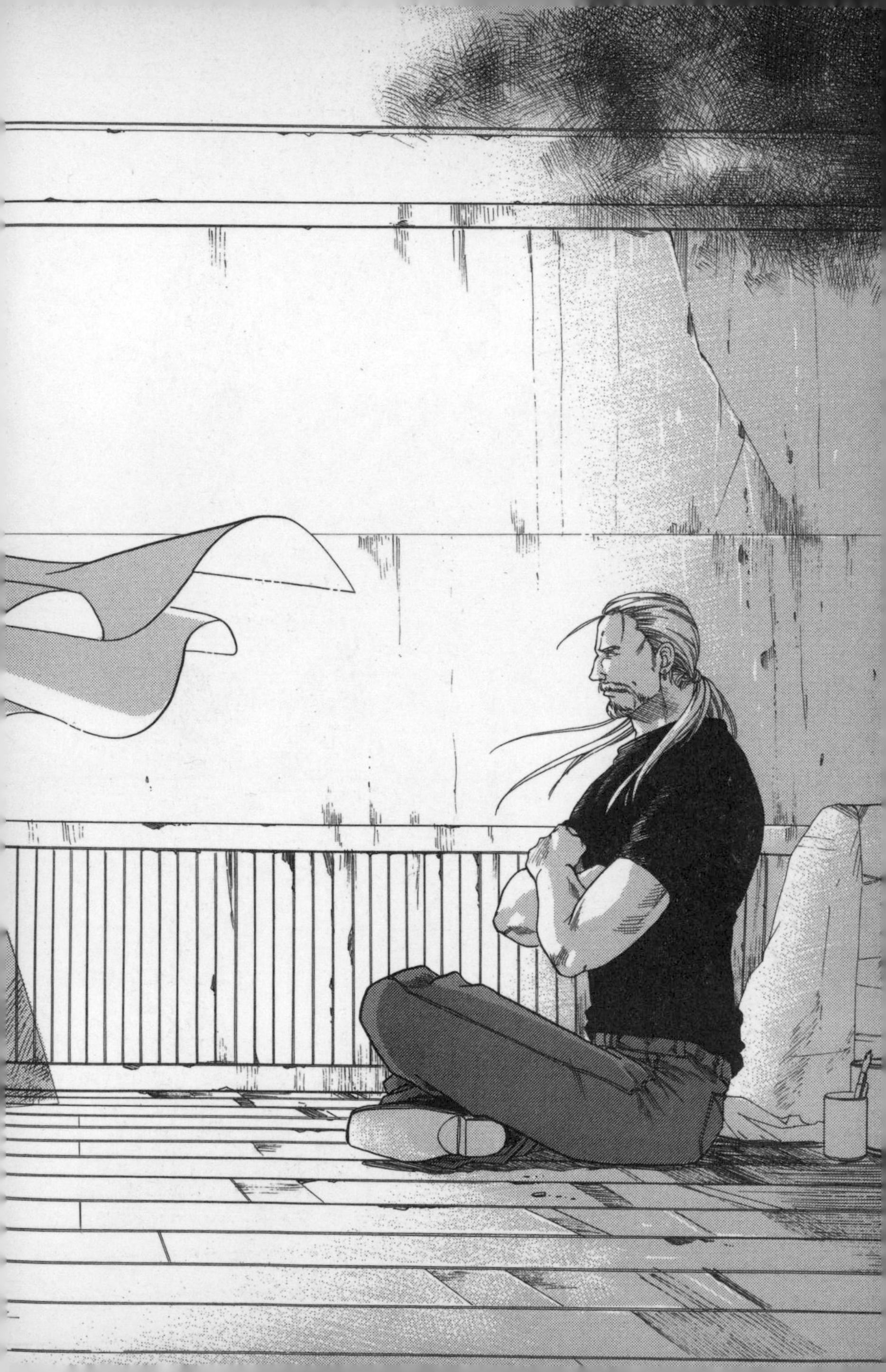

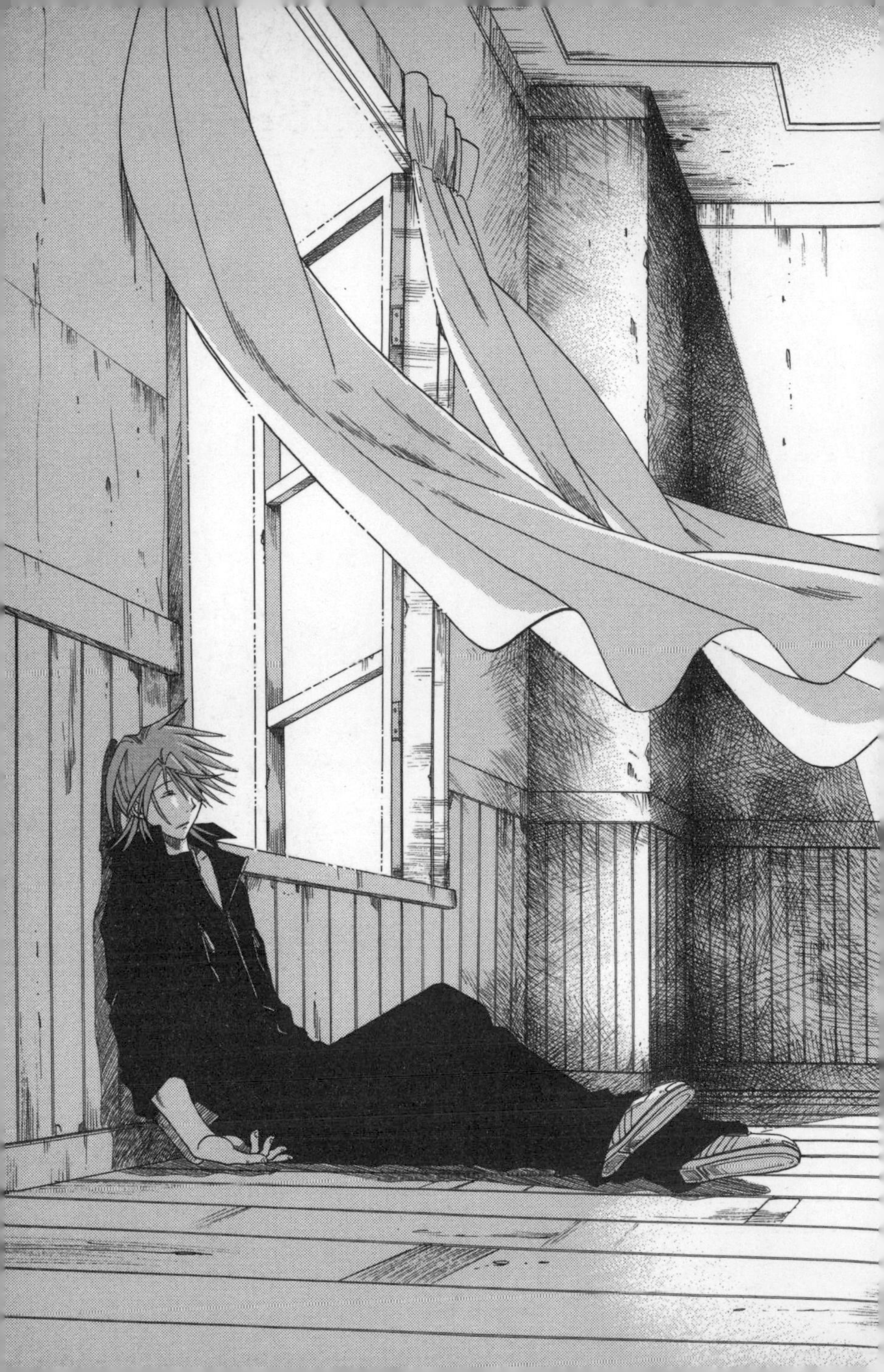

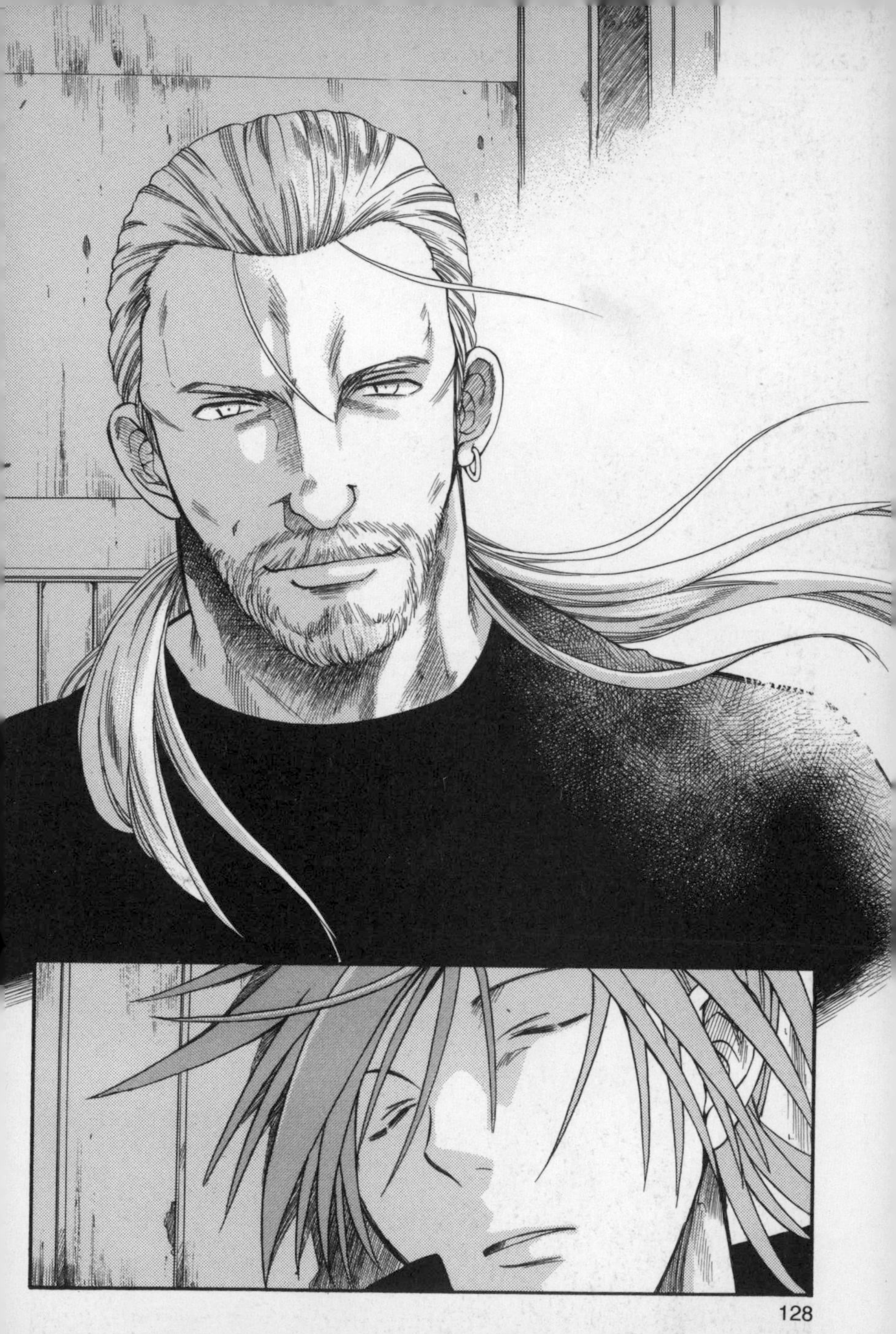

Last Scene: Field of Dreams Redux (Part 2)

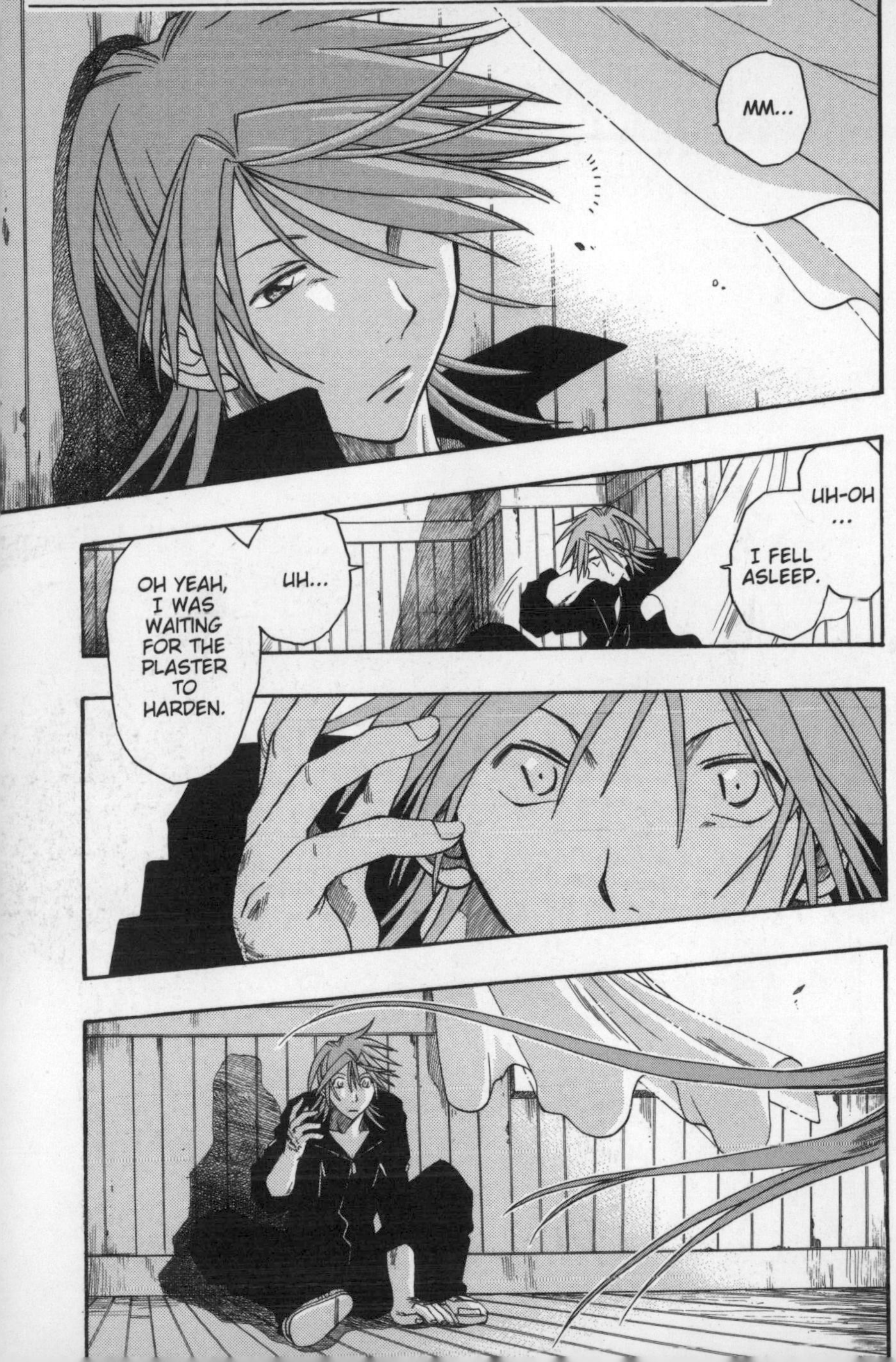
MM...
UH-OH ... I FELL ASLEEP.
UH...
OH YEAH, I WAS WAITING FOR THE PLASTER TO HARDEN.

Last Scene: Field of Dreams Redux (Part 2)

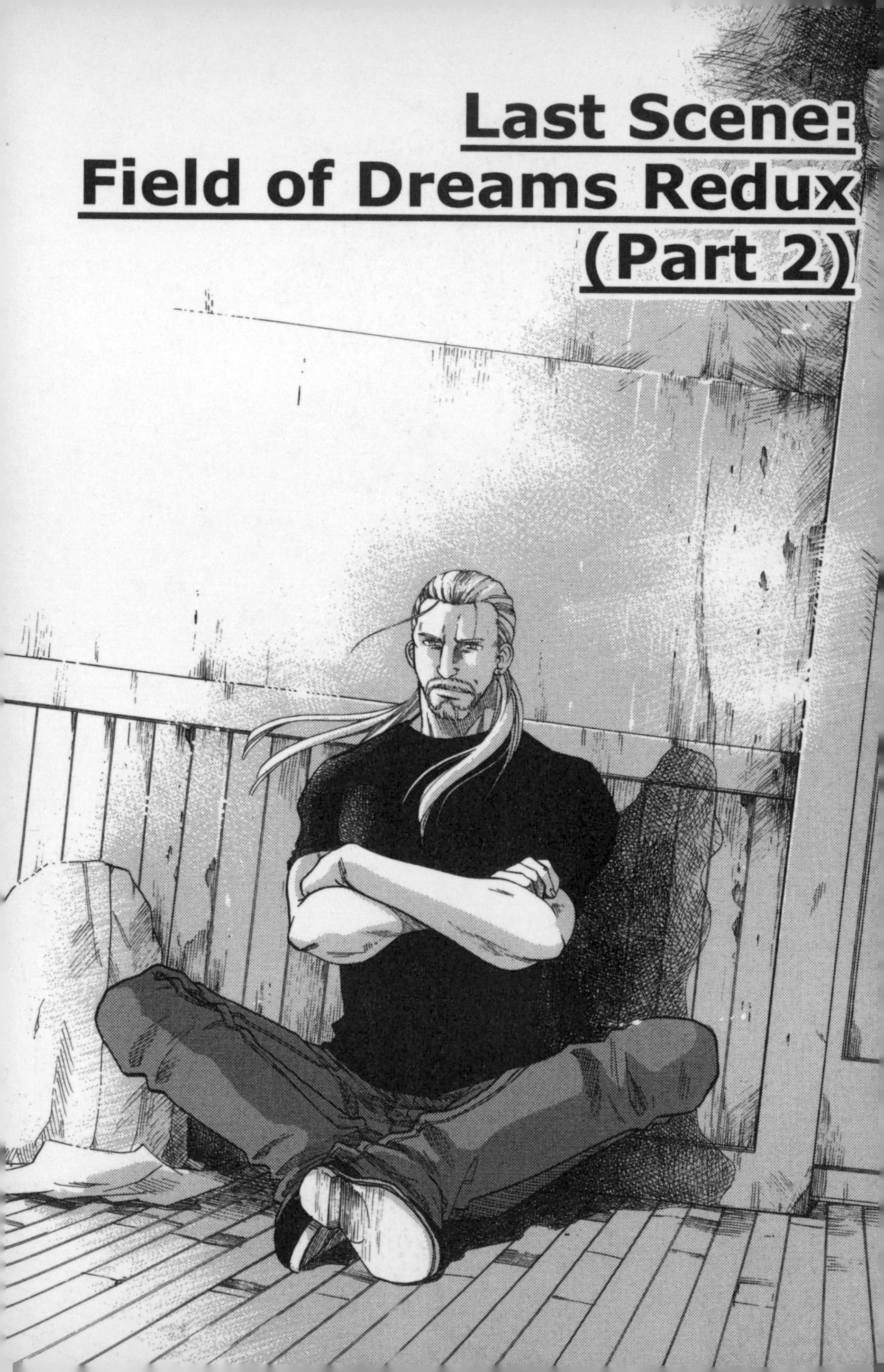

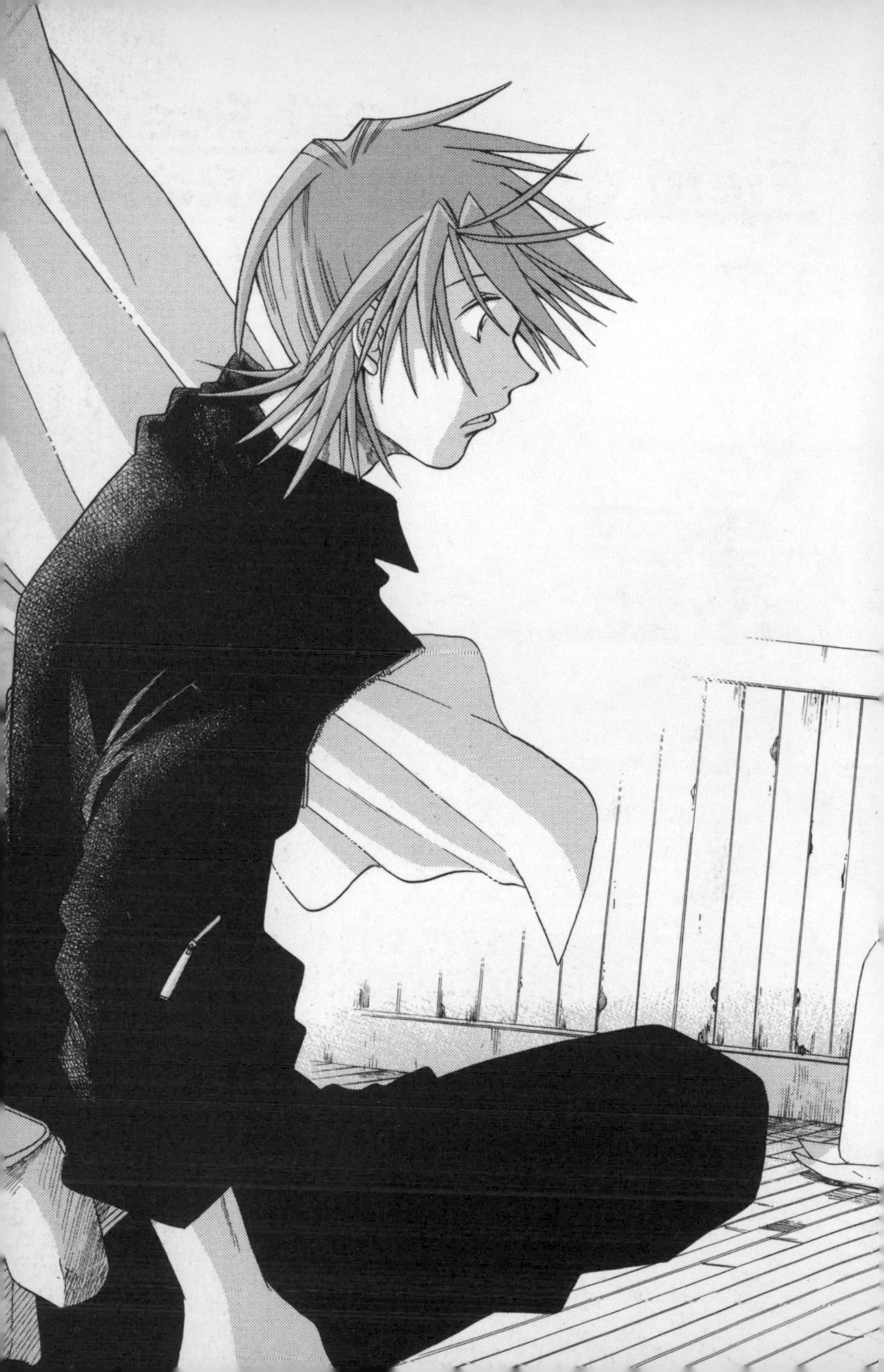

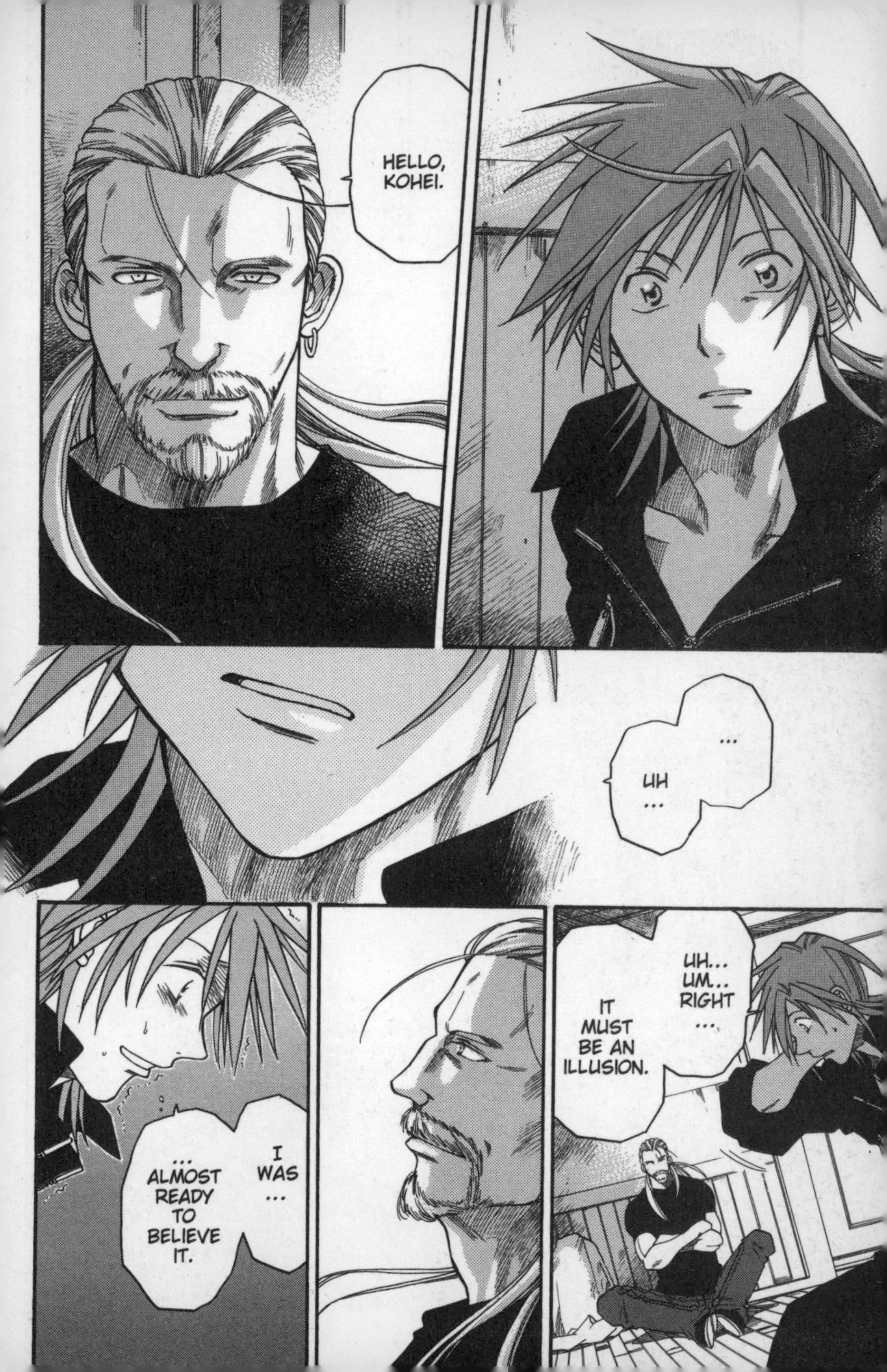
HELLO, KOHEI.
... UH ...
UH... UM... RIGHT ...,
IT MUST BE AN ILLUSION.
I WAS ...
... ALMOST READY TO BELIEVE IT.

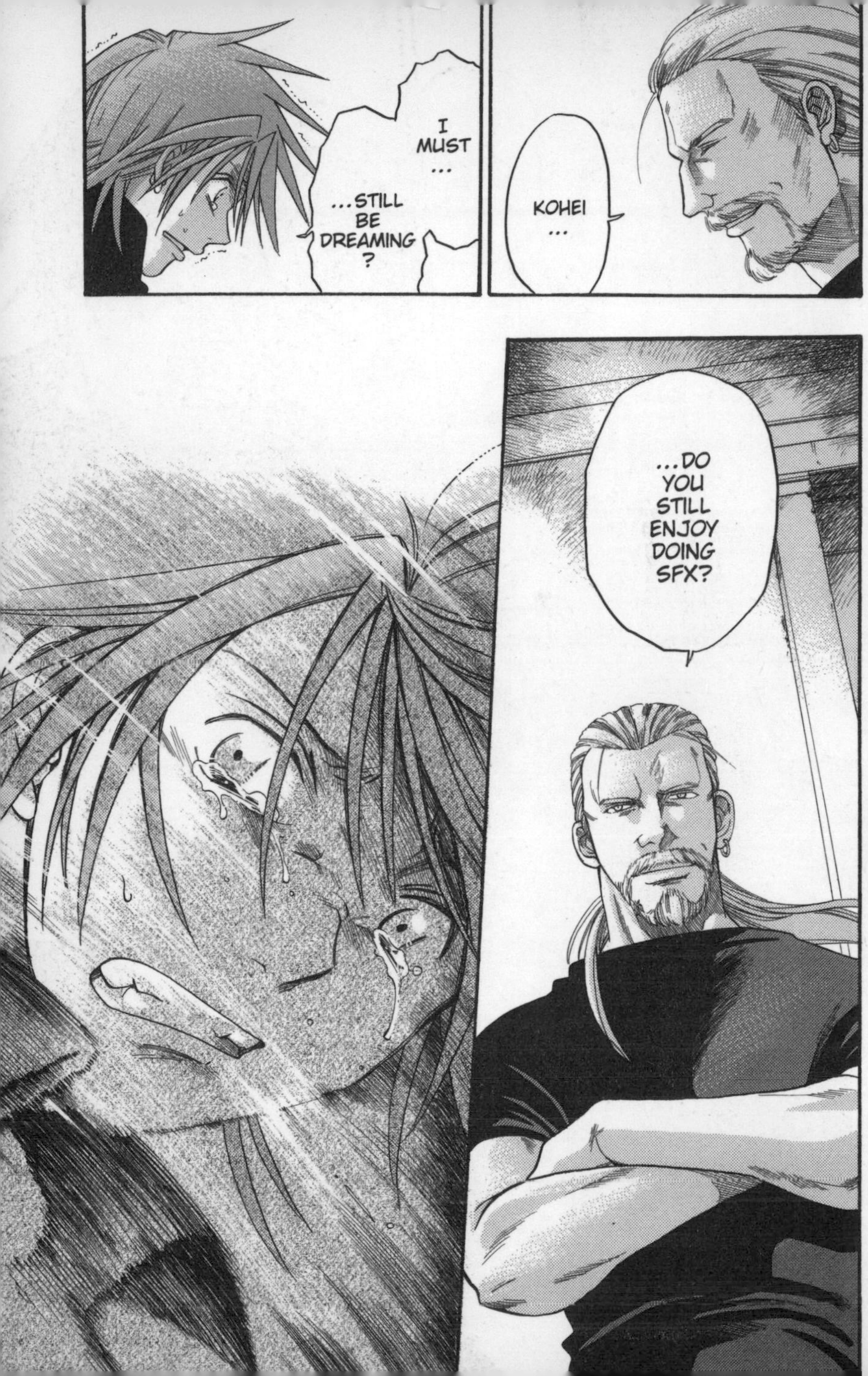
KOHEI ...
I MUST ...
...STILL BE DREAMING?
...DO YOU STILL ENJOY DOING SFX?

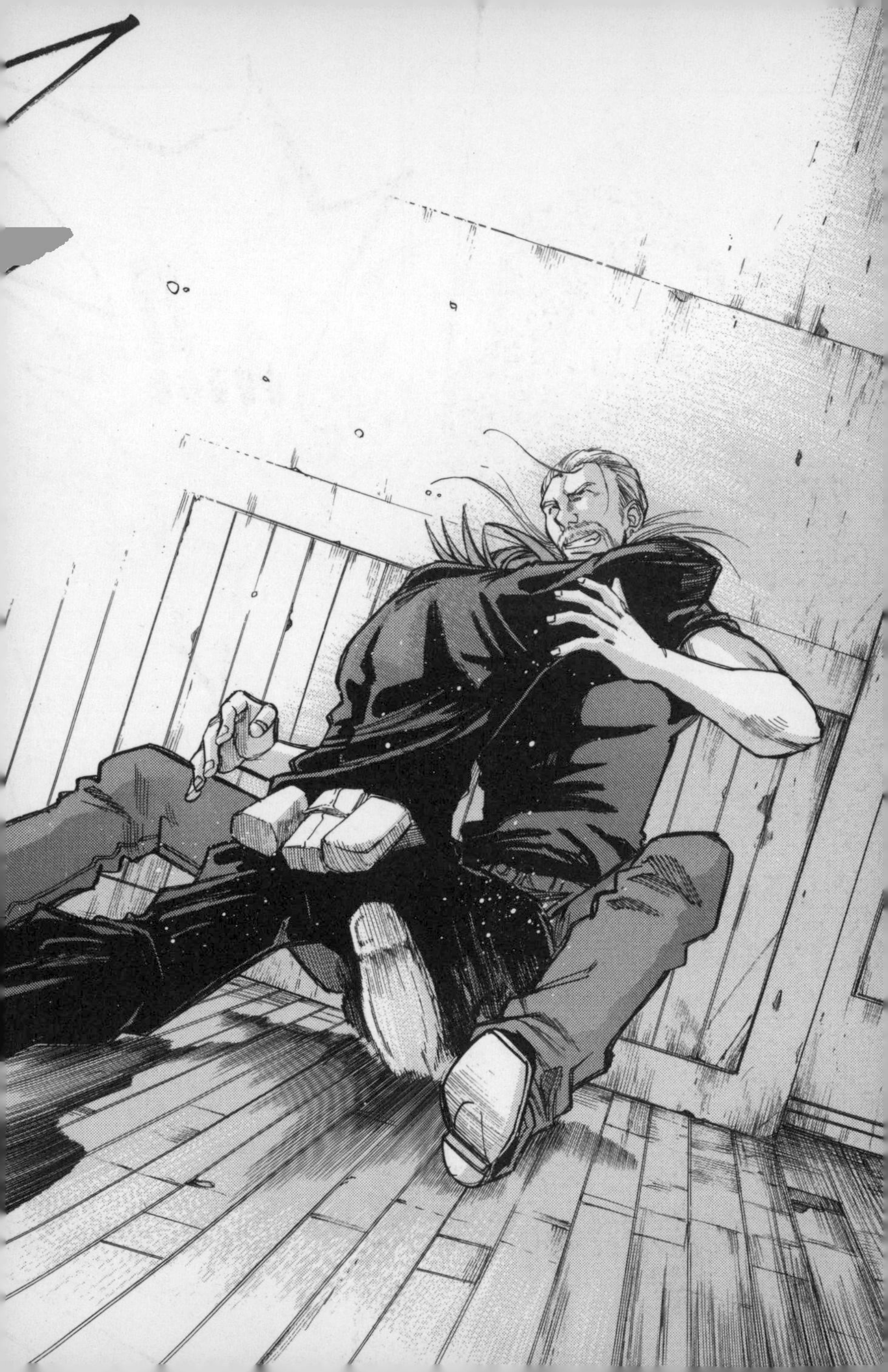

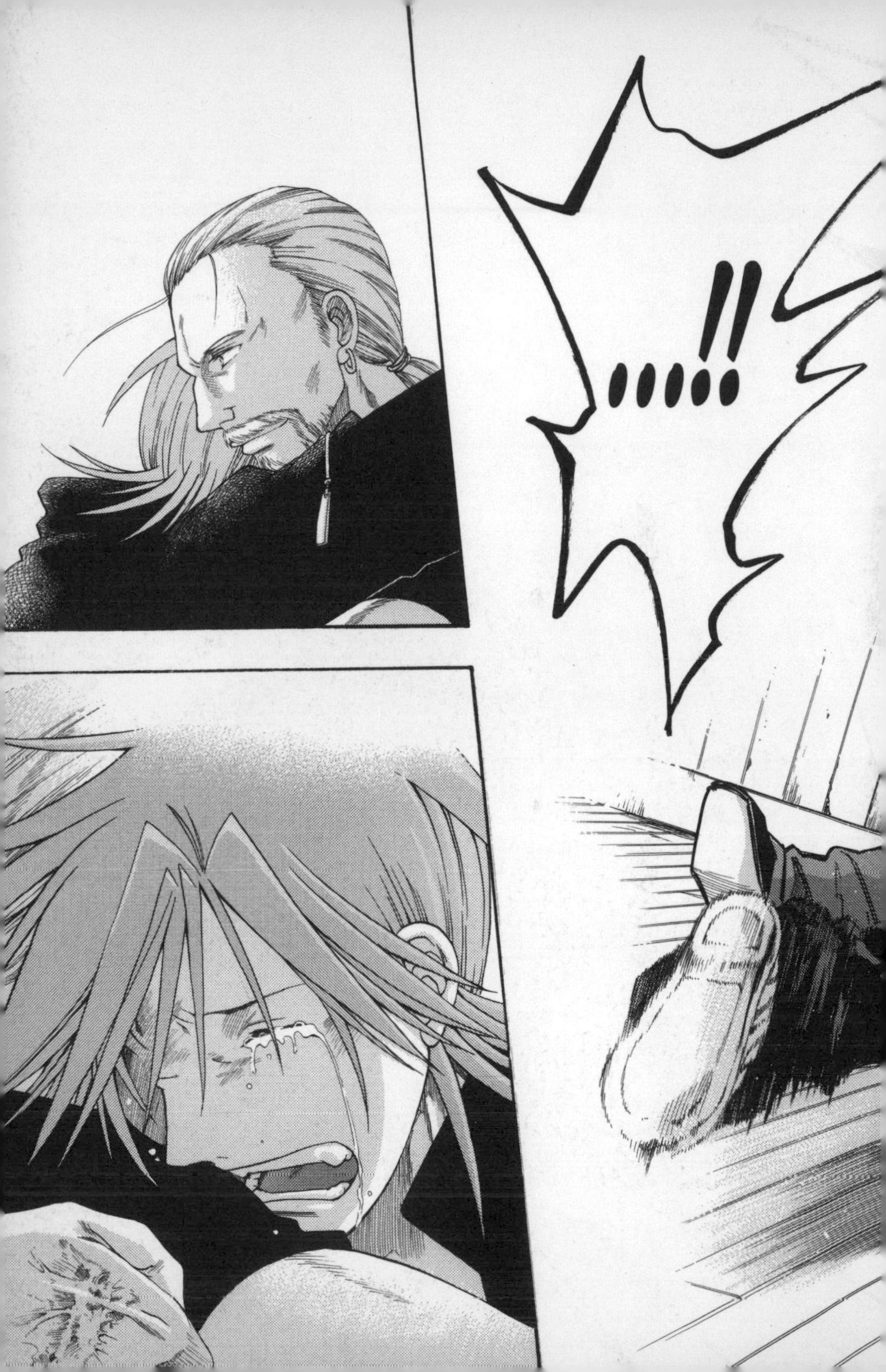
....!!

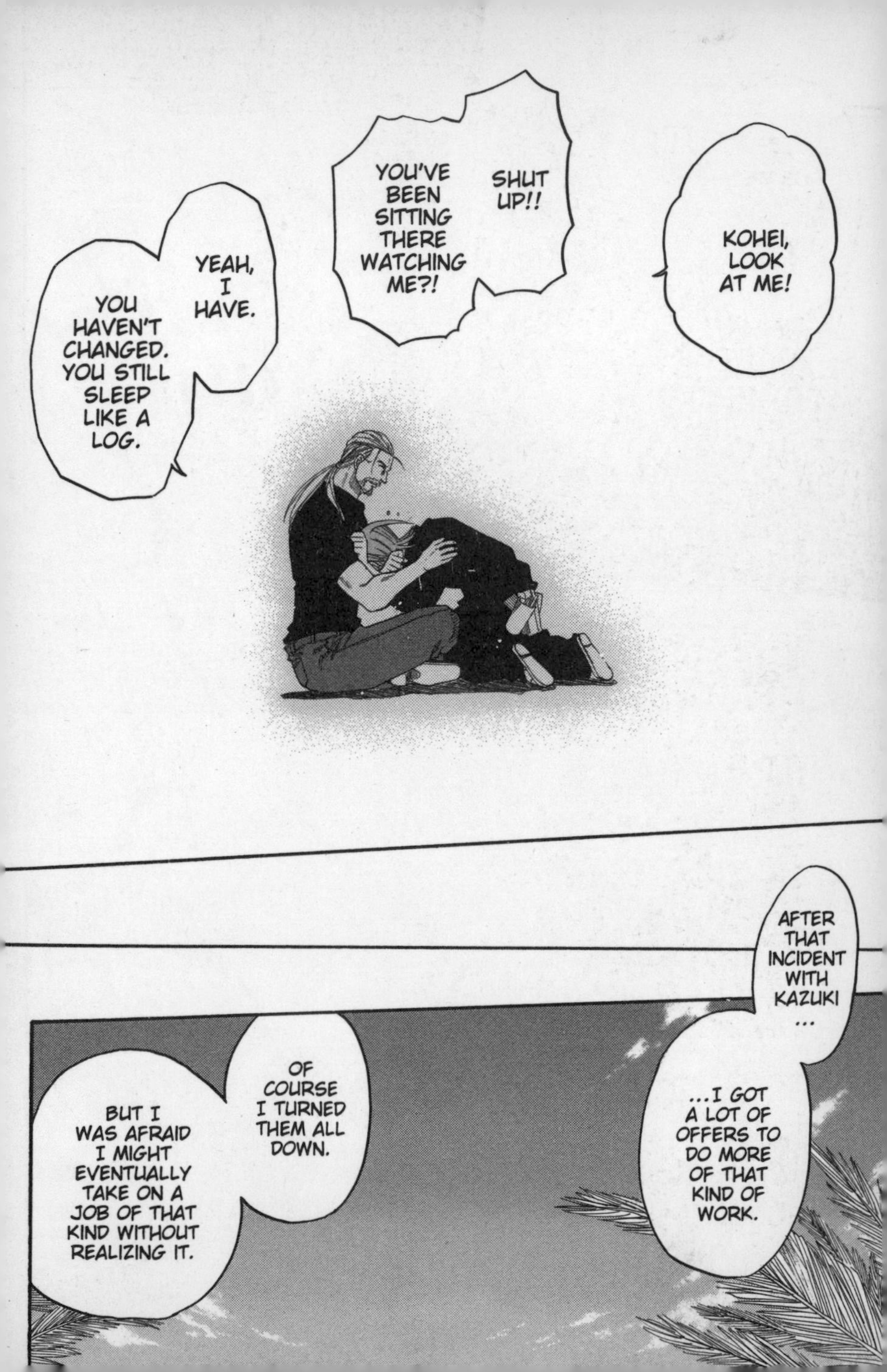
KOHEI, LOOK AT ME!
SHUT UP!!
YOU'VE BEEN SITTING THERE WATCHING ME?!
YEAH, I HAVE.
YOU HAVEN'T CHANGED. YOU STILL SLEEP LIKE A LOG.
AFTER THAT INCIDENT WITH KAZUKI ...
...I GOT A LOT OF OFFERS TO DO MORE OF THAT KIND OF WORK.
OF COURSE I TURNED THEM ALL DOWN.
BUT I WAS AFRAID I MIGHT EVENTUALLY TAKE ON A JOB OF THAT KIND WITHOUT REALIZING IT.

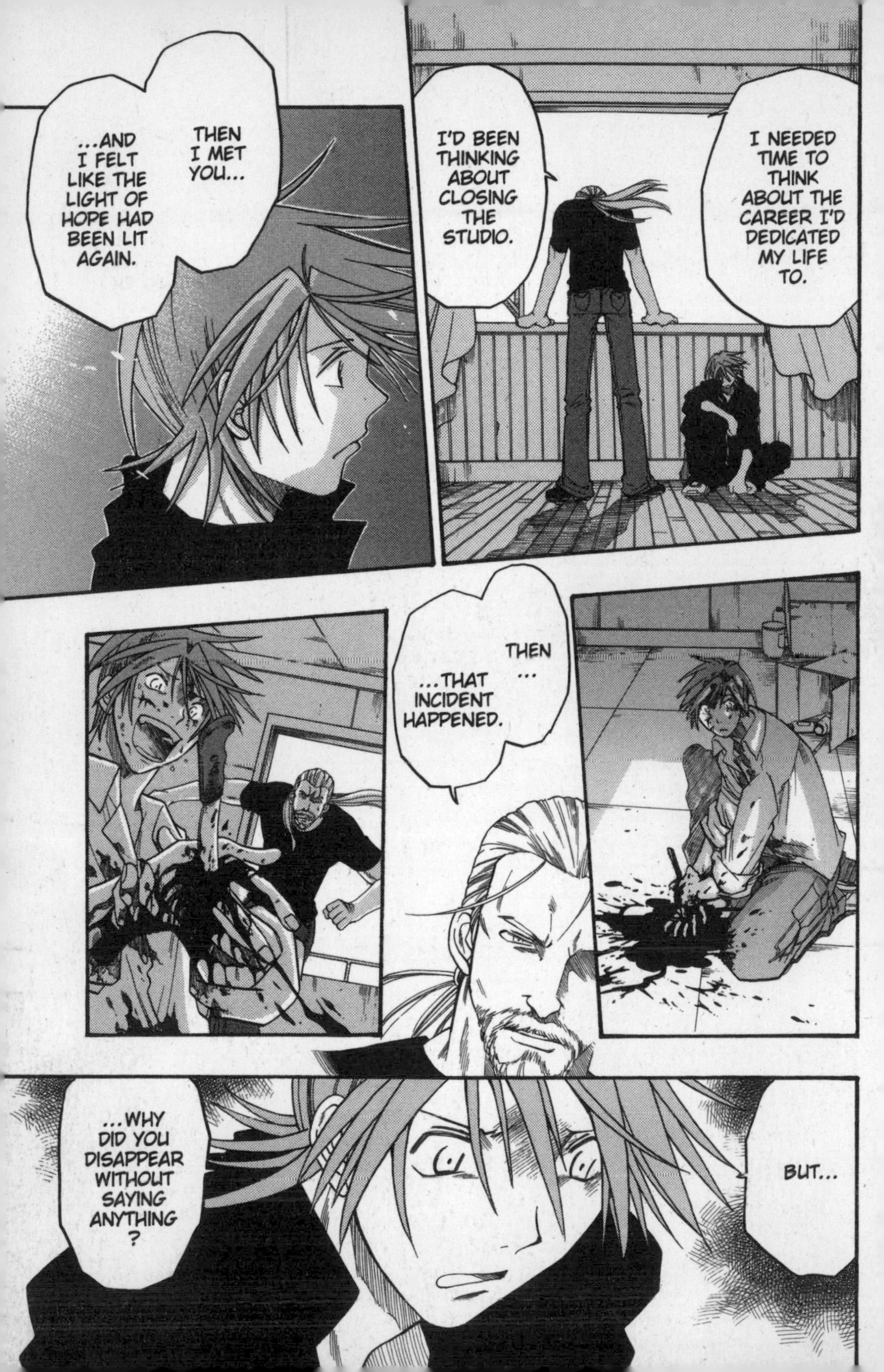
I NEEDED TIME TO THINK ABOUT THE CAREER I'D DEDICATED MY LIFE TO.
I'D BEEN THINKING ABOUT CLOSING THE STUDIO.
THEN I MET YOU...
...AND I FELT LIKE THE LIGHT OF HOPE HAD BEEN LIT AGAIN.
THEN ...
...THAT INCIDENT HAPPENED.
BUT...
...WHY DID YOU DISAPPEAR WITHOUT SAYING ANYTHING?

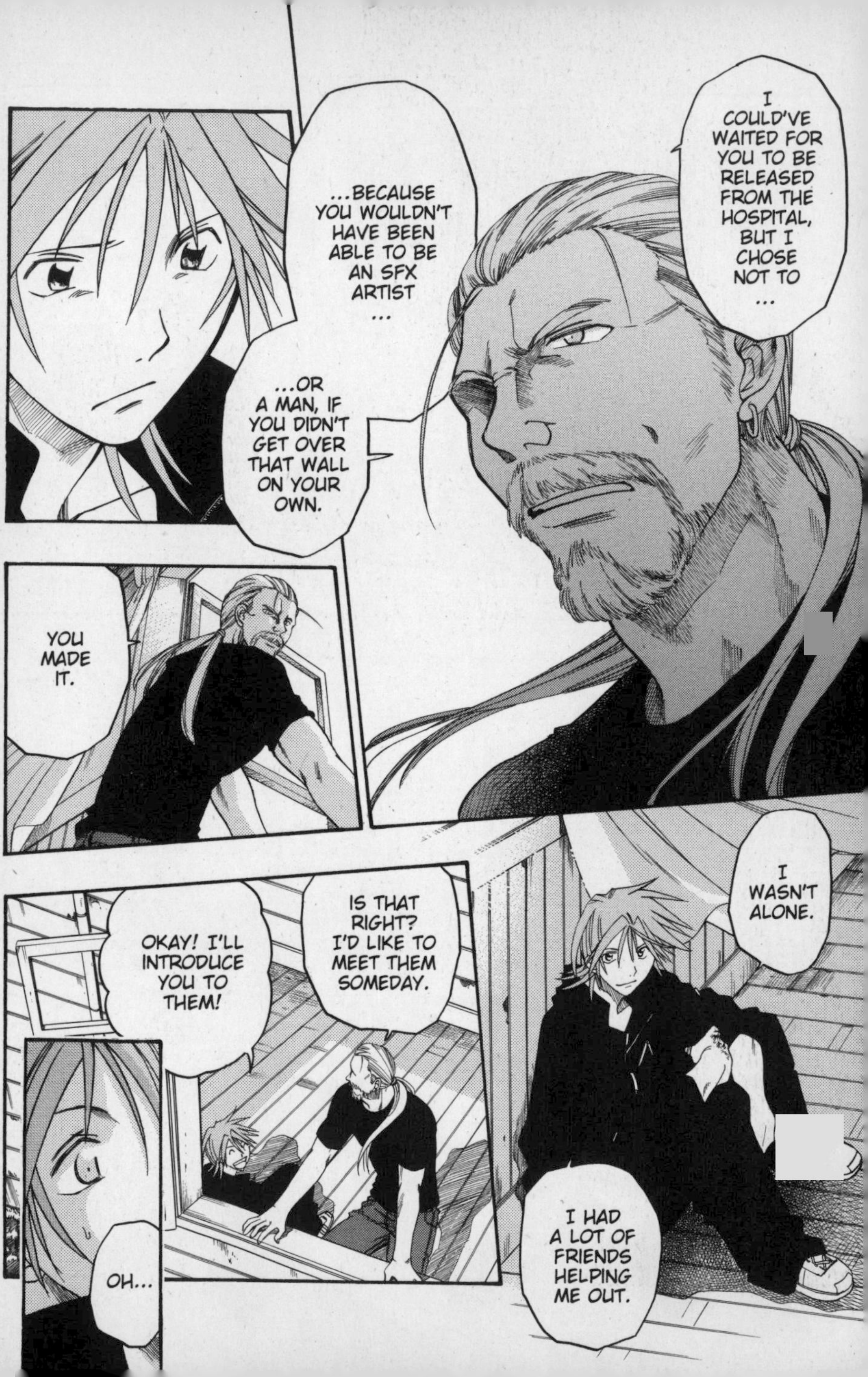
I COULD'VE WAITED FOR YOU TO BE RELEASED FROM THE HOSPITAL, BUT I CHOSE NOT TO ...
...BECAUSE YOU WOULDN'T HAVE BEEN ABLE TO BE AN SFX ARTIST ...
...OR A MAN, IF YOU DIDN'T GET OVER THAT WALL ON YOUR OWN.
YOU MADE IT.
I WASN'T ALONE.
I HAD A LOT OF FRIENDS HELPING ME OUT.
IS THAT RIGHT? I'D LIKE TO MEET THEM SOMEDAY.
OKAY! I'LL INTRODUCE YOU TO THEM!
OH...

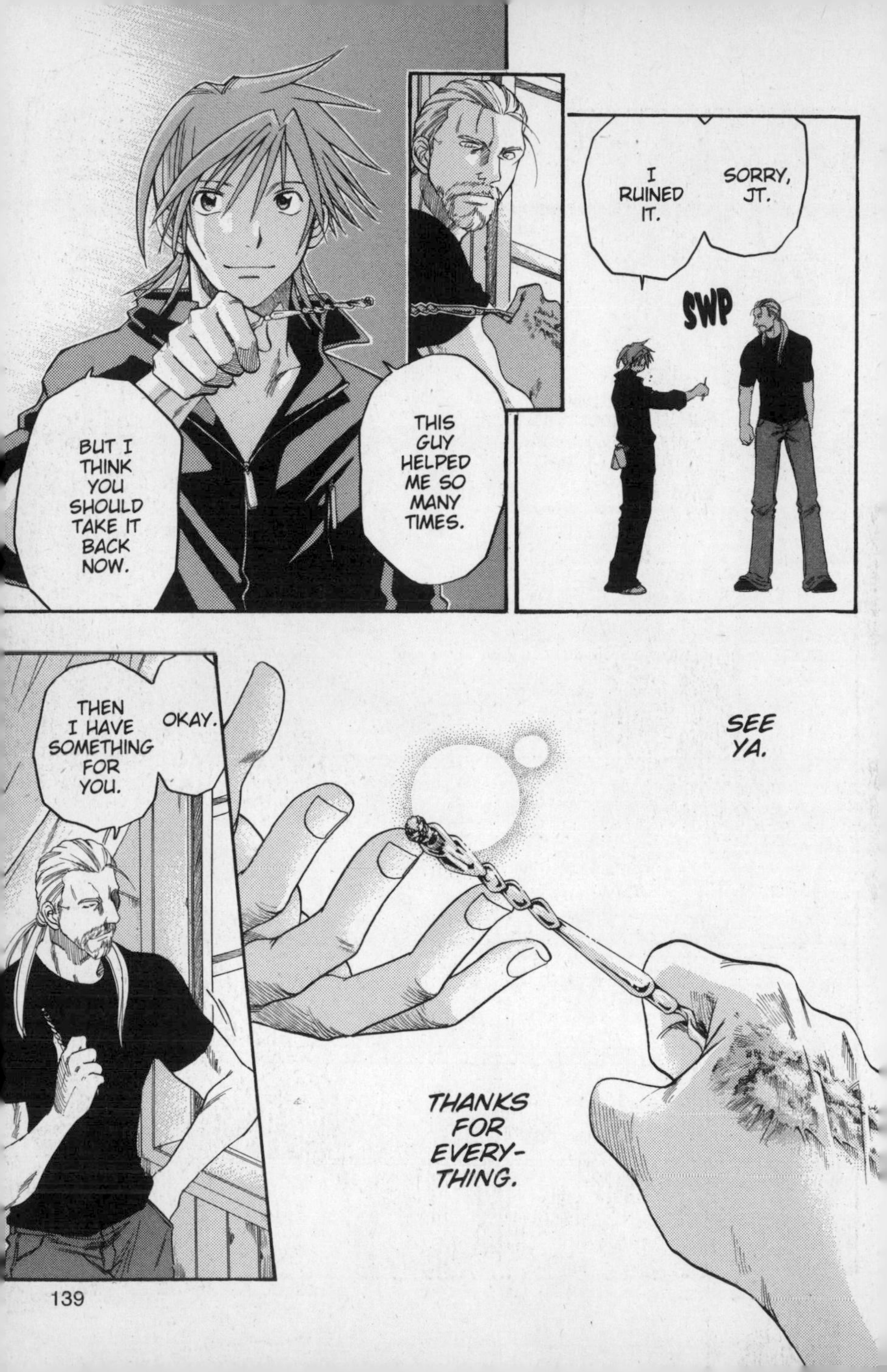
SORRY, JT.
I RUINED IT.
SWP
THIS GUY HELPED ME SO MANY TIMES.
BUT I THINK YOU SHOULD TAKE IT BACK NOW.
SEE YA.
THANKS FOR EVERY-THING.
OKAY.
THEN I HAVE SOMETHING FOR YOU.

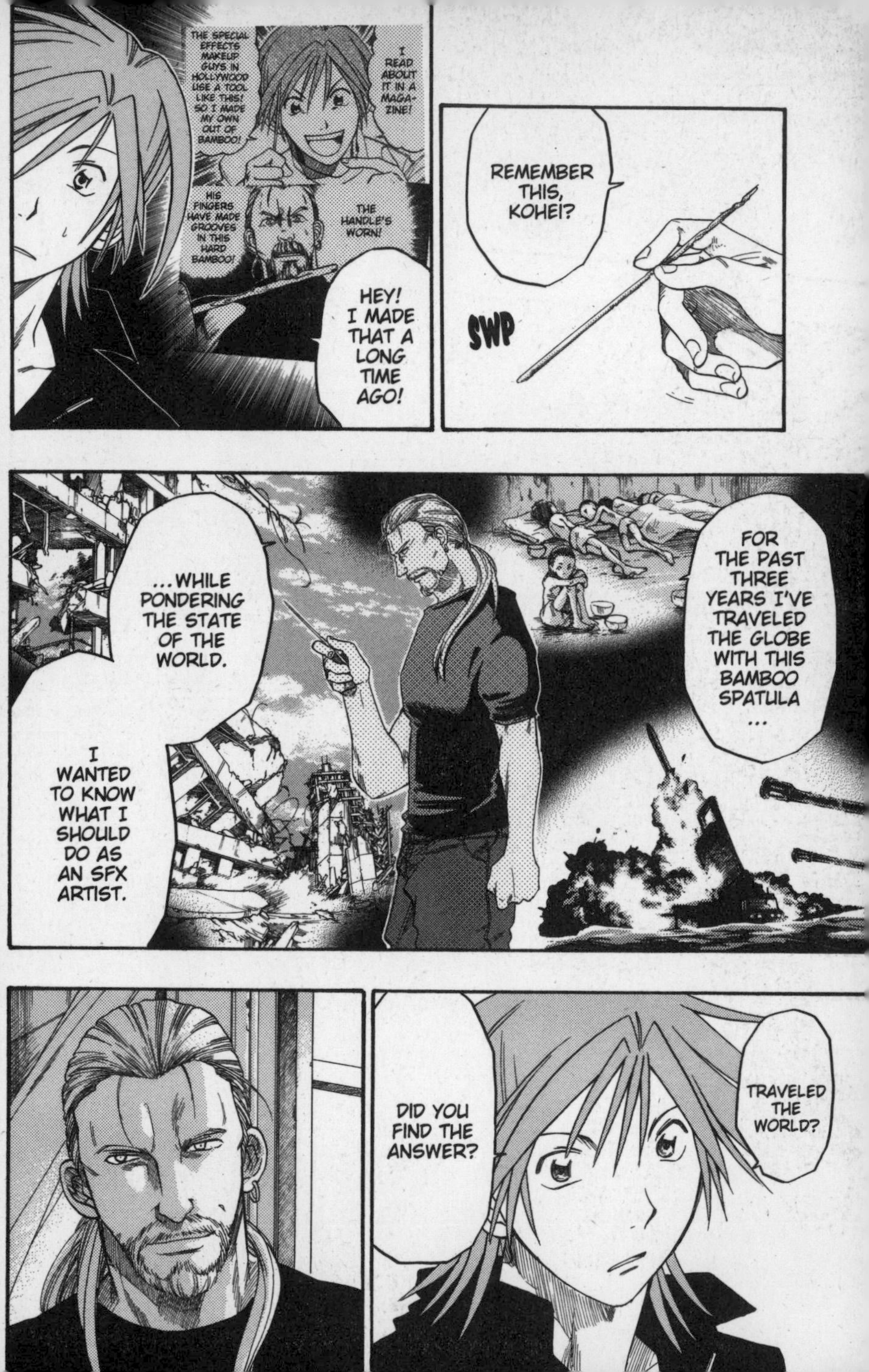
REMEMBER THIS, KOHEI?
SWP
I READ ABOUT IT IN A MAGAZINE!
THE SPECIAL EFFECTS MAKEUP GUYS IN HOLLYWOOD USE A TOOL LIKE THIS! SO I MADE MY OWN OUT OF BAMBOO!
THE HANDLE'S WORN!
HIS FINGERS HAVE MADE GROOVES IN THIS HARD BAMBOO!
HEY! I MADE THAT A LONG TIME AGO!
FOR THE PAST THREE YEARS I'VE TRAVELED THE GLOBE WITH THIS BAMBOO SPATULA ...
...WHILE PONDERING THE STATE OF THE WORLD.
I WANTED TO KNOW WHAT I SHOULD DO AS AN SFX ARTIST.
TRAVELED THE WORLD?
DID YOU FIND THE ANSWER?

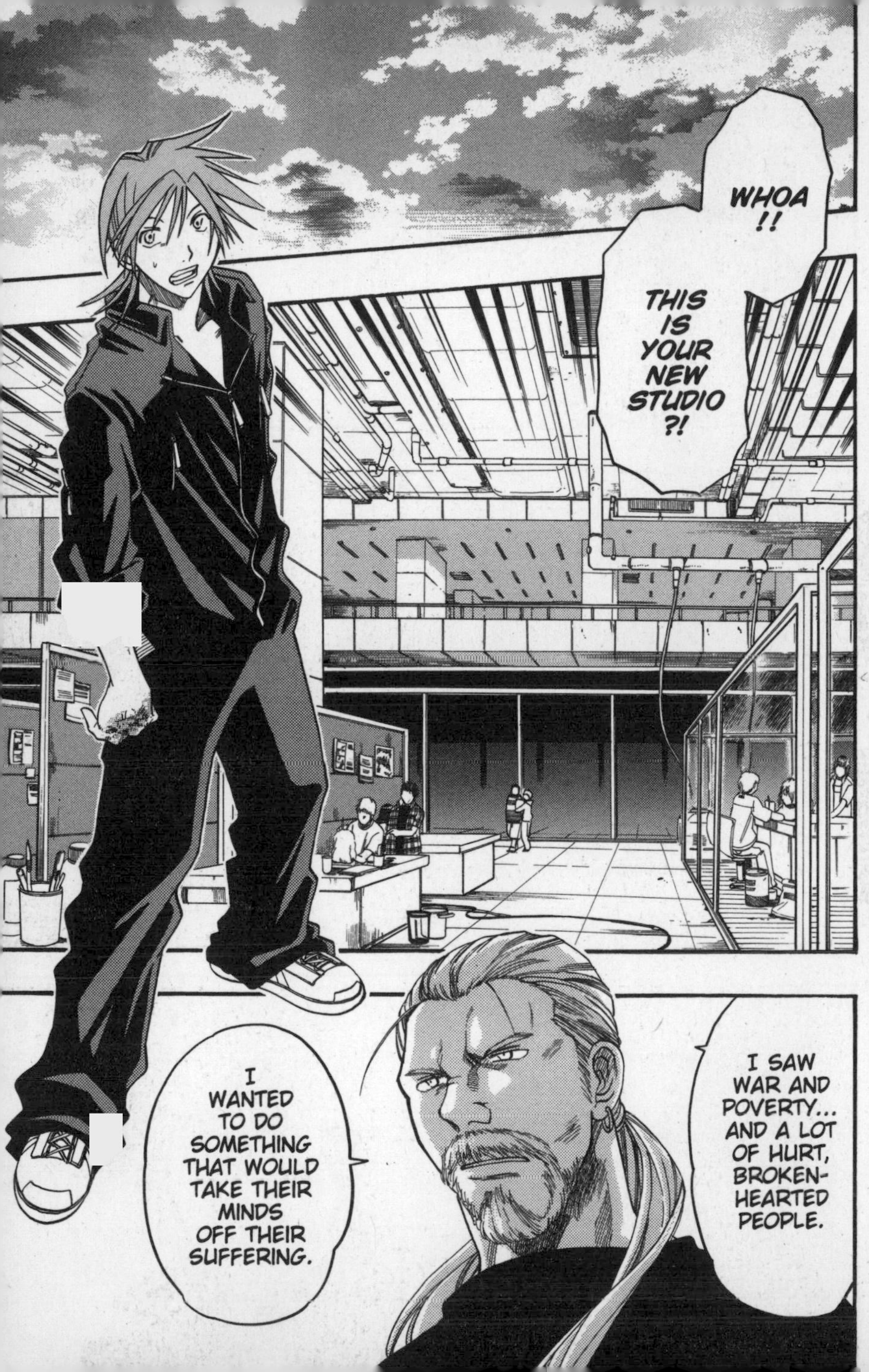
WHOA!!
THIS IS YOUR NEW STUDIO?!
I SAW WAR AND POVERTY... AND A LOT OF HURT, BROKEN-HEARTED PEOPLE.
I WANTED TO DO SOMETHING THAT WOULD TAKE THEIR MINDS OFF THEIR SUFFERING.

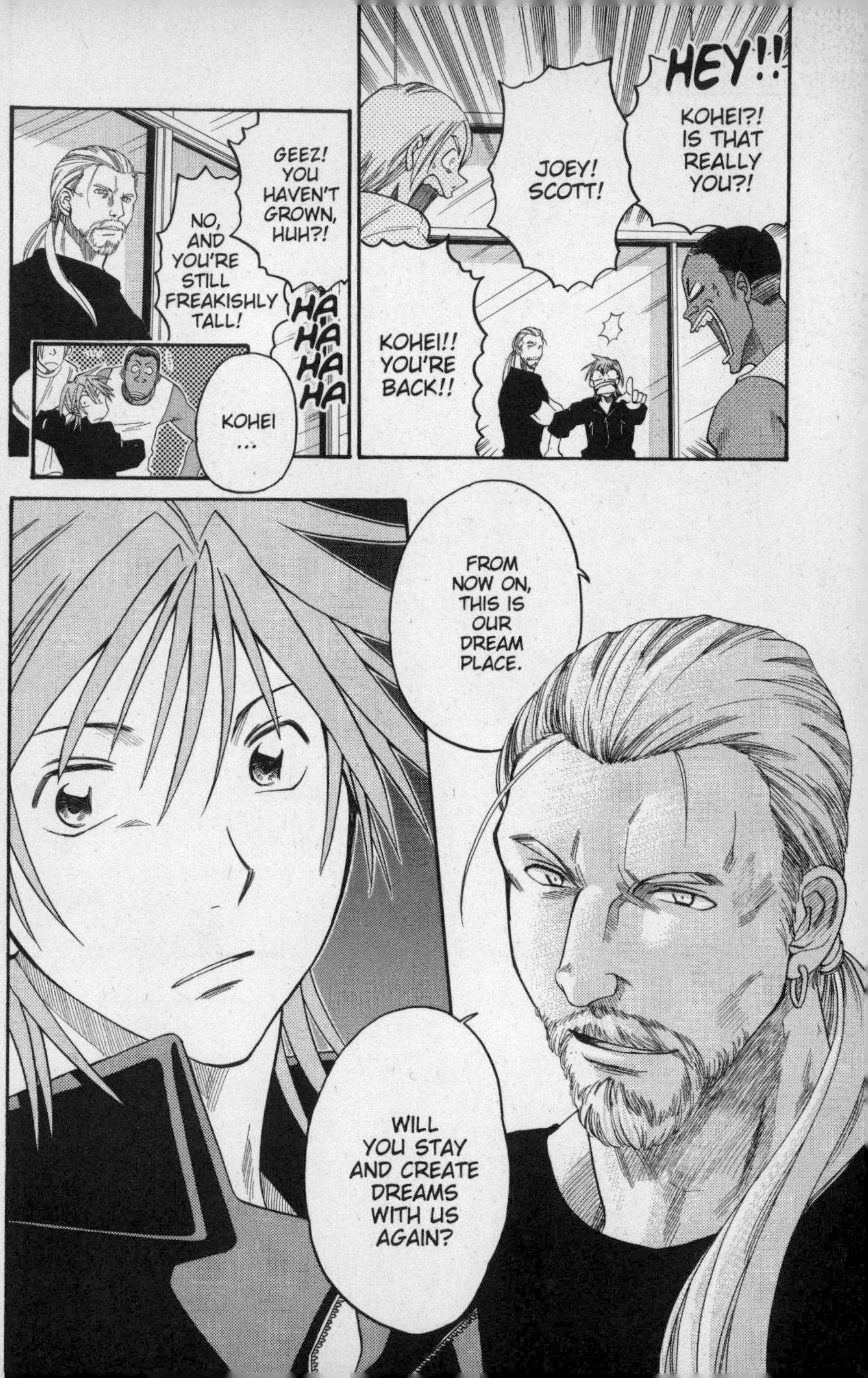
HEY!!
KOHEI?! IS THAT REALLY YOU?!
JOEY! SCOTT!
KOHEI!! YOU'RE BACK!!
GEEZ! YOU HAVEN'T GROWN, HUH?!
NO, AND YOU'RE STILL FREAKISHLY TALL!
HA HA HA HA
KOHEI ...
FROM NOW ON, THIS IS OUR DREAM PLACE.
WILL YOU STAY AND CREATE DREAMS WITH US AGAIN?

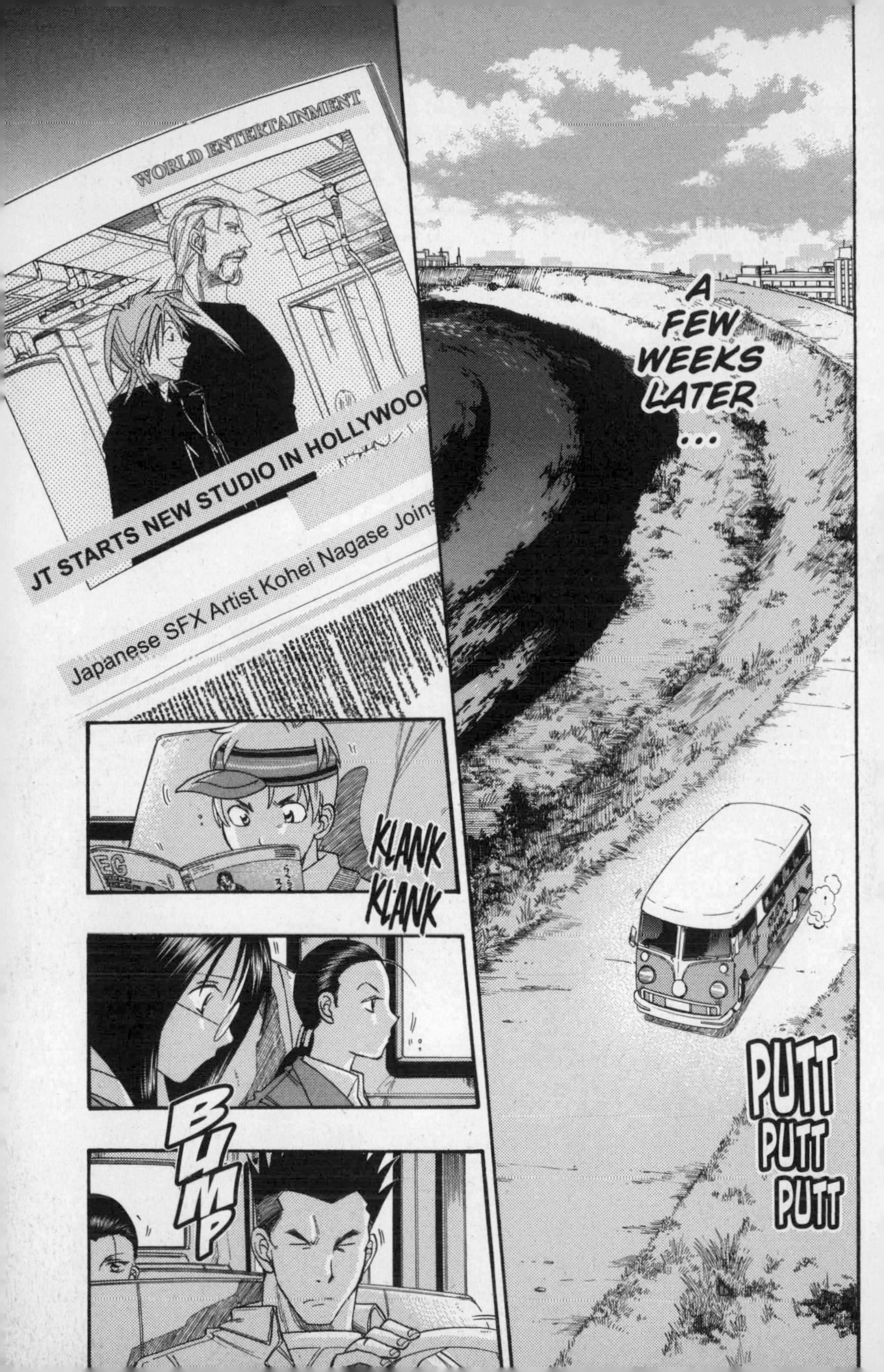
A FEW WEEKS LATER...
PUTT PUTT PUTT
WORLD ENTERTAINMENT
JT STARTS NEW STUDIO IN HOLLYWOO
Japanese SFX Artist Kohei Nagase Joins
KLANK KLANK
BUMP

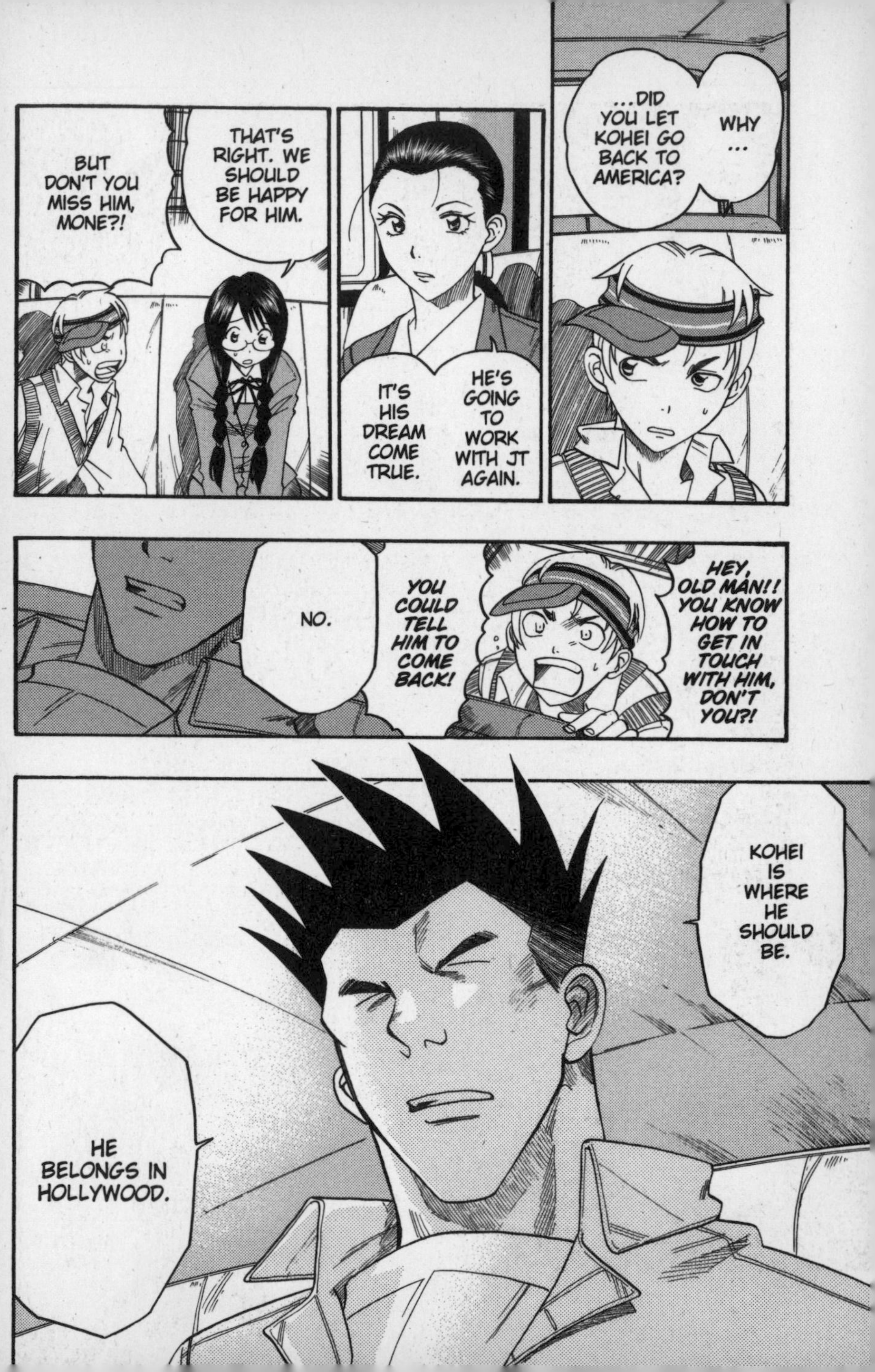
WHY ...
...DID YOU LET KOHEI GO BACK TO AMERICA?
HE'S GOING TO WORK WITH JT AGAIN.
IT'S HIS DREAM COME TRUE.
THAT'S RIGHT. WE SHOULD BE HAPPY FOR HIM.
BUT DON'T YOU MISS HIM, MONE?!
HEY, OLD MAN!! YOU KNOW HOW TO GET IN TOUCH WITH HIM, DON'T YOU?!
YOU COULD TELL HIM TO COME BACK!
NO.
KOHEI IS WHERE HE SHOULD BE.
HE BELONGS IN HOLLYWOOD.

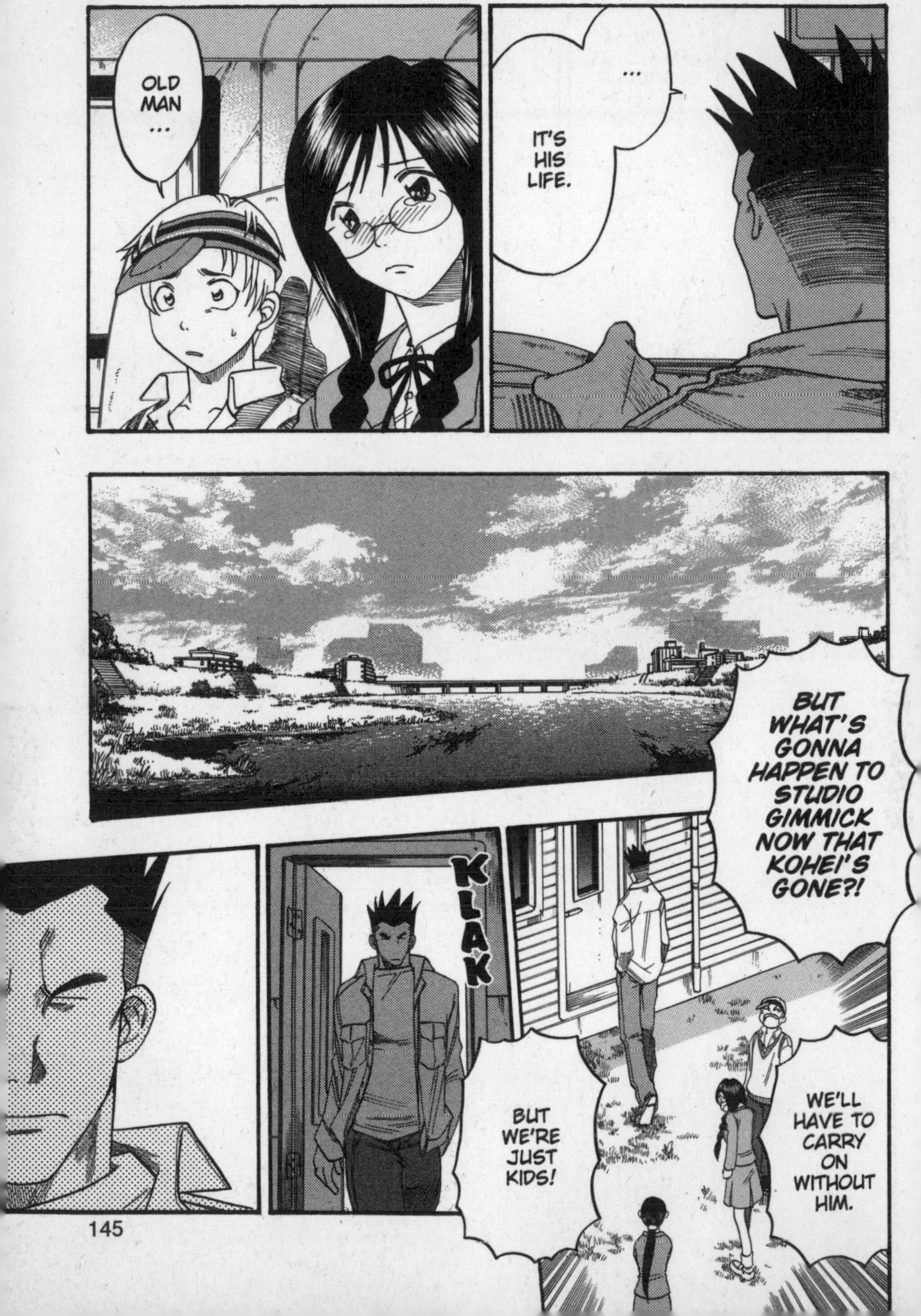

...
IT'S HIS LIFE.
OLD MAN ...
BUT WHAT'S GONNA HAPPEN TO STUDIO GIMMICK NOW THAT KOHEI'S GONE?!
WE'LL HAVE TO CARRY ON WITHOUT HIM.
BUT WE'RE JUST KIDS!
KLAK

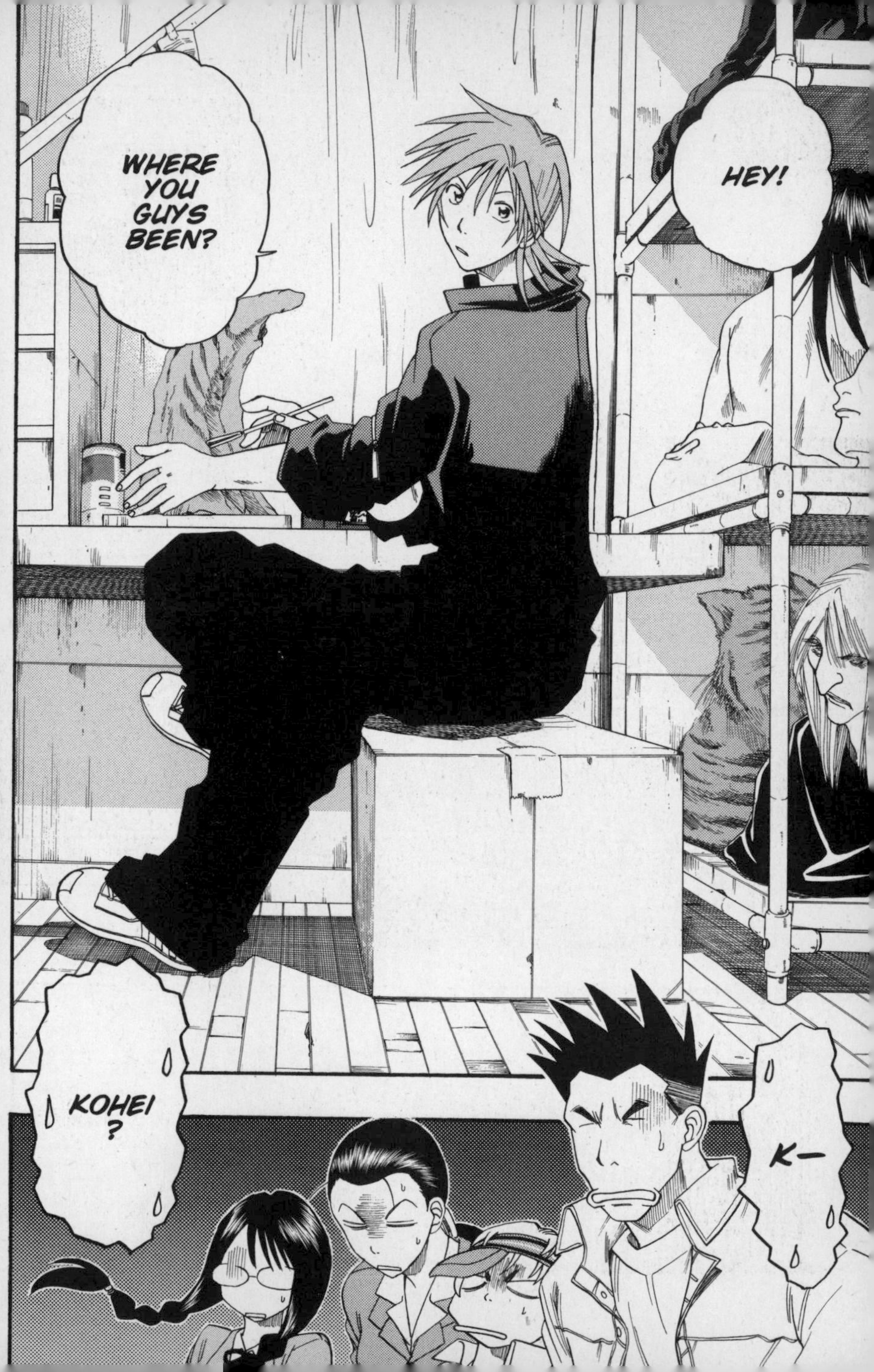
HEY!
WHERE YOU GUYS BEEN?
K—
KOHEI ?

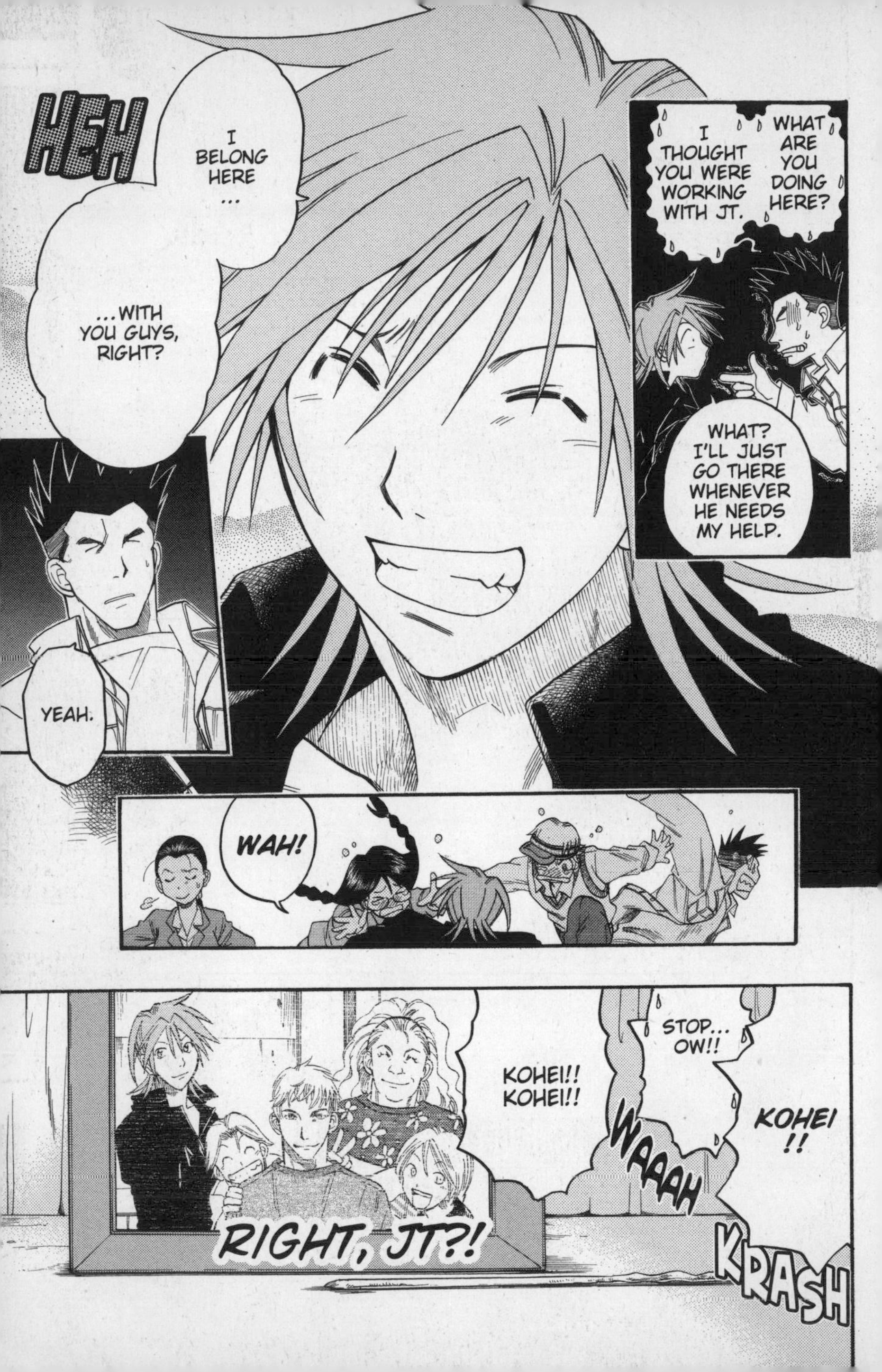
WHAT ARE YOU DOING HERE?
I THOUGHT YOU WERE WORKING WITH JT.
WHAT? I'LL JUST GO THERE WHENEVER HE NEEDS MY HELP.
HEH
I BELONG HERE ...
...WITH YOU GUYS, RIGHT?
YEAH.
WAH!
STOP... OW!!
KOHEI !!
WAAAAH
KOHEI!! KOHEI!!
RIGHT, JT?!
KRASH

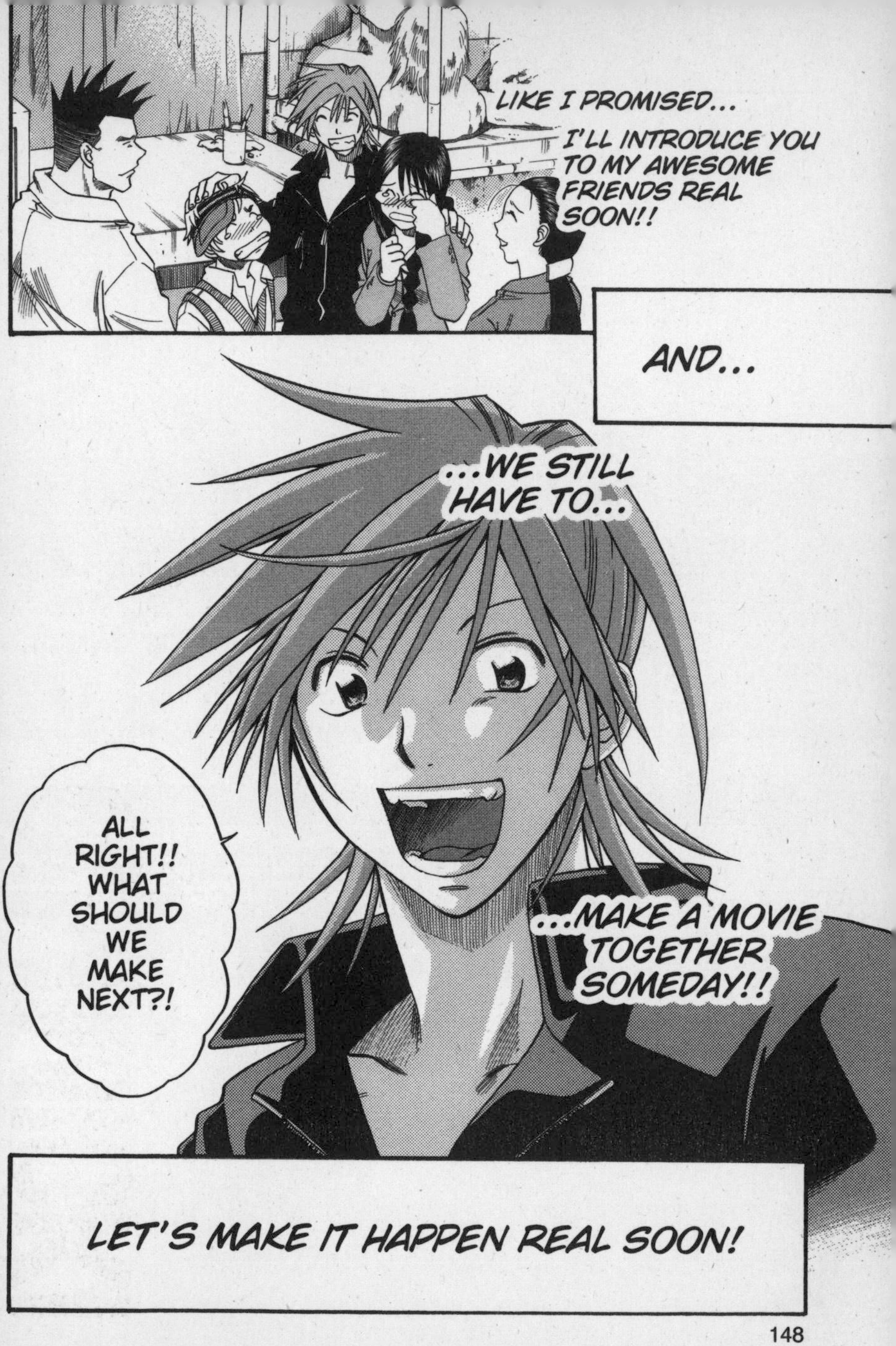
LIKE I PROMISED...
I'LL INTRODUCE YOU TO MY AWESOME FRIENDS REAL SOON!!
AND...
...WE STILL HAVE TO...
...MAKE A MOVIE TOGETHER SOMEDAY!!
ALL RIGHT!! WHAT SHOULD WE MAKE NEXT?!
LET'S MAKE IT HAPPEN REAL SOON!

GIMMICK!

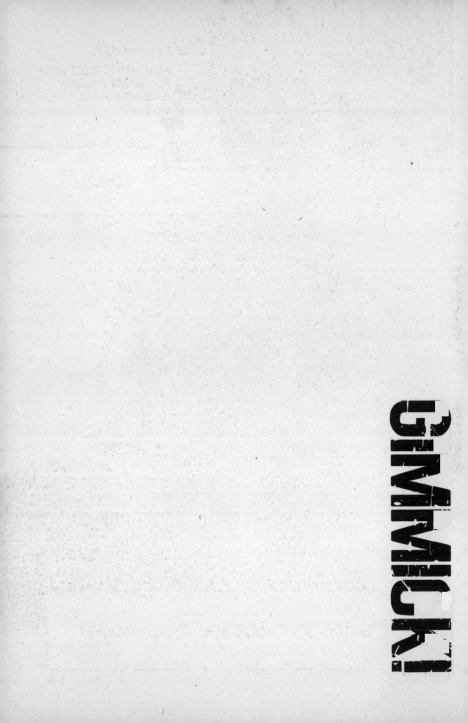

Scene EX2: Fame

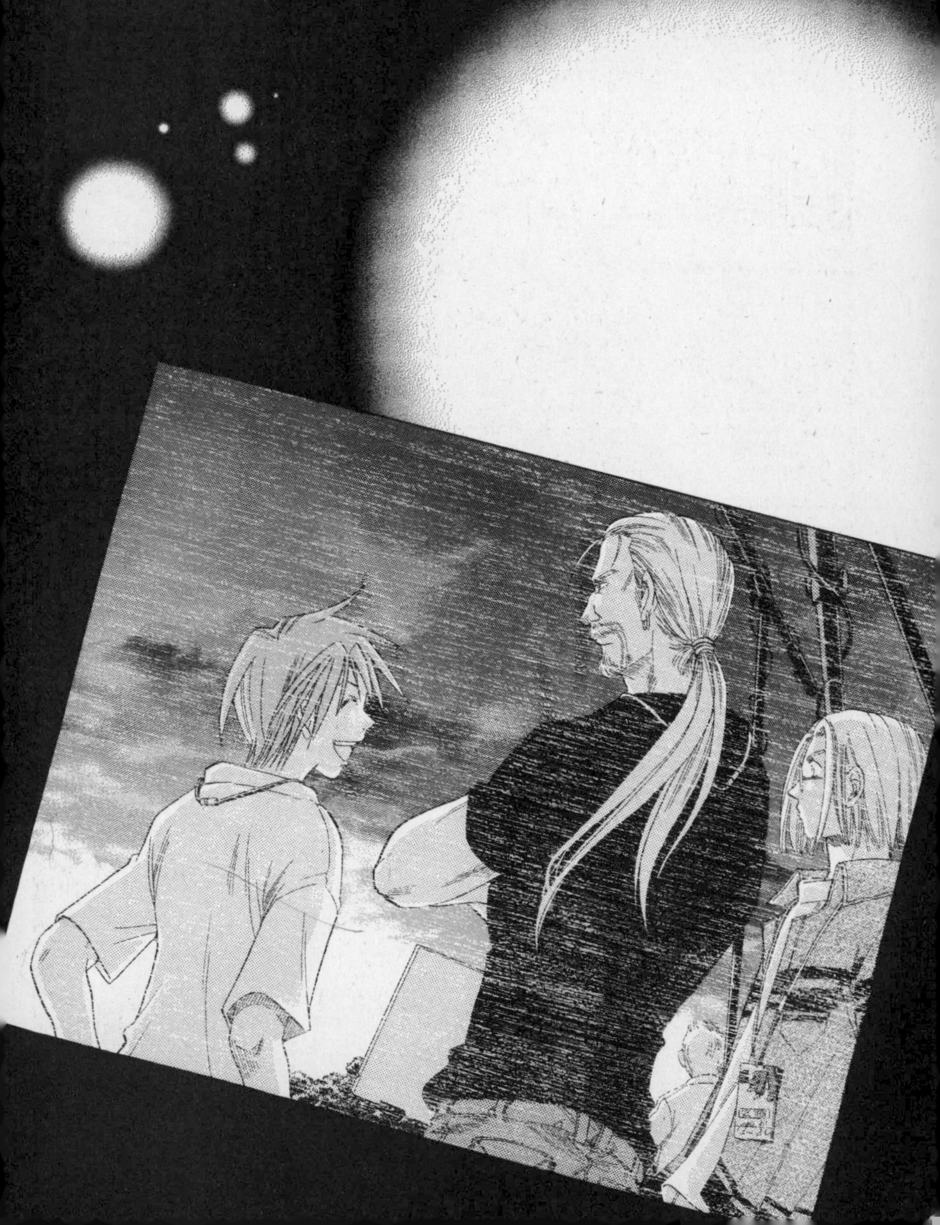

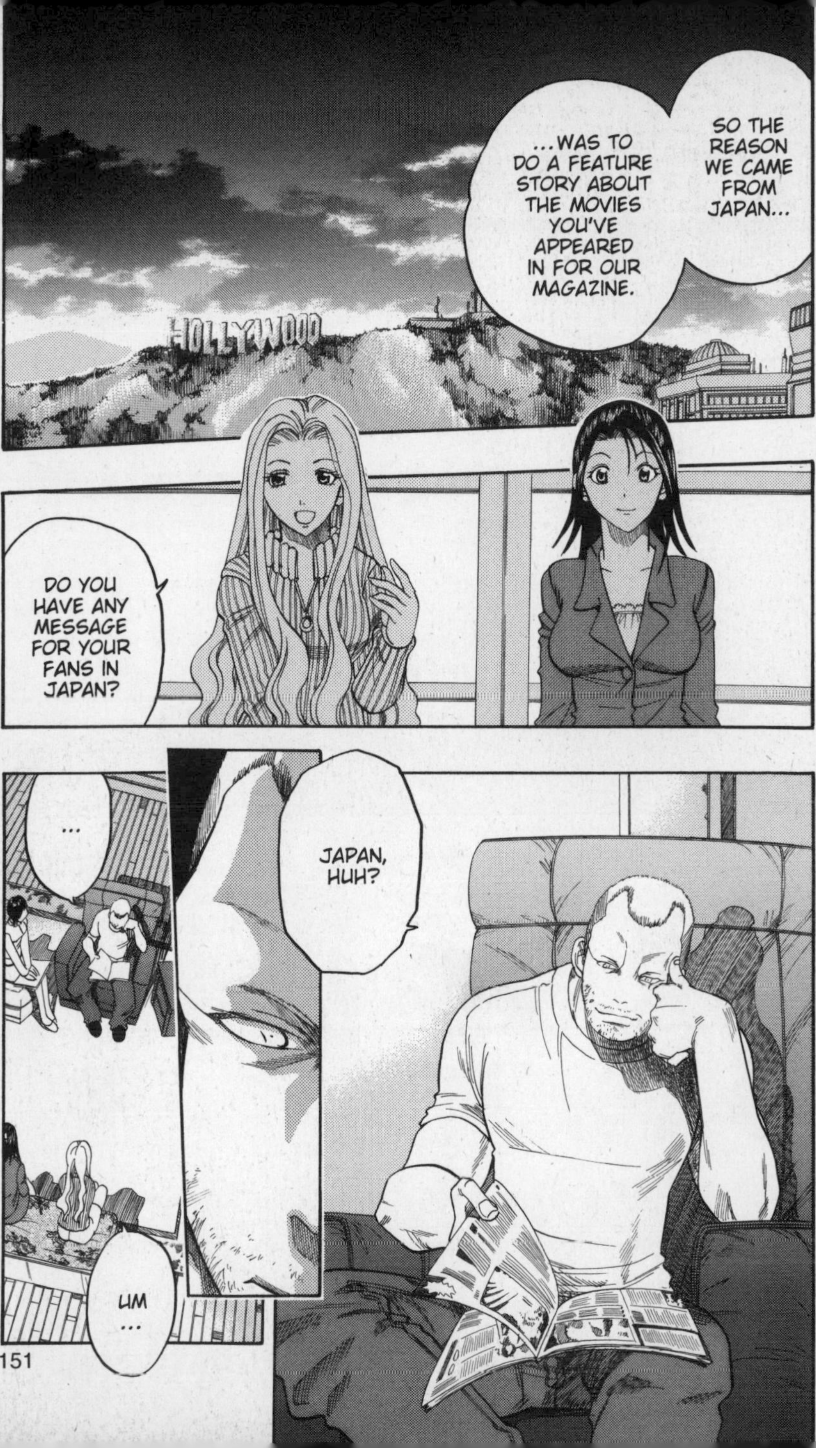
SO THE REASON WE CAME FROM JAPAN...
...WAS TO DO A FEATURE STORY ABOUT THE MOVIES YOU'VE APPEARED IN FOR OUR MAGAZINE.
DO YOU HAVE ANY MESSAGE FOR YOUR FANS IN JAPAN?
JAPAN, HUH?
...
UM ...

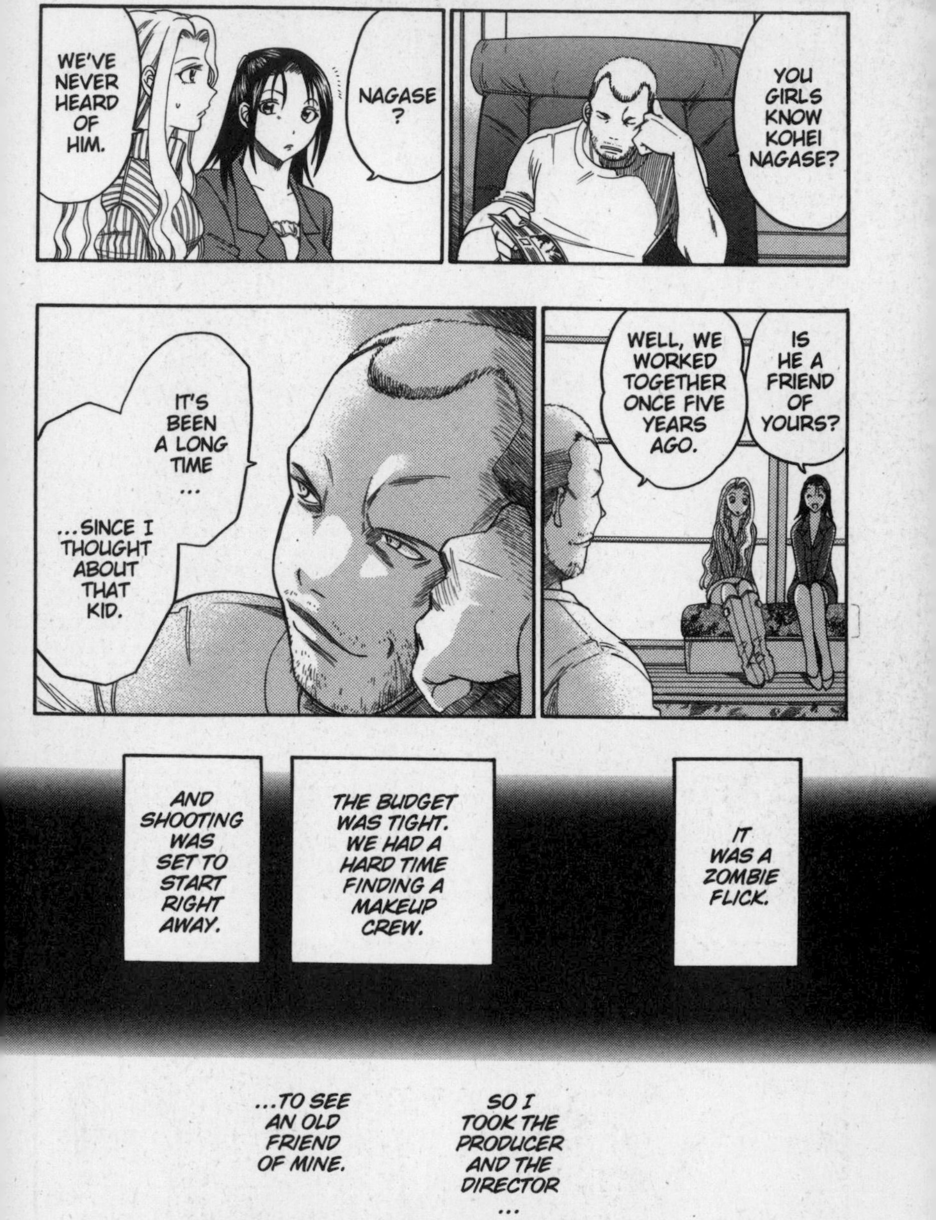
YOU GIRLS KNOW KOHEI NAGASE?
NAGASE?
WE'VE NEVER HEARD OF HIM.
IS HE A FRIEND OF YOURS?
WELL, WE WORKED TOGETHER ONCE FIVE YEARS AGO.
IT'S BEEN A LONG TIME...
...SINCE I THOUGHT ABOUT THAT KID.
IT WAS A ZOMBIE FLICK.
THE BUDGET WAS TIGHT. WE HAD A HARD TIME FINDING A MAKEUP CREW.
AND SHOOTING WAS SET TO START RIGHT AWAY.
SO I TOOK THE PRODUCER AND THE DIRECTOR...
...TO SEE AN OLD FRIEND OF MINE.

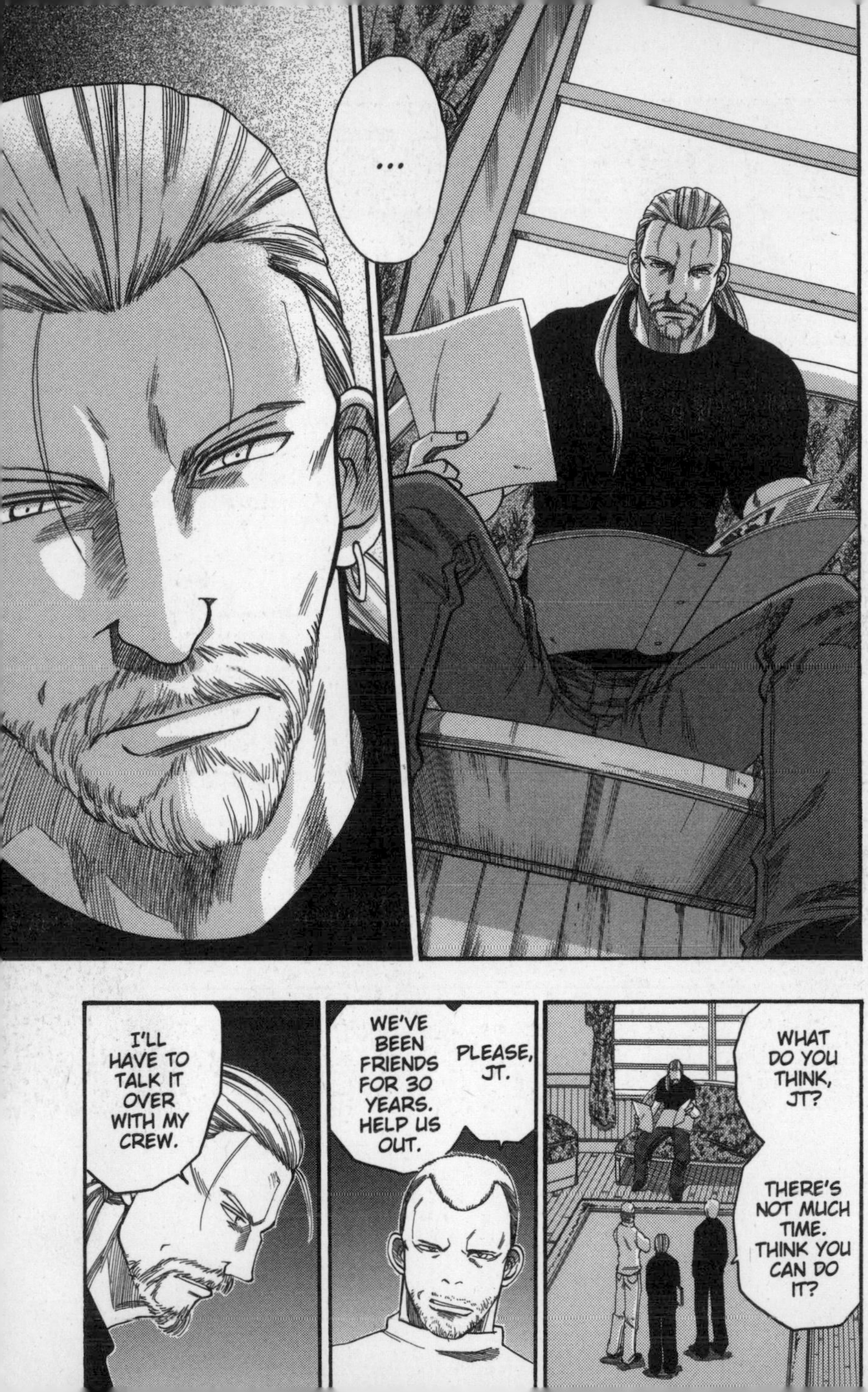
...
WHAT DO YOU THINK, JT?
THERE'S NOT MUCH TIME. THINK YOU CAN DO IT?
PLEASE, JT.
WE'VE BEEN FRIENDS FOR 30 YEARS. HELP US OUT.
I'LL HAVE TO TALK IT OVER WITH MY CREW.

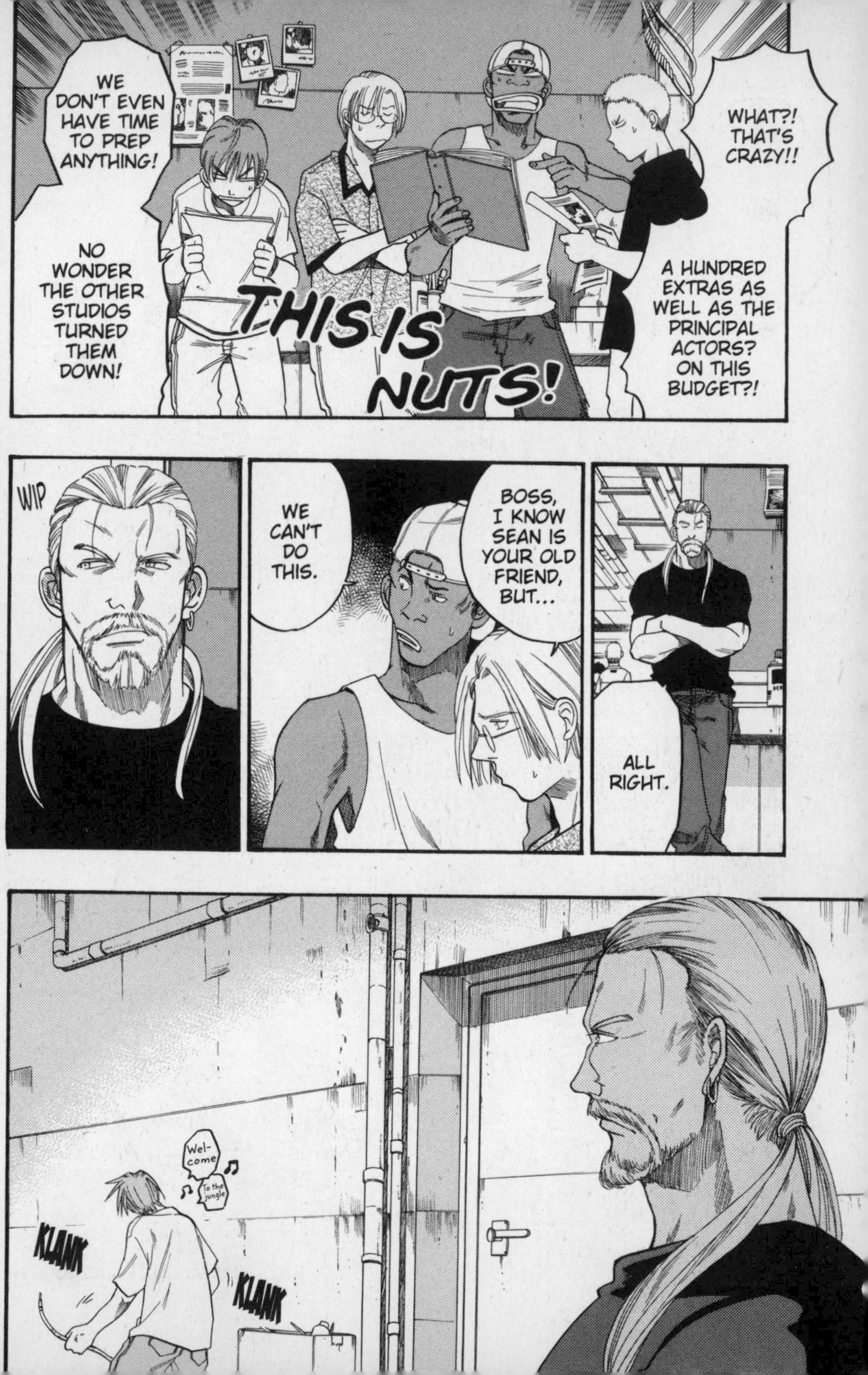
WHAT?! THAT'S CRAZY!!
A HUNDRED EXTRAS AS WELL AS THE PRINCIPAL ACTORS? ON THIS BUDGET?!
THIS IS NUTS!
WE DON'T EVEN HAVE TIME TO PREP ANYTHING!
NO WONDER THE OTHER STUDIOS TURNED THEM DOWN!
ALL RIGHT.
BOSS, I KNOW SEAN IS YOUR OLD FRIEND, BUT...
WE CAN'T DO THIS.
WIP
Wel-come
To the jungle
KLANK
KLANK

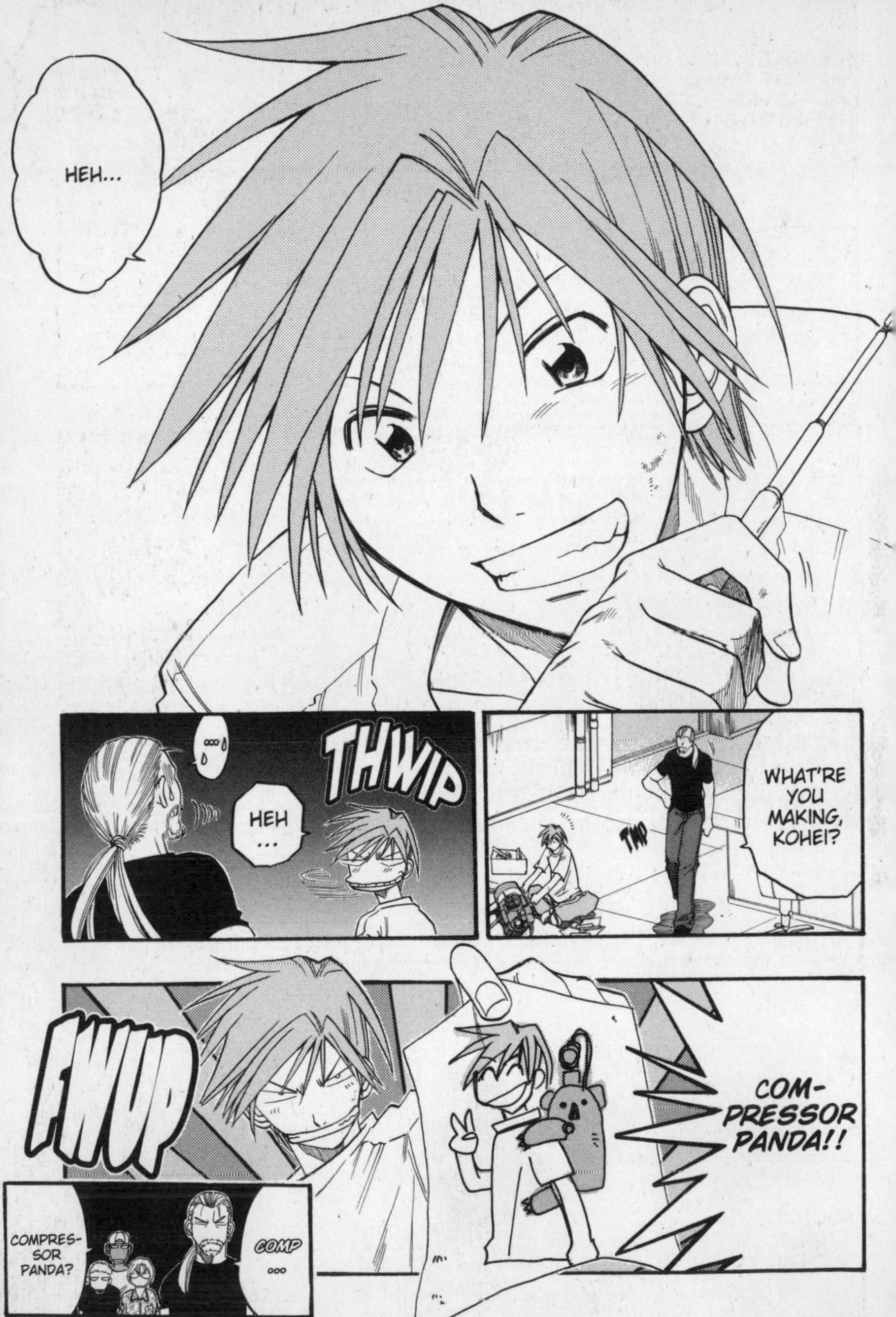
HEH...
WHAT'RE YOU MAKING, KOHEI?
TMP
THWIP
...
HEH ...
FWUP
COM-PRESSOR PANDA!!
COMP ...
COMPRES-SOR PANDA?

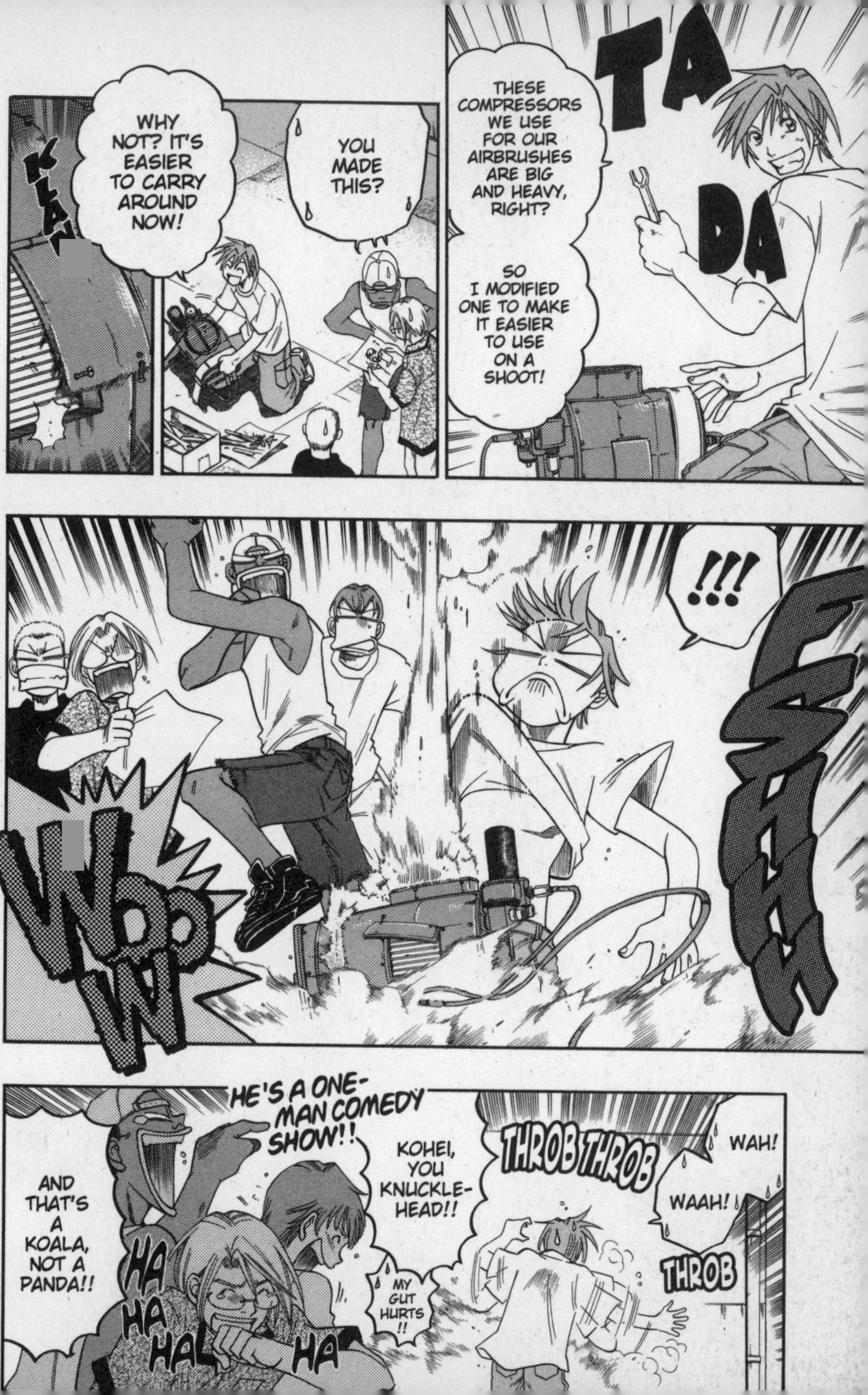
TA DA
THESE COMPRESSORS WE USE FOR OUR AIRBRUSHES ARE BIG AND HEAVY, RIGHT?
SO I MODIFIED ONE TO MAKE IT EASIER TO USE ON A SHOOT!
YOU MADE THIS?
WHY NOT? IT'S EASIER TO CARRY AROUND NOW!
KLAN
!!!
WAH!
WAAH!
THROB THROB
THROB
HE'S A ONE-MAN COMEDY SHOW!!
KOHEI, YOU KNUCKLE-HEAD!!
AND THAT'S A KOALA, NOT A PANDA!!
MY GUT HURTS!!
HA HA HA HA

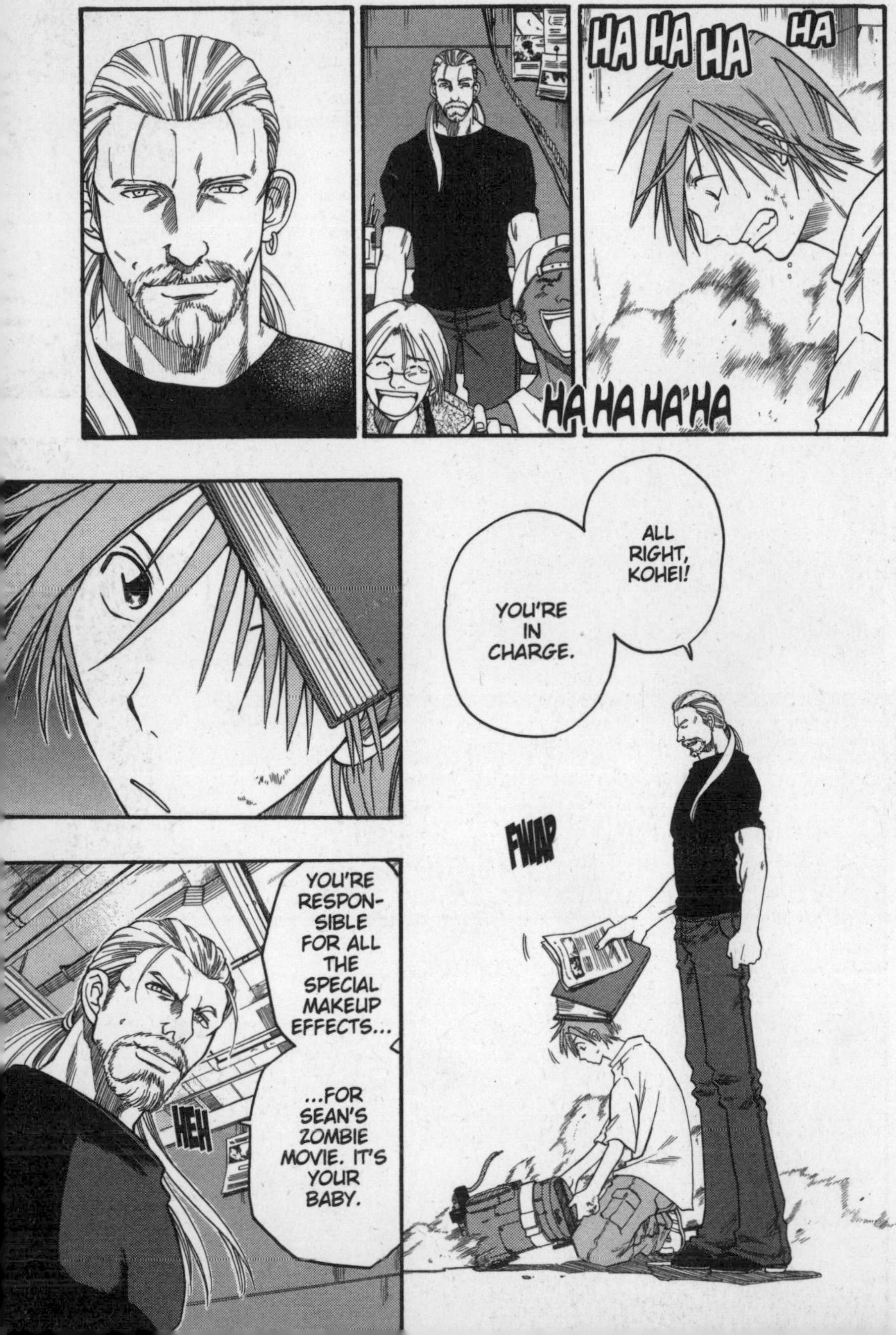
HA HA HA HA
HA HA HA HA
ALL RIGHT, KOHEI!
YOU'RE IN CHARGE.
FWAP
YOU'RE RESPON-SIBLE FOR ALL THE SPECIAL MAKEUP EFFECTS...
HEH
...FOR SEAN'S ZOMBIE MOVIE. IT'S YOUR BABY.

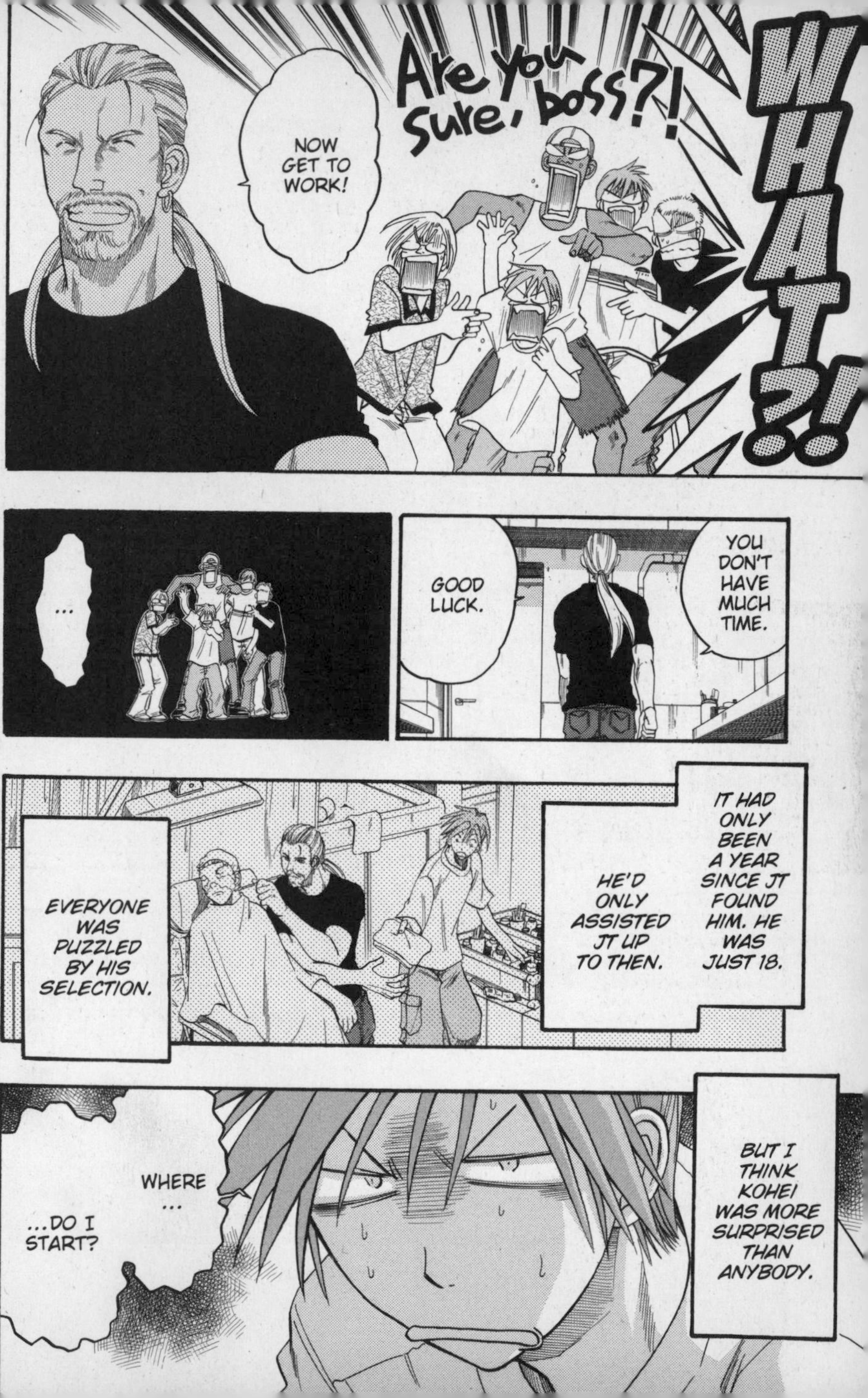
WHAT?!
Are you sure, boss?!
NOW GET TO WORK!
YOU DON'T HAVE MUCH TIME.
GOOD LUCK.
...
IT HAD ONLY BEEN A YEAR SINCE JT FOUND HIM. HE WAS JUST 18.
HE'D ONLY ASSISTED JT UP TO THEN.
EVERYONE WAS PUZZLED BY HIS SELECTION.
BUT I THINK KOHEI WAS MORE SURPRISED THAN ANYBODY.
WHERE...
...DO I START?

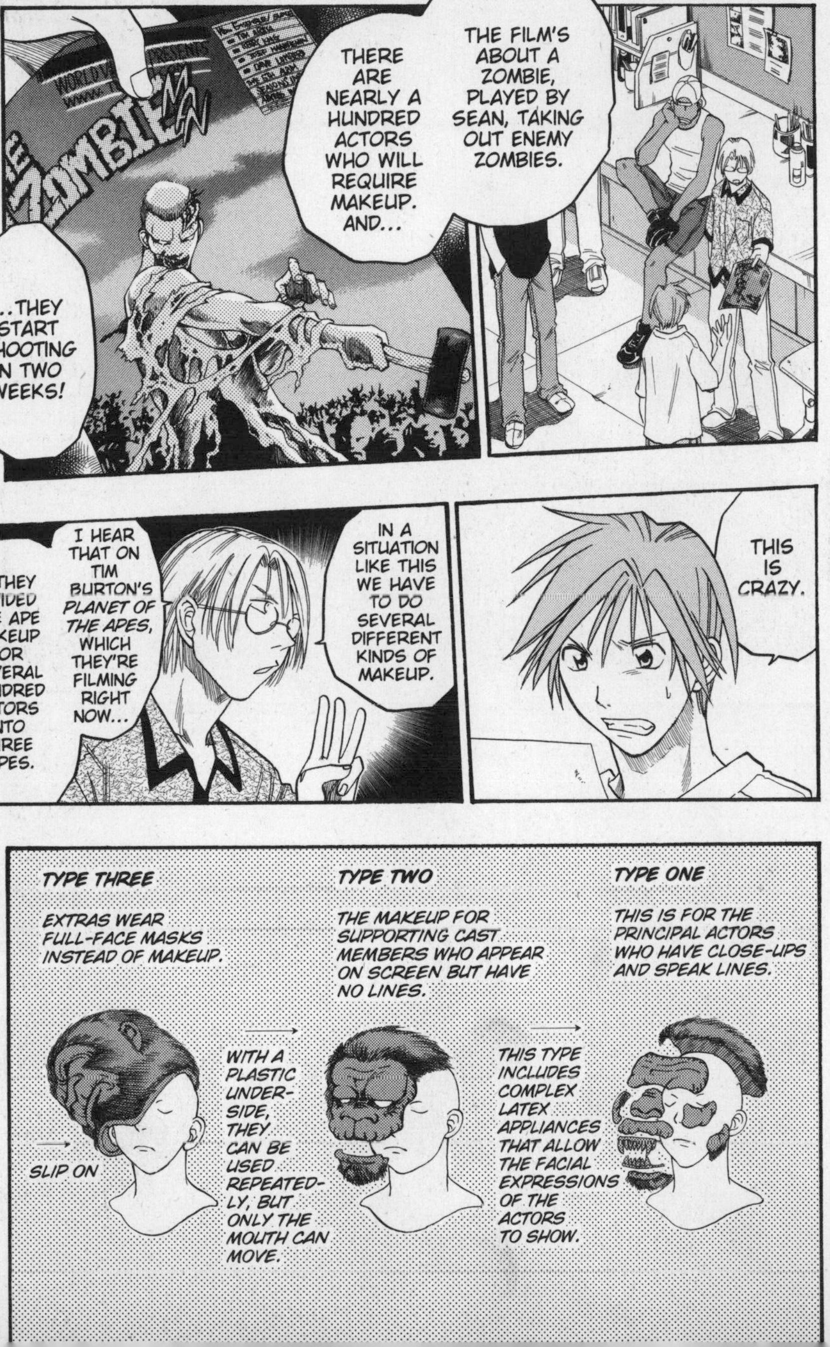
THE FILM'S ABOUT A ZOMBIE, PLAYED BY SEAN, TAKING OUT ENEMY ZOMBIES.
THERE ARE NEARLY A HUNDRED ACTORS WHO WILL REQUIRE MAKEUP. AND...
...THEY START SHOOTING IN TWO WEEKS!
THIS IS CRAZY.
IN A SITUATION LIKE THIS WE HAVE TO DO SEVERAL DIFFERENT KINDS OF MAKEUP.
I HEAR THAT ON TIM BURTON'S *PLANET OF THE APES*, WHICH THEY'RE FILMING RIGHT NOW...
...THEY DIVIDED THE APE MAKEUP FOR SEVERAL HUNDRED ACTORS INTO THREE TYPES.
TYPE ONE
THIS IS FOR THE PRINCIPAL ACTORS WHO HAVE CLOSE-UPS AND SPEAK LINES.
THIS TYPE INCLUDES COMPLEX LATEX APPLIANCES THAT ALLOW THE FACIAL EXPRESSIONS OF THE ACTORS TO SHOW.
TYPE TWO
THE MAKEUP FOR SUPPORTING CAST MEMBERS WHO APPEAR ON SCREEN BUT HAVE NO LINES.
WITH A PLASTIC UNDER-SIDE, THEY CAN BE USED REPEATED-LY, BUT ONLY THE MOUTH CAN MOVE.
TYPE THREE
EXTRAS WEAR FULL-FACE MASKS INSTEAD OF MAKEUP.
SLIP ON

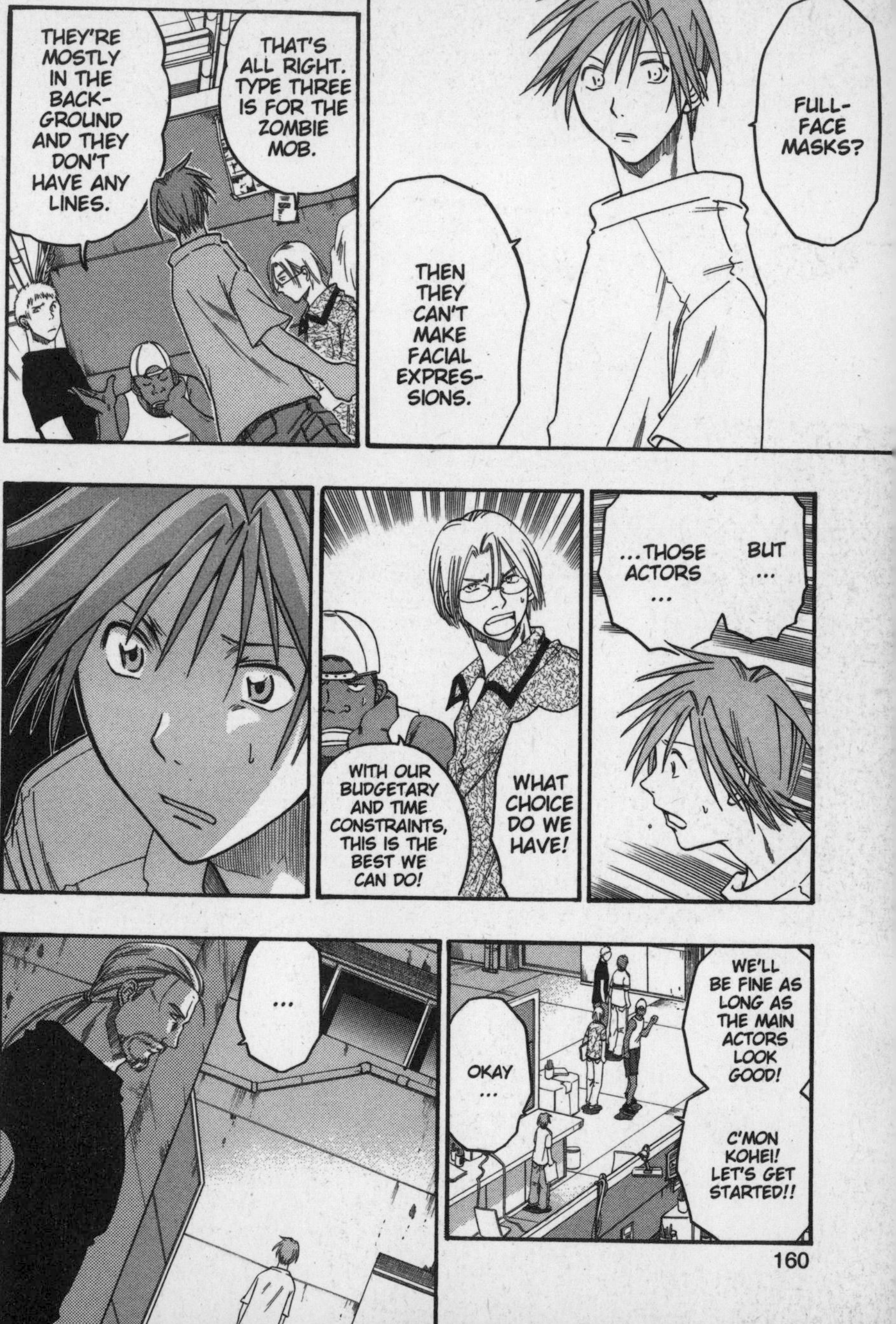
FULL-FACE MASKS?
THEN THEY CAN'T MAKE FACIAL EXPRESSIONS.
THAT'S ALL RIGHT. TYPE THREE IS FOR THE ZOMBIE MOB.
THEY'RE MOSTLY IN THE BACK-GROUND AND THEY DON'T HAVE ANY LINES.
BUT ...
...THOSE ACTORS ...
WHAT CHOICE DO WE HAVE!
WITH OUR BUDGETARY AND TIME CONSTRAINTS, THIS IS THE BEST WE CAN DO!
WE'LL BE FINE AS LONG AS THE MAIN ACTORS LOOK GOOD!
C'MON KOHEI! LET'S GET STARTED!!
OKAY ...
...

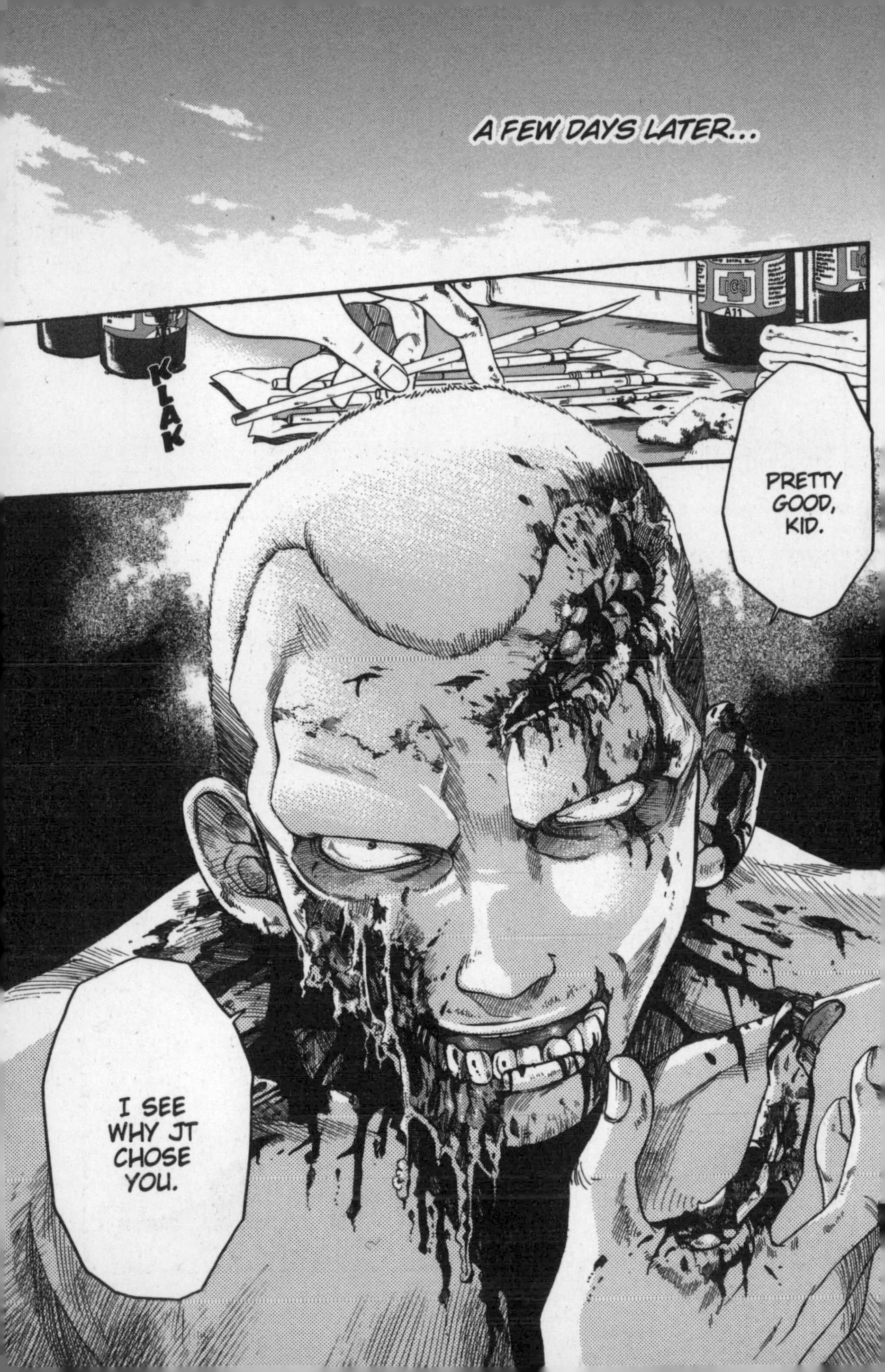
A FEW DAYS LATER...
KLAK
PRETTY GOOD, KID.
I SEE WHY JT CHOSE YOU.

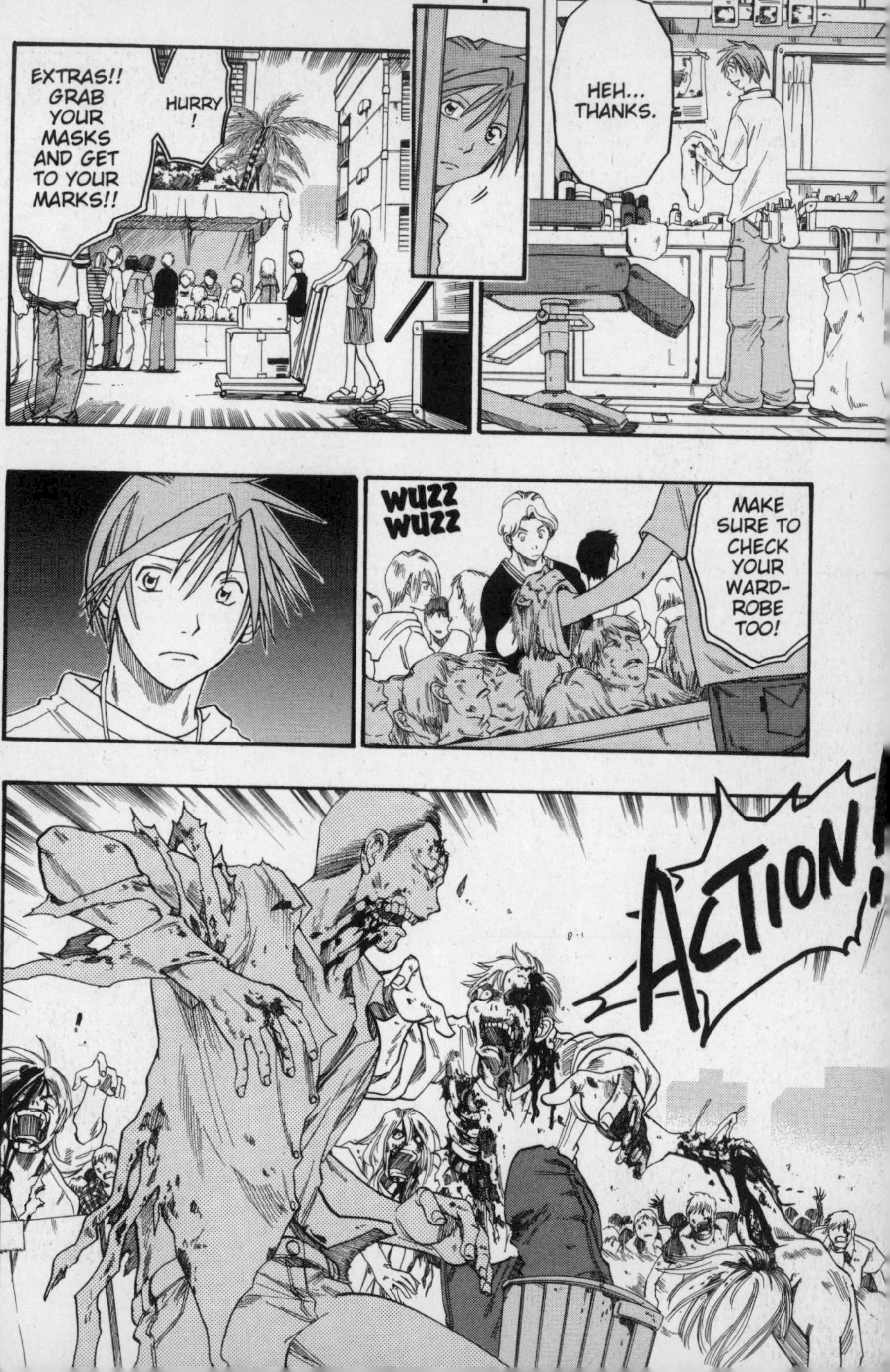
HEH... THANKS.
EXTRAS!! GRAB YOUR MASKS AND GET TO YOUR MARKS!!
HURRY!
MAKE SURE TO CHECK YOUR WARD-ROBE TOO!
WUZZ WUZZ
ACTION!

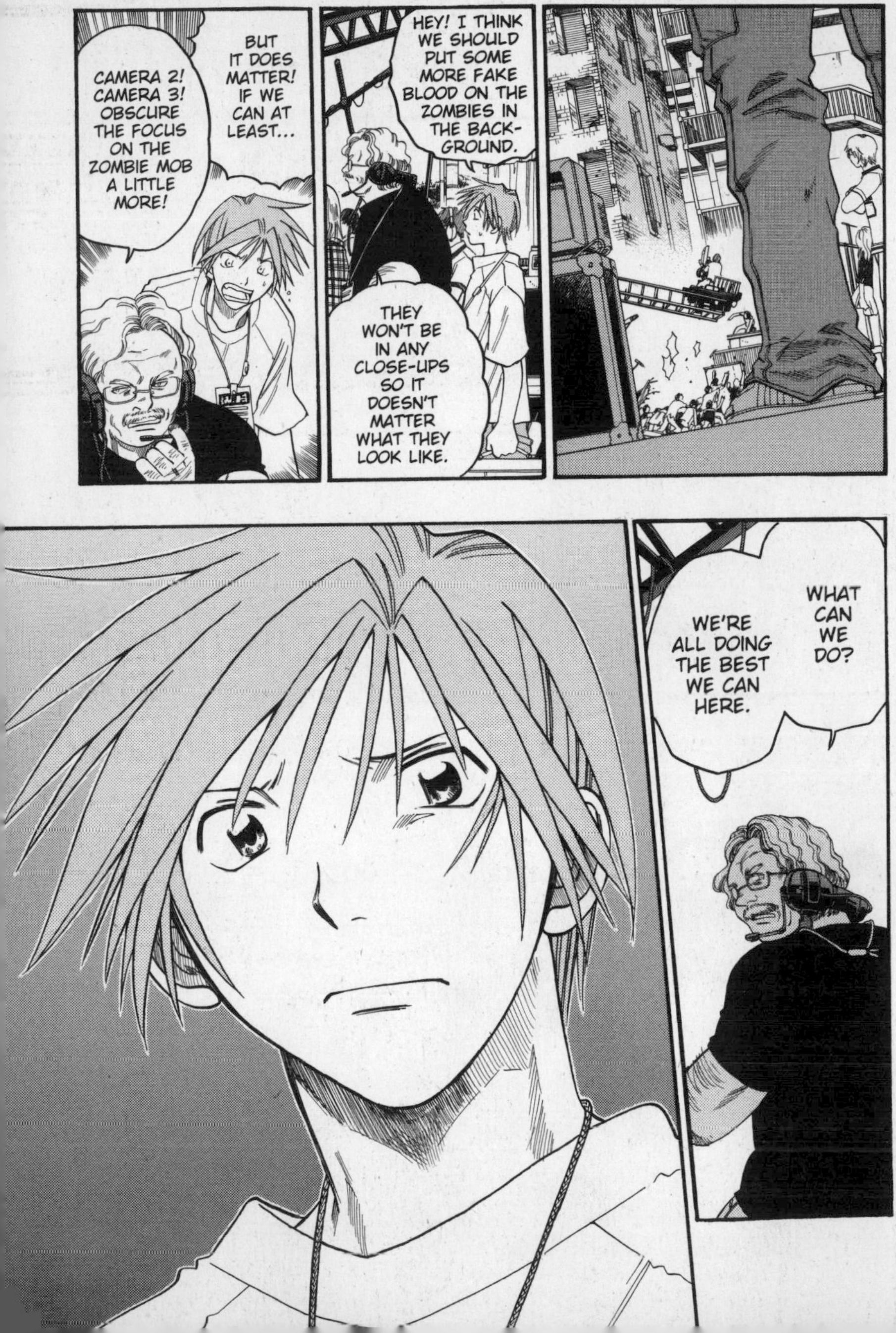
HEY! I THINK WE SHOULD PUT SOME MORE FAKE BLOOD ON THE ZOMBIES IN THE BACK-GROUND.
THEY WON'T BE IN ANY CLOSE-UPS SO IT DOESN'T MATTER WHAT THEY LOOK LIKE.
BUT IT DOES MATTER! IF WE CAN AT LEAST...
CAMERA 2! CAMERA 3! OBSCURE THE FOCUS ON THE ZOMBIE MOB A LITTLE MORE!
WHAT CAN WE DO?
WE'RE ALL DOING THE BEST WE CAN HERE.

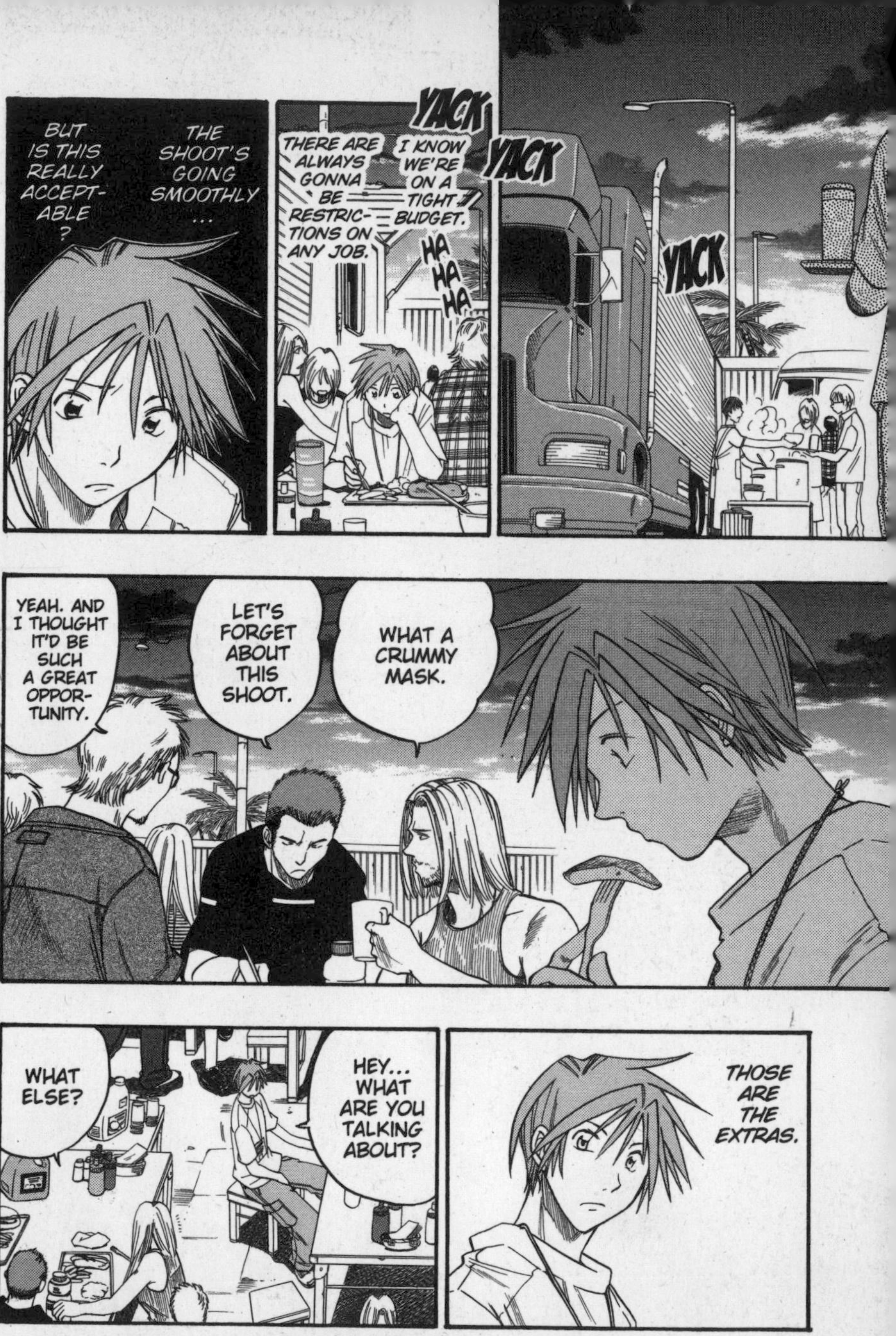
YACK
YACK
YACK
I KNOW WE'RE ON A TIGHT BUDGET.
THERE ARE ALWAYS GONNA BE RESTRICTIONS ON ANY JOB.
HA HA HA
THE SHOOT'S GOING SMOOTHLY...
BUT IS THIS REALLY ACCEPTABLE?
WHAT A CRUMMY MASK.
LET'S FORGET ABOUT THIS SHOOT.
YEAH. AND I THOUGHT IT'D BE SUCH A GREAT OPPORTUNITY.
THOSE ARE THE EXTRAS.
HEY... WHAT ARE YOU TALKING ABOUT?
WHAT ELSE?

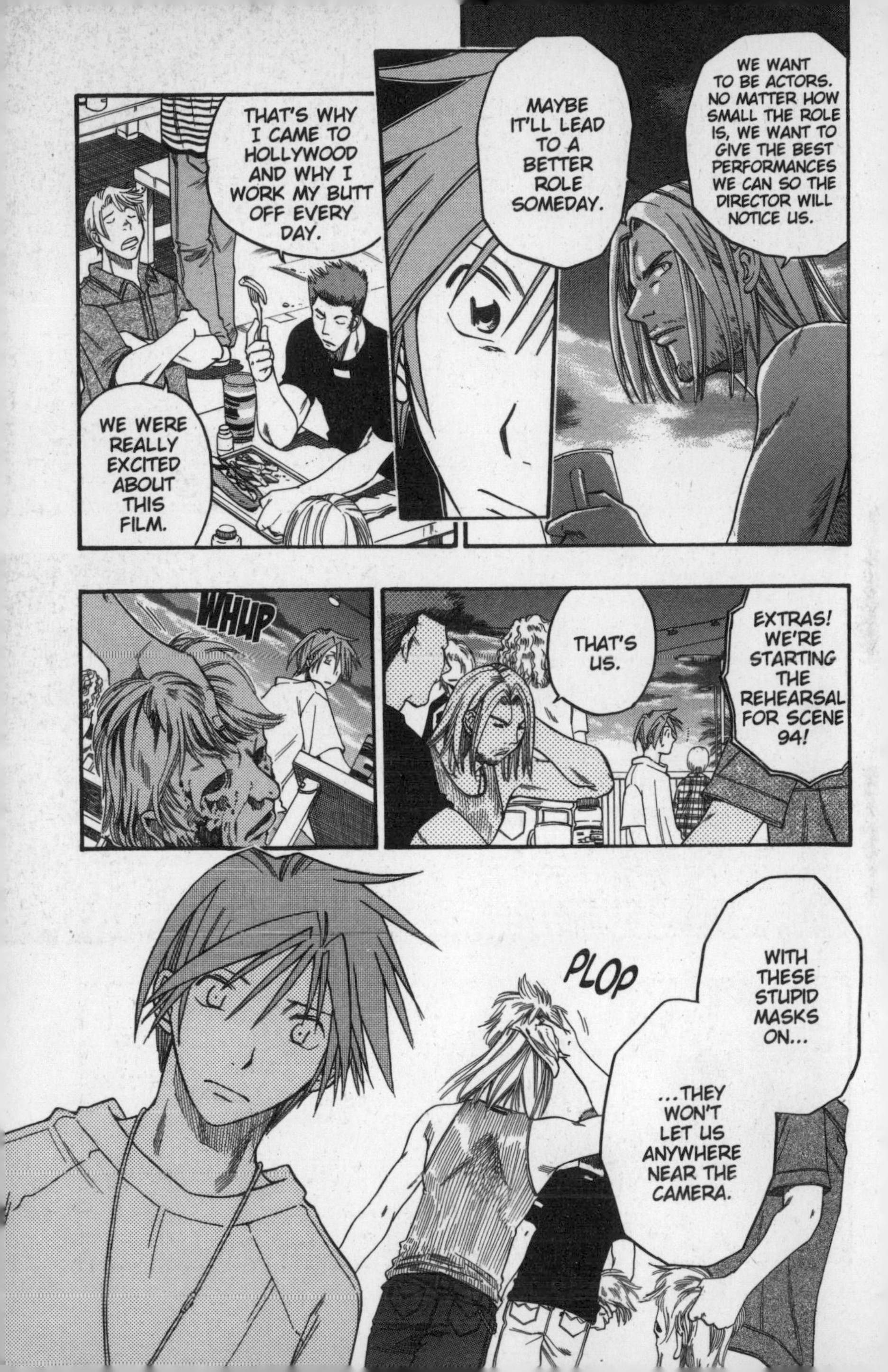
WE WANT TO BE ACTORS. NO MATTER HOW SMALL THE ROLE IS, WE WANT TO GIVE THE BEST PERFORMANCES WE CAN SO THE DIRECTOR WILL NOTICE US.
MAYBE IT'LL LEAD TO A BETTER ROLE SOMEDAY.
THAT'S WHY I CAME TO HOLLYWOOD AND WHY I WORK MY BUTT OFF EVERY DAY.
WE WERE REALLY EXCITED ABOUT THIS FILM.
EXTRAS! WE'RE STARTING THE REHEARSAL FOR SCENE 94!
THAT'S US.
WHUP
WITH THESE STUPID MASKS ON...
PLOP
...THEY WON'T LET US ANYWHERE NEAR THE CAMERA.

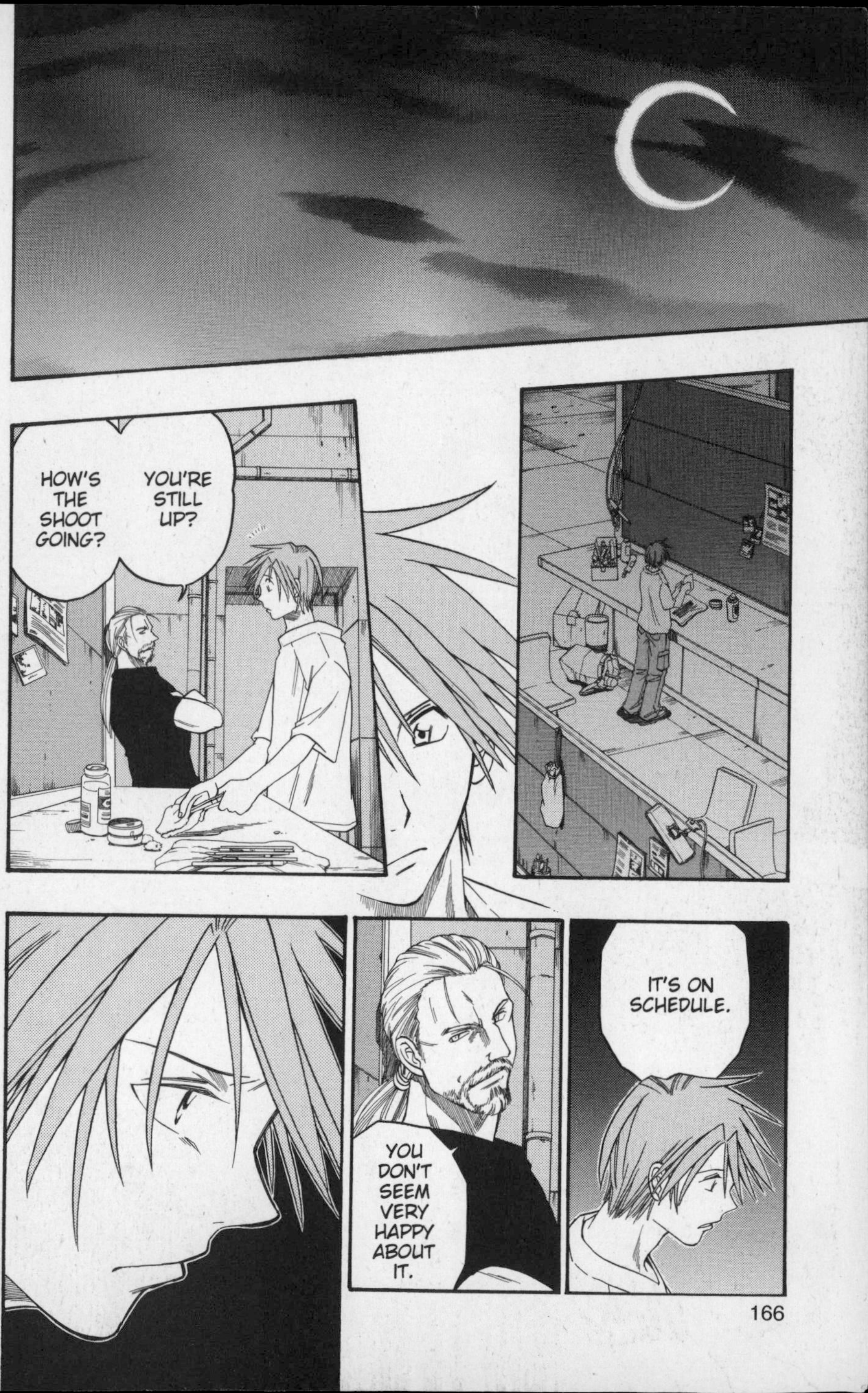
YOU'RE STILL UP?
HOW'S THE SHOOT GOING?
IT'S ON SCHEDULE.
YOU DON'T SEEM VERY HAPPY ABOUT IT.

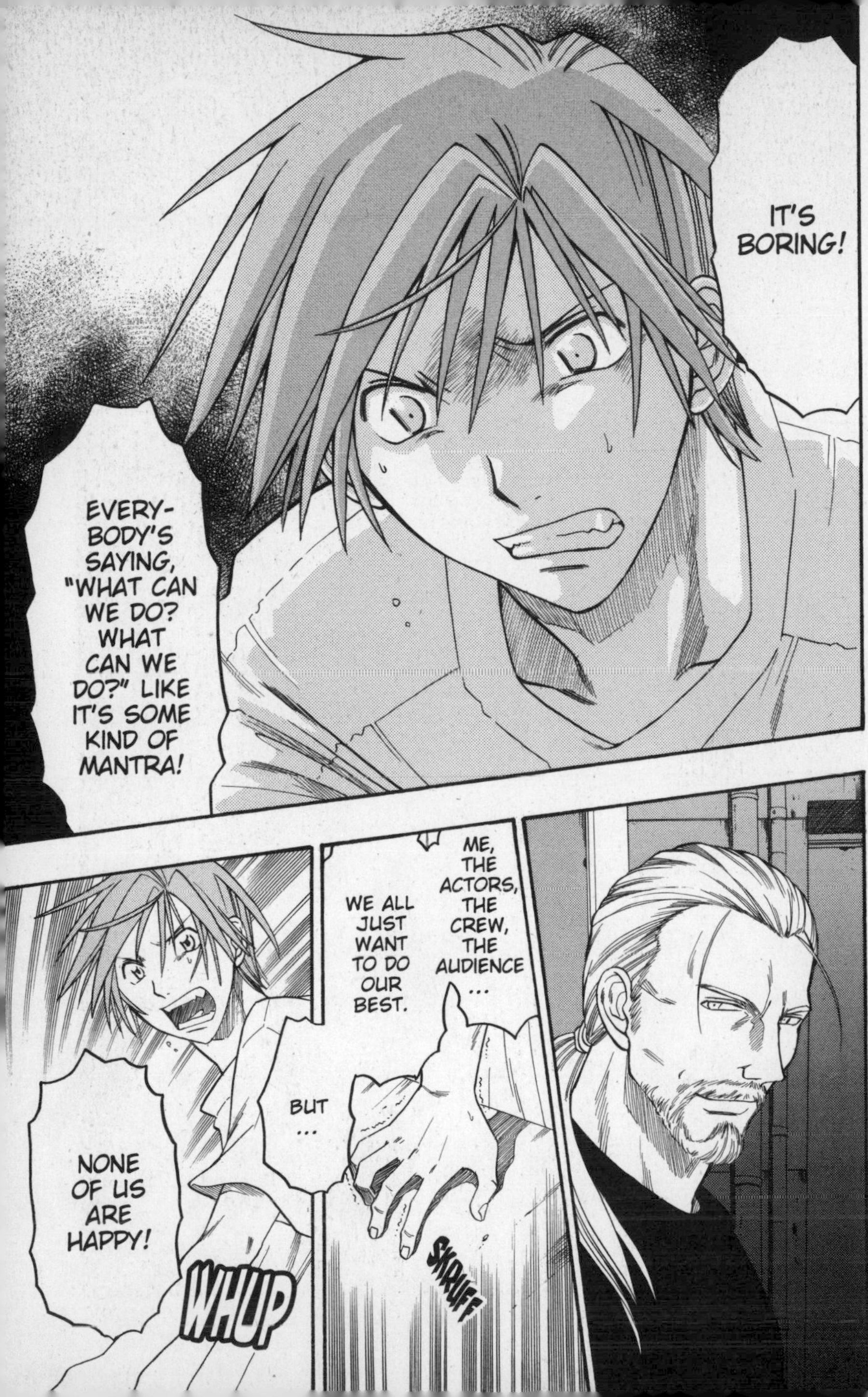
IT'S BORING!
EVERYBODY'S SAYING, "WHAT CAN WE DO? WHAT CAN WE DO?" LIKE IT'S SOME KIND OF MANTRA!
ME, THE ACTORS, THE CREW, THE AUDIENCE ...
WE ALL JUST WANT TO DO OUR BEST.
BUT ...
SKRUFF
NONE OF US ARE HAPPY!
WHUP

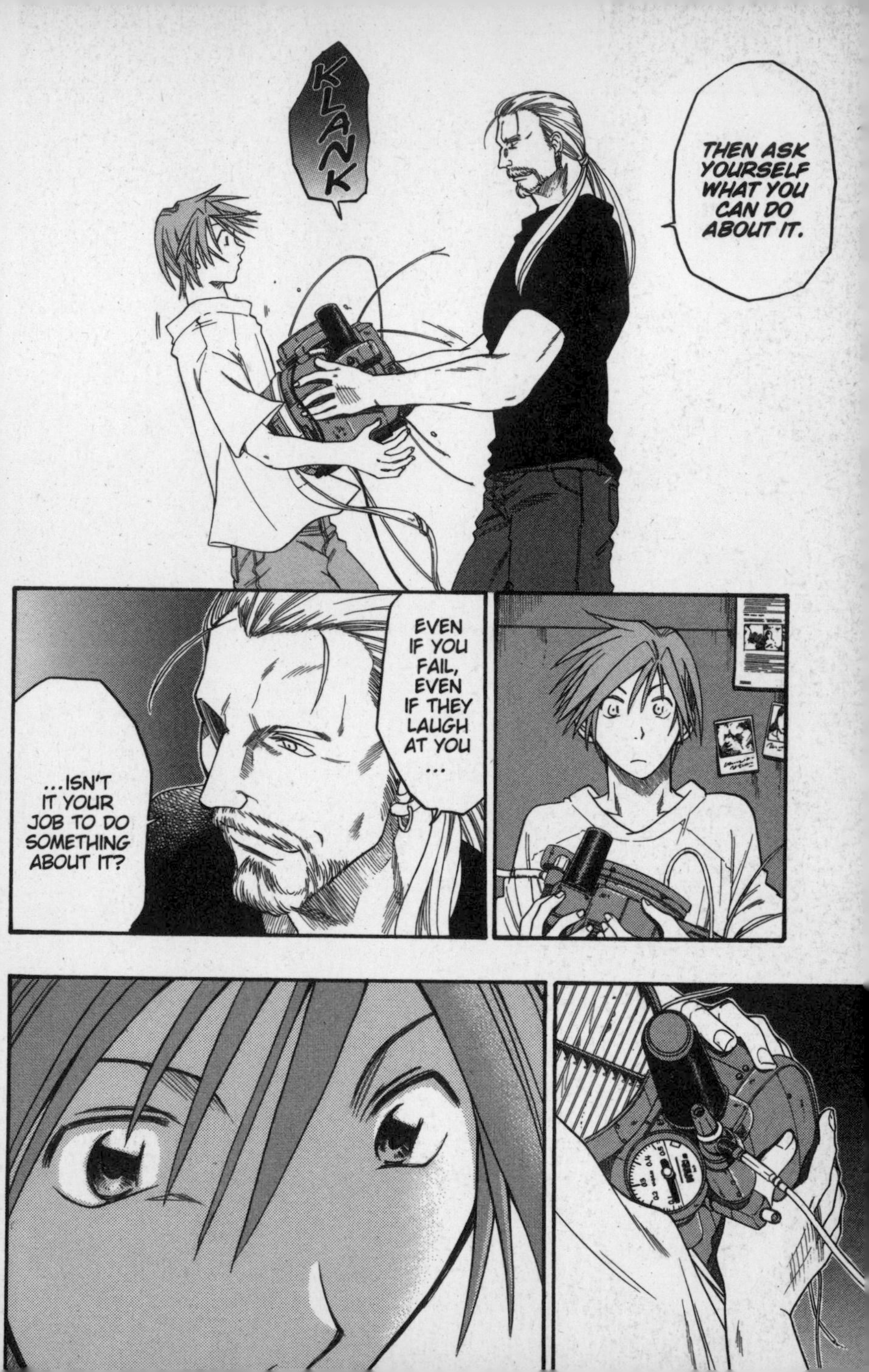
THEN ASK YOURSELF WHAT YOU CAN DO ABOUT IT.
KLANK
EVEN IF YOU FAIL, EVEN IF THEY LAUGH AT YOU ...
...ISN'T IT YOUR JOB TO DO SOMETHING ABOUT IT?

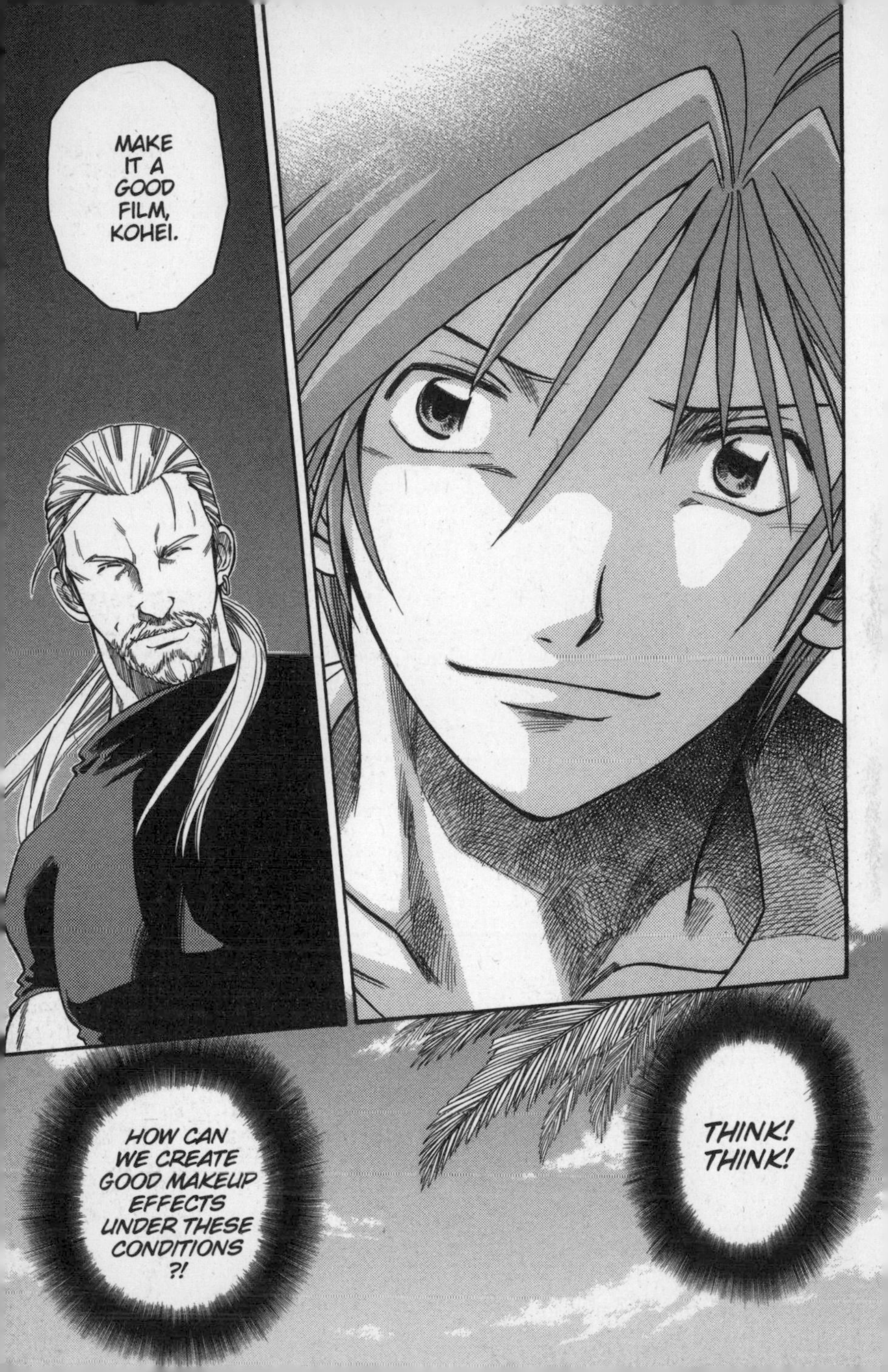
MAKE IT A GOOD FILM, KOHEI.
THINK! THINK!
HOW CAN WE CREATE GOOD MAKEUP EFFECTS UNDER THESE CONDITIONS?!

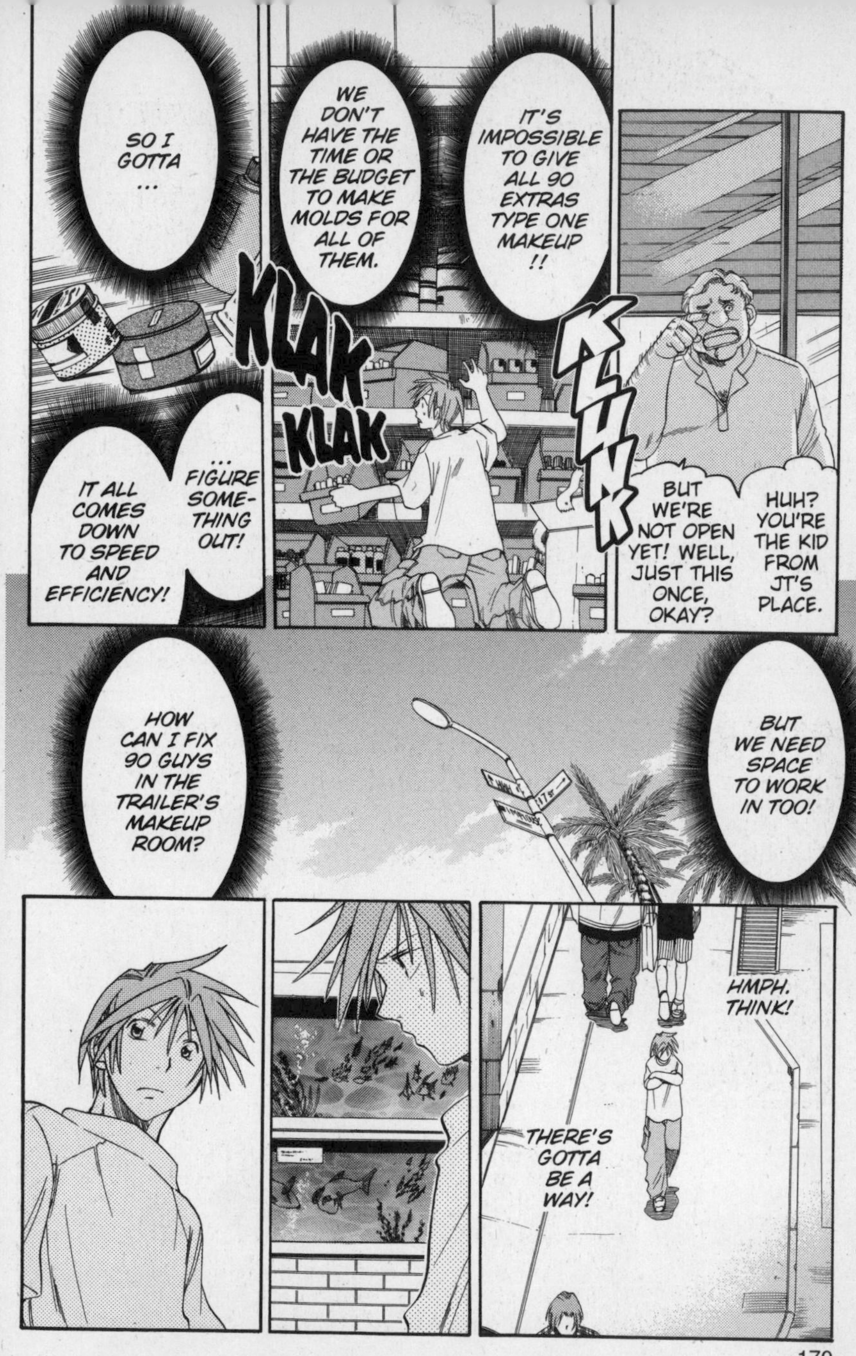
HUH? YOU'RE THE KID FROM JT'S PLACE.
BUT WE'RE NOT OPEN YET! WELL, JUST THIS ONCE, OKAY?
KLUNK
IT'S IMPOSSIBLE TO GIVE ALL 90 EXTRAS TYPE ONE MAKEUP !!
WE DON'T HAVE THE TIME OR THE BUDGET TO MAKE MOLDS FOR ALL OF THEM.
KLAK
KLAK
SO I GOTTA ...
... FIGURE SOME-THING OUT!
IT ALL COMES DOWN TO SPEED AND EFFICIENCY!
BUT WE NEED SPACE TO WORK IN TOO!
HOW CAN I FIX 90 GUYS IN THE TRAILER'S MAKEUP ROOM?
HMPH. THINK!
THERE'S GOTTA BE A WAY!

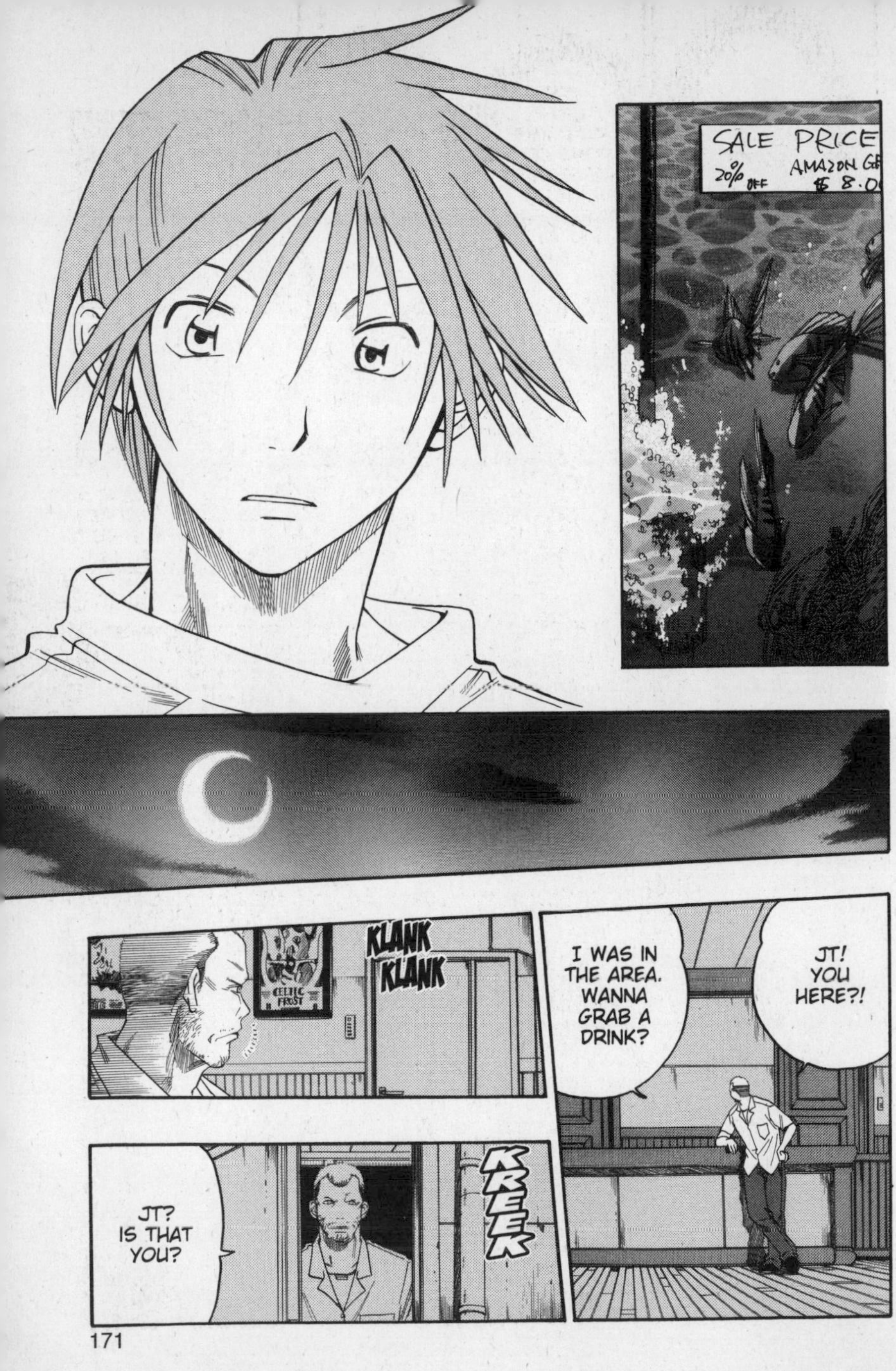
SALE PRICE
20% OFF
AMAZON
JT! YOU HERE?!
I WAS IN THE AREA. WANNA GRAB A DRINK?
CELTIC FROST
KLANK KLANK
KREEK
JT? IS THAT YOU?

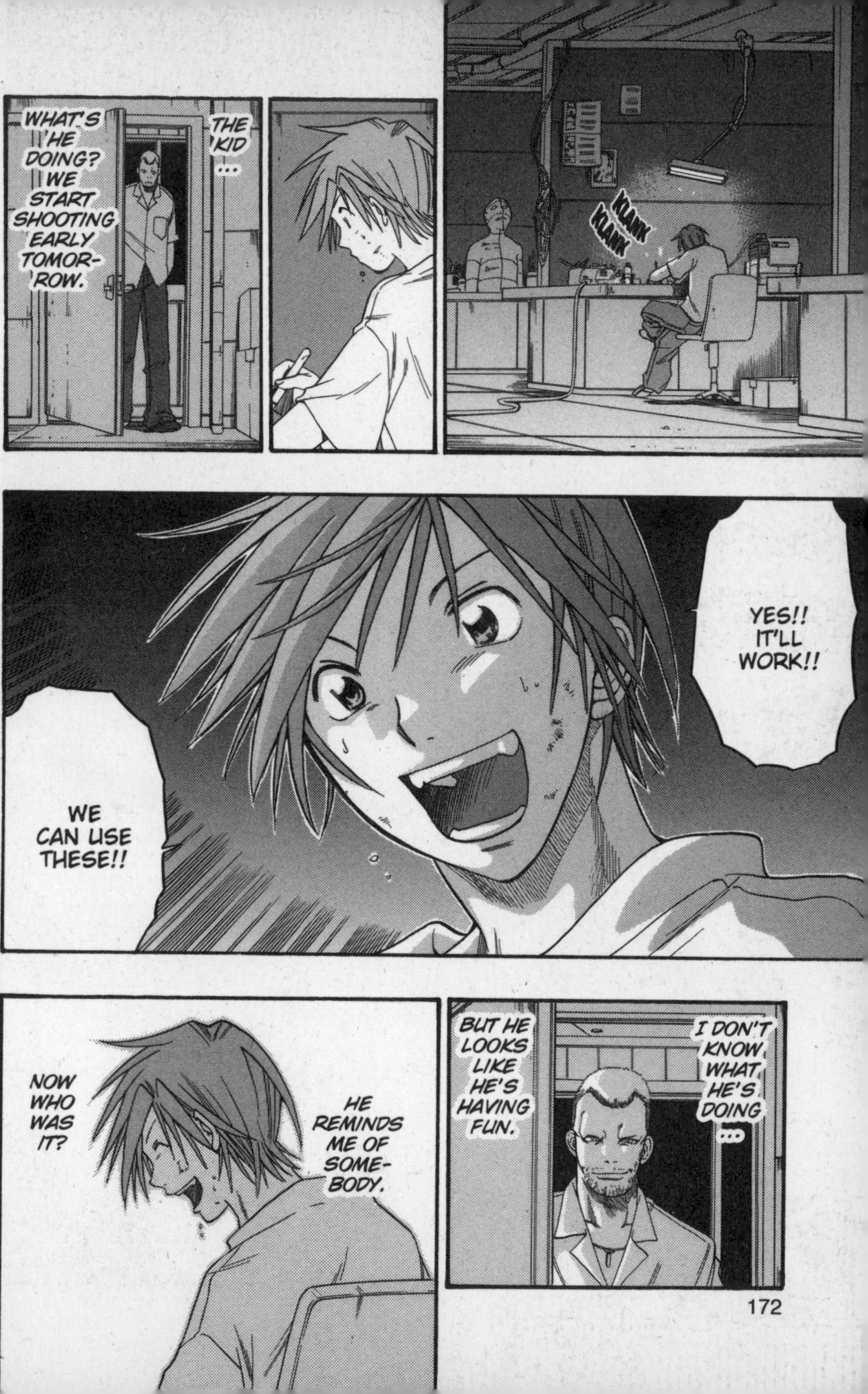
KLANK KLANK
THE KID...
WHAT'S HE DOING? WE START SHOOTING EARLY TOMORROW.
YES!! IT'LL WORK!!
WE CAN USE THESE!!
I DON'T KNOW WHAT HE'S DOING...
BUT HE LOOKS LIKE HE'S HAVING FUN.
HE REMINDS ME OF SOMEBODY.
NOW WHO WAS IT?

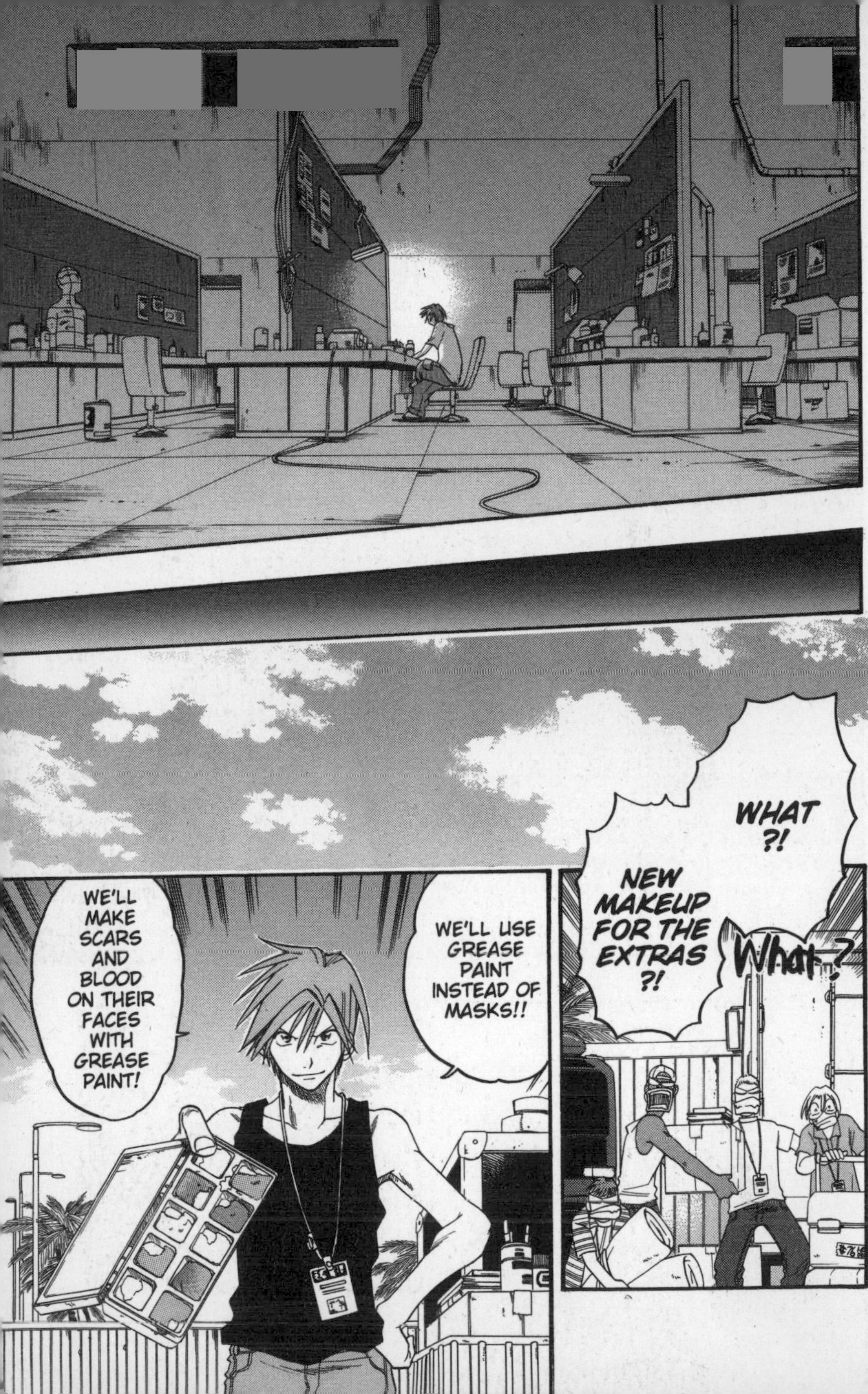
WHAT ?!
NEW MAKEUP FOR THE EXTRAS ?!
What?
WE'LL USE GREASE PAINT INSTEAD OF MASKS!!
WE'LL MAKE SCARS AND BLOOD ON THEIR FACES WITH GREASE PAINT!

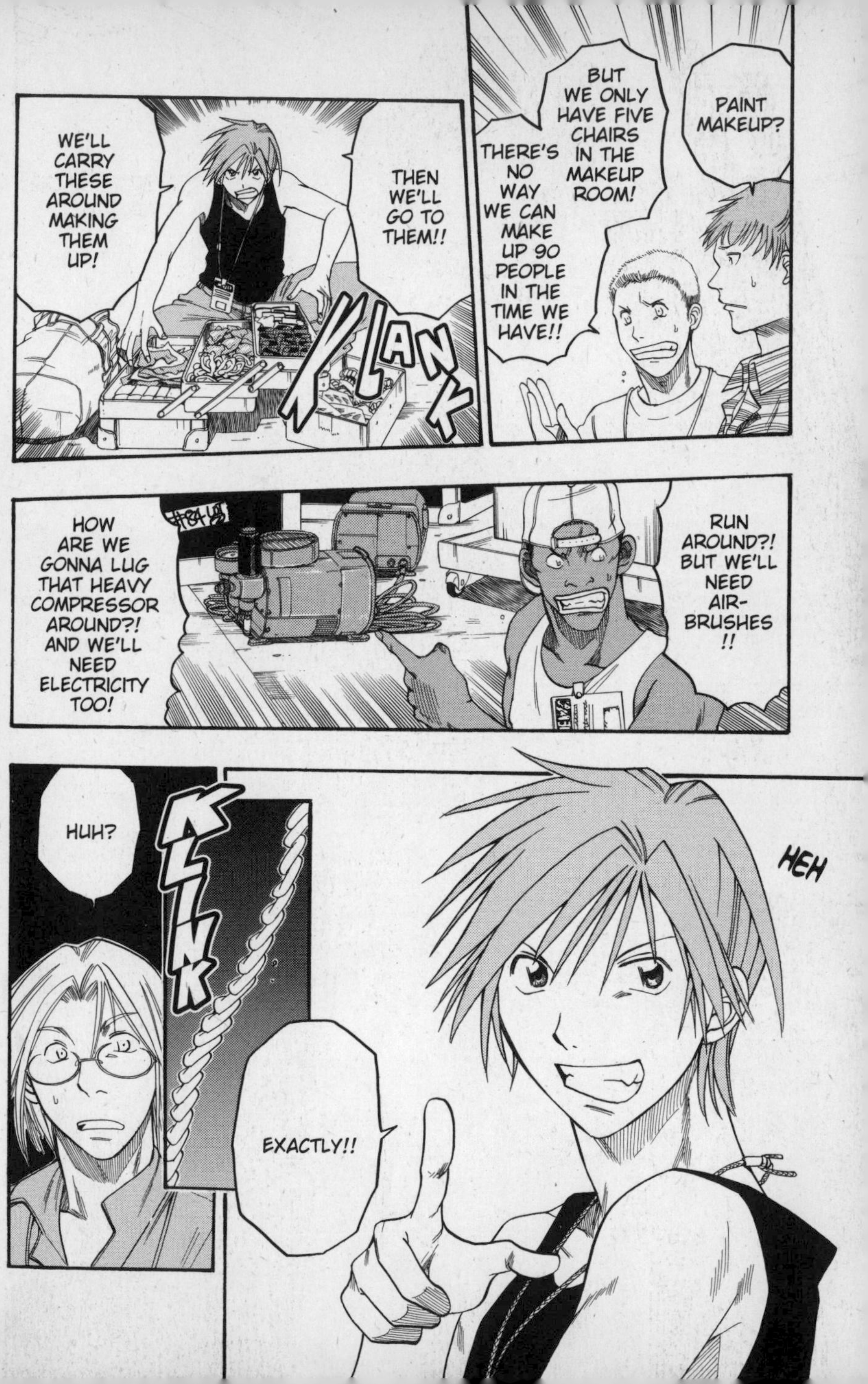
PAINT MAKEUP?
BUT WE ONLY HAVE FIVE CHAIRS IN THE MAKEUP ROOM!
THERE'S NO WAY WE CAN MAKE UP 90 PEOPLE IN THE TIME WE HAVE!!
THEN WE'LL GO TO THEM!!
WE'LL CARRY THESE AROUND MAKING THEM UP!
KLANK
RUN AROUND?! BUT WE'LL NEED AIR-BRUSHES !!
HOW ARE WE GONNA LUG THAT HEAVY COMPRESSOR AROUND?! AND WE'LL NEED ELECTRICITY TOO!
HEH
EXACTLY!!
HUH?
KLINK

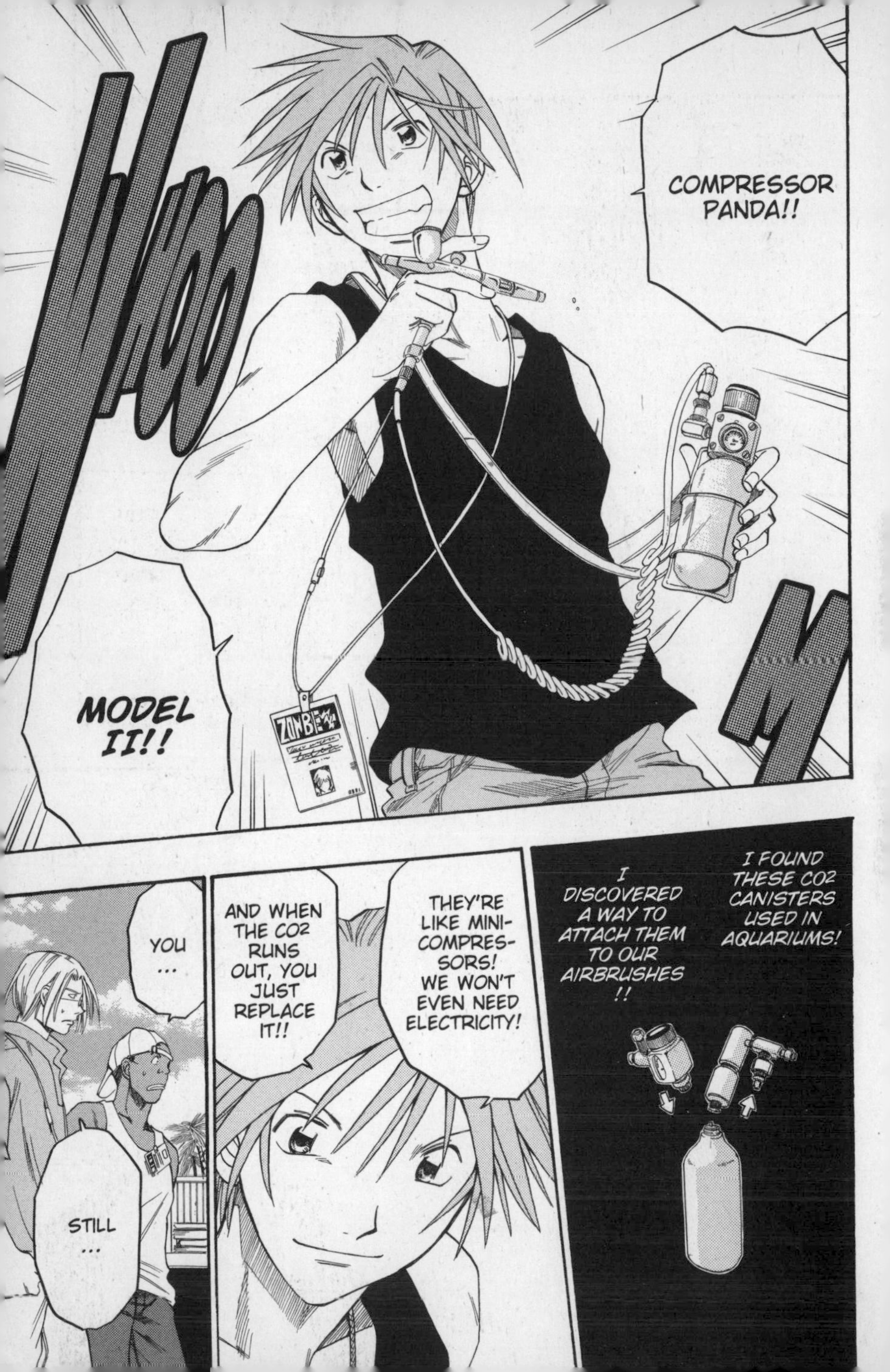
COMPRESSOR PANDA!!
MODEL II!!
I FOUND THESE CO2 CANISTERS USED IN AQUARIUMS!
I DISCOVERED A WAY TO ATTACH THEM TO OUR AIRBRUSHES !!
THEY'RE LIKE MINI-COMPRES-SORS! WE WON'T EVEN NEED ELECTRICITY!
AND WHEN THE CO2 RUNS OUT, YOU JUST REPLACE IT!!
YOU ...
STILL ...

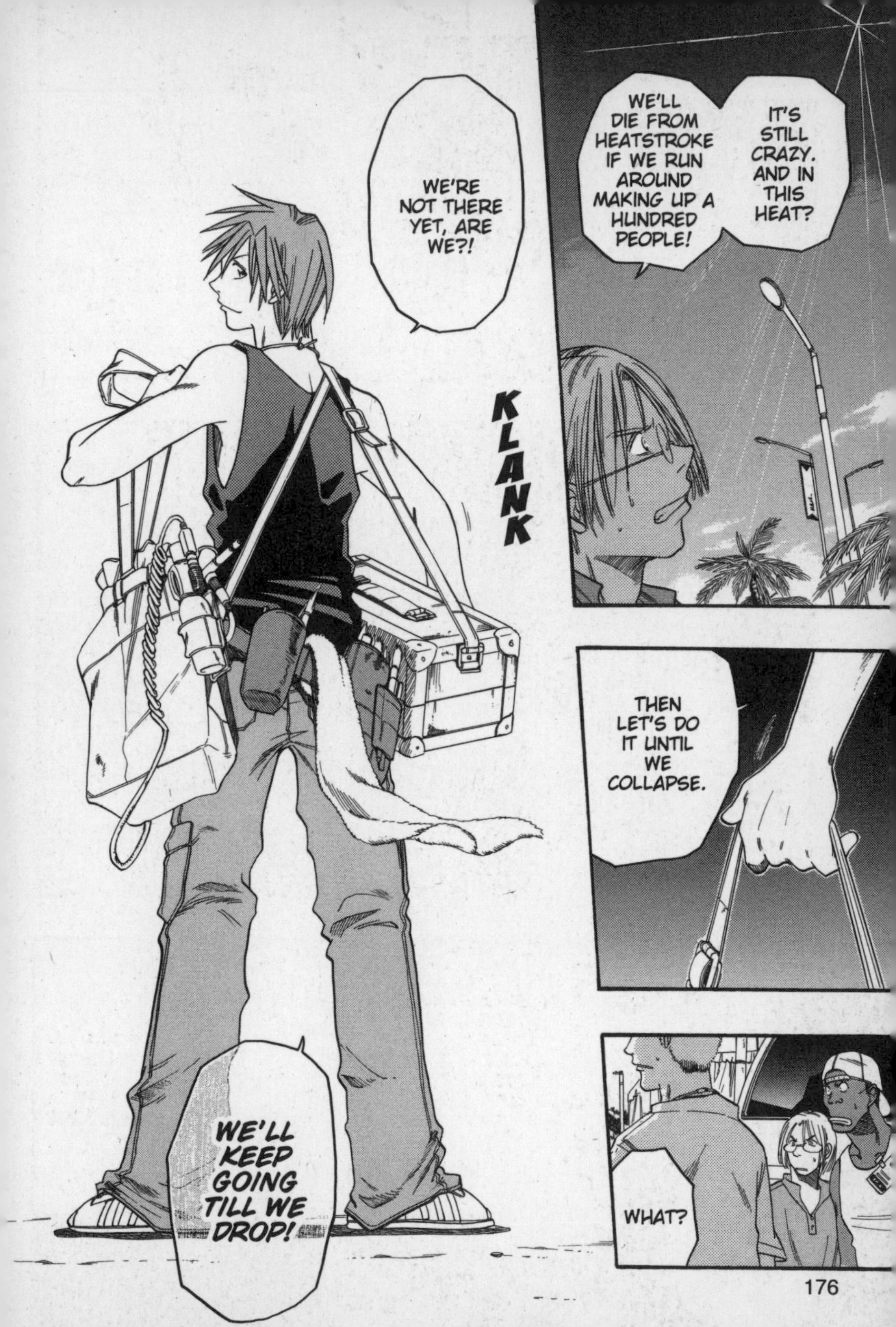
IT'S STILL CRAZY. AND IN THIS HEAT?
WE'LL DIE FROM HEATSTROKE IF WE RUN AROUND MAKING UP A HUNDRED PEOPLE!
THEN LET'S DO IT UNTIL WE COLLAPSE.
WHAT?
WE'RE NOT THERE YET, ARE WE?!
KLANK
WE'LL KEEP GOING TILL WE DROP!

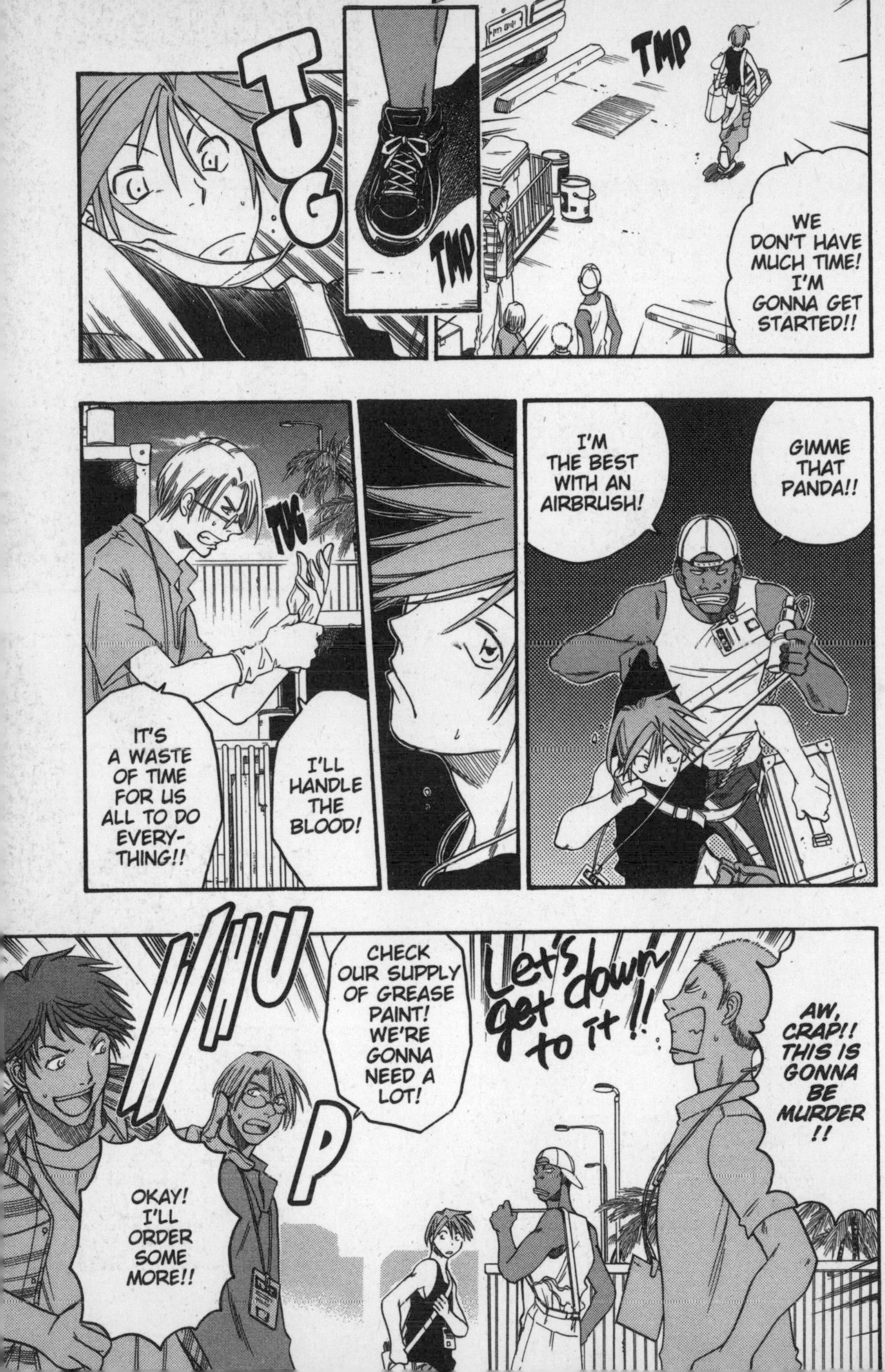
TMP
WE DON'T HAVE MUCH TIME! I'M GONNA GET STARTED!!
TMP
TUG
GIMME THAT PANDA!!
I'M THE BEST WITH AN AIRBRUSH!
TUG
I'LL HANDLE THE BLOOD!
IT'S A WASTE OF TIME FOR US ALL TO DO EVERY-THING!!
AW, CRAP!! THIS IS GONNA BE MURDER!!
Let's get down to it!!
CHECK OUR SUPPLY OF GREASE PAINT! WE'RE GONNA NEED A LOT!
WHUP
OKAY! I'LL ORDER SOME MORE!!

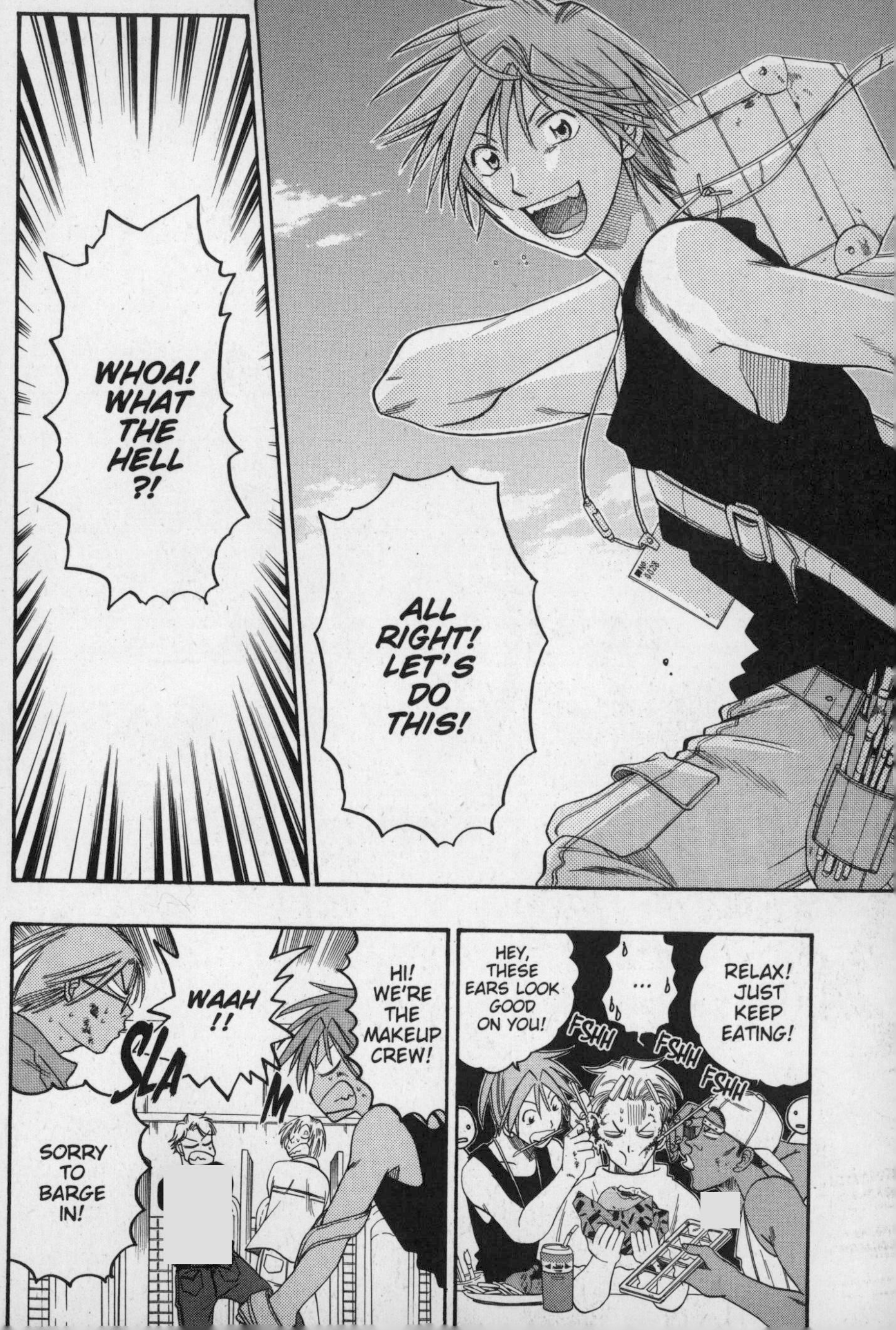
ALL RIGHT! LET'S DO THIS!
WHOA! WHAT THE HELL?!
RELAX! JUST KEEP EATING!
...
HEY, THESE EARS LOOK GOOD ON YOU!
FSHH
FSHH
FSHH
HI! WE'RE THE MAKEUP CREW!
WAAH!!
SLA-M
SORRY TO BARGE IN!

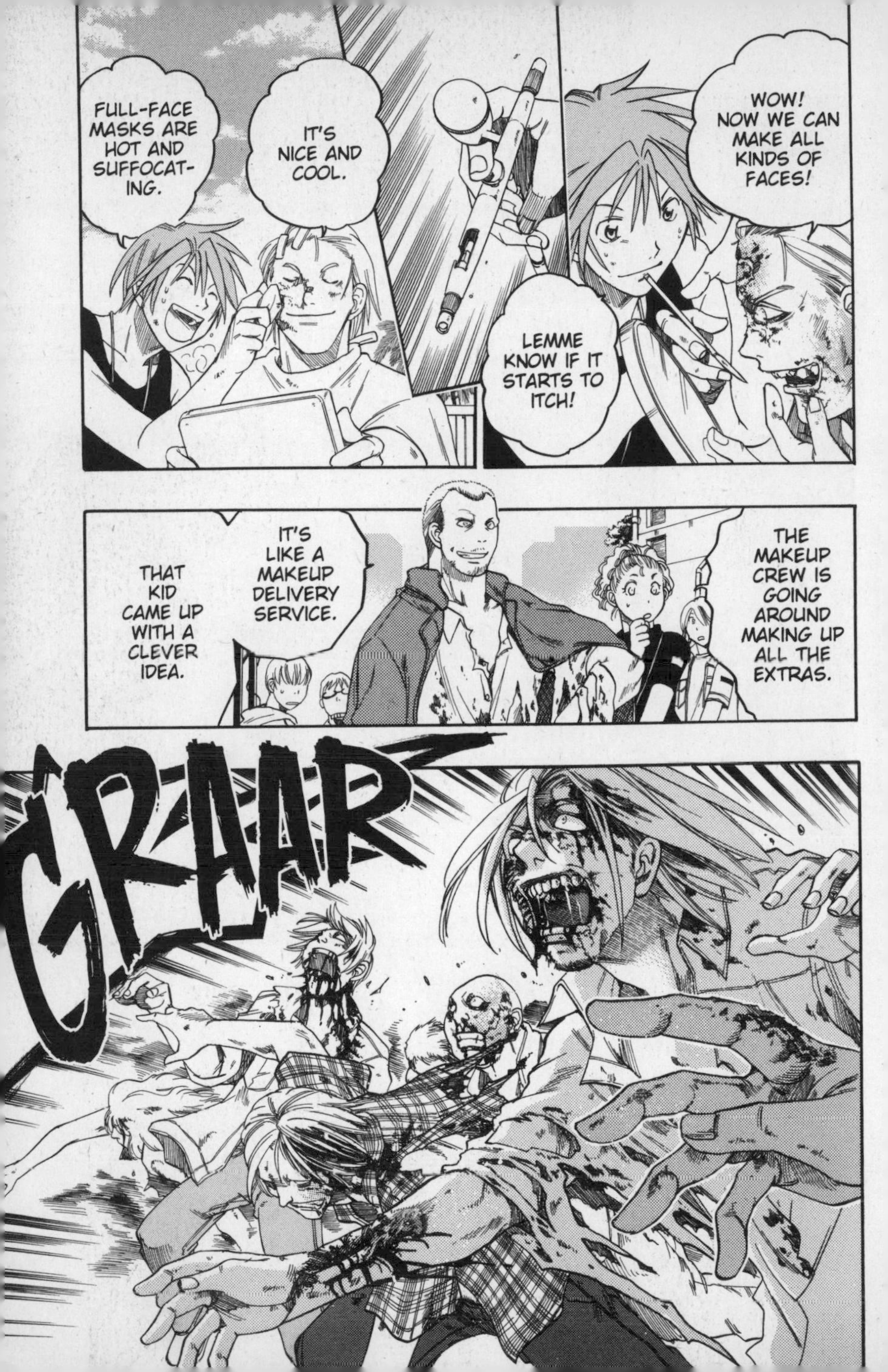
WOW! NOW WE CAN MAKE ALL KINDS OF FACES!
LEMME KNOW IF IT STARTS TO ITCH!
IT'S NICE AND COOL.
FULL-FACE MASKS ARE HOT AND SUFFOCATING.
THE MAKEUP CREW IS GOING AROUND MAKING UP ALL THE EXTRAS.
IT'S LIKE A MAKEUP DELIVERY SERVICE.
THAT KID CAME UP WITH A CLEVER IDEA.
GRAAR

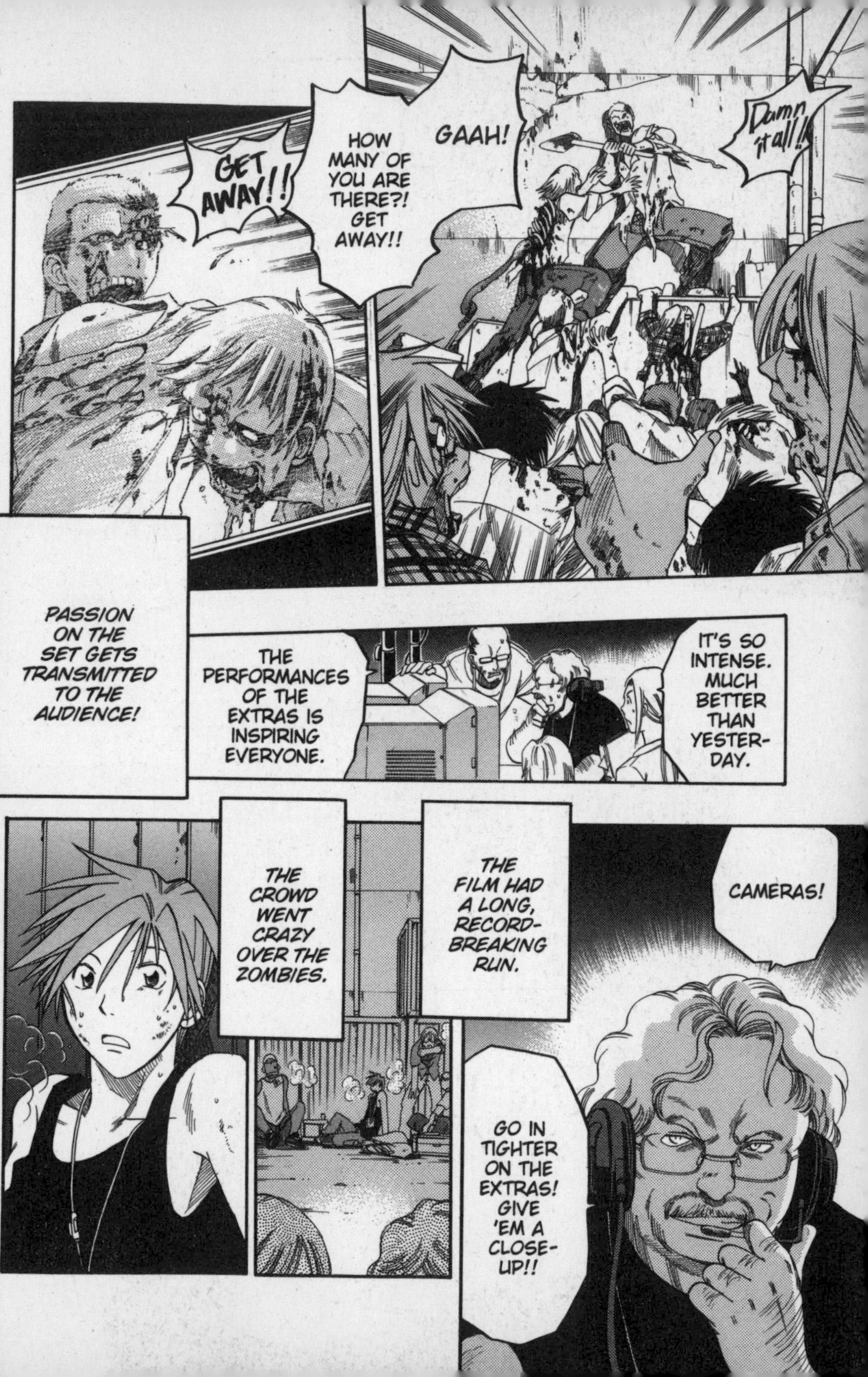
Damn it all!!
GAAH!
HOW MANY OF YOU ARE THERE?! GET AWAY!!
GET AWAY!!
IT'S SO INTENSE. MUCH BETTER THAN YESTER-DAY.
THE PERFORMANCES OF THE EXTRAS IS INSPIRING EVERYONE.
PASSION ON THE SET GETS TRANSMITTED TO THE AUDIENCE!
CAMERAS!
GO IN TIGHTER ON THE EXTRAS! GIVE 'EM A CLOSE-UP!!
THE FILM HAD A LONG, RECORD-BREAKING RUN.
THE CROWD WENT CRAZY OVER THE ZOMBIES.

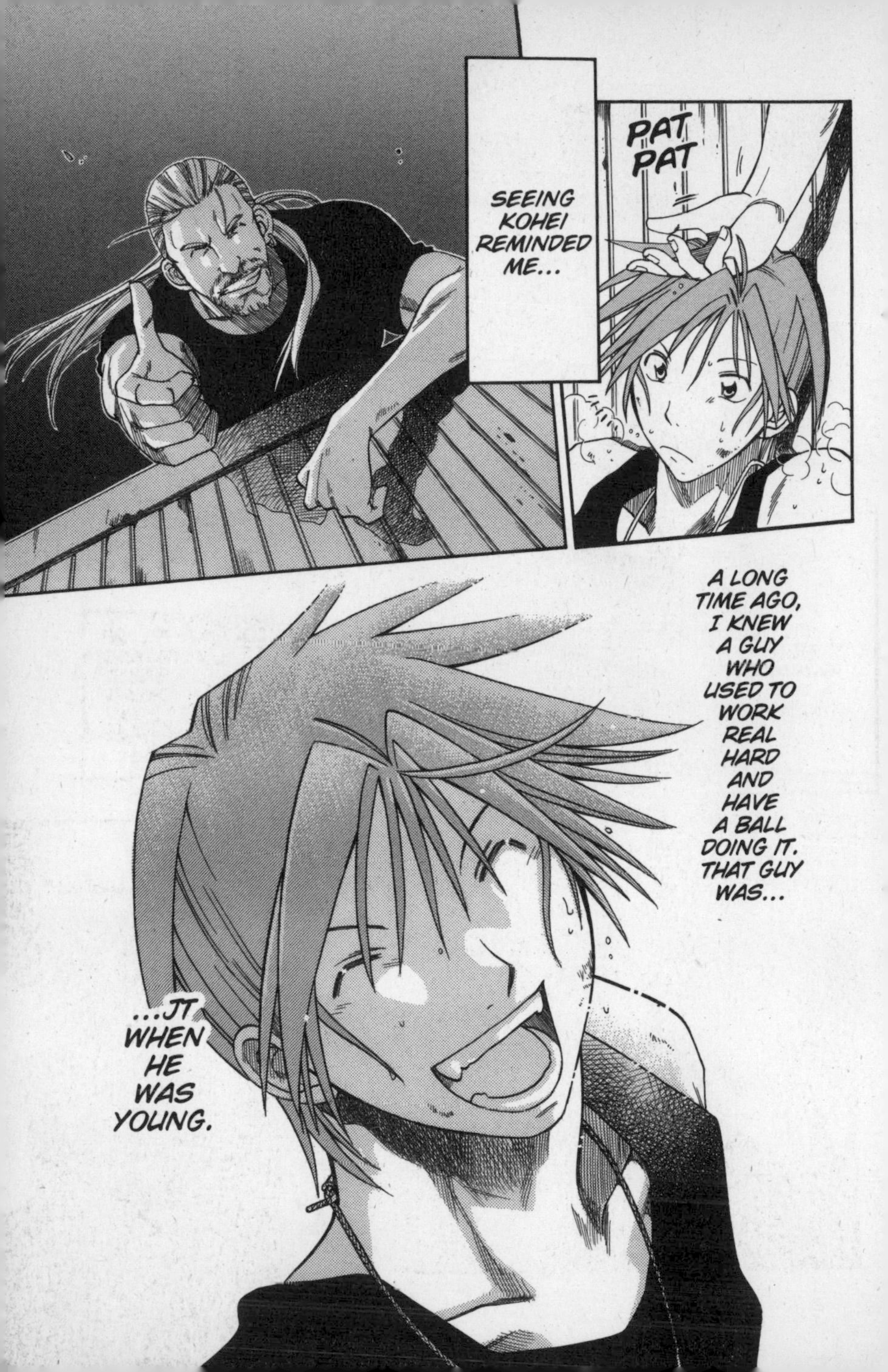
PAT PAT
SEEING KOHEI REMINDED ME...
A LONG TIME AGO, I KNEW A GUY WHO USED TO WORK REAL HARD AND HAVE A BALL DOING IT. THAT GUY WAS...
...JT WHEN HE WAS YOUNG.

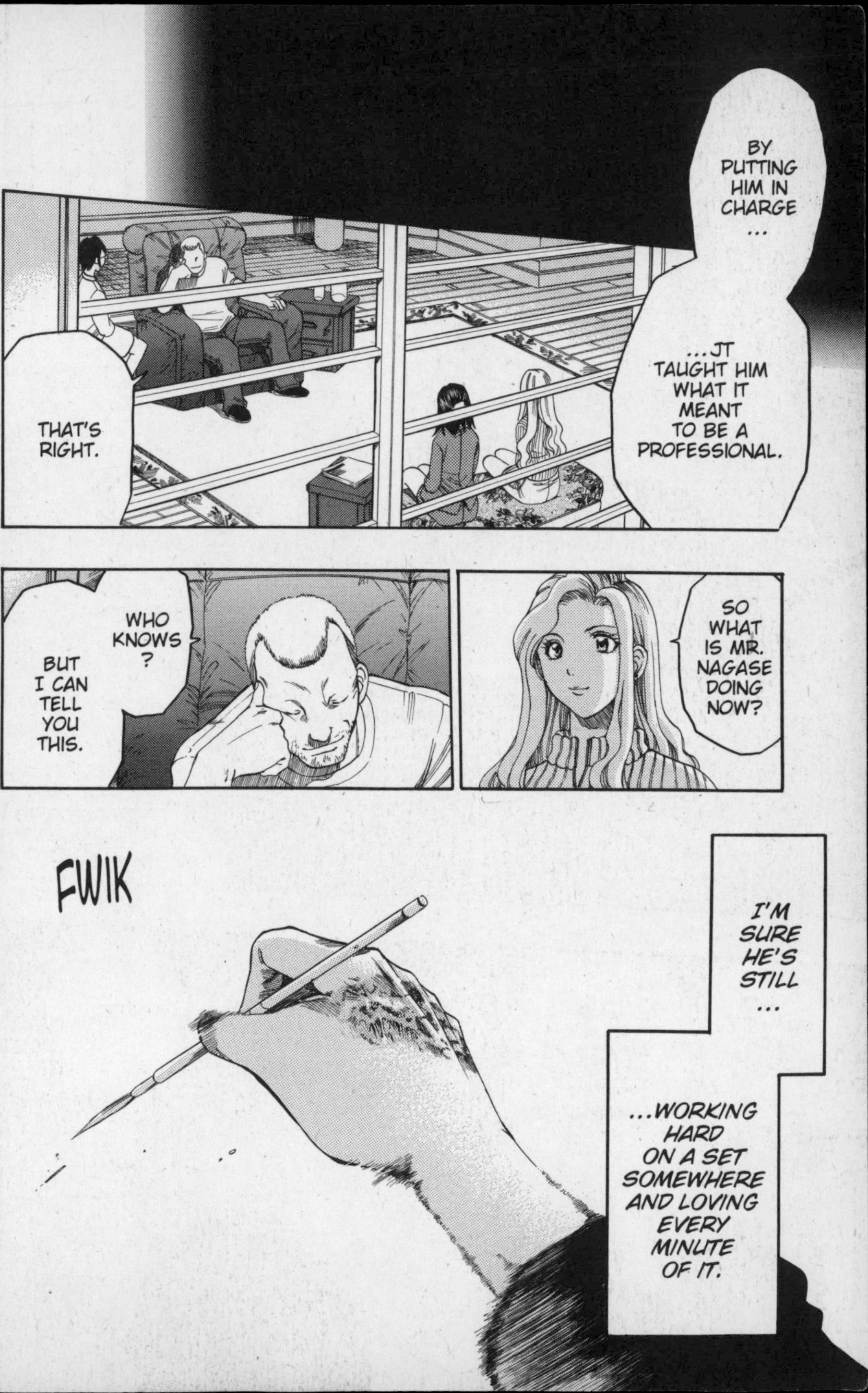
BY PUTTING HIM IN CHARGE...
...JT TAUGHT HIM WHAT IT MEANT TO BE A PROFESSIONAL.
THAT'S RIGHT.
SO WHAT IS MR. NAGASE DOING NOW?
WHO KNOWS?
BUT I CAN TELL YOU THIS.
I'M SURE HE'S STILL...
FWIK
...WORKING HARD ON A SET SOMEWHERE AND LOVING EVERY MINUTE OF IT.

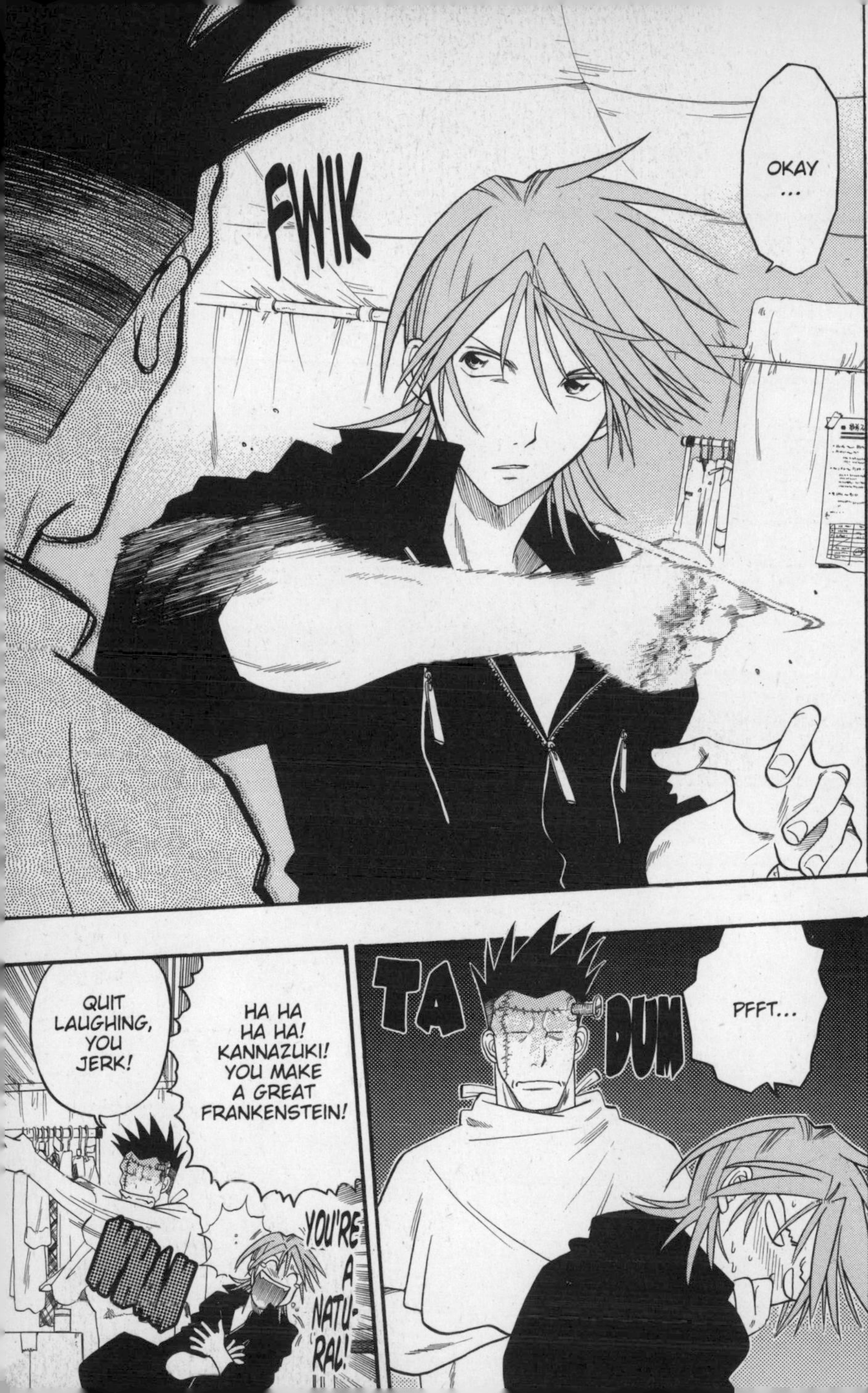
OKAY ...
FWIK
PFFT...
TA DUM
HA HA HA HA! KANNAZUKI! YOU MAKE A GREAT FRANKENSTEIN!
QUIT LAUGHING, YOU JERK!
YOU'RE A NATURAL!

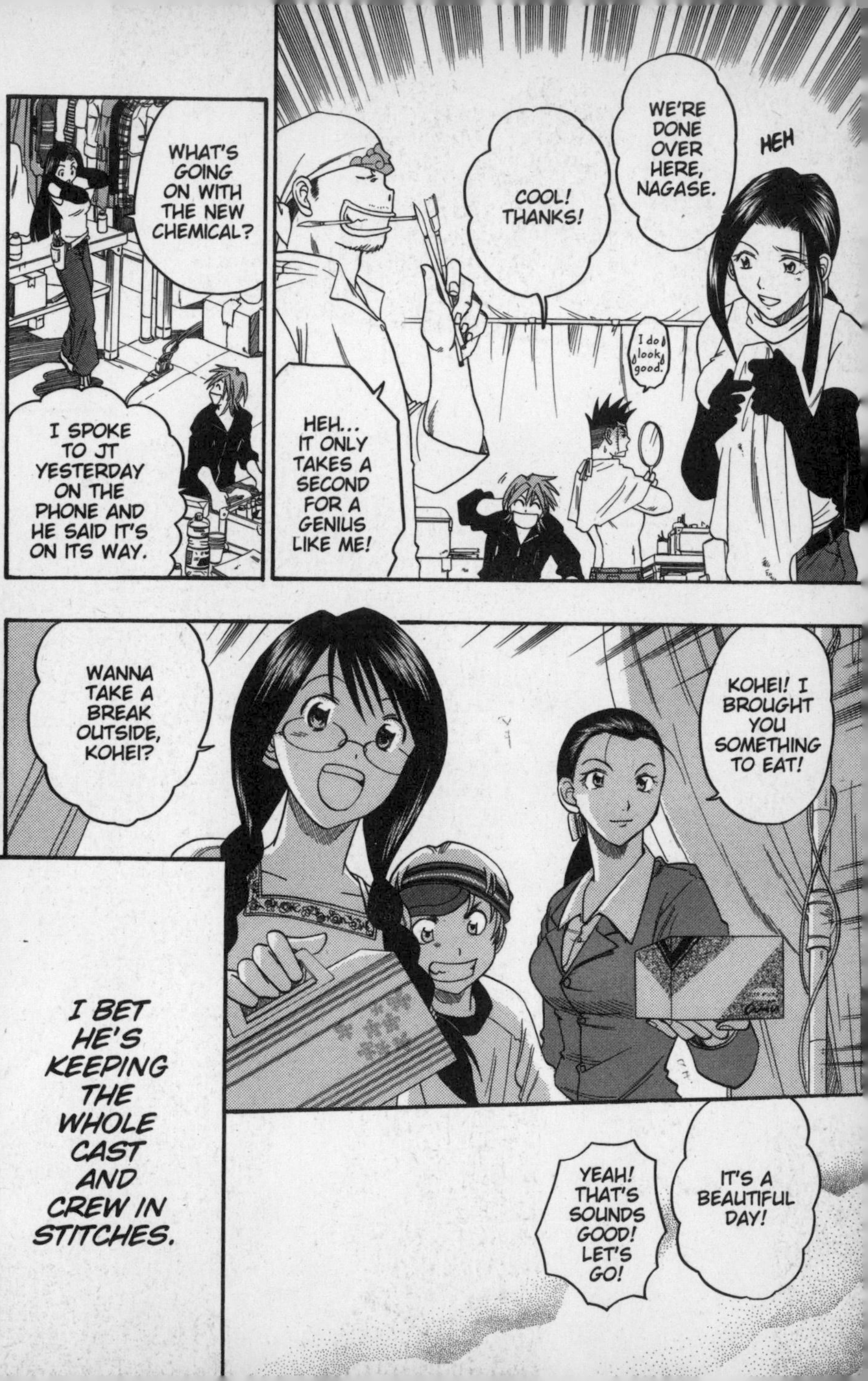
WE'RE DONE OVER HERE, NAGASE.
HEH
COOL! THANKS!
I do look good.
HEH... IT ONLY TAKES A SECOND FOR A GENIUS LIKE ME!
WHAT'S GOING ON WITH THE NEW CHEMICAL?
I SPOKE TO JT YESTERDAY ON THE PHONE AND HE SAID IT'S ON ITS WAY.
KOHEI! I BROUGHT YOU SOMETHING TO EAT!
WANNA TAKE A BREAK OUTSIDE, KOHEI?
IT'S A BEAUTIFUL DAY!
YEAH! THAT'S SOUNDS GOOD! LET'S GO!
I BET HE'S KEEPING THE WHOLE CAST AND CREW IN STITCHES.

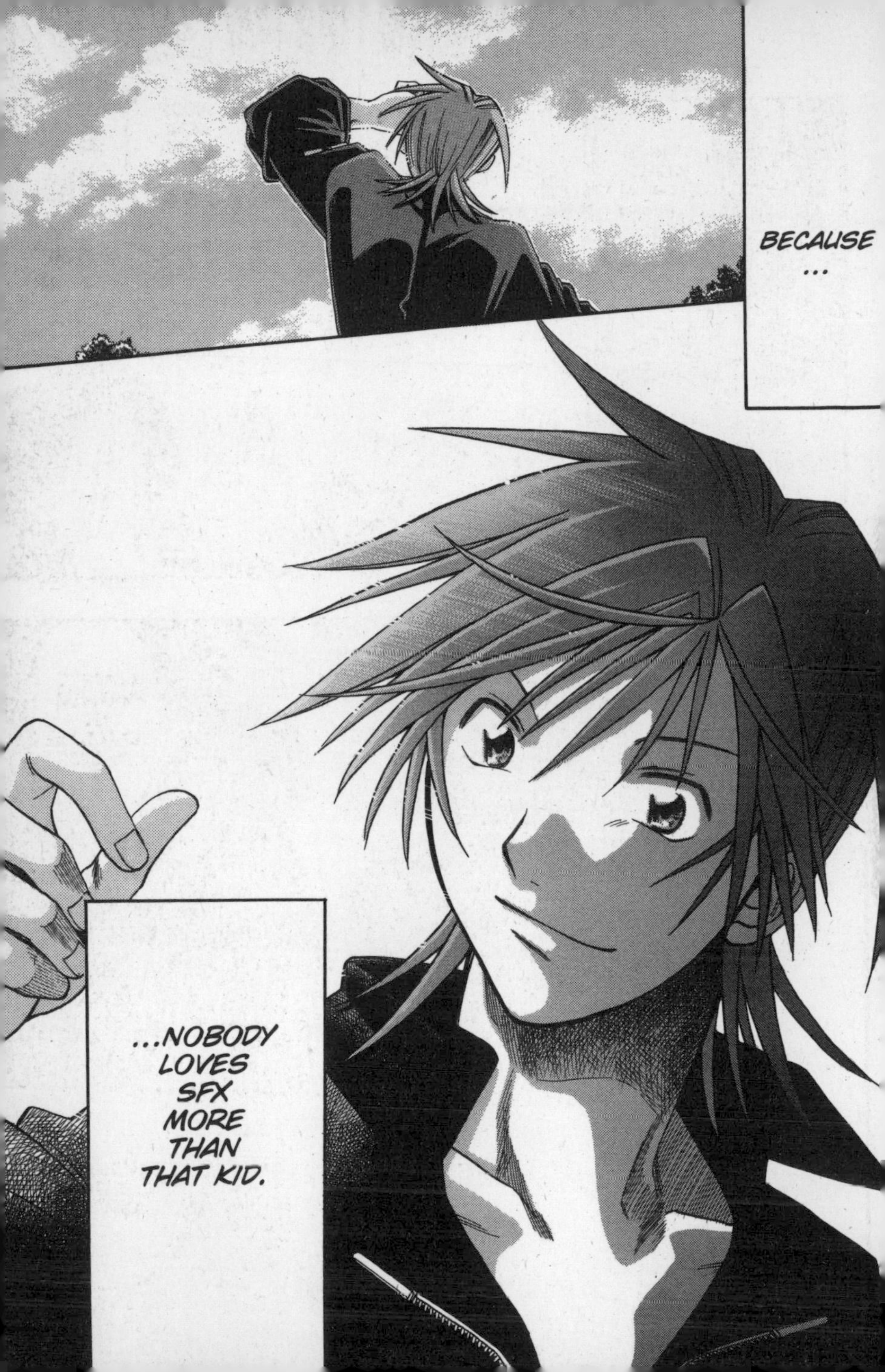
BECAUSE ...
...NOBODY LOVES SFX MORE THAN THAT KID.

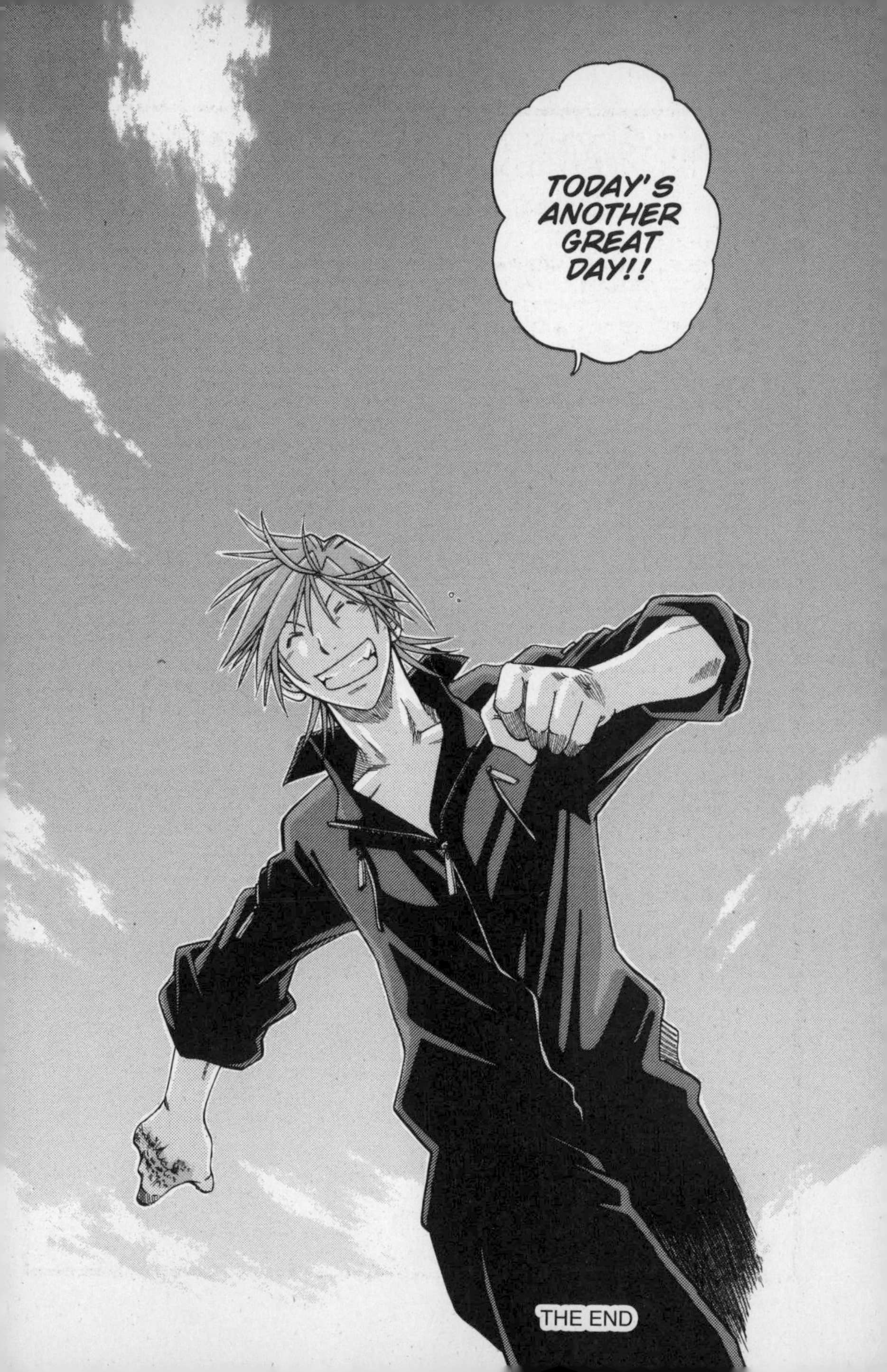
TODAY'S ANOTHER GREAT DAY!!
THE END

THE MAKING OF GIMMICK!

Episode 9 By Youzaburou Kanari

"MR. DOUBT"
I BELIEVE THERE ARE TWO TYPES OF CHARACTERS--THOSE
THAT ARE CREATED AND THOSE THAT ARE BORN. KOSEI
KAGASE WAS DEFINITELY THE LATTER. HE APPEARED OUT OF
NOWHERE DURING A DISCUSSION WITH MY EDITOR. HIS CREATION
WAS INSTANTANEOUS, AS IF HE HAD ALWAYS BEEN THERE.

"ACROSS CASTLE RIVER"
WHETHER IT'S A COMIC, A MOVIE, MUSIC, A PLAY, A PHOTOGRAPH
OR A PAINTING, THE PROCESS OF CREATION IS BASICALLY
COMMUNICATING SOMETHING TO OTHERS. CASTLE RIVER IS THE
NAME OF THE RIVER IN *STAND BY ME* (1986). BY THE WAY,
SCENES OF CROSSING RIVERS OR OCEANS IN HOLLYWOOD
FILMS ARE SUPPOSED TO SYMBOLIZE A CHILD'S PASSAGE
INTO ADULTHOOD.

"GLADIATOR" "48 HOURS" "THE VERDICT" "THE THIRD MAN"
THE J-SMAC ARC WAS THE LONGEST STORY-ARC IN *GIMMICK!*
IT WAS AN EXAMINATION OF ONE OF OUR MAIN THEMES: CRAFTS-
MANSHIP. THE SPECIAL MAKEUP EFFECTS ARTIST MR. U-I WHO
OVERSAW THE STORY IS A REALLY AMAZING MAN. I WOULD THROW
IMPOSSIBLE SITUATIONS AT HIM LIKE "THEY CAN'T USE FOAM
LATEX," OR, "THEY CAN'T USE GREASE PAINT AND PIGMENTS," AND
HE WOULD COME UP WITH GREAT IDEAS. MR. U-I, IF IT WEREN'T FOR
YOU, *GIMMICK!* WOULD NOT HAVE BEEN POSSIBLE. THANK YOU!
THERE'S A LOT I WANT TO SAY ABOUT THE J-SMAC STORY ARC,
BUT...MAYBE SOMEDAY, SOMEWHERE.
THERE'S AN EPISODE TOWARD THE END OF IT WHERE KOHEI
CAN'T USE AN OVEN AND HE IS FORCED TO BOIL HIS APPLIANCE.
SOME PEOPLE SAID THAT WAS IMPOSSIBLE, BUT IT REALLY CAN
BE DONE. I HEARD THAT A FILM CREW COULDN'T GET AN OVEN
ONCE SO THEY HEATED THEIR APPLIANCES LIKE THAT ON THE
SET. GIVE IT A TRY!

"FIELD OF DREAMS REDUX"
AND FINALLY IT CAME, *GIMMICK!*'S LAST STORY, FOUR YEARS
AFTER THE PROJECT WAS FIRST DISCUSSED. DURING THAT WHOLE
TIME, I WAS ALWAYS THINKING ABOUT KOHEI. BY THE END, IT FELT
LIKE HE WAS A CLOSE FRIEND OF MINE. THAT'S WHY IN THE LAST
STORY I WANTED TO FREE HIM FROM ALL THE PAIN AND SADNESS
THAT HAD BEEN TYING HIM DOWN. I WANTED HIM TO BE FREE. BUT
THE DREAM PLACE KOHEI CHOSE WASN'T WITH JT, BUT THE
TRAILER BY THE RIVER IN JAPAN WHERE ALL HIS FRIENDS WERE.
A HAPPY ENDING IS ALWAYS NICE AFTER A LONG JOURNEY.

"FAME"
EVEN THOUGH *GIMMICK!* IS FINISHED, KOHEI AND KANNAZUKI WILL
ALWAYS BE THERE BY THE RIVER. THEY WILL ALWAYS BE INVOLVED
WITH MOVIES, SMILING AND LAUGHING AND LIVING FREE. I HOPE
ALL OUR FAITHFUL READERS ALWAYS IMAGINE THEM THAT WAY.
THAT'S WHY I WROTE THIS STORY.

• TONS OF THANKS •

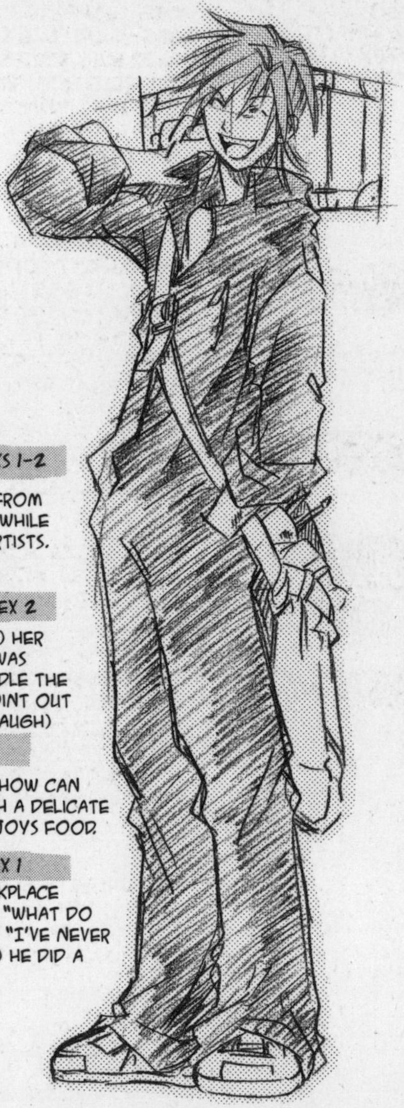

• STAFF •

TATEBUE NAMETA CHAPTERS 1-87, EXS 1-2

HANDLED THE FINISHING TOUCHES FROM THE TWO-PART ONE-SHOT STORY WHILE WORKING FOR MANY DIFFERENT ARTISTS. THANK YOU!!

SACHIKO OGATA CHAPTERS 64-87, EX 2

HEAVY DRINKER. JUST KIDDING! (HA) HER WORK WAS ALWAYS THOROUGH. I WAS NEVER AFRAID TO ASK HER TO HANDLE THE FINISHING TOUCHES. SHE WOULD POINT OUT MISTAKES IN MY DRAWINGS TOO. (LAUGH)

RYU HONJO CHAPTERS 50-63

WHAT ARE YOU, A MARTIAL ARTIST?! HOW CAN YOU LOOK SO TOUGH YET HAVE SUCH A DELICATE TOUCH? HE EATS LIKE HE REALLY ENJOYS FOOD.

TOSHIYA SATO CHAPTERS 3-49, EX 1

HE FRIGHTENED THE ENTIRE WORKPLACE WHEN HE SAID ON THE FIRST DAY, "WHAT DO I USE TO APPLY BLACK INK?" AND, "I'VE NEVER USED WHITEOUT BEFORE." (LAUGH) HE DID A REALLY GREAT JOB.

MR. USUI, MR. TAKAHASHI AT-ILLUSION	THEY HELPED US IN SO MANY AREAS SINCE THE ONE-SHOT STORY. THEY TOOK TIME OUT FROM THEIR BUSY SCHEDULES TO ACCOMPANY US ON OUR RESEARCH TRIPS, ANSWER OUR QUESTIONS, AND TELL US SO MANY INTERESTING STORIES. AND THEY DIDN'T GET MAD WHEN I PUT THEM IN ONE OF MY COMIC STRIPS. (OR DID THEY?) I WISH THEM ALL THE BEST.
MITALLICA	THE BIGGEST CONTRIBUTOR TO VOLUME 5. BUT I FORGOT TO INCLUDE HIM IN THE THANK YOU AT THE END OF THE VOLUME. I FEEL TERRIBLE ABOUT THAT. THANK YOU FOR YOUR HELP ON THE SPECIAL STORY AT THE VERY LAST MINUTE! AND THANKS FOR POINTING OUT ALL THE MISTAKES. (LAUGH)
KIYOHUMI ITO	SORRY FOR MISSPELLING YOUR NAME. THANK YOU FOR HELPING OUT WITH THE DESIGN OF THE NOVEL AND THE ENGLISH TRANSLATION.
SATOSHI IWASE (CURE)	A LONG-TIME ACQUAINTANCE, BUT I NEVER THOUGHT WE'D END UP WORKING TOGETHER. (LAUGH) THANK YOU FOR FABRICATING THE SACRED SILVER SPATULA!!
YOKO + MIYUKI	NUTRITIONISTS AND THE BIGGEST CONTRIBUTORS TO THE SUPERMARKET STORY ARC. THAT STORY WOULDN'T HAVE BEEN POSSIBLE WITHOUT YOU TWO. SORRY FOR REPEATEDLY CALLING YOU DURING YOUR TRAVELS AND DEMANDING ANSWERS TO MY QUESTIONS! AND THANKS FOR ANSWERING MY SURVEYS.

THANK YOU, MR. KANARI AND MR. ITATANI (THE WRITER AND THE EDITOR), FOR ALL YOUR HARD WORK. BUT MOSTLY I'D LIKE TO THANK ALL THE FANS THAT READ *GIMMICK!* YOU HAVE MY UNDYING GRATITUDE.

KUROKO YABUGUCHI

• DRAFT MANUSCRIPT •

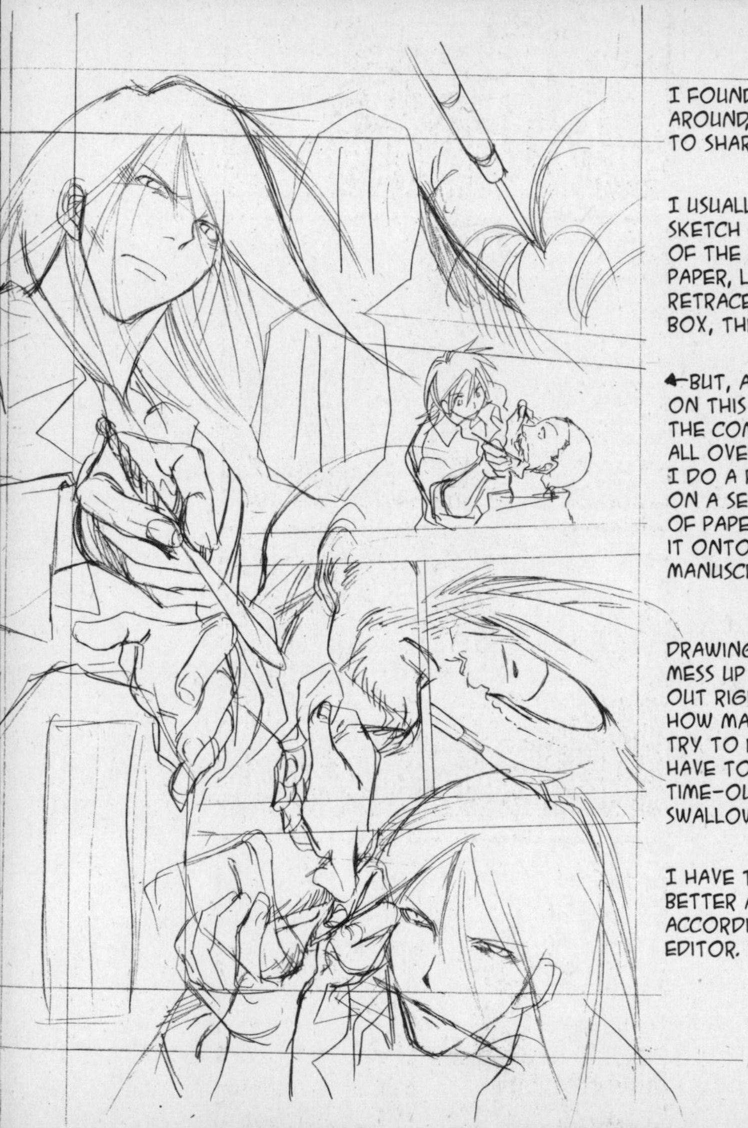

I FOUND THIS LYING AROUND, SO I DECIDED TO SHARE IT WITH YOU.

I USUALLY DO A ROUGH SKETCH ON THE BACK OF THE MANUSCRIPT PAPER, LIGHTLY RETRACE IT ON A LIGHT BOX, THEN INK IT.

←BUT, AS YOU CAN SEE ON THIS PAGE, WHEN THE COMPOSITION IS ALL OVER THE PLACE, I DO A ROUGH SKETCH ON A SEPARATE PIECE OF PAPER THEN COPY IT ONTO THE MANUSCRIPT PAPER.

DRAWINGS THAT YOU MESS UP NEVER TURN OUT RIGHT NO MATTER HOW MANY TIMES YOU TRY TO FIX THEM. YOU HAVE TO TAKE A TIME-OUT AND SWALLOW YOUR SHAME.

I HAVE TO GET A LOT BETTER AT DRAWING, ACCORDING TO MY EDITOR. IT'S TRUE.

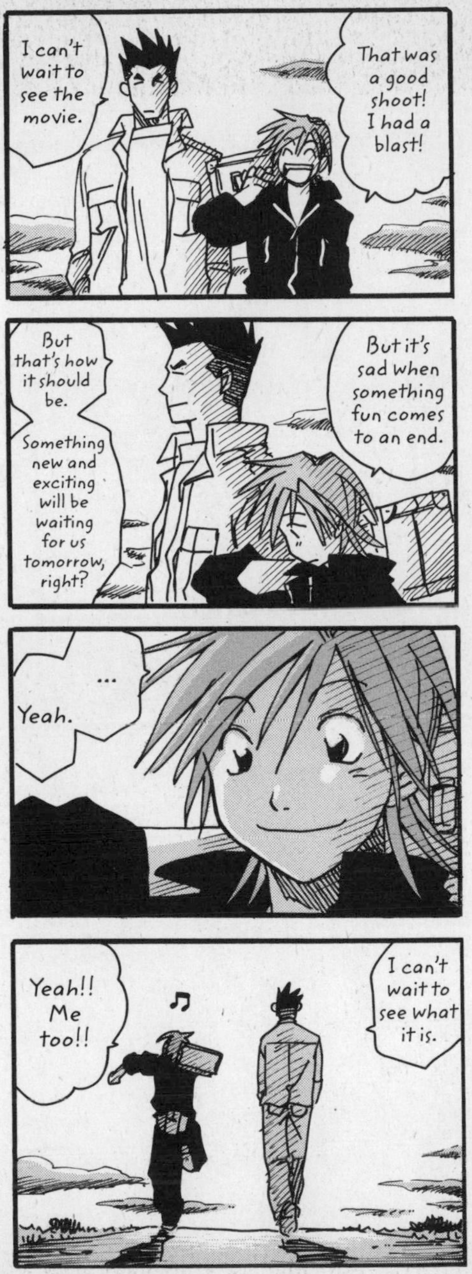
That was a good shoot! I had a blast!
I can't wait to see the movie.
But it's sad when something fun comes to an end.
But that's how it should be.
Something new and exciting will be waiting for us tomorrow, right?
...
Yeah.
I can't wait to see what it is.
Yeah!! Me too!!

GIMMICK!
THE END

THANK YOU!

Thanks to everybody who helped us on our research trips, the staff, and all the readers! Thank you!
—Kanari

I look forward to the day we meet again.
—Yabuguchi

GIMMICK!
Vol. 9

Story by Youzaburou Kanari
Art by Kuroko Yabuguchi

English Adaptation/Lance Caselman
Translation/Joe Yamazaki
Touch-up Art & Lettering/Rina Mapa
Design/Amy Martin
Editor/Megan Bates

VP, Production/Alvin Lu
VP, Publishing Licensing/Rika Inouye
VP, Sales & Product Marketing/Gonzalo Ferreyra
VP, Creative/Linda Espinosa
Publisher/Hyoe Narita

GIMMICK! © 2005 by Youzaburou Kanari, Kuroko Yabuguchi. All rights reserved.
First published in Japan in 2005 by SHUEISHA Inc., Tokyo. English translation
rights arranged by SHUEISHA Inc. The stories, characters and incidents
mentioned in this publication are entirely fictional.

Printed in the U.S.A.

Published by VIZ Media, LLC
P.O. Box 77010
San Francisco, CA 94107

10 9 8 7 6 5 4 3 2 1
First printing, October 2009

www.viz.com

store.viz.com

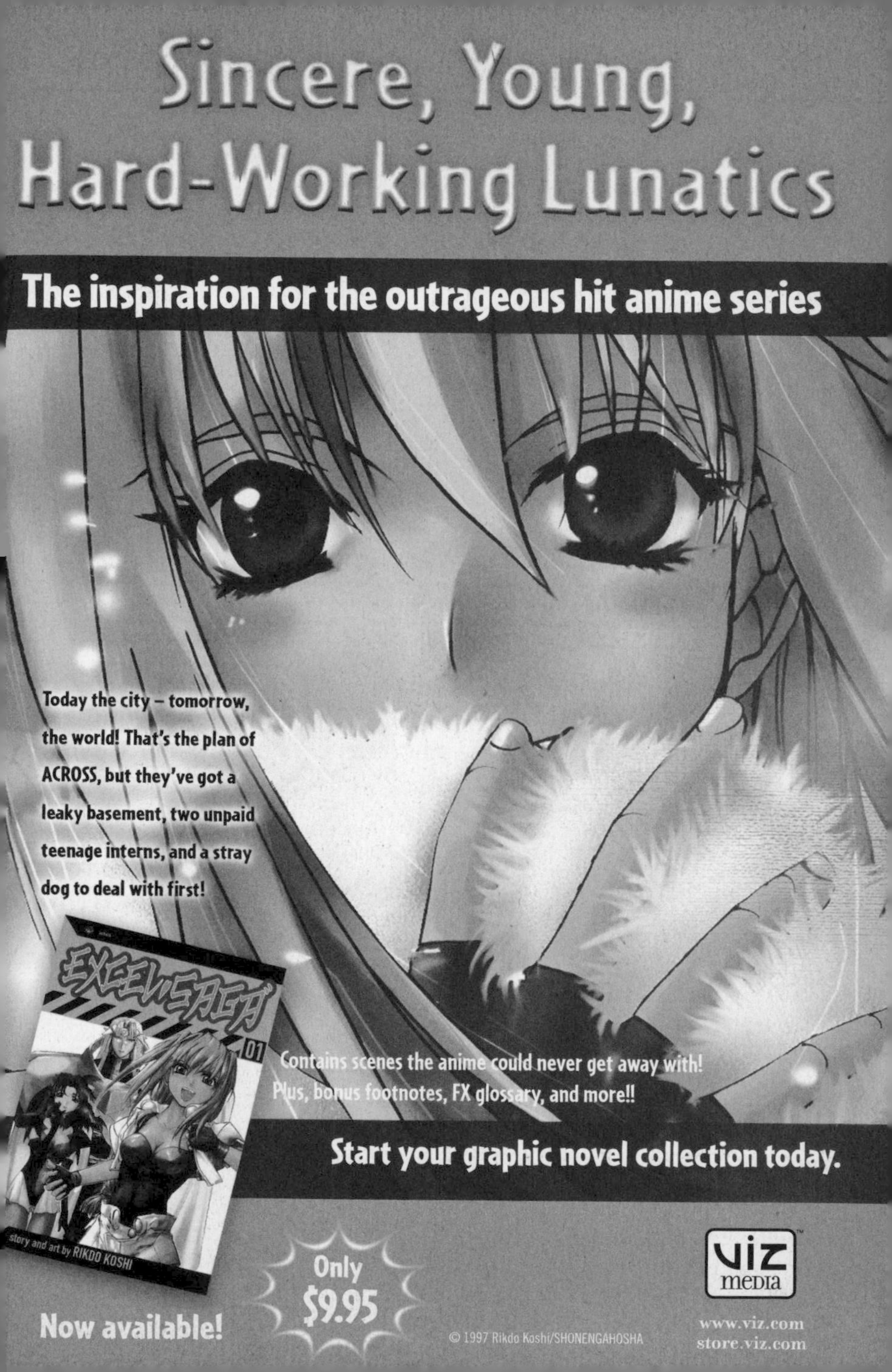
Sincere, Young, Hard-Working Lunatics
The inspiration for the outrageous hit anime series
Today the city – tomorrow, the world! That's the plan of ACROSS, but they've got a leaky basement, two unpaid teenage interns, and a stray dog to deal with first!
EXCEL SAGA
01
story and art by RIKDO KOSHI
Contains scenes the anime could never get away with!
Plus, bonus footnotes, FX glossary, and more!!
Start your graphic novel collection today.
Only $9.95
Now available!
© 1997 Rikdo Koshi/SHONENGAHOSHA
VIZ MEDIA
www.viz.com
store.viz.com

InuYasha

Read the action from the start with the original manga series

Full color adaptation of the popular TV series

The Art of
InuYasha

Original Illustrations by
Rumiko Takahashi

Art book with cel art, paintings, character profiles and more

TV SERIES & MOVIES ON DVD!

See more of the action in *Inuyasha* full-length movies

www.viz.com
inuyasha.viz.com

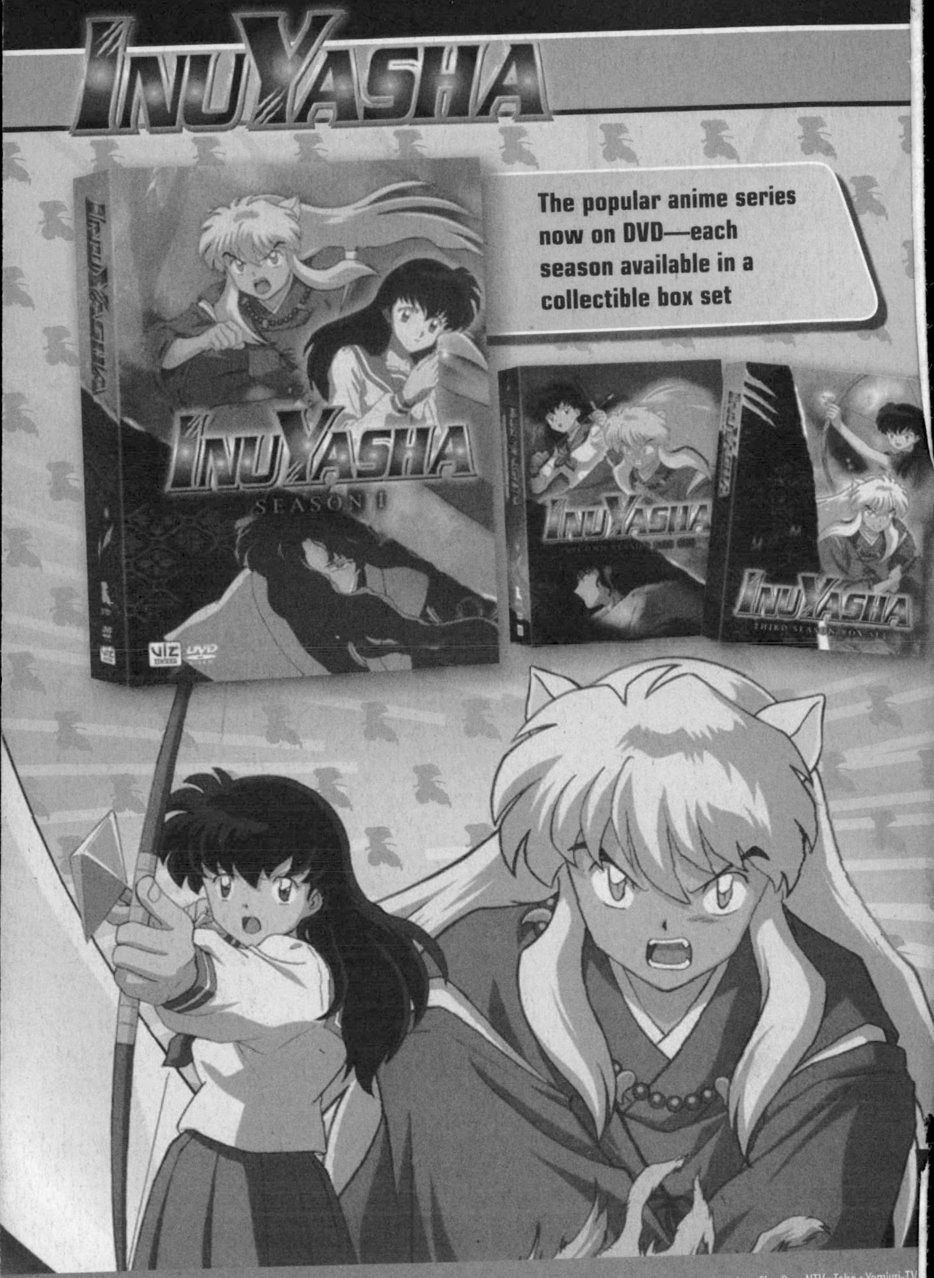
InuYasha
The popular anime series now on DVD—each season available in a collectible box set
InuYasha
Season 1
InuYasha
InuYasha

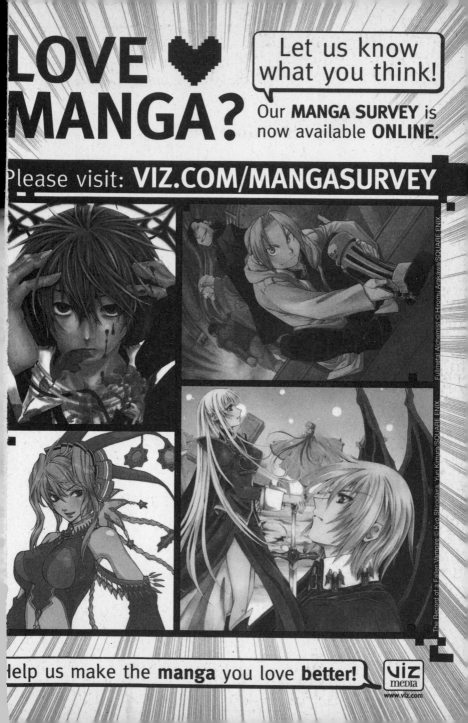